Western Civilization

BEYOND BOUNDARIES

D1403538

Western Civilization

BEYOND BOUNDARIES

Sixth Edition   VOLUME B: 1300–1815

Thomas F. X. Noble
University of Notre Dame

Barry Strauss
Cornell University

Duane J. Osheim
University of Virginia

Kristen B. Neuschel
Duke University

Elinor A. Accampo
University of Southern California

David D. Roberts
University of Georgia

William B. Cohen
Late of Indiana University

WADSWORTH
CENGAGE Learning™

Australia • Brazil • Japan • Korea • Mexico • Singapore • Spain • United Kingdom • United States

WADSWORTH
CENGAGE Learning

Western Civilization: Beyond Boundaries,
Volume B, Sixth Edition
Thomas F. X. Noble, Barry Strauss, Duane J. Osheim, Kristen B. Neuschel, Elinor A. Accampo, David D. Roberts, William B. Cohen

Senior Publisher: Suzanne Jeans

Senior Sponsoring Editor: Nancy Blaine

Associate Editor: Adrienne Zicht

Editorial Assistant: Emma Goehring

Senior Media Editor: Lisa Ciccolo

Executive Marketing Manager:
Diane Wenckebach

Marketing Coordinator: Lorreen Pelletier

Marketing Communications Manager:
Christine Dobberpuhl

Senior Content Project Manager: Jane Lee

Senior Art Director: Cate Rickard Barr

Senior Print Buyer: Judy Inouye

Senior Rights Acquisition Account Manager:
Mollika Basu

Production Service: Elm Street Publishing
Services

Text Designer: Henry Rachlin

Senior Photo Editor: Jennifer Meyer Dare

Cover Designer: Harold Burch

Volume B cover image: *Winter* by Pieter Brueghel,
the Younger (c. 1564–1638). Pushkin Museum,
Moscow, Russia/The Bridgeman Art Library

Compositor: Integra Software Services Pvt. Ltd.

For product information and technology assistance, contact us at
Cengage Learning, Customer & Sales Support, 1-800-354-9706

For permission to use material from this text or product,
submit all requests online at **www.cengage.com/permissions.**
Further permissions questions can be e-mailed to
permissionrequest@cengage.com.

Library of Congress Control Number: 2009934607

ISBN-13: 978-1-424-06959-0
ISBN-10: 1-424-06959-9

Wadsworth
20 Channel Center Street
Boston, MA 02210
USA

Cengage Learning is a leading provider of customized learning solutions with office locations around the globe, including Singapore, the United Kingdom, Australia, Mexico, Brazil, and Japan. Locate your local office at **international.cengage.com/region.**

Cengage Learning products are represented in Canada by Nelson Education, Ltd.

For your course and learning solutions, visit **www.cengage.com.**

Purchase any of our products at your local college store or at our preferred online store **www.ichapters.com.**

Printed in the United States of America
1 2 3 4 5 6 7 13 12 11 10 09

BRIEF CONTENTS

CONTENTS

MAPS

DOCUMENTS

THE VISUAL RECORD

PREFACE

An old adage says that each generation must write history for itself. If the adage is true, then it would also be true that each generation must teach and learn history for itself. The history, of course, does not change, although new discoveries come to light all the time. What does change is us, each succeeding generation of us. What causes us to change, and thus to experience and understand history in ever new ways, are the great developments of our own times. Think of the world-changing events of the last century: two world wars, the Great Depression, the cold war, nuclear weapons, the civil rights movement, the women's movement, the explosion in scientific knowledge, and the media revolutions involving radio and television, the computer, and the Internet. The pace of change has accelerated in our time, but the process of change always affects people's view of their world.

As we launch the sixth edition of this book we are once again acutely aware of the need to address big questions in ways that make sense to teachers and students right now, in the world we live in today. As these words are being written, the news is full of reports from Afghanistan, Iraq, Iran, Darfur, Somalia, and North Korea. The world's economy is in a perilous state. The United States has elected an African American as its president. In such circumstances we might well ask, What is the West; what is Western? Some believe that we are engaged in a "Clash of Civilizations." Is one of these Western Civilization? If so, who or what is its adversary? The West is sometimes understood geographically and sometimes culturally. For most people, the West means western Europe. And yet western Europe itself is the heir of the peoples and cultures of antiquity, including the Sumerians, Egyptians, Persians, Greeks, Romans, Jews, Christians, and Muslims. In fact, Europe is the heir of even earlier civilizations in Asia and Africa. As a cultural phenomenon, "Western" implies many things: freedom and free, participatory political institutions; economic initiative and opportunity; monotheistic religious faiths (Judaism, Christianity, and Islam); rationalism and ordered thought in the social, political, and philosophical realms; an aesthetic sensibility that aspires to a universal sense of beauty. But the West has felt free to evoke tradition as its guiding light and also to innovate brilliantly, to accommodate slavery and freedom simultaneously, and to esteem original thought and persecute people who deviate from the norm. "Western" indeed has meant many things in various places at different times. This book constantly and explicitly attempts to situate its readers in place, time, and tradition.

Another big question is this: What exactly is civilization? No definition can win universal acceptance, but certain elements of a definition are widely accepted. Civilization is the largest unit within which any person might feel comfortable. It is an organizing principle that implies common institutions, economic systems, social structures, and values that extend over both space and time. Cities are crucial; with cities emerge complex social organizations that involve at least a minimal division of labor. Some people work in the fields, some in the home. Soldiers defend the city, and artisans provide its daily goods. Governing institutions have a wide measure of acceptance and have the ability to enforce their will. Civilizations also develop religious ideas and authorities; literatures and laws that may be oral or written; monumental architecture, especially fortifications, palaces, and temples; and arts such as music, painting, and sculpture. Every civilization enfolds many cultures, a term that may be applied to the full range of expressions of a people in a given place and time. So, for example, the cultures of Egypt, Greece, and Rome were distinctive but all fit under the broad umbrella of Western Civilization.

Western Civilization has had an influence on almost every person alive today. The West deserves to be studied because its tale is compelling, but it demands to be studied because its story has been so central to the development of the world in which we live. Many of the world's dominant institutions are Western in their origin and in their contemporary manifestations—most notably parliamentary democracy. Commercial capitalism, a Western construct, is the world's dominant form of economic organization. The Internet, fast food, and hip-hop music are all western in origin but world-wide in reach today.

Until a generation or so ago, Western Civilization was a staple of college and university curricula and was generally studied in isolation. Although it was, and is, important for us to know who we are, it is also important for us to see that we have changed in dramatic ways and that we can no longer understand ourselves in isolation from the world around us. Accordingly, this book repeatedly sets the experience of the West into its global context. This is not a World History book. But it is a book that sees Western Civilization as one significant segment of the world's history.

BASIC APPROACH

Nearly two decades ago the six original authors of *Western Civilization: Beyond Boundaries* set out to create a textbook for a course that would, as a total effort, inform students about essential developments within a tradition that has powerfully, though not always positively, affected everyone in the contemporary world. Although each of us found something to admire in all of the existing textbooks, none of us was fully happy with any of them. We were disappointed with books that claimed "balance" but actually stressed a single kind of history. We regretted that so many texts were uneven in their command of recent scholarship. Although we were convinced of both the inherent interest of Western Civilization and the importance of teaching the subject, we were disconcerted by the celebratory tone of some books, which portrayed the West as resting on its laurels instead of creatively facing its future.

We decided to produce a book that is balanced and coherent; that addresses the full range of subjects that a Western Civilization book needs to address; that provides the student reader with interesting, timely material; that is up-to-date in terms of scholarship and approach; and that is handsome to look at—in short, a book that helps the instructor to teach and the student to learn. We have kept our common vision fresh through frequent meetings, correspondence, critical mutual readings, and expert editorial guidance. The misfortune of the untimely death of one member of our team has brought us the fortune of a new colleague who has inspired and challenged the rest of us in new ways. Because each of us has focused on his or her own area of specialization, we believe that we have attained a rare blend of competence, confidence, and enthusiasm. Moreover, in moving from plans for a first edition to the preparation of a sixth, we have been able to profit from the experience of using the book, the advice and criticism of dozens of colleagues, and the reactions of thousands of students.

Western Civilization is a story. Therefore, we aimed at a strong chronological narrative line. Our experience as teachers tells us that students appreciate this clear but gentle orientation. Our experience tells us, too, that an approach that is broadly chronological will leave instructors plenty of room to adapt our narrative to their preferred organization, or to supplement our narrative with one of their own.

Although we maintain the familiar, large-scale divisions of a Western Civilization book, we also present some innovative adjustments in arrangement. For instance, we incorporate a single chapter on Late Antiquity, the tumultuous and fascinating period from about A.D 300 to 600 that witnessed the transformation of the Roman Empire into three successors: Byzantine, Islamic, and European. One chapter studies those three successors, thereby permitting careful comparisons. But we also assign chapters to some of the greatest issues in Western Civilization, such as the Renaissance, the age of European exploration and conquest, the Scientific Revolution, and the industrial transformation. Our twentieth-century chapters reflect an understanding of the last century formed in its closing years rather than in its middle decades. What is new in our organization represents adjustments grounded in the best scholarship, and what is old represents time-tested approaches.

In fashioning our picture of the West, we took two unusual steps. First, our West is itself bigger than the one found in most textbooks. We treat the Celtic world, Scandinavia, and the Slavic world as integral parts of the story. We look often at the lands that border the West—Anatolia/Turkey, western Asia, North Africa, the Eurasian steppes—in order to show the to-and-fro of peoples, ideas, technologies, and products. Second, we continually situate the West in its global context. Just as we recognize that the West has influenced the rest of the world, we also carefully acknowledge how the rest of the world has influenced the West. We begin this story of mutual interaction with the Greeks and Romans, carry it through the European Middle Ages, focus on it in the age of European exploration and conquest, and analyze it closely in the modern world of industry, diplomacy, empire, immigration, and questions of citizenship and identity.

Another approach that runs like a ribbon throughout this textbook involves balance and integration. Teachers and students, just like the authors of this book, have their particular interests and emphases. In the large and diverse American academy, that is as it should be. But a textbook, if it is to be helpful and useful, should incorporate as many interests and emphases as possible. For a long time, some said, Western Civilization books devoted excessive coverage to high politics—"the public deeds of great men," as an ancient Greek writer defined the historian's subject. Others felt that high culture—all the Aristotles and Mozarts—was included to the exclusion of supposedly lesser figures and ordinary men and women. In the 1970s, books began to emphasize social history. Some applauded this new emphasis even as they debated fiercely over what to include under this heading.

In this book, we attempt to capture the Western tradition in its full contours, to hear the voices of all those who have made durable contributions. But because we cannot say everything about everybody at every moment, we have had to make choices about how and where to array key topics within our narrative. Above all, we have tried to be integrative. For example, when we talk about government and politics, we present the institutional structures through which power was exercised, the people who possessed power as well as the people who did not, the ideological foundations for the use of power, and the material conditions that fostered or hindered the real or the would-be powerful. In other words, instead of treating old-fashioned "high politics" in abstract and descriptive ways, we take an approach that is organic and analytical: How did things work? Our approach to the history of women is another example. A glance at this book's table of contents and then at its index is revealing. The former reveals very few sections devoted explicitly and exclusively to women. The latter shows that women appear constantly in every section of this book. Is there a contradiction here? Not at all. Women and men have not been historical actors in isolation from one another. Yet gender, which is relational, reciprocal, and mutual, is an important variable that has shaped individual and collective experience. Hence we seek to explain why certain political, economic, or social circumstances had differing impacts on men and women, and how such conditions led them to make different choices.

Similarly, when we talk of great ideas, we describe the antecedent ideas from which seemingly new ones were built up, and we ask about the consequences of those ideas. We explore the social positions of the authors of those ideas to see if this helps us explain the ideas themselves or gauge their influence. We try to understand how ideas in one field of human endeavor prove to be influential in other fields. For instance, gender is viewed as connected to and part of the larger fabric of ideas including power, culture, and piety.

We invite the reader to look at our narrative as if it were a mosaic. Taken as a whole, our narrative contains a coherent picture. Viewed more closely, it is made up of countless tiny bits that may have their individual interest but do not even hint at the larger picture of which they are parts. Finally, just as the viewer of a mosaic may find his or her eye drawn especially to one area, feature, color, or style, so too the reader of this book will find some parts more engaging or compelling than others. But it is only because there is, in this book as in a mosaic, a complete picture that the individual sections make sense, command our attention, excite our interest.

One word sums up our approach in this book: "balance." We tell a good story, but we pause often to reflect on that story, to analyze it. We devote substantial coverage to the typical areas of Greece, Rome, Italy, France, Great Britain, and so forth, but we say more about western Europe's frontiers than any other book. We do not try to disguise our Western Civilization book as a World History book, but we take great pains to locate the West within its global context. And we always assume that context means mutuality and reciprocity. We have high politics and big ideas alongside household management and popular culture. We think that part of the fascination of the past lies in its capacity to suggest understandings of the present and possibilities for the future.

Our subtitle, "Beyond Boundaries," is intended to suggest growth, challenge, and opportunity. The West began in Mesopotamia but soon spread to all of western Asia. Gradually the Greeks entered the scene and disseminated their ideas throughout the Mediterranean world. The Romans, always heirs of the Greeks, carried ideas and institutions from Britain to Mesopotamia. As the Roman order collapsed, Rome's imprint was left on a small segment of Europe lying west of the Rhine and south of the Danube. Europeans then crashed through those boundaries to create a culture that extended from Iceland to the Russian steppes. At the dawn of the modern age Europe entered into a complex set of commercial, colonial, military, and political relations with the rest of the globe. Our contemporary world sees Western influences everywhere. No western "boundary" has ever been more than temporary, provisional.

DISTINCTIVE FEATURES

To make this book as accessible as possible to students, we have constantly been aware of its place in a program of teaching and learning. In the preceding paragraphs something has been said about this book's distinctive substantive features and how, we believe, they will contribute to the attainment of a deeper understanding of Western Civilization, as well as of its importance and place in the wider history of the earth's peoples. Teaching and learning also involve pedagogical techniques and innovations. We have attended conscientiously to pedagogical issues from the start, and we have made some significant changes in this edition.

Our chapters have always begun with a vignette that is directly tied to an accompanying picture. These vignettes alert the reader to one or more of the key aspects of the chapter. Thus the readers have encountered a thematic introduction that evokes interest while pointing clearly and in some detail to what follows.

To make our chapter introductions more effective, which means to give students greater confidence as they proceed through the book, we have taken numerous steps. First, as in past editions, we reviewed and revised our opening vignettes to connect text and picture more closely and to use both to invite the reader into the chapter.

Second, the first page of each chapter contains a succinct Outline that immediately and dramatically tells the reader what he or she is going to encounter in the following pages. Third, the chapter introductions conclude with a list of Focus Questions that both echo the introduction and set the reader off on the right path into the following pages. Fourth, as the student begins to read the chapter proper, a Chronology serves as yet another orientation to the material contained in the chapter. Subject-specific chronologies still appear in various parts of the book, but we felt readers would benefit from a chronological guide at the beginning of each chapter.

In this edition, we have repeated each Focus Question at the head of the section to which it pertains. At the end of each major section, we provide a succinct Section Summary. Each chapter concludes with a Chapter Summary that reiterates the Focus Questions and then briefly answers them once again.

As a complement to text coverage, a ready reference, and a potential study guide, all of the Key Terms have been gathered into a Glossary included in the website that accompanies the book. For this edition, we have also placed definitions on the pages where the Key Terms first appear.

In addition to this fundamental attention to chapter themes and contents, we have sought to improve the book's teachability by adding a pronunciation guide. Whenever we use an unfamiliar name or term, we show the reader how to pronounce it. Instead of using the intricate rules of phonetics, we provide commonsense guides to pronunciation in parentheses directly following the word.

This edition is a bit shorter than its predecessors. Relevance, "teachability," and "learnability" were our guides in streamlining our coverage at many points. Virtually every chapter experienced some slimming in the interest of keeping major points and themes front and center.

Having always been conscious of this book's physical appearance, we have this time adopted a dynamic, single-column design to enhance the reader's experience of the book. Attractively laid-out pages, a handsome full-color design, engaging maps, and beautifully reproduced pictures enhance the book's appearance. In keeping with our desire to integrate the components of the book into a coherent whole, we carefully anchor the maps and pictures into the volume. Our maps, always chosen and conceptualized by the authors, have for the sixth edition been completely redesigned to make them fresher, more attractive, and more informative. Map captions have been carefully written, and revised, to make them effective elements of the book's teaching program. The same is true of the pictures: the authors selected them, worked with the book's designers to place them advantageously (and not just decoratively), and wrote all the captions. For this edition, we paid particular attention to reviewing all the captions and to revising many of them. All of the maps are cross-referenced in the text, some of them several times, and the text often refers directly to the pictures.

From the start, every chapter in this book has had boxed documents, one of which treated a "global" theme, as well as a two-page feature entitled "Weighing the Evidence." For this edition, we thought hard about our features and decided to take some decisive steps to make them work better for teachers and students. First, we reduced the number of features to three per chapter. Second, we introduced a uniform structure and format. One feature, entitled "The Global Record," presents a significant document that sets some aspect of Western Civilization within the global perspective. These documents are substantial, are carefully introduced, and conclude with study questions. Another feature is called "The Written Record." This feature contains a significant document relevant to the text materials then under discussion with a careful introduction and study questions. The third feature is called "The Visual Record." This feature represents a reconceptualization of our former "Weighing the Evidence" feature. Most of those features did focus on visual evidence, but now the Visual Record features all do so. As with the Global Record and Written Record features, the Visual Records have helpful questions. Whereas the Weighing the Evidence features always concluded our chapters, now the Visual Records are placed into the chapters at the most appropriate position. For the fifth edition, we cast a careful eye over all the Visual Record features and prepared eight new ones, and for the sixth edition, we have prepared two new ones. Finally, we took two last steps. We deleted the "Looking Ahead" sections because reviewers suggested that this "telegraphing" of what was to come might confuse the student reader as to what he or she has just read. And we moved the "Suggested Readings" to the book's website.

ORGANIZATION AND CONTENT CHANGES

Throughout the book, the authors have made changes to improve the narrative and to incorporate new ways of talking about particular topics. Chapter 1 has been trimmed by cutting the short section "The First Cities" and by eliminating the larger section "Widening Horizons: The Levant and Anatolia, 2500–1150 B.C." The original subsection "War Abroad, Reform at Home, 1786–1075 B.C." has been divided into two separate sections and the material on the Amarna Archives and the Hittites has been moved to the new "War Abroad" section.

Chapter 2 gained a new main section, "Traders Invent the Alphabet: Canaanites and Phoenicians, ca. 1400–450 B.C.," with new subsections on "The Canaanite City-States, ca. 1400–1200 B.C." and "The Phoenicians, ca. 1050–450 B.C." Material on the Phoenicians, formerly found under "Assyrians and Babylonians," has been moved to the new section. These revisions create sharper focus and clearer organization. A new Visual Record feature, "The Siege of Lachish," has been introduced. The entire main section on "Early Greece" has been moved to Chapter 3, once again in the interest of sharpening the focus.

In Chapter 5, two subsections, "The Roman Household" and "Patrons and Clients," have been combined and shortened into one new section entitled "Families and Patronage." The sections on Roman expansion, both in Italy and in the wider Mediterranean, have been recast as follows: The former section on "The Latin League and Beyond" has been replaced by a section entitled "Keeping the Peace," which has been moved to the section "Republican Expansion: The Conquest of Italy, ca. 509–265 B.C." The sections on "Rome Versus Carthage: The Punic Wars, 264–146 B.C." and "Victories in the Hellenistic East, ca. 200–133 B.C." have been combined into one new section, "Punic Wars and the Conquest of the Greek East." The sections on "The Gracchi" and on "Marius and Sulla" have been recast as "Reformers and Revolutionaries." Chapter 6 has a new Written Record feature on "Boudicca's Revolt."

Chapter 8 has been substantially revised. The long and largely introductory section "Catholic Kingdoms in the West" has been deleted. Its material, much abbreviated, has been recast as the opening subsection, "Medieval Europe takes Shape," under the main section "The Rise of the Carolingian Empire." This main section includes revised and trimmed subsections entitled "The Carolingian Dynasty," "Carolingian Government," "The Carolingian Renaissance," and "The Fragmentation of Charlemagne's Empire." The former subsections "Social Patterns" and "The Experiences of Women" have been combined into a new section, "Social Patterns."

In Chapter 12, the section "Renaissance Court and Society" has been revised as "Politics and Renaissance Culture." In Chapter 14, the map "Reform in Germany, 1517–1555" has been replaced by a new map, "The Global Empire of Charles V." Chapter 15 has been significantly reorganized. The material in the subhead "The Failure of the Invincible Armada" has been moved into the section on "The Formation of the United Provinces." Material from the former subhead "Henry IV and the Fragile Peace" has been moved into the section "Decades of Civil War." The main heading "Religious and Political Conflict in Central and Eastern Europe" has been recast as "The Holy Roman Empire and the Thirty Years' War." The subheads in this main section have been revised, shortened, and renamed. The social and cultural sections of this chapter have been revised and reorganized. One old map 15.4 ("Two Empires in Eastern Europe, ca. 1600") has been deleted. In Chapter 16, material on "The Dutch War" has been moved into the section on "The Burdens of War and the Limits of Power." The section on "Competition Around the Baltic" has been tightened.

Chapter 17 has a new subsection, "Women Scientists and Institutional Constraints," and the former section on "Pierre Bayle" has been revised as "Skepticism and the Spread of Scientific Rationality" to signal the central issues more clearly. Similarly, in Chapter 18, the old section "Adam Smith and David Hume" has been recast as "Economic Thought and the Scottish Enlightenment." Some subsections within the former section on "Monarchy and Constitutional

Government" have been eliminated and the whole section reorganized under "Monarch and Parliament in Great Britain." The subheads in the rest of this chapter have been revised, and two main headings "The Widening World of Commerce" and "Economic Expansion and Social Change" have been eliminated with some of their material reorganized and placed in other sections and other material retained under the new main heading "The Widening World of Trade and Production." Finally, this chapter acquires the new main heading "The Widening World of Warfare" that pulls together military history issues. In Chapter 19, several minor subheads have been shortened and combined into other sections, but a new subhead on "Revolution in the Atlantic World" has been added to the section "The Legacy of Revolution for France and the World" and an old section, "The View from Britain," has been deleted. In general, the revisions in Chapters 15 to 19 aim to gather like with like, to streamline the narrative, and to make topics more explicit.

Two important sections in Chapter 20 have been renamed: "Advances in the Cotton Industry" to "Mass Production" and "Iron, Steam, and Factories" to "New Energy Sources and Their Impacts." Several small, fifth-edition subheads have been incorporated into the larger section on "The Spread of Industry to the Continent." The former subhead "The Working Classes and Their Lot" has been renamed "Social Class and Family Structure," which also gained some material from the deleted section "Industrialization and the Family." This chapter acquired a new Visual Record feature, "St. Giles," while material from the former Visual Record "Collective Action" has been creatively reintegrated into the chapter.

Chapters 21 and 22, which deal with the tangled political history of the nineteenth century, received significant attention in this edition. The first major heading in Chapter 21, "The Congress of Vienna," has been reorganized under a heading entitled "Restoration and Reaction." This move permits new subheads, "The Congress of Vienna," "Restored Monarchs in Western Europe," "Eastern Europe," and "Spain and Its Colonies," to carry the political story effectively down to 1830. Then, the former main heading "Restoration, Reform, and Reaction" has been recast as "The Quest for Reform." In other words, the chapter now establishes Europe's restored regimes and then looks inside them to understand their internal political dynamics. Accordingly, the old heading "Western Europe: From Reaction to Liberalism, 1815–1830" has been deleted because its essential material has already been presented. The chapter does receive a new heading entitled "The Revolution of 1830 and the July Monarchy in France," but a number of smaller subheads have been eliminated and their material redistributed. In Chapter 22, the former main heads "Italian Unification, 1859–1870" and "German Unification, 1850–1871" have been combined into one major section, "Forging New States," that itself contains subsections on the main stages in Italian and German unification subordinated to central themes. The main heading on "The Emergence of New Political Forms in the United States and Canada, 1840–1880" has been eliminated, along with its maps. As in earlier chapters, the aim has been to streamline and focus the narratives in these two as well.

In Chapter 23, some headings received new titles, for instance "The Declining Aristocracy" became "The Adapting Aristocracy," while "The Workers' Lot" shifted to "Improving Conditions Among the Workers and the Poor." The former main heading "Social and Political Initiatives" has been deleted with its most important material, particularly "Educational and Cultural Opportunities," redistributed elsewhere. Old Map 23.1, "European Rails, 1850–1880," has been cut.

Chapter 24 has a new title: "Imperialism and Escalating Tensions, 1880–1914." Its first main heading, "The New Imperialism and the Spread of Europe's Population," has been changed to "The New Imperialism and the Spread of Europe's Influence." This change permitted deletion of the subsection on "Overseas Migration and the Spread of European Values." A new subhead on "Unanticipated Consequences: Rebellion and Colonial War" has been added. Former Map 24.3, "European Migrations," has been replaced by a new map on the Ottoman Empire. In Chapter 25, two maps (25.1 and 25.2) have been combined into one new map called "The War in Europe, 1914–1918," and a new map has been added, "The European Peace Settlement and the Peace in the Middle East." In Chapter 26, one main head, "Weimar Germany and the Trials of New Democracies," has been renamed "The Trials of the New Democracies." In Chapter 28, the main heading "The Victory of Nazi Germany, 1939–1941" received a new title, "German Military Successes, 1939–1941." In Chapter 29, the subhead "The Energy Crisis and the Changing Economic Framework" has been moved under the main heading "Prosperity and Democracy in Western Europe." The subhead "New Nations in Asia" has been deleted with its most important information transferred to "The Varieties of Decolonization."

Our attempt to bring the story up to date means that Chapter 30, as always, received considerable attention. This begins with a new opening photo and vignette on the financial crisis, the meeting of the G-20 in London in April 2009. Several subheads received new titles, for example "Origins of the Union" became "Renewing the Union," "War Crimes Tribunals" became "War Crimes Trials," "Unemployment and Economic Challenges in Western Europe" became "Responding to New Economic Challenges," and "Immigration, Assimilation, and the New Right" became "Immigration, Assimilation, and Citizenship." The subhead "The Post-Communist Experiment" has been expanded with new material on Vladimir Putin and the confrontation between Russia and Georgia. One subhead, "Consensus in the Established Democracies" was deleted. The last section, "The West in the Global Age," has been rewritten, especially the subsection "Questioning the Meaning of the West."

ANCILLARIES

Instructor Resources

PowerLecture CD-ROM with ExamView® and JoinIn® This dual platform, all-in-one multimedia resource includes the Instructor's Resource Manual; Test Bank, revised to reflect the new material in the text by Dolores Grapsas of New River Community College (includes key term identification, multiple-choice, short answer, essay, and map questions); Microsoft® PowerPoint® slides of both lecture outlines and images and maps from the text that can be used as offered, or customized by importing personal lecture slides or other material; and *JoinIn®* PowerPoint® slides with clicker content. Also included is ExamView, an easy-to-use assessment and tutorial system that allows instructors to create, deliver, and customize tests in minutes. Instructors can build tests with as many as 250 questions using up to 12 question types, and using ExamView's complete word-processing capabilities, they can enter an unlimited number of new questions or edit existing ones.

HistoryFinder This searchable online database allows instructors to quickly and easily download thousands of assets, including art, photographs, maps, primary sources, and audio/video clips. Each asset downloads directly into a Microsoft® PowerPoint® slide, allowing instructors to easily create exciting PowerPoint presentations for their classrooms.

Instructor's Resource Manual Prepared by Janusz Duzinkiewicz of Purdue University North Central, the Instructor's Resource Manual has been revised to reflect the new material in the text. This manual has many features, including instructional objectives, chapter outlines and summaries, lecture suggestions, suggested debate and research topics, cooperative learning activities, and suggested readings and resources. The Instructor's Resource Manual is available on the instructor's companion site.

WebTutor™ on Blackboard® With WebTutor's text-specific, pre-formatted content and total flexibility, instructors can easily create and manage their own custom course website. WebTutor's course management tool gives instructors the ability to provide virtual office hours, post syllabi, set up threaded discussions, track student progress with the quizzing material, and much more. For students, WebTutor offers real-time access to a full array of study tools, including animations and videos that bring the book's topics to life, plus chapter outlines, summaries, learning objectives, glossary flashcards (with audio), practice quizzes, and weblinks.

WebTutor™ on WebCT® With WebTutor's text-specific, pre-formatted content and total flexibility, instructors can easily create and manage their own custom course website. WebTutor's course management tool gives instructors the ability to provide virtual office hours, post syllabi, set up threaded discussions, track student progress with the quizzing material, and much more. For students, WebTutor offers real-time access to a full array of study tools, including animations and videos that bring the book's topics to life, plus chapter outlines, summaries, learning objectives, glossary flashcards (with audio), practice quizzes, and weblinks.

Student Resources

Book Companion Site A website for students that features a wide assortment of resources, which have been revised to reflect the new material in the text, to help students master the subject matter. The website, prepared by David Paradis of the University of Colorado, Boulder, includes a glossary, flashcards, crossword puzzles, tutorial quizzes, essay questions, weblinks, and suggested readings.

CL eBook This interactive multimedia eBook links out to rich media assets such as video and MP3 chapter summaries. Through this eBook, students can also access self-test quizzes, chapter outlines, focus questions, chronology and matching exercises, essay and critical thinking questions (for which the answers can be emailed to their instructors), primary source documents with critical thinking questions, and interactive (zoomable) maps. The CL eBook is available on ichapters.

Wadsworth Western Civilization Resource Center Wadsworth's Western Civilization Resource Center gives your students access to a "virtual reader" with hundreds of primary sources including speeches, letters, legal documents and transcripts, poems, maps, simulations, timelines, and additional images that bring history to life, along with interactive assignable exercises. A map feature including Google Earth™ coordinates and exercises will aid in student comprehension of geography and use of maps. Students can compare the traditional textbook map with an aerial view of the location today. It's an ideal resource for study, review, and research. In addition to this map feature, the resource center also provides blank maps for student review and testing.

Rand McNally Historical Atlas of Western Civilization, 2e This valuable resource features over 45 maps, including maps that highlight classical Greece and Rome; maps document European civilization during the Renaissance; follow events in Germany, Russia, and Italy as they lead up to World Wars I and II; show the dissolution of Communism in 1989; document language and religion in the western world; and maps that describe the unification and industrialization of Europe.

Document Exercise Workbook Prepared by Donna Van Raaphorst, Cuyahoga Community College. A collection of exercises based around primary sources. This workbook is available in two volumes.

Music of Western Civilization Available free to adopters, and for a small fee to students, this CD contains many of the musical selections highlighted in the text and provides a broad sampling of the important musical pieces of Western civilization.

Exploring the European Past A collection of documents and readings that give students first-hand insight into the period. Each module also includes rich visual sources that help put the documents into context, helping the students to understand the work of the historian.

Writing for College History, 1e Prepared by Robert M. Frakes, Clarion University. This brief handbook for survey courses in American history, Western Civilization/European history, and world civilization guides students through the various types of writing assignments they encounter in a history class. Providing examples of student writing and candid assessments of student work, this text focuses on the rules and conventions of writing for the college history course.

The History Handbook, 1e Prepared by Carol Berkin of Baruch College, City University of New York and Betty Anderson of Boston University. This book teaches students both basic and history-specific study skills such as how to read primary sources, research historical topics, and correctly cite sources. Substantially less expensive than comparable skill-building texts, *The History Handbook* also offers tips for Internet research and evaluating online sources.

Doing History: Research and Writing in the Digital Age, 1e Prepared by Michael J. Galgano, J. Chris Arndt, and Raymond M. Hyser of James Madison University. Whether you're starting down the path as a history major, or simply looking for a straightforward and systematic guide to writing a successful paper, you'll find this text to be an indispensible handbook to historical research. This text's "soup to nuts" approach to researching and writing about history addresses every step of the process, from locating your sources and gathering information, to writing clearly and making proper use of various citation styles to avoid plagiarism. You'll also learn how to make the most of every tool available to you—especially the technology that helps you conduct the process efficiently and effectively.

The Modern Researcher, 6e Prepared by Jacques Barzun and Henry F. Graff of Columbia University. This classic introduction to the techniques of research and the art of expression is used widely in history courses, but is also appropriate for writing and research methods courses in other departments. Barzun and Graff thoroughly cover every aspect of research, from the selection of a topic through the gathering, analysis, writing, revision, and publication of findings presenting the process not as a set of rules but through actual cases that put the subtleties of research in a useful context. Part One covers the principles and methods of research; Part Two covers writing, speaking, and getting one's work published.

Reader Program Cengage Learning publishes a number of readers, some containing exclusively primary sources, others a combination of primary and secondary sources, and some designed to guide students through the process of historical inquiry. Visit Cengage.com/history for a complete list of readers.

Custom Options Nobody knows your students like you, so why not give them a text that is tailor-fit to their needs? Cengage Learning offers custom solutions for your course—whether it's making a small modification to *Western Civilization: Beyond Boundaries* to match your syllabus or combining multiple sources to create something truly unique. You can pick and choose chapters, include your own material, and add additional map exercises along with the *Rand McNally Atlas* to create a text that fits the way you teach. Ensure that your students get the most out of their textbook dollar by giving them exactly what they need. Contact your Cengage Learning representative to explore custom solutions for your course.

ACKNOWLEDGMENTS

The authors have benefited throughout the process of revision from the acute and helpful criticisms of numerous colleagues. We thank in particular: **Stephen Andrews,** Central New Mexico Community College; **Sascha Auerbach,** Virginia Commonwealth University; **Jonathan Bone,** William Paterson University; **Kathleen Carter,** High Point University; **Edmund Clingan,** Queensborough Community College/CUNY; Gary Cox, Gordon College; **Padhraig Higgins,** Mercer County Community College; **John Kemp,** Meadows Community College; **Michael Khodarkovsky,** Loyola University; **William Paquette,** Tidewater Community College; **David Paradis,** University of Colorado, Boulder; **Sandra Pryor,** Old Dominion University; **Ty Reese,** University of North Dakota; **Michael Saler,** University of California, Davis; **Janette VanBorsch,** Midlands Technical College; and **Matthew Zembo,** Hudson Valley Community College.

Each of us has benefited from the close readings and careful criticisms of our coauthors, although we all assume responsibility for our own chapters. Barry Strauss has written Chapters 1–6; Thomas Noble, 7–10; Duane Osheim, 11–14; Kristen Neuschel, 15–19; and David Roberts, 25–30. Originally written by William Cohen, Chapters 20–24 have been substantially revised and updated by Elinor Accampo.

Many colleagues, friends, and family members have helped us develop this work as well. Thomas Noble continues to be grateful for Linda Noble's patience and good humor. Noble's coauthors and many colleagues have over the years been sources of inspiration and information. He also thanks several dozen teaching assistants and more than 4,000 students who have helped him to think through the Western Civilization experience.

Barry Strauss is grateful to colleagues at Cornell and at other universities who offered advice and encouragement and responded to scholarly questions. He would also like to thank the people at Cornell who provided technical assistance and support. Most important have been the support and forbearance of his family. His daughter, Sylvie; his son, Michael; and, above all, his wife, Marcia, have truly been sources of inspiration.

Duane Osheim thanks family and friends who continue to support and comment on the text. He would especially like to thank colleagues at the University of Virginia who have engaged him in a long and fruitful discussion of Western Civilization and its relationship to other cultures. They make clear the mutual interdependence of the cultures of the wider world. He particularly wishes to thank H. C. Erik Midelfort, Arthur Field, Brian Owensby, Joseph C. Miller, Chris Carlsmith, Beth Plummer, and David D'Andrea for information and clarification on a host of topics.

Kristen Neuschel thanks her colleagues at Duke University for sharing their expertise. She is especially grateful to Sy Mauskopf, Bill Reddy, John Richards, Tom Robisheaux, Alex Roland, Barry Gaspar, and Peter Wood. She also thanks her husband and fellow historian, Alan Williams, for his wisdom about Western Civilization and his support throughout the project, and her children, Jesse and Rachel, for their patience and interest over many years.

Elinor Accampo is deeply indebted to the late Bill Cohen whose chapters in the first four editions offered a model of expertise and prose, and she continues to carry on what he originated with pride and respect. She owes special thanks to Kristen Neuschel and Rachel Fuchs for friendship and advice, to her daughter, Erin Hern, for her expert input as a consumer of college textbooks, and, as always, to her husband Robert Hern for his encouragement and enduring support.

David Roberts wishes to thank Sheila Barnett, Vici Payne, and Brenda Luke for their able assistance and Walter Adamson, Timothy Cleaveland, Karl Friday, Michael Kwass, John Morrow, Miranda Pollard, Judith Rohrer, John Short, William Stuek, and Kirk Willis for sharing their expertise in response to questions. He also thanks Beth Roberts for her constant support and interest and her exceedingly critical eye.

The first plans for this book were laid in 1988, and over the course of twenty-one years there has been remarkable stability in the core group of people responsible for its development. The author team lost a member, Bill Cohen, but Elinor Accampo stepped into Bill's place with such skill and grace that it seemed as though she had been with us from the start. Our original sponsoring editor, Jean Woy, moved up the corporate ladder but never missed an author meeting with us. Through five editions we had the pleasure of working with production editor Christina Horn and photo researcher Carole Frohlich. For this edition Jane Lee and Catherine Schnurr filled those roles, and we are grateful for their efforts. Our sponsoring editor for more than a decade, Nancy Blaine, has been a tower of strength. She believes in us, as we believe in her. We have been fortunate in our editors, Elizabeth Welch, Jennifer Sutherland, Julie Swasey, and Adrienne Zicht. All these kind and skillful people have elicited from us authors a level of achievement that fills us at once with pride and humility.

Thomas F. X. Noble

ABOUT THE AUTHORS

Thomas F. X. Noble   After receiving his Ph.D. from Michigan State University, Thomas Noble taught at Albion College, Michigan State University, Texas Tech University, and the University of Virginia. In 1999 he received the University of Virginia's highest award for teaching excellence and in 2008 Notre Dame's Edmund P. Joyce, C.S.C., Award for Excellence in Undergraduate Teaching. In 2001 he became Robert M. Conway Director of the Medieval Institute at the University of Notre Dame and in 2008 chairperson of Notre Dame's history department. He is the author of *The Republic of St. Peter: The Birth of the Papal State, 680–825; Religion, Culture and Society in the Early Middle Ages; Soldiers of Christ: Saints and Saints' Lives from Late Antiquity and the Early Middle Ages; From Roman Provinces to Medieval Kingdoms; Images, Iconoclasm, and the Carolingians;* and *Charlemagne and Louis the Pious: Five Lives.* He was a member of the Institute for Advanced Study in 1994 and the Netherlands Institute for Advanced Study in 1999–2000. He has been awarded fellowships by the National Endowment for the Humanities (twice) and the American Philosophical Society. He was elected a Fellow of the Medieval Academy of America in 2004.

Barry Strauss   Professor of history and Classics at Cornell University, Barry Strauss holds a Ph.D. from Yale. He has been awarded fellowships by the National Endowment for the Humanities, the American School of Classical Studies at Athens, The MacDowell Colony for the Arts, the Korea Foundation, and the Killam Foundation of Canada. He is the recipient of the Clark Award for excellence in teaching from Cornell. He is Chair of Cornell's Department of History, Director of Cornell's Program on Freedom and Free Societies, and Past Director of Cornell's Peace Studies Program. His many publications include *Athens After the Peloponnesian War: Class, Faction, and Policy, 403–386 B.C.; Fathers and Sons in Athens: Ideology and Society in the Era of the Peloponnesian War; The Anatomy of Error: Ancient Military Disasters and Their Lessons for Modern Strategists* (with Josiah Ober); *Hegemonic Rivalry from Thucydides to the Nuclear Age* (co-edited with R. New Lebow); *War and Democracy: A Comparative Study of the Korean War and the Peloponnesian War* (co-edited with David R. McCann); *Rowing Against the Current: On Learning to Scull at Forty; The Battle of Salamis, the Naval Encounter That Saved Greece – and Western Civilization; The Trojan War: A New History;* and *The Spartacus War.* His books have been translated into six languages. His book *The Battle of Salamis* was named one of the best books of 2004 by the Washington Post.

Duane J. Osheim   A Fellow of the American Academy in Rome with a Ph.D. in History from the University of California at Davis, Duane Osheim is professor of history at the University of Virginia. He has held American Council of Learned Societies, American Philosophical Society, National Endowment for the Humantities and Fulbright Fellowships. He is author and editor of *A Tuscan Monastery and Its Social World; An Italian Lordship: The Bishopric of Lucca in the Late Middle Ages; Beyond Florence: The Contours of Medieval and Early Modern Italy;* and *Chronicling History: Chroniclers and Historians in Medieval and Renaissance Italy.*

Kristen B. Neuschel   After receiving her Ph.D. from Brown University, Kristen Neuschel taught at Denison University and Duke University, where she is currently associate professor of history and Director of the Thompson Writing Program. She is a specialist in early modern French history and is the author of *Word of Honor: Interpreting Noble Culture in Sixteenth-Century France* and articles on French social history and European women's history. She has received grants from the Josiah Charles Trent Memorial Foundation, the National Endowment for the Humanities, and the American Council of Learned Societies. She has also received the Alumni Distinguished Undergraduate Teaching Award, which is awarded annually on the basis of student nominations for excellence in teaching at Duke.

Elinor A. Accampo   Professor of history and gender studies at the University of Southern California, Elinor Accampo completed her Ph.D. at the University of California, Berkeley. Prior to her career at USC, she taught at Colorado College and Denison University. She specializes in modern France and is the author of *Blessed Motherhood; Bitter Fruit: Nelly Roussel and the Politics of Female Pain in Third Republic France;* and *Industrialization, Family, and Class Relations: Saint Chamond, 1815–1914.* She has also published *Gender and the Politics of Social Reform in France* (co-edited with Rachel Fuchs and Mary Lynn Stewart) and articles and book chapters on the history of reproductive rights and birth control movements. She has received fellowships and travel grants from the German Marshall Fund, the Haynes Foundation, the American Council of Learned Societies, and the National Endowment for the Humanities, as well as an award for Innovative Undergraduate Teaching at USC.

David D. Roberts After receiving his Ph.D. in modern European history at the University of California, Berkeley, David Roberts taught at the Universities of Virginia and Rochester before becoming professor of history at the University of Georgia in 1988. At Rochester he chaired the Humanities Department of the Eastman School of Music, and he chaired the History Department at Georgia from 1993 to 1998. A recipient of Woodrow Wilson and Rockefeller Foundation fellowships, he is the author of *The Syndicalist Tradition and Italian Fascism; Benedetto Croce and the Uses of Historicism; Nothing but History: Reconstruction and Extremity After Metaphysics; The Totalitarian Experiment in Twentieth-Century Europe: Rethinking the Poverty of Great Politics;* and *Historicism and Fascism in Modern* Italy, as well as two books in Italian and numerous articles and reviews. He is currently Albert Berry Saye Professor of History *Emeritus* at the University of Georgia.

Western Civilization

Beyond Boundaries

CHAPTER OUTLINE

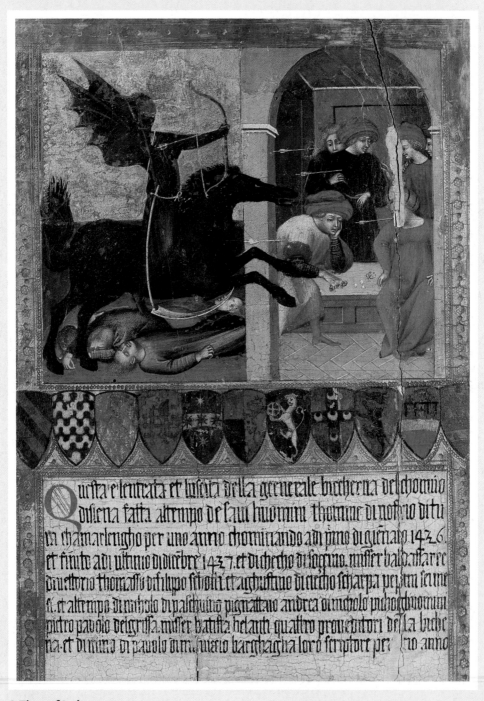

A Time of Judgment

On this cover for a fifteenth-century government account book, symbols of death—arrows, a scythe, and a horse—carry the angel of death from place to place. (Bildarchiv Preussischer Kulturbesitz/Art Resource, NY)

Crisis and Recovery in Late Medieval Europe, 1300–1500

In the fourteenth century, Europeans sang an old Franciscan hymn, "Day of Wrath, Day of Burning." Its verses described the fear and disorder that would accompany the end of the world and God's judgment of the saved and the damned. That hymn could well have been in the mind of the painter of the facing illustration. When countless Europeans, such as these poor souls beneath the winged angel of death, fell victim to epidemic disease, many people thought they knew why. The illustrator seems to believe it was God's judgment against sinners, including these gamblers sickened by the angel's plague-tipped arrows. The flood, fire, and pestilence that ravaged late medieval Europe were thought to be premonitions of the breakdown of the world and a time of judgment.

FOCUS QUESTIONS

- How did the Great Schism change the church and the papacy?

- What forces limited the political power of rulers in England, France, and Italy?

- How were economic and social structures changed by plague and economic crisis?

- How did the political makeup of Europe in 1500 differ from that in 1300?

The late Middle Ages (ca. 1300–1500) are often described as a period of continued crisis and decline that put an end to the growth and expansion of the previous three centuries. In truth, however, the years of crisis in the fourteenth and early fifteenth centuries gave way to a dramatic economic, social, and political recovery in the fifteenth century. The cultural and intellectual changes that accompanied the crisis and recovery are the focus of Chapter 12, "The Renaissance."

Military, political, religious, economic, and social crises burdened Europe in the fourteenth and early fifteenth centuries. Between 1337 and 1453, France and England fought a war that touched most of the states of western Europe. The Hundred Years' War, as it has come to be known, was fought primarily over English claims to traditionally French lands. Aristocrats in many parts of Europe challenged the hereditary rights of their rulers. In the towns of Germany and Italy, patrician classes moved to reduce the influence of artisans and laborers in government, instituting oligarchies or even aristocratic lordships in place of more democratic governments.

Questions of power and representation also affected the Christian church as ecclesiastical claims to authority came under attack. Secular governments challenged church jurisdictions. Disputed papal elections led to the so-called Great Schism, a split between rival centers of control in Rome and Avignon (a city in what is now the south of France). In the aftermath of the crisis, the papacy was forced to redefine its place in both the religious life and the political life of Europe.

A series of economic and demographic shocks worsened these political and religious difficulties. Part of the problem was structural: The population of Europe had grown too large to be supported by the resources available. Famine and the return of the plague in 1348 sent the economy into long-term decline. In almost every aspect of political, religious,

This icon will direct you to additional materials on the website: www .cengage.com/history/ noble/westciv6e.

See our interactive eBook for map and primary source activities.

and social life, then, the fourteenth and early fifteenth centuries marked a pause in the growth and consolidation that had characterized the earlier medieval period.

Yet, out of the crises, a number of significant changes emerged. By 1500, the European population and economy were again expanding. England and France emerged strengthened by military and political conflicts, and the consolidation of the Spanish kingdoms, the Ottoman Empire, and the states of eastern Europe altered the political and social makeup of Europe. None of the transformations could have been predicted in 1300, as Europe entered a religious, political, and social whirlwind.

THE CRISIS OF THE WESTERN CHRISTIAN CHURCH

How did the Great Schism change the church and the papacy?

Early in the fourteenth century, the king of France attempted to kidnap the pope. His act initiated a series of crises that challenged traditional ideas about church government and the role of the church in the various countries of Europe. First, the popes and their entourages abandoned their traditional residences in central Italy and moved to Avignon, an imperial enclave in the south of modern France. Then, in the wake of a disputed election, two and later three rivals claimed the papal throne. Simultaneously, the church hierarchy faced challenges from radical reformers who wished to change it. At various times, all the European powers became entangled in the problems of the church. In the wake of the crisis, the papacy realized that it needed a stronger, independent base. Papal recovery in the fifteenth century was predicated on political autonomy in central Italy.

The Babylonian Captivity, 1309–1377

The Christian church was in turmoil as a result of an attack on Pope Boniface VIII (r. 1294–1303) by King Philip IV (r. 1285–1314) of France. The king attempted to kidnap Boniface, intending to try him for heresy because of the pope's challenges to the king's authority within his own kingdom. The outstanding issues revolved around the powers of the pope and the responsibilities of the clergy to political leaders. It was, in fact, largely because of tensions with the northern kingdoms that the French archbishop of Bordeaux (bor-DOE) was elected Pope Clement V (r. 1305–1314). Clement chose to remain north of the Alps in order to seek an end to warfare between France and England and to protect, to the extent possible, the wealthy religious order of the Knights of the Temple, or Templars (see page 261), which Philip was in the process of suppressing. After the death of Boniface, it was clear that the governments of Europe had no intention of recognizing papal political authority as absolute.

Clement's pontificate marked the beginning of the so-called Babylonian Captivity, a period from 1309 to 1378, when popes resided almost continuously outside of Italy. In 1309, Clement moved the papal court to Avignon, on the Rhône River in a region that was still part of the Holy Roman Empire—the name that, by the fourteenth century, was given to the medieval empire whose origin reached back to Charlemagne.

The papacy and its new residence in Avignon became a major religious, diplomatic, and commercial center. The size of the court changed as dramatically as its venue: Although the thirteenth-century papal administration required only two hundred or so officials, the bureaucracy in Avignon grew to about six hundred. It was not just the pope's immediate circle that expanded the population of Avignon. Artists, writers, lawyers, and merchants from across Europe were drawn to the new center of administration and hub of patronage. Papal administrators intervened actively in local ecclesiastical affairs, and the pope's revenues from annates (generally a portion of the first year's revenues from an ecclesiastical office granted by papal letter), court fees, and provisioning charges continued to grow.

Not everyone approved of this situation. It was the Italian poet and philosopher Francesco Petrarch (1304–1374) who first referred to the Avignon move as a **Babylonian Captivity of the Papacy**.

Babylonian Captivity of the Papacy Term used to describe the period from 1309 to 1378 when popes resided outside of Italy, relating the pontificate's move to the period when the tribes of Israel lived in exile.

Recalling the account in the Hebrew Bible of the exile of the Israelites and New Testament images of Babylon as the center of sin and immorality, he complained of

> [an] unholy Babylon, Hell on Earth, a sink of iniquity, the cesspool of the world. There is neither faith, nor charity, nor religion. ... [1]

Two of the most vigorous critics were Saint Catherine of Siena (1347–1380) and Saint Bridget of Sweden (1303–1373). They were part of a remarkable flowering of religious feeling among women who were strong moral critics within their communities. Unlike others, Catherine and Bridget left their homes and neighborhoods and led the call for religious reform and a return of the papacy to Rome.

The Great Schism, 1378–1417

In 1377, Pope Gregory XI (r. 1370–1378) bowed to critics' pressure and did return to Rome. He was shocked by what he found: churches and palaces in ruin and the city violent and dangerous. By the end of 1377, he had resolved to retreat to Avignon, but he died before he could flee Rome. During a tumultuous election, the Roman populace entered the Vatican Palace and threatened to break into the conclave itself, demanding that there be an Italian pope. The subsequent election of the archbishop of Bari, Urban VI (r. 1378–1389), was soon challenged by dissidents who then elected a French cardinal who took the name Clement VII (r. 1378–1394). The church now had two popes.

After some hesitation, Western Christians divided into two camps, initiating the **Great Schism** (SKIZ-em), a period of almost forty years during which no one knew for sure who was the true pope. This was a deadly serious issue for all. The true pope had the right to appoint church officials, decide important moral and legal issues, and allow or forbid taxation of the clergy by the state.

The crisis gave impetus to new discussions about church government: Should the pope be considered the sole head of the church? Debates within the church followed lines of thought already expressed in the towns and kingdoms of Europe. Representative bodies—the English Parliament, the French Estates General, the Swedish Riksdag (RIX-dog)—already claimed the right to act for the realm, and in the city-states of Italy, ultimate authority was thought to reside in the body of citizens. Canon lawyers and theologians similarly argued that authority resided in the whole church, which had the right and duty to come together in council to correct and reform the church hierarchy. Even the most conservative of these **conciliarists** agreed that the "universal church" had the right to respond in periods of heresy or schism. More radical conciliarists argued that the pope as bishop of Rome was merely the first among equals in the church hierarchy and that he, like any other bishop, could be corrected by a gathering of his peers—that is, by an ecumenical council.

The rival popes resisted international pressure to end the schism. In exasperation, the cardinals, the main ecclesiastical supporters of the rival popes, called a general council in Pisa, which deposed both popes and elected a new one. Since the council lacked the power to force the rivals to accept deposition, the result was that three men now claimed to be the rightful successor of Saint Peter. Conciliarists, by themselves, could not mend the split in the church.

Resolution finally came when the Holy Roman emperor Sigismund (r. 1411–1437) forced the diplomatically isolated third papal claimant, John XXIII (r. 1410–1415), to call a general council of the church. The council, which met from 1414 to 1418 in the German imperial city of Constance, could never have succeeded without Sigismund's support. At one point, he forced the council to remain in session even after Pope John had fled the city in an attempt to end deliberations.

CHRONOLOGY

1303	Pope Boniface VIII attacked at Anagni and dies
1305	Election of Pope Clement V
1309	Clement V moves papal court to Avignon; beginning of Babylonian Captivity
1337	Beginning of Hundred Years' War between England and France
1348–1351	Black Death
1356	German emperor issues Golden Bull
1378	Great Schism
1381	English Rising
1397	Union of Kalmar unites Denmark, Norway, and Sweden
1410	Battle of Tannenberg
1414–1418	Council of Constance
1415	Battle of Agincourt
1420	Treaty of Troyes
1431	Execution of Joan of Arc
1438	Pragmatic Sanction of Bourges
1453	End of the Hundred Years' War Ottoman Turks conquer Constantinople
1469	Marriage of Ferdinand and Isabella unites kingdoms of Aragon and Castile
1480	Ivan III ends Tatar overlordship of Moscow
1485	Tudor dynasty established in England
1492	Spanish conquest of Granada Jews expelled from Spanish lands Columbus commissioned to discover new lands
1494	Charles VIII invades Italy

Great Schism The period from 1378 to 1417 when there were two and eventually three claimants to the papal throne.

conciliarists People who argued that the pope was merely "the first among equals" and that therefore a council of church leaders could correct or discipline a pope.

**Gregory XI Returns
to Rome** This highly
stylized painting conveys
the hopes of European
Christians when Gregory
XI returned from Avignon
in 1377. Saint Catherine of
Siena, who had pleaded for
the pope's return, is seen in
the foreground. (Scala/Art
Resource, NY)

Heresy and the Council of Constance, 1414–1418

Sigismund hoped that a council could help him heal deep religious and civil divisions in
Bohemia, the most important part of his family's traditional lands (see **MAP 11.3**). Far from
healing religious division, however, the actions of the council exacerbated tensions in central Europe and created a climate of religious distrust that poisoned relations for more than a
century. Bohemia and its capital, Prague, were Czech-speaking. Prague was also the seat of the
Luxemburg dynasty of German emperors and the site of the first university in German or Slavic
lands. Religious and theological questions quickly became entangled with the competing claims
of Czech and German factions. The preaching and teaching of the Czech reformer **Jan Hus**
(ca. 1370–1415) were at the center of the debate. As preacher in the Bethlehem Chapel in Prague
from 1402 and eventually as rector of the university, Hus was the natural spokesman for the
non-German townspeople in Prague and the Czech faction at the university. His criticisms of the

Jan Hus Czech reformer
who attacked clerical privileges
and advocated church reform.
He was executed as a heretic
at the Council of Constance in
1415.

church hierarchy, which in Prague was primarily German, fanned into flames the smoldering embers of Czech national feeling. It was Sigismund's hope that a council might clarify the orthodoxy of Hus's teachings and heal the rift within the church of Bohemia.

The council's response to the theological crisis was based on the church's experience with heresy over the previous forty years, primarily the teachings of John Wyclif (1329–1384). In the 1370s, Wyclif, an Oxford theologian and parish priest, began to criticize in increasingly angry terms the state of the clergy and the abuses of the church hierarchy. By 1387, his ideas had been declared heretical and his followers were hunted out. Wyclif believed that the church could be at once a divine institution and an earthly gathering of individuals. Thus, in his opinion, individual Christians need not unquestioningly obey the pronouncements of the church hierarchy. Final authority lay only in the Scriptures, insisted Wyclif, who sponsored the first translations of the Bible into English. He gathered about himself followers called "Lollards," who emphasized Bible reading and popular piety; some even supported public preaching by women. According to one disciple, "Every true man and woman being in charity is a priest."[2]

Wyclif's influence continued on the Continent, especially in the circle of Jan Hus and the Czech reformers. By 1403, the German majority in the university had condemned Hus's teaching as Wycliffite, thus initiating almost a decade of struggle between Czechs and Germans, Hussites and Catholics. This was the impasse that Sigismund hoped the **Council of Constance** could settle. Accordingly, he offered a suspicious Hus a safe conduct pass to attend the council. The council, however, revoked the pledge of safe conduct and ordered Hus to recant his beliefs. He refused and the council condemned him as a heretic and burned him at the stake on July 6, 1415.

Far from ending Sigismund's problems with the Bohemians, the actions of the council provided the Czechs with a martyr and hero. The execution of Hus provoked a firestorm of revolution in Prague. Czech forces roundly defeated an imperial army sent in to restore order. The Hussite movement gathered strength and spread throughout Bohemia. Moderate Hussites continued Hus's campaign against clerical abuses and claimed the right to receive both the bread and the wine during the sacrament of Communion. Radical Hussites argued that the true church was the community of spiritual men and women; they had no use for ecclesiastical hierarchy of any kind. The German emperors were unable to defeat a united Hussite movement. In 1433, a new church council and moderate Hussites negotiated an agreement that allowed the Hussites to continue some of their practices, including receiving both bread and wine at Communion, while returning to the church. Radical Hussites refused the compromise, and the war dragged on until 1436. Bohemia remained a center of religious dissent, and the memory of Hus's execution at a church council would have a chilling effect on discussions of church reform during the Reformation in the sixteenth century.

Council of Constance
General council of the church convened by the Holy Roman emperor to deal with schism and church reform. It elected Pope Martin V to end the Great Schism.

The Execution of Jan Hus
Stripped of the signs of ecclesiastical office, Jan Hus was forced to wear a paper hat indicating he was a heresiarch, the leader of heretics. This and similar images were meant to show the legitimacy of his execution, but in Bohemia he was revered as a martyred saint. (The Art Archive/University Library Prague/Gianni Dagli Orti/Picture Desk)

The Reunion and Reform of the Papacy, 1415–1513

To most of the delegates at the Council of Constance, the reunion and reform of the papacy were more important than the issue of heresy. And as we will see, attempts to deal with reform and reunion seemed in the eyes of the popes to threaten the political independence and the moral leadership of the papacy itself. This too would remain a problem well into the sixteenth century.

The council deposed two claimants and forced the third to resign. Then, in 1417, the council elected a Roman nobleman as Pope Martin V (r. 1417–1431).

The council justified its actions in what was perhaps its most important decree, *Haec sancta synodus* ("This sacred synod"): "This sacred synod of Constance ... declares ... that it has its power immediately from Christ, and that all men, of every rank and position, including even the pope himself are bound to obey it in those matters that pertain to the faith."[3] Popes could no longer expect to remain unchallenged if they made claims of absolute dominion, and ecclesiastical rights and jurisdictions increasingly were matters for negotiation.

Reform was more difficult. Both the cardinals and the popes viewed any reforms to the present system as potential threats to their ability to function. The council, however, recognized the need for further reforms. A second reform council met at Basel from 1431 to 1449, but with modest results. The council again tried to reduce papal power, but this time, it received little support from European governments.

Because of the continuing conciliarist threat, the papacy needed the support of the secular rulers of Europe. Thus, the papacy was forced to accept compromises on the issues of reform, on ecclesiastical jurisdictions and immunities, and on papal revenues. Various governments argued that it was they, and not the pope, who should be responsible for ecclesiastical institutions and jurisdictions within their territories.

Lay rulers wanted church officials in their territories to belong to local families. They wanted ecclesiastical institutions to be subject to local laws and administration. By the 1470s, it was clear that they wanted to have local prelates named as cardinal-protectors. These were not churchmen who could serve the church administration in Rome; rather they functioned as mediators between local governments and the papacy.

The reunited papacy had to accept claims it would have staunchly opposed a century earlier. One of the most important of these was the Pragmatic Sanction of Bourges of 1438. The papacy was unable to protest when the French clergy, at the urging of the king, abolished papal rights to annates, limited appeals to the papal court, and reduced papal rights to appoint clergy within France without the approval of the local clergy or the Crown. Similar concessions diminished church authority throughout Europe.

With reduced revenues from legal fees, annates, and appointments, the popes of the fifteenth century were forced to derive more and more of their revenue and influence from the Papal States. By 1430, the Papal States accounted for about half of the annual income of the papacy. Papal interests increasingly centered on protecting the papacy's influence as a secular ruler of a large territory in central Italy. Further, it saw political independence as essential to its continued moral leadership. Thus, the papacy had to deal with many of the same jurisdictional, diplomatic, and military challenges that faced other medieval governments.

SECTION SUMMARY

- A political crisis forced the papacy to abandon central Italy and move to the south of France.

- A disputed papal election left two claimants—one French, the other Italian—and no clear way to resolve the issue.

- The religious beliefs of John Wyclif and Jan Hus challenged the basis of papal authority.

- In addition to resolving the disputed election, conciliarists claimed authority to correct and reform the papacy.

- By 1450, the papacy was reunited but weakened in relation to the European kingdoms.

WAR AND THE STRUGGLE OVER POLITICAL POWER, 1300–1450

What forces limited the political power of rulers in England, France, and Italy?

A lawyer who served King Philip IV of France (r. 1285–1314) observed that "everything within the limits of his kingdom belongs to the lord king, especially protection, high justice and dominion."[4] Royal officials in England and France generally believed that "liberties"—that is, individual rights to local jurisdictions—originated with the king. These ideas were the result of several centuries of centralization of political power in royal hands. At almost the same time, however, an English noble challenged royal claims on his lands, saying, "Here, my lords, is my warrant," as he brandished a rusty long sword. "My ancestors came with William the Bastard [that is, William the Conqueror, in 1066] and conquered their lands with the sword, and by the sword I will defend them against anyone who tries to usurp them."[5] The views of the royal lawyer and the feisty earl exemplify the central tension over power in the late Middle Ages. The struggle over political power was played out in the context of the **Hundred Years' War**, which affected not just England and France but also most of western Europe, especially Italy, as mercenary soldiers traveled south during temporary lulls in the fighting. In England and France, the crisis led to strengthened monarchies. In Italy, however, local and regional entities exercised many of those liberties the old Englishman wanted to protect with his sword.

Hundred Years' War
Series of conflicts, 1337–1453, fought over English claims within the French monarchy. It ended with the nearly complete expulsion of the English from French lands.

The Hundred Years' War, 1337–1453

In the twelfth and thirteenth centuries, centralization of royal power in England and France had proceeded almost without interruption. In the fourteenth century, matters changed in both countries. Questions of the nature of royal power, common responsibility, and hereditary rights to rule challenged the power of the English and French monarchs. In both countries, competition began largely over dynastic issues, but by the mid-fifteenth century, resolution of the wars led to governments with a more distinctly national tone to them.

ENGLAND

In England, fears arising from the growing power of the English crown and the weakness of a gullible king brought issues to a head during the reign of Edward II (r. 1307–1327). By the early fourteenth century, resident justices of the peace (JPs) were replacing the expensive and inefficient system of traveling justices. In theory, the JPs were royal officials doing the king's bidding, but this was often not the case in reality. These unpaid local officials were modestly well-to-do gentry, who were often clients of local magnates. When the king was not vigilant, justices were prone to use their offices to carry out local vendettas and feuds and to protect the interests of the wealthy and powerful.

The barons, the titled lords of England, were interested in controlling more than just local justices. Fearing that Edward II would continue many of the centralizing policies of his father, the barons passed reform ordinances in 1311, limiting the king's right to wage war, leave the realm, grant lands or castles, or appoint chief justices and chancellors without the approval of Parliament, which they dominated. Special taxes or subsidies were to be paid to the public Exchequer rather than into the king's private treasury. Some of these ordinances were later voided, but the tradition of parliamentary consent remained a key principle of English constitutional history.

The baronial influence grew because Edward II was a weak and naive king, easily influenced by court favorites. After a humiliating defeat at the hands of the Scots at the Battle of Bannockburn (1314), his position steadily deteriorated until he was deposed in 1327 by a coalition of barons led by his wife, Queen Isabella. After a short regency, their son, Edward III (r. 1327–1377), assumed the throne. He was a cautious king, ever aware of the violence and rebelliousness of the baronage.

FRANCE

French kings seemed significantly more powerful in the early fourteenth century. A complex succession crisis, however, made clear the limits of French kingship. In 1328, the direct Capetian line, which had sired the kings of France since the election of Hugh Capet in 987, finally died out. The last Capetians did produce daughters, but by the fourteenth century, many argued that according to custom the French crown should pass through the male line only. Thus, the French nobility selected as king Philip of Valois (Philip VI; r. 1328–1350), a cousin of the last king through the male line (Charles IV; r. 1322–1328). He was chosen in preference to the daughters of the last Capetian kings and, more significantly, in preference to King Edward III of England, whose mother, Isabella, was the daughter of King Philip IV (r. 1285–1314).

Controversy over succession was just one of the disputes between the French and English. An even longer-standing issue was the status of lands within France that belonged to the English kings. In 1340, climaxing a century of tensions over English possessions in France, Edward III of England formally claimed the title "King of France," and the Hundred Years' War was on.

The war was marked by quick English raids and only occasional pitched battles. With a population of about 16 million, France was far richer and more populous than England. On at least one occasion, the French managed to field an army of over 50,000; the English mustered only 32,000

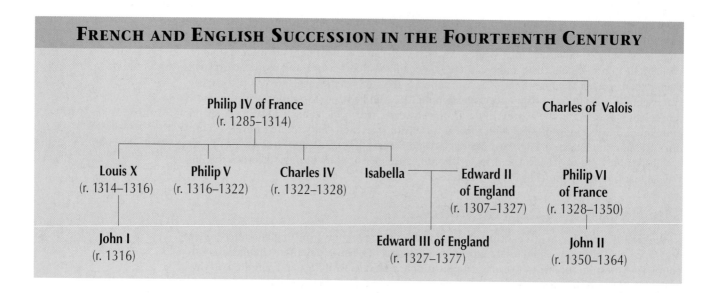

at most. These armies were easily the largest ever assembled by a medieval European kingdom. In almost every engagement, the English were outnumbered. Their strategy, therefore, was to avoid pitched battles except on the most advantageous terms. Edward III engaged in extremely destructive raids, hoping to lure the French into ill-considered attacks. The English stole what they could, destroyed what they could not steal, and captured enemy knights to hold for ransom.

STAGES OF THE WAR The war can be divided into four stages. The first stage (1337–1360) was characterized by a rapid series of English assaults and victories. The few pitched battles, including Crécy (1346) and Poitiers (1356), show how Edward's strategy worked (see **MAP 11.1**). In these cases, the English gathered their forces in careful defensive positions and took advantage of an individualistic French chivalric ethos according to which, in the words of one knight, "who does the most is worth the most." The key to the English defensive position was the use of longbowmen and cannon. Arrows from the longbow had more penetrating power than a bolt from a crossbow, and the longbow could be fired much more rapidly. By 1300, Europeans had forged cannon for use in siege warfare and to protect defensive positions. Although there is a debate over how effective they were, when used in combination with the longbow, they effectively disrupted and scattered advancing troops.

In the second stage of the war (1360–1396), French forces responded more cautiously to the English tactics and slowly regained much of the territory they had lost. However, during this stage, the disruptions and expenses of war placed a huge burden on both French and English society. First, in the wake of the French defeat at Poitiers in 1356, France was rocked by a series of urban and rural revolts and protests. Later, in 1381, the English faced a similar series of protests over taxes and the costs of war. Finally, because of stress over the war and general noble dissatisfaction, Richard II was forced to abdicate the English throne. Parliament then elected as king Henry IV (r. 1399–1413), the first ruler from the House of Lancaster. Richard died in prison under mysterious circumstances in 1400.

A fateful shift occurred in the third stage of the war (1396–1422). King Charles VI (r. 1380–1422) of France suffered bouts of insanity throughout his long reign, which made effective French government almost impossible. The English king Henry V (r. 1413–1422) renewed his family's claim to the French throne.

The Battle at Agincourt The English victory at Agincourt marked the high point of English influence in France. Once again English archers defeated a larger, mounted force.
(The Granger Collection, New York)

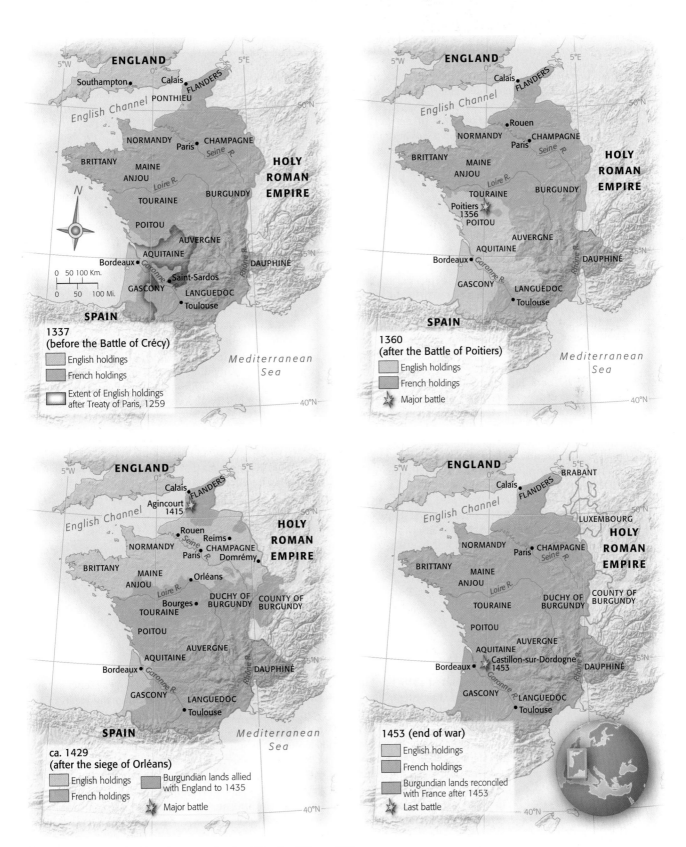

🌐 **Map 11.1—England and France in the Hundred Years' War**

The succession of maps suggests both why hit-and-run tactics worked for the English early in the war and why the English were ultimately unable to defeat the French and take control of all of France.

The Inquisition of Joan of Arc

An important question at the trial of Joan of Arc was whether her acts had any authoritative value: Did the voices she heard originate with God or the Devil? The judges wanted to demonstrate to their own satisfaction that Joan was one of "the sowers of deceitful inventions" of which the Gospels warned. They fully expected that external signs could reveal hidden truths. The following memorandum is a summation of the commission's case against the maid.

You said that your king received a sign by which he knew you were sent from God, that it was St. Michael, in the company of a host of angels. ... You have said that you are certain of future and contingent events that you recognized men you had never seen, through the voices of St. Catherine and St. Margaret. ... Regarding this article, the clergy find superstition, divination, ... and vain boasting.

You said that you wore and still wear man's dress at God's command and to His good pleasure, for you had instruction from God to wear this dress, and so you put on a short tunic, jerkin, and hose with many points. You even wear your hair cut above the ears, without keeping about you anything to denote your sex, save what nature has given you. ... The clergy declare that you blaspheme against God, despising Him and His sacraments, that you transgress divine law, Holy Scripture and the canons of the Church, ... that you are given to idolatry and worship of yourself and your clothes, according to the customs of the heathen.

You have declared that you know well that God loves certain living persons better than you, and that you learned this by revelation from St. Catherine and St. Margaret; also that those saints speak French, not English, as they are not on the side of the English. And since you knew that your voices were for your king, you began to dislike the Burgundians. ... Such matters the clergy pronounce to be a rash and presumptuous assertion, a superstitious divination, a blasphemy uttered against St. Catherine and St. Margaret, and a transgression of the commandment to love our neighbors. ...

You declared that to those whom you call St. Michael, St. Catherine and St. Margaret, you did reverence, bending the knee ... vowing them your virginity ... now touching these matters, the clergy affirm. ... You are an idolatress, an invoker of demons, an apostate from the faith, a maker of rash statements, a swearer of an unlawful oath.

And you have said ... that you know that all the deeds of which you have been accused in your trial were wrought according to the command of God and that it was impossible for you to do otherwise. ... Wherefore the clergy declare you to be schismatic, an unbeliever in the unity and authority of the Church, apostate and obstinately erring from the faith. ... [The inquisitor admonished her,] "You have believed in apparitions lightly, instead of turning to God in devout prayer to grant you certainty; and you have not consulted prelates or learned ecclesiastics to enlighten yourself: although, considering your condition and the simplicity of your knowledge, you ought to have done so."

QUESTIONS

1. What are the signs that indicated to the judges that Joan was a heretic?

2. Why do the judges believe that Joan's "voices" are false?

Source: "The Inquisition of Joan of Arc" from *The Trial of Jeanne d'Arc*, trans. W.P. Barrett, 1932. Reprinted by permission of Gotham House.

At Agincourt in 1415, the English (led by Henry himself) again enticed a larger French army into attacking an English position fortified by longbows and cannon. By the terms of the Treaty of Troyes (1420), Charles VI's son (the future Charles VII) was declared illegitimate and disinherited; Henry married Catherine, the daughter of Charles VI, and he was declared the legitimate heir to the French throne. A final English victory seemed assured, but both Charles VI and Henry V died in 1422, leaving Henry's infant son, Henry VI (r. 1422–1461), to inherit both thrones.

The kings' deaths ushered in the final stage of the Hundred Years' War (1422–1453), the French reconquest. In 1428, military and political power seemed firmly in the hands of the English and the great aristocrats. Yet, in a stunning series of events, the French were able to reverse the situation.

JOAN OF ARC   In 1429, with the aid of the mysterious **Joan of Arc** (d. 1431), the French king, Charles VII, was able to raise the English siege of Orléans (or-lay-OHN) and begin the reconquest of the north of France. Joan was the daughter of prosperous peasants from an area of Burgundy that had suffered under the English and their Burgundian allies. Her "voices" told her to go to the king and assist him in driving out the English. Like many late medieval mystics, she reported regular visions of divine revelation. Even politically or militarily important female leaders depended initially on religious charisma. One of the tests that supported Joan's claim to divine direction was her identification of Charles, who had disguised himself among his courtiers. Dressed as a man, she was Charles's most famed and feared military leader. With Joan's aid, the king was crowned in the cathedral at Reims, the traditional site of French coronations. Joan was captured during an audacious attack on Paris itself and eventually fell into English hands. Because of her "unnatural dress" and her claim to divine guidance, she was condemned and burned as a heretic in 1431. (See the feature, "The Written Record: The Inquisition of Joan of Arc.") A heretic only to the English and their supporters, Joan almost instantly became a symbol of French resistance. Pope Calixtus III reversed the condemnation in 1456, and Joan was canonized in 1920. The heretic became Saint Joan, patron of France.

Despite Joan's capture, the French advance continued. By 1450, the English had lost all their major centers except Calais (ca-LAY). In 1453, the French armies captured the fortress of Castillon-sur-Dordogne (kasti-YON sir dor-DON-ya) in what was to be the last battle of the war (see **Map 11.1**). There was no treaty, only a cessation of hostilities.

The war touched almost every aspect of life in western Europe: political, religious, economic, and social. It ranged beyond the borders of France, as Scotland, Castile, Aragon, and German principalities were, at various times, drawn into the struggle. French and English support for rival popes prevented early settlement of the Great Schism in the papacy (see page 291). Further, the war caused a general rise in the level of violence in society. As Henry V casually observed, "War without fire is as bland as sausages without mustard."[6] Because of the highly profitable lightning raids, this war was never bland. During periods of truce, many soldiers simply ranged through France, pillaging small towns and ravaging the countryside. Others went in search of work as mercenaries, especially in Germany, Poland, and Italy. Truces in France did not necessarily mean peace in Europe.

Italy

Compared with France and England, fourteenth- and fifteenth-century Italy was a land of cities. In northern Europe, a town of over 20,000 or 30,000 people was unusual; only Paris and London boasted more than 100,000 people in the fourteenth century. Yet, at one time or another, in the late Middle Ages, Milan, Venice, Florence, and Naples all had populations near or exceeding 100,000, and countless other Italian towns boasted populations of well over 30,000. Unlike northern European states with their kings or emperors, however, the Italian peninsula lacked a unifying force. The centers of power were in Italy's flourishing cities. Political life revolved around the twin issues of who should dominate city governments and how cities could learn to coexist peacefully.

By the late thirteenth century, political power in most Italian towns was divided among three major groups. First was the old urban nobility that could trace its wealth back to grants of property and rights from kings, emperors, and bishops in the tenth and eleventh centuries. Second was the merchant families who had grown wealthy in the twelfth and thirteenth centuries, as Italians led the European economic expansion into the Mediterranean. Third, challenging these entrenched urban groups were the modest artisans and merchants who had organized trade, neighborhood, or militia groups and referred to themselves as the *popolo*, or "people." Townspeople gathered together in factions based on wealth, family, profession, neighborhood, and even systems of clientage that reached back into the villages from which many of them had come. "War and hatred have so multiplied among the Italians," observed one Florentine, "that in every town there is a division and enmity between two parties of citizens."

Riven with factions, townspeople often would turn control of their government over to a *signor* (sin-YOUR), a "lord" or "tyrant," often a local noble with a private army. Once firmly in power, the tyrant often allowed the government to continue to function as it had, requiring only that he control all major political appointments. The process might appear democratic, but it represented a profound shift in power. In the case of Milan, the noble Viscontis (vis-KON-tees) used support from the emperor Henry VII (r. 1308–1313) to drive their opponents out of the city. Eventually granting Milan and its territories as a duchy, the Viscontis, and later their Sforza successors, made marriage alliances with the French crown and created a splendid court culture. In a series of wars between the 1370s and 1450s, the dukes of Milan expanded their political control throughout most of Lombardy, Liguria, and, temporarily, Tuscany. The Viscontis maintained control of the city and much of the region of Lombardy until the last scion of the family died in 1447.

Joan of Arc Charismatic peasant who heard voices telling her to assist the French crown in its war against England. She was captured and eventually executed as a heretic.

CITY-STATES

THE REPUBLICS The great republics of Venice and Florence escaped domination by signori, but only by undertaking significant constitutional change. In both republics, political life had been disrupted by the arrival of immigrants and by the demands of recently enriched merchants and speculators for a voice in government. In 1297, reacting to increased competition for influence, the Venetian government began a series of reforms that would come to be known as the "Closing of the Grand Council." This enlarged the council to about eleven hundred members from those families eligible for public office, but its eventual effect was to freeze out subsequent arrivals from ever rising to elite status. The Venetian patriciate became a closed urban nobility. Political, factional, and economic tensions were hidden beneath a veneer of serenity as Venetians developed a myth of public-spirited patricians who governed in the interests of all the people, leaving others free to enrich themselves in trade and manufacture.

In Florence, the arguments over citizenship and the right of civic participation disrupted public life. Violent wealthy families, immigrants, and artisans of modest background were cut off from civic participation. A series of reforms, culminating in the Ordinances of Justice of 1293 to 1295, restricted political participation in Florence to members in good standing of certain merchant and artisan guilds. Members of violence-prone families were defined as *Magnate* (literally, "the powerful") and disqualified from holding public office. In spite of the reforms, political power remained concentrated in the hands of the great families, whose wealth was based primarily on banking and mercantile investments. These families used their political influence and economic power to dominate Florentine life.

There were short-lived attempts to reform the system and extend the rights of political participation to include the more modest artisans and laborers. The most dramatic was in 1378, when the Ciompi (CHOMP-ee), unskilled workers in Florence's woolen industry, led a popular revolution hoping to expand participation in government and limit the authority of the guild masters over semiskilled artisans and day laborers. They created new guilds to represent the laborers who had no voice in government. Barely six weeks after the Ciompi insurrection, however, wealthy conservatives began a reaction suppressing, exiling, or executing the leaders of the movement and eventually suppressing the new guilds. Political and economic power was now even more firmly in the grip of influential patricians.

Following a crisis in 1434, brought on by war and high taxes, virtual control of Florentine politics fell into the hands of Cosimo de' Medici (day-MAY-di-chi), the wealthiest banker in the city. From 1434 to 1494, Cosimo, his son Piero, his grandson Lorenzo, and Lorenzo's son dominated the government in Florence. Although the Medicis were always careful to pay homage to Florentine republican traditions, their control was virtually as complete as that of the lords of towns such as Ferrara and Milan.

Indeed, by the middle of the fifteenth century, little differentiated the republics—Florence and Venice—from cities, such as Milan and Mantua, where lords held sway. Although Florentines maintained that they intervened to protect Florentine and Tuscan "liberty" when the Viscontis of Milan threatened Tuscany and central Italy, their interests went beyond simple defense. Relations among the great cities of Milan, Venice, Florence, Rome, and Naples were stabilized by the Peace of Lodi and the creation of the Italian League in 1454. In response to endemic warfare in Italy and the looming threat of the Ottoman Turks in the eastern Mediterranean (see pages 312–314), the five powers agreed to the creation of spheres of influence that would prevent any one of them from expanding at the expense of the others.

The Journey of the Magi The story of the journey of the Magi to Bethlehem to find the baby Jesus seemed a perfect image of the power and wisdom of rulers. This painting (a detail) of the Magi was commissioned for the private chapel of Cosimo de' Medici, the de facto ruler of Florence. (Palazzo Medici Riccardi, Florence/Scala/Art Resource, NY)

The limits of these territorial states became clear when King Charles VIII of France invaded Italy in 1494 to assert his hereditary claim to the kingdom of Naples. The French invasion touched off a devastating series of wars called the Habsburg-Valois Wars (1496–1559). French claims were challenged by the Habsburg emperors and also by the Spanish, who themselves made claims on southern Italy and much of Lombardy. The cost of prolonged warfare kept almost all governments in a state of crisis.

In Florence, the wars destroyed the old Medici-dominated regime and brought in a new republican government. Anti-Medici efforts were initially led by the popular Dominican preacher Girolamo Savonarola (1452–1498). In the constitutional debates after 1494, Savonarola argued that true political reform required a sweeping purge of the evils of society. Gangs of youth flocked to his cause, attacking prostitutes and homosexuals. Many of his followers held "bonfires of vanities," burning wigs, silks, and other luxuries. In 1498, when his followers had lost influence in the government, Savonarola was arrested, tortured, and executed.

In spite of republican reforms, new fortresses, and a citizen militia, the Florentine government was unable to defend itself from papal and imperial armies. In 1512, the Habsburg emperor restored Medici control of Florence. The Medicis later became dukes and then grand dukes of Tuscany. The grand duchy of Tuscany remained an independent, integrated, and well-governed state until the French Revolution of 1789. Venice also managed to maintain its republican form of government and its territorial state until the French Revolution, but like the grand dukes of Tuscany, the governors of Venice were no longer able to act independently of the larger European powers.

The Habsburg-Valois Wars ended with the Treaty of Cateau-Cambrésis (kah-toe kam-bray-SEE) in 1559, which left the Spanish kings in control of Milan, Naples, Sardinia, and Sicily. Thus, the Spanish dominated Italy, but without the centralizing control typical of England and France. Venice, Tuscany, the Papal States, and even lesser republics and principalities retained significant influence, as Italy remained a land of regional governments.

SECTION SUMMARY

- The Hundred Years' War was fought over English dynastic claims within the French kingdom.

- The costs of war contributed to social and political unrest in both countries.

- As a result of the war, the English lost all their significant possessions within the French kingdom.

- Italy was a land of populous, independent cities and regional states.

- By the fifteenth century, most Italian governments were dominated by merchant oligarchies or by lords.

CRISIS IN ECONOMY AND SOCIETY

How were economic and social structures changed by plague and economic crisis?

After nearly three centuries of dramatic growth, Europe, in 1300, was seriously overpopulated, with estimates ranging from about 80 million to as high as 100 million. In some parts of Europe, population would not be this dense again until the late eighteenth century. Opportunities dwindled because of overpopulation, famine, war, and epidemic, which also brought changes in trade and commerce. As the population began to decline, this trend, along with deflation and transformed patterns of consumption, affected agriculture, which was still the foundation of the European economy. Recovery from all these crises altered the structure and dynamics of families, the organization of work, and the culture in many parts of Europe. As a result of the crises, there had been a relative shift in economic and demographic vitality from Italy to England, France, and central Europe.

Famine and Declining Births

People in many parts of Europe were living on the edge of disaster in 1300. Given the low level of agricultural technology and the limited amount of land available for cultivation, it became increasingly difficult for the towns and countryside to feed and support the expanding population.

Growing numbers of people competed for land to farm and for jobs. Farm sizes declined throughout Europe, as parents tended to divide their land among their children. Rents for farmland increased, as landlords found that they could play one land-hungry farmer against another. Competition for jobs kept urban wages low, and when taxes were added to high rents and low wages, many peasants and artisans found it difficult to marry and raise families. Thus, because of reduced opportunities brought on by overpopulation, poor townspeople and peasants tended to marry late and have smaller families.

More dramatic than this crisis of births were the deadly famines that occurred in years of bad harvests. The great famine of 1315 to 1322 marks a turning point in the economic history of Europe. Wet and cold weather repeatedly ruined crops in much of northern Europe. Food stocks were quickly exhausted, and mass starvation followed. At Ypres, in Flanders, 2,800 people (about 10 percent of the population) died in just six months and shortages continued. Seven other severe famines were reported in the south of France or Italy during the fourteenth century.

Black Death An epidemic, possibly of bubonic plague, that wiped out one-third or more of Europe's population between 1348 and 1351. It initiated almost three centuries of epidemics.

If Europe's problem had merely been one of famine brought on by overpopulation, rapid recovery should have been possible. However, the difficulties of overpopulation were exacerbated by war and plague. As noted previously, the devastation of cities and the countryside was a common tactic in the Hundred Years' War. It was also typical of the local wars in parts of Spain, Germany, and especially Italy. The destruction of trees and vineyards and the theft of livestock made it difficult for rural populations to survive. Then, in 1348, the **Black Death** or "the great Mortality," as contemporaries called it, struck Europe.

The Black Death

Today there is no consensus as to what caused the Black Death. In the early twentieth century, after the bacillus that causes bubonic plague was identified by French and Japanese physicians in Hong Kong, it was assumed that bubonic plague was the cause. Subsequently, there have been controversial claims that DNA fragments of bubonic plague have been found in mass graves. Yet, bubonic plague usually travels slowly and infects a relatively small portion of a given population. By contrast, the Black Death seemed to race across Europe, wiping out entire families and infecting whole cities. Because of this evidence, some historical epidemiologists have speculated that the cause may actually have been anthrax or even a "hemorrhagic plague" similar to the Ebola virus.

THE SPREAD OF THE DISEASE

Although the historical identification of the Black Death remains controversial, contemporaries had little doubt about the source of the disease. Genoese traders, they believed, contracted the plague in Caffa, on the Black Sea coast. Infected sailors carried the disease south into Egypt and west into Sicily, then on to Genoa and Venice. From there, it followed established trade routes first into central Italy; later to the south of France, the Low Countries, and England; and finally, through the North and Baltic Seas, into Germany and the Slavic lands to the east (see **MAP 11.2**).

Mortality rates varied, but generally 60 percent or more of those infected died. In the initial infestation of 1348 to 1351, 25 to 35 percent of Europe's population may have died. In some of Europe's larger cities, the death rate may have been as high as 60 percent. In Florence, for example, the population probably declined from about 90,000 to about 50,000 or even less. The shock and disruption were immense. Governments in some towns simply ceased to function at the height of the epidemic. Chroniclers reported that no one could be found to care for the sick or bury the dead. Although abandonment of the sick was probably more a fear than a reality, the epidemic nonetheless significantly disrupted daily life.

Just as areas were rebounding from the initial outbreak of the plague, it returned between 1360 and 1363, and then, for three centuries thereafter, almost no generation could avoid it. It has been calculated that in central Italy, where the best records are available, the plague returned on average every eleven years between 1350 and 1400. Less is known about the plague in Muslim lands and in the eastern Mediterranean, but the situation seems to have been similar to the European experience. Because the plague tended to carry off the young, the almost generational return of the disease accounts for the depressed population levels found in many parts of Europe until the late fifteenth century and in western Asia until the late seventeenth or eighteenth century.

Lacking an understanding of either contagion or infection, fourteenth-century doctors depended on traditional theories inherited from the Greeks, especially the work of Galen (GAY-len), to treat the plague. In Galenic medicine, good health depended on the proper balance of bodily and environmental forces; it could be upset by corrupt air, the movement of planets, and even violent

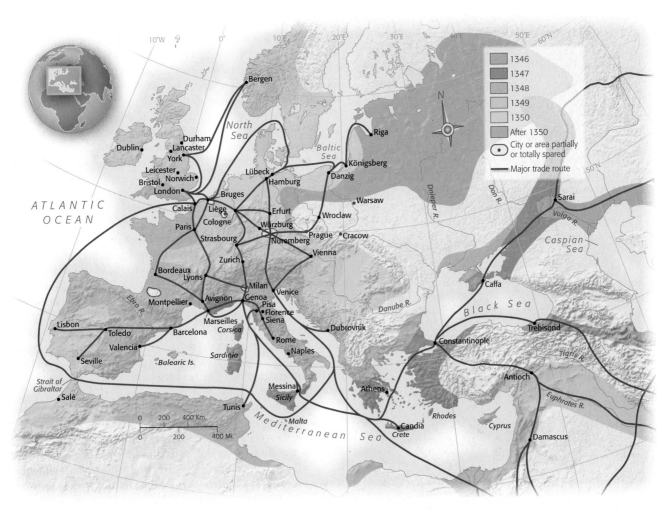

🌐 **MAP 11.2—The Progress of the Black Death**
The Black Death did not advance evenly across Europe; rather, as is clear from the dates at which it struck various regions, it followed the main lines of trade and communication.

shifts in emotions. Yet, in the fifteenth and sixteenth centuries, as the rhythms of the infestations became clearer, towns and, later, territorial governments perceived the contagious nature of the disease. Officials instituted increasingly effective quarantines and embargoes to restrict the movement of goods and people from areas where the plague was raging. Some argue that it was the eventual extension of these efforts throughout Europe that led to the gradual reduction and then disappearance of the plague from western Europe by the early eighteenth century.

Alongside medical theory, however, another class of explanations developed. Taking a lead from miracle stories in which Jesus linked illness and sin, many Christians considered the Black Death a signal of the Last Judgment, or at least a sign of the severe judgment of God on a sinful world. Given that view, a traditional, and logical, religious response was to urge various moral reforms and penitential acts, such as charitable gifts, special prayers, and holy processions. (See the feature, "The Visual Record: A Painting of the Plague.") Many Muslim theologians also concluded that "the plague is part of Allah's punishment." Women were often thought to be a source of moral pollution and hence one of the causes of God's wrath. In Muslim Egypt, women were ordered off the streets; in Christian Europe prostitutes were driven out of towns.

A movement of penitents called "flagellants" arose in Hungary and spread quickly into Germany and across France and the Low Countries. In an imitation of Christ's life and sufferings, they sought to atone in their own bodies for the sins of the world. Following an ancient Christian tradition, they ritually beat (flagellated) themselves between the shoulders with metal-tipped whips. Through their

processions and sufferings, these pilgrims hoped to bring about a moral and religious transformation of society. The arrival of flagellants was often an occasion for an end of feuds and political violence within a community. But their arrival, just as often, was an occasion for political and even religious unrest. Authorities recognized the flagellants and the leaders of the religious riots as dangerous and drove them from towns.

In a quest for a purer, truly Christian society, the flagellants brought suspicion on all those who were not Christian or who were otherwise suspect. Some parts of Europe witnessed murderous attacks on outsiders, especially lepers and Jews, who were suspected of spreading the contagion in an attempt to bring down Latin Christendom. These attacks probably have more to do with tensions and fears already existing in parts of Europe than with the provocations of the flagellants. Like many other anti-Semitic myths, the rumors of wells poisoned by lepers and Jews seemed to arise in the south of France and spread in their most virulent forms to German towns along the Rhine. In Strasbourg attacks on Jews preceded the arrival of the plague. Except in a few districts, officials opposed attacks on Jews, lepers, and heretics. Doctors and churchmen often observed that Jews were unlikely culprits, since the plague claimed Jewish as well as Christian victims. Despite official rejection of popular rumors and fears, from the mid-fourteenth century, life became more difficult for the Jews of Christian Europe.

It was a commonplace among contemporary chroniclers that "so many did die that everyone thought it was the end of the world." Yet it was the very young, the elderly, and the poor—those least likely to pay taxes, own shops, or produce children—who were the most common victims. And even in towns, such as Florence, where mortality rates were extraordinarily high, recovery from the initial epidemic was rapid. Government offices were closed at most for only a few weeks; markets reopened as soon as the death rate began to decline; and within two years, tax receipts were back at preplague levels. Yet plague, fear of plague, and social and economic disruption caused by epidemic disease became a regular feature of European life. Thus, famine, warfare, plague, and population decline fueled the economic and social transformations of the late Middle Ages.

Trade and Agriculture

In the aftermath of plague, the economy of Europe changed in a number of profound ways. Disruptions brought on by population decline were accompanied by changes in the basic structure of economic life. In particular, Italy's domination of the European economy was challenged by the growth of trade and manufacturing in many other parts of Europe. Further, by 1500, the relative power of Italian bankers declined as they came to face competition from equally astute northern bankers.

Saint Roch Cured by an Angel Saint Roch is often shown with an exposed plague bubo. The image offered Christians comfort since he was cured because of his faith and charity. It offers modern historians evidence that bubonic plague was responsible for at least some of the mortality. (Courtesy, Bayerisches Nationalmuseum)

Discussions of the economy must begin with Italy because it was the key point of contact between Europe and the international economy. In 1300, Italian merchants sold woolens produced in Flanders and Italy to Arab traders in North Africa, who sold them along the African coast and as far south as the Niger Delta. The Italians used the gold that they collected in payment to buy spices and raw materials in Byzantium, Egypt, and even China. They resold these highly prized goods in the cities and at regional fairs of northern Europe. Italian traders also sold spices, silks, and other luxuries throughout Europe, from England to Poland.

Because of their expertise in moving bullion and goods and their ready sources of capital, Italian merchants, such as the Ricciardis of Lucca who flourished in England, were ideal bankers and financial advisers to the popes and European rulers, who appreciated sources of ready capital. In times of war, rulers tended to trade the rights to various revenues to Italian bankers, who had cash at hand. Merchants from Cremona, Genoa, Florence, and Siena forged commercial agreements with the kings of France, Aragon, and Castile, and with the papacy. The most powerful bank in fifteenth-century Europe was the Medici bank of Florence. Founded in 1397 by Giovanni de' Medici (1360–1429), the bank grew quickly because of its role as papal banker. Medici agents transferred papal revenues from all parts of Europe to Rome and managed papal alum mines, which provided an essential mineral to the growing cloth industry.

The dramatic career of the Frenchman Jacques Coeur (1395?–1456) demonstrates that by the mid-fifteenth century, Italian merchants were not the only Europeans who understood international trade. After making a fortune trading in southern France, Coeur managed the French royal mint and became the financial adviser of King Charles VII (r. 1422–1461). He put the French monarchy back on a solid financial footing after the Hundred Years' War, in the process, becoming the wealthiest individual in France.

By 1500, Italians faced increased competition from local merchants throughout Europe. From as early as the late thirteenth century, trade along the North and Baltic Seas in northern Europe was dominated by the **Hanseatic League**, an association of over a hundred trading cities centered on the German city of Lübeck. By the late fourteenth and early fifteenth centuries, the Hansa towns controlled grain shipments from eastern Europe to England and Scandinavia. The league's domination waned in the second half of the fifteenth century, however, as Dutch, English, and even southern German merchants gained shares of the wool, grain, and fur trades.

In contrast to the Hanseatic League of towns, merchants in southern Germany adopted Italian techniques of trade, manufacture, and finance to expand their influence throughout central Europe. German merchants regularly bought spices in the markets of Venice and distributed them in central and eastern Europe. By the fifteenth century, the townspeople of southern Germany also produced linen and cotton cloth, which found ready markets in central and eastern Europe.

The Fugger (FOO-ger) family of Augsburg in southern Germany was the most prosperous of the German commercial families. Jacob Fugger (1459–1525) was a dominant figure in the spice trade and also participated in a number of unusually large loans to a succession of German princes. Jacob Fugger's wealth increased fourfold between 1470 and 1500. The Fuggers were indispensable allies of the German emperors. Jacob himself ensured the election of Charles V as Holy Roman emperor in 1519, making a series of loans that allowed Charles to buy the influence that he needed to win election.

As wealthy as the great merchants were, in most parts of Europe, prosperity was still tied to agriculture and the production of food grains. In northern and western Europe, foodstuffs were produced on the manorial estates of great churchmen and nobles. These estates were worked by a combination of farmers paying rents, serfs who owed a variety of labor services, and day laborers who were hired during planting and harvesting. In the face of a decimated population, landlords and employers found themselves competing for the reduced number of laborers who had survived the plague.

Cloth manufacture, not agriculture, was the part of the European economy that changed most dramatically in the late Middle Ages. First in Flanders, then later in England, Germany, and the rest of Europe, production shifted from urban workshops to the countryside. Industries in rural areas tended to be free of controls on quality or techniques. Rural production, whether in Flanders, England, or Lombardy, became the most dynamic part of the industry.

Rural cloth production was least expensive because it could be done as occasional or part-time labor by farmers, or by their wives or children, during slack times of the day or season.

ITALIAN AND NORTHERN MERCHANTS

NEW TRADING PATTERNS

Hanseatic League An association of over a hundred German trading towns, which dominated trade in the North Sea and Baltic Sea regions during the fourteenth and fifteenth centuries.

THE RURAL ECONOMY

A Painting of the Plague

Writers who survived the coming of pestilential disease in 1348 described a world of terror in which things seemed changed forever. Look at this painting, St. Sebastian Interceding for the Plague-Stricken, created by the Flemish artist Josse Lieferinxe between 1497 and 1499. One dying man seems to be falling terrified to the ground, while a female bystander in the background screams in alarm. Images of Christ, Saint Sebastian (pierced by arrows), a devil, and a priest seem to indicate that something terrifying and undreamed-of is happening. But what exactly was the terror, and what had changed?

The art of the later Middle Ages is an extremely valuable source for understanding social and religious values. As you look at St. Sebastian Interceding for the Plague-Stricken, the first step is to understand what men and women in the fourteenth and fifteenth centuries thought about death. After 1400 European Christians often depicted the universality of death in paintings showing the Dance of Death. The motif varies, but typically Death grasps the hands of men and women, rich and poor, noble and peasant, and leads them away. Deathbed scenes were another popular motif. In the late Middle Ages most people believed that at death the good and evil acts committed by an individual were tallied in the Book of Life and the person was either granted eternal life, first in Purgatory and then Paradise, or consigned to eternal suffering in Hell. Judgment scenes often depict the Virgin Mary or another saint pleading before God or contending with the Devil or demons over the souls of the dying.

It was essential for people to prepare for a good death. Individuals studied the artes moriendi, or "arts of dying." A lingering, painful illness was often interpreted as an opportunity for penitential suffering that would benefit the soul. At the point of death, the dying person could confess and receive absolution for sins and the last sacraments of the church. From that moment on, he or she needed to maintain a calm faith, free from fear. Salvation and eternal life depended on avoiding further sin, especially the questioning of God's forgiveness and mercy. Death was a public event. Clergy, family, religious societies, even neighbors helped the dying person to avoid losing faith at the end. The person might pray, "Virgin Mary, Mother of God, I have placed my hope in you. Free my soul from care, and from Hell, and bitter death."*

The concept of a good death is critical to understanding the European response to the plague. To be sure, individuals rarely look forward to death, then or now. Numerous writers and chroniclers lamented the suddenness of death and the lack of priests to hear confessions. Individuals who were healthy in the morning might be dead by nightfall. The suddenness, the lack of time to prepare for a good death, heightened the dread that accompanied the onset of the illness.

Medieval Christians turned to saints to represent them before God at the point of death and to stop the onslaught of the plague. Three patron saints were especially popular. The Virgin Mary was often shown using her cloak to shelter towns and individuals from arrows carrying pestilence. Saint Roch, himself a victim of the plague, was thought to intercede and protect those who prayed in his name. And Saint Sebastian, an early Christian who as part of his elaborate martyrdom survived being shot with arrows (later understood as symbols of death caused by the plague), was thought to be an especially effective patron during epidemics. In times of plague, people went on pilgrimages to local shrines dedicated to these or local saints, carried images of the saints in processions, and built churches and chapels in honor of the saints in thanks for deliverance from the plague.

With these issues in mind, what do we see in Lieferinxe's painting? The painting portrays an outbreak of the plague. We note first the body of the dead person, carefully shrouded.

Because production was likely to be finished in the countryside (beyond guild supervision), the merchant was free to move the cloth to wherever it could be sold most easily and profitably; guild masters had no control over price or quality.

Two other developments also changed the woolen trade of the fifteenth century: the rise of Spain as an exporter of unprocessed wool and the emergence of England, long recognized as a source of prime wool, as a significant producer of finished cloth. Spain was an ideal region for the pasturing of livestock. By the fifteenth century, highly prized Spanish wool from merino sheep was regularly exported to Italy, Flanders, and England. By 1500, over three million sheep grazed in Castile alone, and revenues from duties on wool formed the backbone of royal finance.

In England, in contrast, economic transformation was tied to cloth production. During the fifteenth century, England reduced its export of its high-quality raw wool and began instead to export its own finished cloth. In 1350, the English exported just over 5,000 bolts of cloth. By the 1470s, exports had risen to 63,000 bolts, and they doubled again by the 1520s. The growth of cloth exports contributed enormously to the expansion of London. During the fourteenth and fifteenth centuries, English commerce became increasingly controlled by London merchant-adventurers. Soon after 1500, over 80 percent of the cloth for export passed through the hands

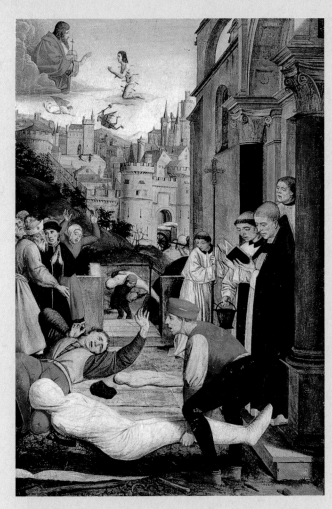

Lieferinxe: St. Sebastian Interceding for the Plague-Stricken (Collection of The Walters Art Museum. Photo © The Walters Art Museum, Baltimore)

Ideally the dead, like the corpse here, were taken to a church by friends and relatives and given a Christian burial. This was an important part of the ritual meant to ease the suffering of the soul in Purgatory. But chroniclers often reported that so many died, and died so quickly, that no one could be found to bury them properly. In many towns the dead were gathered on carts and hauled to gaping common graves outside the towns. We can see one such cart leaving the castle in the background. In a series of images, then, Lieferinxe shows what mattered most to people. In the foreground is the shrouded body attended by a priest and other clerics bearing a cross. This person experienced a good death. In contrast, the man who has fallen behind the body is suffering a bad death, one that caught him unaware. He is the object of the concern and grief of those near him. In the sky just above the castle walls, a white-robed angel and a horned, ax-wielding demon contend over the souls of the dead and dying. At the top of the painting Christ listens to the prayers of Saint Sebastian. The painting thus portrays the impact and horror of plague and also the way Christians were expected to respond to it.

Returning to our original question, we can conclude that the terror of epidemic plague was not entirely like a modern panic. Medieval people saw the Black Death, its ghastly devastation, and its only possible solution or meaning in terms of traditional religious values: The true terror was to be caught unaware.

QUESTIONS

1. What is a good death?
2. What responses to epidemic diseases can you find in this image?
3. Which parts of the image illustrate panic and which do not?

*Quoted in Philippe Ariès, *The Hour of Our Death* (New York: Knopf, 1981), p. 108.

---

of the Londoners. This development, coupled with the rise of London as a center of administration and consumption, laid the foundation for the economic and demographic growth that would make London the largest and most prosperous city in western Europe by the eighteenth century.

The new structures of agriculture, manufacture, and trade in the fifteenth century challenged customs and institutions by admitting new entrepreneurs into the marketplace. However, Europe was still a conservative society in which social and political influence was more prized than economic wealth. Patricians in many European towns acted to dampen competition and preserve traditional values. Great banking families, such as the Medicis of Florence, tended to avoid competition and concentrations of capital. They did not try to drive their competitors out of business because the leaders of rival banks were their political and social peers. In northern Europe, governments in towns, such as Leiden, restricted the concentration of resources in the hands of the town's leading cloth merchants. Their aim was to ensure full employment for the town's laborers, political power for the guild masters, and social stability in the town.

In the wake of plague, the patricians' role, literally as "city fathers," was challenged by artisans and laborers. As wages rose because of population decline, workers demanded more voice in public life. Famed revolts, like the English Rising of 1381 (see page 296) or the Ciompi Revolt in

PATTERNS OF ECONOMIC LIFE

Street Life in Medieval Towns In a world dependent on natural lighting, shops were entirely open to the street. It made social and economic life much more public than it is in the modern world. (Bibliothèque nationale de France)

Italy (see page 300) are only the tip of the iceberg. Numerous other rebellions are recorded across Europe in the second half of the fourteenth century. Laborers attempted to use demand for labor to social and political advantage.

Full employment was not just for men. Although men had controlled the guilds and most crafts in the thirteenth and early fourteenth centuries, women's guilds existed in several European cities, including Paris and Cologne. In Italy, some women could be found among the more prosperous crafts. Women often practiced their trades in the context of the family. In Cologne, for instance, women produced the linen yarn and silk cloths that their husbands sold throughout Europe. Speaking of the silkmakers of Cologne, a report noted that "the women are much more knowledgeable about the trade than are the men." Unlike southern Europe, where women had no public roles, some northern towns apparently allowed women's guilds to protect their members' activities as artisans and even peddlers. Because they often worked before marriage, townswomen in northern Europe tended to marry at a later age than did women in Italy. Many women earned their own marriage dowries. Since they had their own sources of income and often managed the shop of a deceased husband, women could be surprisingly independent. They were consequently under less pressure to remarry at the death of a spouse. Although their economic circumstances varied considerably, up to a quarter of the households in northern towns such as Bern and Zurich were headed by women. Many of them were widows, but many others, perhaps a third, were women who had never married.

If plague and population decline created new opportunities for women, the fifteenth century brought new restrictions to women's lives. In England, brewing ale had been a highly profitable

part-time activity that women often combined with the running of a household. Ale was usually produced in small batches for household use and whatever went unconsumed would be sold. The introduction of beer changed matters. Because hops were added as a preservative during brewing, beer was easier to produce, store, and transport in large batches. Beer brewing became a lucrative full-time trade, reducing the demand for the alewife's product and providing work for men as brewers. At the same time, the rights of women to work in urban crafts and industries were reduced. Wealthy fathers became less inclined to allow wives and daughters to work outside the home. Guilds banned the use of female laborers in many trades and severely limited the rights of widows to supervise their spouses' shops.

Despite the narrowing of economic opportunities for women, the overall economic prospects of peasants and laborers improved. Lower rents and increased wages in the wake of the plague meant a higher standard of living for small farmers and laborers. Before the plague struck in 1348, most poor Europeans had subsisted on bread or grain-based gruel, consuming meat, fish, and cheese only a few times a week. A well-off peasant in England had lived on a daily ration of about two pounds of bread and a cup or two of oatmeal porridge washed down with three or four pints of ale. Poorer peasants generally drank water except on very special occasions. After the plague, laborers were more prosperous. Adults in parts of Germany may have consumed nearly a liter of wine, a third of a pound of meat, and a pound or more of bread each day. Elsewhere, people could substitute an equivalent portion of beer, ale, or cider for the wine. Hard times for landlords were good times for peasants and day laborers.

Landlords in England responded to the shortage of labor by converting their lands to grazing in order to produce wool for the growing textile market. In parts of Italy, landlords invested in canals, irrigation, and new crops in order to increase profits. In eastern Germany and Poland, landlords were able to take advantage of political and social unrest to force tenants into semi-free servile status. This so-called second serfdom created an impoverished workforce whose primary economic activity was in the lord's fields, establishing commercial grain farming. Increasingly in the second half of the century, grains cultivated in Poland and Prussia found their way to markets in England and the Low Countries. Europe east of the Elbe River became a major producer of grain, but at a heavy social cost.

SECTION SUMMARY

- The Black Death may have killed one-third or more of Europe's population.

- In response to the epidemics many groups attacked outsiders, lepers, and Jews.

- Italy's medieval bankers and merchants dominated trade between Europe, North Africa, and the eastern Mediterranean.

- By the late fifteenth century, north European merchants challenged Italian economic leadership.

- Cloth production, arranged by a putting-out system, was Europe's most important industry.

- By the end of the fifteenth century, women found it increasingly difficult to maintain a significant role in Europe's craft industries.

The loss of perhaps a third of the urban population to the plague had serious consequences in the towns of Europe. Because of lower birthrates and higher death rates, late medieval towns needed a constant influx of immigrants to expand or even to maintain their populations. These immigrants did not find life in the cities easy, however. Citizenship in most towns was restricted to masters in the most important guilds, and local governments were in their hands, if not under their thumbs. In many towns, citizens constructed a system of taxation that worked to their own economic advantage and fell heavily on artisans and peasants living in territories controlled by the towns. Unskilled laborers and members of craft guilds depended for their economic well-being on personal relationships with powerful citizens who controlled the government and the markets. Peace and order in towns and in the countryside required a delicate balance of the interests of the well-to-do and the more humble. When that balance was shattered by war, plague, and economic depression, the result was often a popular revolt, such as the Ciompi insurrection of 1378 in Florence and the Rising of 1381 in England.

THE CONSOLIDATION OF POLITICAL POWER, 1450–1500

How did the political makeup of Europe in 1500 differ from that in 1300?

By 1500, it seemed that the French royal lawyer's claim that all within the kingdom belonged to the king was finally accepted. With the exception of Italy and Germany, strong central governments recovered from the crises of war and civil unrest that wracked the fourteenth and fifteenth centuries. The Hundred Years' War and the resulting disorganization in France and England seemed to strike at the heart of the monarchies. However, through the foundation of standing armies and the careful consolidation of power in the royal court, both countries seemed stronger and more able to defend themselves in the second half of the century. And as the Italians learned in the wars following the French invasion of 1494, small regional powers were no match for the mighty monarchies.

France, England, and Scandinavia

In France, recovery from a century of war was based on a consolidation of the monarchy's power. A key to French military successes had been the creation of a paid professional army, which replaced the feudal host and mercenary companies of the fourteenth century. Charles VII created Europe's first standing army, a cavalry of about eight thousand nobles under the direct control of royal commanders. Charles also expanded his judicial claims. He and his son, Louis XI (r. 1461–1483), created new provincial *parlements*, or law courts, at Toulouse, Grenoble, Bordeaux, and Dijon. They also required that local laws and customs be registered and approved by the parlements.

A second key to maintaining royal influence was the rise of the French court as a political and financial center. Through careful appointments and judicious offers of annuities and honors, Charles VII and Louis XI drew the nobility to the royal court and made the nobles dependent on it. "The court," complained a frustrated noble, "is an assembly of people who, under the pretense of acting for the good of all, come together to diddle each other; for there's scarcely anyone who isn't engaged in buying and selling and exchanging … and sometimes for their money we sell them our … humanity."[7] By 1500, France had fully recovered from the crisis of war and was once again a strong and influential state.

The fate of the English monarchy was quite different. Henry VI (r. 1422–1461) turned out to be weak-willed, immature, and prone to bouts of insanity—inherited, perhaps, from his French grandfather, Charles VI (see pages 296–298). The infirmity of Henry VI and the loss of virtually all French territories in 1453 led to factional battles known as the Wars of the Roses—the red rose symbolized Henry's House of Lancaster, the white the rival House of York. Edward of York eventually deposed Henry and claimed the Crown for himself as Edward IV (r. 1461–1483). He faced little opposition because few alternatives existed. English public life was again thrown into confusion, however, at Edward's death. The late king's brother, Richard, duke of Gloucester, claimed the protectorship over the 13-year-old king, Edward V (r. April–June 1483), and his younger brother. Richard seized the boys, who were placed in the Tower of London and never seen again. He proclaimed himself king and was crowned Richard III (r. 1483–1485). He withstood early challenges to his authority but in 1485 was killed in the Battle of Bosworth Field, near Coventry, by Henry Tudor, a leader of the Lancastrian faction. Henry married Elizabeth, the surviving child of Edward IV. Symbolically at least, the struggle between the rival claimants to the Crown appeared over.

Henry VII (r. 1485–1509), like Edward IV who preceded him, recognized the importance of avoiding war and taxation. Following Edward's example, Henry controlled local affairs through the traditional system of royal patronage. He also imitated Edward in emphasizing the dignity of the royal office. Henry solidified ties with Scotland and Spain by marrying his daughter, Margaret Tudor, to James IV of Scotland and his sons, Arthur and (after Arthur's death) Henry, to Catherine of Aragon, daughter of the Spanish rulers Ferdinand and Isabella. The English monarchy of the late fifteenth century departed little from previous governments. The success of Henry VII was based on several factors: the absence of powerful opponents; lower taxation thanks to twenty-five years of peace; and the desire, shared by ruler and ruled alike, for an orderly realm built on the assured succession of a single dynasty.

Public authority varied greatly across Scandinavia. In Norway, Denmark, and Sweden the power of the king was always mediated by the influence of the council, made up of the country's leading landowners. Power was based on ownership or control of lands and rents. All the Scandinavian countries were home to a significant class of free peasants, and they were traditionally represented in the popular assemblies that had the right to elect kings, authorize taxes, and make laws. Scandinavians spoke similar Germanic languages and were linked by close social and economic ties. Thus, it is not surprising that the crowns of the three kingdoms were joined during periods of crisis. In 1397, the dowager queen Margaret of Denmark was able to unite the Scandinavian crowns by the Union of Kalmar, which would nominally endure until 1523.

Eastern Europe and Russia

Two phenomena had an especially profound effect on the governments of eastern Europe. One was the emergence of a newly important ruling dynasty. The other was the decline of Mongol, or Tatar, influence in the region. Since the thirteenth century, much of eastern Europe had been forced to acknowledge Tatar dominion and pay annual tribute. Now, the Tatar subjugation was challenged and finally ended.

As in much of Europe, political power was segmented and based on personal relationships between family members, communities, clients, and friends. Life in the East was further complicated by the mix of languages, cultures, and religions. Native Catholic and Orthodox Christian populations were further diversified in the fourteenth century by the arrival of Muslims in the Balkans and Ashkenazi Jews throughout most of the region. Escaping growing persecution in their traditional homelands in France and western Germany, the Ashkenazim migrated to Poland, Lithuania, and Ruthenian lands (parts of modern Russia), where they lived under their own leaders and followed their own laws.

This mix of cultures and religions played a role in the growth of new states. Under the pretext of converting their pagan neighbors to Christianity, the mostly German Teutonic knights sought to expand eastward against the kingdom of Poland and the Lithuanian state. They were

POLAND AND LITHUANIA

thwarted, however, by a profound dynastic shift. In 1386, Grand Duke Jagiello (yahg-YELL-loh) of Lithuania, who reigned from 1377 to 1434, converted to Catholic Christianity and married Hedwig, the daughter and heir of King Louis of Poland (r. 1370–1382). The resulting dynastic union created a state with a population of perhaps six million that reached from the Baltic nearly to the Black Sea. Polish-Lithuanian power slowed and finally halted the German advance to the east. The descendants of Jagiello, called Jagiellonians, had no hereditary right to rule Poland, and the Lithuanians opposed any Polish administrative influence in their lands. Yet, because of Jagiellonian power, the Poles continued to select them as kings. At various times, Jagiellonians also sat on the thrones of Bohemia and Hungary.

Poland and Lithuania remained more closely tied to western Europe than to the Russian East. They tended to be Catholic rather than Orthodox Christians. They wrote in a Roman rather than a Cyrillic script, and their political institutions resembled those of western Europe. Polish nobles managed to win a number of important concessions, the most significant being freedom from arbitrary arrest and confinement. This civil right was secured in Poland well before the more famous English right of habeas corpus. It was during this period, and under the influence of the Polish kings, that Cracow emerged as the economic and cultural center of Poland. Cracow University was founded in 1364, in response to the foundation of Prague University by the emperor Charles IV in 1348. After the dynastic union of Poland and Lithuania, Polish language and culture increasingly influenced the Lithuanian nobility. This union laid the foundation for the great Polish-Lithuanian commonwealth of the early modern period.

THE RISE OF MOSCOW Lithuania had never been conquered by the Tatars, and its expansion contributed to the decline of Tatar power. The rise of Moscow, however, owed much to the continuing Tatar domination. Since the Mongol invasions in the thirteenth century, various towns and principalities of Kievan Rus had been part of a Tatar sphere of influence. This primarily meant homage and payment of an annual tribute.

A key to the emergence of Moscow occurred when Ivan I (r. 1328–1341), Prince of Moscow, was named Grand Prince and collector of tribute from the other Russian princes. It was not for nothing that he was called "the Moneybag." It was during this same period that the head of the Russian Orthodox Church was persuaded to make his home in Moscow, and in 1367, the princes began to rebuild the Kremlin walls in stone.

The decisive change for Moscow, however, was the reign of Ivan III (r. 1462–1505). By 1478, Ivan III, called "Ivan the Great," had seized the famed trading center of Novgorod. Two years later, he was powerful enough to renounce Mongol overlordship and refuse further payments of tribute. After his marriage to an émigré Byzantine princess living in Rome, Ivan began to call himself "Tsar" (Russian for "Caesar"), implying that in the wake of the Muslim conquest of Constantinople, Moscow had become the new Rome.

The Ottoman Empire

The most profound political and cultural transformation of the late Middle Ages took place in the Balkans with the conquest of Constantinople (1453) and the emergence of the Ottoman Turks as a major European power (see **MAP 11.3**). They solidified a fragmented and unstable area and from their base spread their influence throughout the Mediterranean and Europe.

The eastern Mediterranean region was a politically tumultuous area in the fourteenth century, when the Ottoman Turks were first invited into the Balkans by the hard-pressed Byzantine emperor. In the 1420s, as the Turks and the Hungarians fought for influence in Serbia, the Serbian king moved easily from alliance with one to alliance with the other. Elites often retained their political and economic influence by changing religion.

An Ottoman victory over a Christian crusading army at Varna, on the Black Sea coast, in 1444 changed the dynamics and virtually sealed the fate of Constantinople. It was only a matter of time before the Turks took the city. When Mehmed (MEH-met) II (r. 1451–1481) finally turned his attention to Constantinople in 1453, the siege of the city lasted only fifty-three days. The destruction of the last vestiges of the Roman imperial tradition that reached back to the emperor Augustus sent shock waves through Christian Europe and brought forth calls for new crusades to liberate the East from the evils of Islam. It also stirred anti-Christian feelings among the Turks. The rise of the Ottoman Turks transformed eastern Europe and led to a profound clash between Christian and Muslim civilizations.

MAP 11.3—Turkey and Eastern Europe

With the conquest of Constantinople, Syria, and Palestine, the Ottoman Turks controlled the eastern Mediterranean and dominated Europe below the Danube River. The Holy Roman emperors, rulers of Italy, and kings of Spain had to be concerned about potential invasions by land or by sea.

After the fall of Constantinople, the Turks worked to consolidate their new territories. Through alliance and conquest, Ottoman hegemony extended through Syria and Palestine, and by 1517, to Egypt. Even the Muslim powers of North Africa were nominally under Turkish control. In short order, they expanded to the west and north, seizing Croatia, Bosnia, Dalmatia, Albania, eastern Hungary, Moldavia, Bulgaria, and Greece. Turkish strength was based on a number of factors. The first was the loyalty and efficiency of the sultan's crack troops, the Janissaries. These troops were young boys forcibly taken from the subject Christian populations, trained in the Turkish language and customs, and converted to Islam. Although they functioned as special protectors of the Christian community from which they were drawn, they were separated from it by their new faith. Because the Turkish population viewed them as outsiders, they were particularly loyal to the sultan.

The situation of the Janissaries underlines a secondary explanation for Ottoman strength: the unusually tolerant attitudes of Mehmed, who saw himself not only as the greatest of the *ghazi* (crusading warriors who were considered the "instruments of Allah"), but also as emperor, heir to Byzantine and ancient imperial traditions. Immediately after the conquest of Constantinople, he repopulated the city with Greeks, Armenians, Jews, and Muslims. Mehmed especially welcomed Sephardic Jews from Spain and Portugal to parts of his empire. Thessalonica (Salonika), for example, was second only to Amsterdam as a Sephardic Jewish center until the community was destroyed in World War II. Religious groups in the cities lived in separate districts centered on a church or synagogue, and each religious community retained the right to select its own leaders. (See the feature, "The Global Record: A Disputation.") Mehmed made Constantinople the capital of the new Ottoman Empire, and by building mosques, hospitals, hostels, and bridges, he breathed new life into the city, which he referred to as Istanbul—that is, "the city." In the

The Siege of Constantinople The siege of Constantinople by the Turks required the attackers to isolate the city both by sea and by land. This miniature from the fifteenth century shows the Turkish camps, as well as the movements of Turkish boats, completing the isolation of the city. (Bibliothèque nationale de France)

fifty years following the conquest, the population of the city grew an extraordinary 500 percent, from about 40,000 to over 200,000, making it the largest city in Europe, as it had been in Late Antiquity.

At a time when Christian Europe seemed less and less willing to tolerate non-Christian minorities, the Ottoman Empire's liberal attitude toward outsiders seemed striking. Muslims and non-Muslims belonged to the same trade associations and traveled throughout the empire. Mehmed had no qualms about making trade agreements with the Italian powers in an attempt to consolidate his control. In Serbia, Bulgaria, Macedonia, and Albania, he left in place previous social and political institutions, requiring only loyalty to his empire.

The Union of Crowns in Spain

While expanding across the Mediterranean, the Turks came in contact with the other new state of the fifteenth century, the newly unified kingdom of Spain. As in Poland-Lithuania, the Spanish monarchy was only a dynastic union. In 1469, Ferdinand, heir to the kingdom of Aragon and Catalonia, married Isabella, daughter of the king of Castile. Five years later, Isabella became queen of Castile, and in 1479, Ferdinand took control of the kingdom of Aragon. This union of Crowns eventually would lead to the creation of a united Spain, but true integration was still a distant dream in 1469.

CASTILE AND ARAGON The permanence of the union was remarkable because the two kingdoms were so different. Castile was a much larger and more populous state. It had taken the lead in the Reconquista, the fight begun in the eleventh century to reclaim Iberia from Muslim rule. As a result, economic power within Castile was divided among the groups most responsible for the Reconquista: military orders and nobles. The military orders of Calatrava, Santiago, and Alcantara were militias formed by men who had taken a religious vow similar to that taken by a monk, with an added commitment to fight against the enemies of Christianity. In the course of the Reconquista, the military orders assumed control of vast districts. Lay nobles who aided in the Reconquista also held large tracts of land and proudly guarded their independence.

Castile's power stemmed from its agrarian wealth. During the Reconquista, Castilians took control of large regions and turned them into ranges for grazing merino sheep, producers of the prized merino wool exported to the markets of Flanders and Italy (see page 306). To maximize the profits from wool production, the kings authorized the creation of the Mesta, a brotherhood of sheep producers. The pastoral economy grew to the point that, by the early sixteenth century, Castilians owned over three million sheep.

Economic power in Castile lay with the nobility, but political power rested with the monarch. Because the nobility was largely exempt from taxation, nobles ignored the Cortes (cor-TEZ), the popular assembly, which could do little more than approve royal demands. The towns of Castile were important only as fortresses and staging points for militias, rather than as centers of trade and commerce.

The kingdom of Aragon was dramatically different. The center of the kingdom was Barcelona, an important trading center in the Mediterranean. In the fourteenth and fifteenth centuries, the kings of Aragon concentrated their efforts on expanding their influence in the

A Disputation

Konstantin Mihailovic, a Serb by birth, was captured by the Turks during the conquest of Constantinople in 1453. He later served with the Turks until he returned to the Christian forces in 1463. His description of a typical Turkish disputation, or debate, taking place in the presence of the sultan or another dignitary is an interesting example of how the Muslim, Jewish, and Christian peoples of the Balkans tried to understand one another.

The masters and scribes have among themselves this custom: they arrange their deliberations before the highest lord after the emperor. ... And then they begin to argue one against the other, speaking mostly about the prophets. Some [of these Turkish scribes] recognize Our Lord Jesus Christ as a prophet, and others as an archprophet, alongside God the Creator of Heaven and earth. And also the Lord, from the time when the Mohammedan faith began, created eight hundred camels, like invisible spirits, which go around every night and gather evil *Busromane* [i.e., the Muslim, or the Chosen People of God] from our [Muslim] graves and carry them to *kaur* graves [the Kaury are "the Confused People," i.e., the Christians]; and then gather good kaury and carry them to our graves. And now the good kaury will stand with our Busroman council and the evil Busromane will stand with the kaur council on Judgment Day before God. For [a pious one] says ... , "The Christians have a faith but have no works." Therefore Mohammed will lead the Busromane to Paradise and Jesus will order the Christians to hell. Moses will sorrow for the Jews that they have not been obedient to him. ... He [one of the scribes] spoke in this way: "Elias and Enoch are both in body and soul in paradise; but before Judgment Day they must die. But Jesus both in body and in soul is in heaven. He is the only one who will not die a death but will be alive forever and ever. Mohammed both in body and soul was in heaven, but remained with us on earth." And then the masters began to dispute, one in one way and one in another, and there were many words among them. And having raised a cry one against another, they began to throw books at one another. [Then the official in charge of the disputation] ... told them to cease this disputation and he ordered that food be brought them according to their custom and they gave them water to drink, since they do not drink wine. And then, having eaten their fill, they gave thanks to God, praying for the souls of the living and the dead and for those who fight against the kaury or Christians.

QUESTIONS

1. Like many people, the scribes in the debate are aware that good and evil behavior is not the special preserve of one people. How do they explain that individuals will be punished or rewarded for their deeds?

2. Christian theologians traditionally considered Muslims to be heretics who could not be saved. How do these debaters evaluate Christians?

Source: Konstantin Mihailovic, *Memoirs of a Janissary*, translated by Benjamin Stolz. Copyright © 1975. Reprinted by permission of Michigan Slavic Publications.

Mediterranean, especially south of France and Italy. By the middle of the fifteenth century, the Aragonese empire included the kingdom of Naples, Sicily, the Balearic (ba-LEER-ik) Islands, and Sardinia.

The power of the Aragonese king, in sharp contrast to the Castilian monarchy, was limited because the Crown was not unified. The ruler was king in Aragon and Navarre but only count in Catalonia. Aragon, Catalonia, and Valencia each maintained its own Cortes. In each area, the traditional nobility and the towns had a great deal more influence than did their counterparts in Castile. The power of the Cortes is clear in the coronation oath taken by the Aragonese nobility: "We who are as good as you and together are more powerful than you, make you our king and lord, provided that you observe our laws and liberties, and if not, not."[8] The distinction between Aragon and Castile could not be stronger.

Initially, the union of the crowns of Aragon and Castile did little to unify the two monarchies. Nobles fought over disputed boundaries, and Castilian nobles felt exploited by Aragonese merchants. Trade duties and internal boundaries continued to be disputed. The two realms even lacked a treaty to allow for the extradition of criminals from one kingdom to the other. Castilians never accepted Ferdinand as more than their queen's consort. After the death of Isabella in 1504, he ruled in Castile only as regent for his infant grandson, Charles I (r. 1516–1556). "Spain" would not emerge in an institutional sense until the late sixteenth century.

Nonetheless, the reign of Isabella and Ferdinand marked a profound change in politics and society in the Iberian kingdoms and in Europe in general. Ferdinand and Isabella married their daughter Joanna to Philip of Habsburg in 1496 to draw the Holy Roman Empire into the Italian wars brought on by the French invasion (see page 301). The marriage of their daughter Catherine of Aragon to Prince Arthur of England in 1501 was designed to obtain yet another ally against the

French. Those two marriages would have momentous consequences for European history in the sixteenth century.

1492: MUSLIMS AND JEWS　The reign of Ferdinand and Isabella is especially memorable because of the events of 1492. In January of that year, a crusading army conquered Granada, the last Muslim stronghold in Iberia. In March, Ferdinand and Isabella ordered the Jews of Castile and Aragon to convert or leave the kingdom within four months. In April, Isabella issued her commission authorizing Christopher Columbus "to discover and acquire islands and mainland in the Ocean Sea" (see pages 362–364).

The conquest of Granada and the expulsion of the Jews represented a radical shift in the Spanish mentality. Until the beginning of the fifteenth century, Spain maintained a level of religious tolerance unusual in Christendom. In the fourteenth century, perhaps 2 percent of the population of Iberia was Jewish, and the Muslim population may have been as high as 50 percent. The various groups were inextricably mixed. The statutes of the Jewish community in Barcelona were written in Catalan, a Spanish dialect, rather than in Hebrew. *Maranos*, Jewish converts to Christianity, and *moriscos*, Muslim converts, mixed continuously with Christians and with members of their former religions. It was difficult at times to know which religion these converts, or *conversos*, actually practiced. One surprised northern visitor to Spain remarked that one noble's circle was filled with "Christians, Moors, and Jews and he lets them live in peace in their faith."

This tolerant mingling of Christians, Muslims, and Jews had periodically occasioned violence. All three communities, in fact, preferred clear boundaries between the groups. In 1391, however, a series of violent attacks had long-lasting and unfortunate effects on Iberian society. An attack on the Jews of Seville led to murders, forced conversions, and suppression of synagogues throughout Spain. In the wake of the assault, large portions of the urban Jewish population either converted to Christianity or moved into villages away from the large commercial cities. The Jewish population in Castile may have declined by a fourth. Although the anti-Jewish feelings were expressed in religious terms, the underlying cause was anger over the economic prominence of some Jewish or converso families. After 1391, anti-Jewish feeling increasingly became racial. As one rebel said, "The converso remains a Jew and therefore should be barred from public office."[9]

Hostility and suspicion toward Jews grew throughout the fifteenth century, until Ferdinand and Isabella concluded that the only safe course was to order all Jews to accept baptism. Jews who would not convert would have to leave the kingdom within four months. The order was signed on March 31, 1492, and published in late April, after an unsuccessful attempt by converso and Jewish leaders to dissuade the monarchs from implementing it.

Many Jews could not dispose of their possessions in the four months allowed and so chose to convert and remain. But it is estimated that about ten thousand Jews left Aragon and that even more left Castile. Many moved to Portugal and then to North Africa. Some went east to Istanbul or north to the Low Countries. A number of others moved to the colonies being established in the New World in the vain hope of avoiding the Inquisition, which was already underway when the expulsion order was issued (see below). In 1504, the expulsion order was extended to include all Muslims.

The economic and social costs of the expulsion were profound. Not every Muslim or Jew was wealthy and cultured, but the exiles did include many doctors, bankers, and merchants. Spanish culture, long open to influences from Muslim and

Alfonso de Espina's Fortress of Faith (1474)　The diatribe against heretics, Muslims, and Jews fanned religious tensions in Spain. In this image from the book, Jews, Muslims, heretics, and demons are depicted as related threats to Christianity. Blindfolded Jews (blind to Christian Truth), Muslim warriors, and the Devil himself are seen assaulting the fortress of faith.　(© Topham/The Image Works)

Jewish sources, became narrower and less willing to accept new ideas. After the expulsion, a chasm of distrust opened between the "Old Christians" and the "New Christians"—that is, those newly converted. As early as the first decades of the fifteenth century, some religious orders had refused to accept "New Christians." They required that their members demonstrate *limpieza de sangre*, a purity of blood. By 1500, the same tests of blood purity became prerequisites for holding most religious and public offices. Thus, by the end of the fifteenth century, the Iberian kingdoms had created more powerful, unified governments, but at a terrible cost to the only portion of Christendom that had ever practiced religious tolerance.

Complaints that led to the expulsion arose from a variety of sources. The fact that many of the most important financiers and courtiers were Jews or conversos bred jealousies and tensions among the communities. All three religious communities favored distinct dress and identifying behaviors. Old Christians seemed concerned that many of the conversos might reconvert to Judaism, and the fear of reconversion, or "judaizing," led many to advocate the institution of the **Spanish Inquisition**.

Inquisitions were well known in many parts of Europe, but the Spanish Inquisition was unique because in 1478, Pope Sixtus IV placed the grand inquisitor under the direct control of the monarchs. Like most Christian rulers, Ferdinand and Isabella believed that uniform Christian orthodoxy was the only firm basis for a strong kingdom. Inquisitors attacked those aspects of converso tradition that seemed to make the conversos less than fully Christian. They were concerned that many conversos and maranos had converted falsely and were secretly continuing to follow Jewish or Muslim rituals—a fear that some recent scholars have argued was unfounded.

Because its administration, finances, and appointments were in Spanish, not papal, hands, the Spanish Inquisition quickly became an important instrument for the expansion of state power. Many inquisitors used their offices to attack wealthy or politically important converso families not just to drive them from public life but also to fill the royal treasury, which was where the estates of those judged guilty wound up. "This inquisition is as much to take the conversos' estates as to exalt the faith," concluded one despairing conversa woman.[10]

Spanish Inquisition
A church court under monarchical control established in 1478 to look for "false Christians" among the newly converted Muslims and Jews.

The Limits of Consolidation: Germany

The issue of central versus local control played a key role in German affairs as well. The Holy Roman Empire of the late Middle Ages was dramatically different from the empire of the early thirteenth century. Emperors generally were unable to claim lands and preside over jurisdictions outside Germany, and within Germany, power shifted eastward. Imperial power had previously rested on lands and castles in southwestern Germany. These strongholds melted away, as emperors willingly pawned and sold traditional crown lands in order to build up the holdings of their own families. Emperor Henry VII (r. 1308–1313) and his grandson, Charles IV (r. 1347–1378), for example, liquidated imperial lands west of the Rhine in order to secure the House of Luxemburg's claims to the crown of Bohemia and other lands in the east. The Habsburgs in Austria, the Wittelsbachs in Bavaria, and a host of lesser families staked out power bases in separate parts of the empire. As a result, Germany unraveled into a loose collection of territories. More seriously, the power of each emperor depended almost entirely on the wealth and power of his dynastic lands.

The power of regional authorities in the empire was further cemented by the so-called **Golden Bull** of 1356, the most important constitutional document of late medieval German history. In it, Charles IV declared that henceforth the archbishops of Cologne, Mainz, and Trier, plus the secular rulers of Bohemia, the Rhenish Palatinate, Saxony, and Brandenburg, would be the seven electors responsible for the choice of a new emperor. He further established that the rulers of these seven principalities should have full jurisdictional rights within their territories. The Golden Bull acknowledged the power of regional princes, but it did nothing to solve the inherent weakness of an electoral monarchy. Between 1273 and 1519, Germany elected fourteen emperors from six different dynasties, and only once, in 1378, did a son follow his father. The contrast between Germany and the monarchies of Iberia, France, and England is striking. By 1350, Germany had no hereditary monarchy, no common legal system, no common coinage, and no representative assembly. Political power rested in the hands of the territorial princes.

Golden Bull   Edict of Holy Roman Emperor Charles IV establishing the method of electing a new emperor. It acknowledged the political autonomy of Germany's seven regional princes.

- By the end of the fifteenth century, both England and France had stronger, more centralized governments.

- By the fifteenth century a strong Polish-Lithuanian state had emerged to halt German expansion to the east.

- The rise of Moscow marked the end of Tatar domination in eastern Europe.

- Ottoman Turks established a strong empire that came to dominate the eastern Mediterranean and the Balkans.

- The union of the Aragonese and Castilian crowns created a Spanish monarchy intent on enforcing political unity and religious uniformity.

- In German lands, regional powers emerged to challenge and limit the power of the empire.

Territorial integration was least effective in what is now Switzerland, where a league of towns, provincial knights, and peasant villages successfully resisted a territorial prince. The Swiss Confederation began modestly enough in 1291, as a voluntary association to promote regional peace. By 1410, the confederation had conquered most of the traditionally Habsburg lands in the Swiss areas. Though still citizens of the Holy Roman Empire, the Swiss maintained an independence similar to that of the princes. Their expansion culminated with the Battle of Nancy in Lorraine in 1477, when the Swiss infantry defeated a Burgundian army and killed Charles the Bold, the duke of Burgundy. From then on "turning Swiss" was a common threat made by German towns and individuals who hoped to slow territorial centralization.

CHAPTER SUMMARY

The Europe of 1500 was profoundly different from the Europe of two centuries earlier. The religious, political, and economic crises of the fourteenth and early fifteenth centuries seemed about to destroy the progress of the previous centuries. But the recovery of the second half of the fifteenth century was nearly as dramatic as the preceding disasters.

In the aftermath of schism and conciliar reform, the church also was transformed. Because of conciliar challenges to papal authority, popes had to deal much more carefully with the governments of Europe. They found themselves vulnerable to pressures from the other European powers. Recognizing that, in the end, popes could count on support only from those areas they controlled politically, the papacy became an Italian regional power.

The Hundred Years' War between England and France was a continuation of a long struggle between two royal houses. The English won dramatic battles, but they could not control the territory. As a result, by the end the English lost all their significant possessions in France. The result contributed to the eventual centralization and growth of royal power in the two kingdoms.

The economy had grown more complex in the wake of the epidemic disease and dramatic population decline. Changes included the relative decline of the Italian economy as new patterns of trade and banking and new manufacturing techniques spread throughout Europe. Commerce and manufacture were now more firmly rooted in northern Europe. Italian merchants and bankers faced stiff competition from local counterparts throughout Europe.

Recovery was equally dramatic for the governments of Europe. After the Hundred Years' War and challenges from aristocrats, townsmen, and peasants, governments grew stronger as kings, princes, and town patricians used royal courts and patronage to extend their control. Military advances in the fifteenth century, such as the institution of standing armies, gave the advantage to larger governments. This was as true in Hungary as it was in France. Yet recovery among the traditional Western powers was largely overshadowed by the emergence of the tsars in Moscow and the rise of the Ottoman and Spanish Empires. These three emergent powers upset the political and diplomatic balance in Europe and would dominate politics and diplomacy in the next century.

- How did the Great Schism change the church and the papacy?

- What forces limited the political power of rulers in England, France, and Italy?

- How were economic and social structures changed by plague and economic crisis?

- How did the political makeup of Europe in 1500 differ from that in 1300?

KEY TERMS

Babylonian Captivity of the Papacy   (p. 290)

Great Schism   (p. 291)

conciliarists   (p. 291)

Jan Hus   (p. 292)

Council of Constance   (p. 293)

Hundred Years' War   (p. 295)

Joan of Arc   (p. 299)

Black Death   (p. 302)

Hanseatic League   (p. 305)

Spanish Inquisition   (p. 317)

Golden Bull   (p. 317)

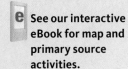 This icon will direct you to additional materials on the website: www .cengage.com/history/ noble/westciv6e.

NOTES

1. Quoted in Guillaume Mollat, *The Popes at Avignon, 1305–1378* (London: Thomas Nelson, 1963), p. 112.

2. Quoted in Mary Aston, *Lollards and Reformers: Images and Literacy in Late Medieval Religion* (Ronceverte, W.V.: Hambledon, 1984), p. 60.

3. Quoted in Francis Oakley, *The Western Church in the Later Middle Ages* (Ithaca, N.Y.: Cornell University Press, 1979), pp. 65–66.

4. Quoted in Charles T. Wood, *Joan of Arc and Richard III* (New York: Oxford University Press, 1988), pp. 56–57.

5. Quoted in Michael T. Clanchy, "Law, Government, and Society in Medieval England," *History* 59 (1974): 75.

6. A. Buchon, *Choix des Chroniques* (Paris, 1875), p. 565, as quoted in John Gillingham and J. C. Holt, eds., *War and Government in the Middle Ages* (Totowa, N.J.: Barnes & Noble, 1984), p. 85.

7. Quoted in Peter Shervey Lewis, *Later Medieval France: The Polity* (New York: Macmillan, 1968), p. 15.

8. Quoted in Angus MacKay, *Spain in the Middle Ages: From Frontier to Empire, 1000–1500* (London: Macmillan, 1977), p. 105.

9. Quoted in Angus MacKay, "Popular Movements and Pogroms in Fifteenth-Century Spain," *Past & Present* 55 (1972): 52.

10. Haim Beinart, ed., *Records of the Trials of the Spanish Inquisition in Ciudad Real*, vol. 1 (Jerusalem: Israel Academy of Sciences and Humanities, 1974), p. 391, trans. Duane Osheim.

e See our interactive eBook for map and primary source activities.

CHAPTER OUTLINE

Humanism and Culture in Italy, 1300–1500

Painting and the Arts, 1250–1550

The Spread of the Renaissance, 1350–1536

Politics and Renaissance Culture

Raphael: School of Athens (detail)
Raphael created this classical setting by using the technique of linear
perspective. (Scala/Art Resource, NY)

The Renaissance

The painting on the left, *School of Athens* by Raphael (1483–1520), was commissioned for the Stanze (STAN-zay), the papal apartments in the Vatican. At the center, Plato and Aristotle advance through a church-like hall, surrounded by the great thinkers and writers of the ancient world. But Raphael portrayed more than just ancient wisdom. The figure of Plato is, in fact, a portrait of Leonardo da Vinci. A brooding Michelangelo leans on a marble block in the foreground. In a companion painting on the opposite wall, Raphael depicted a gathering of the greatest scholars of Christendom. In this way, he brought together Christian and classical, writers and artists, and captured the entire cultural reform plan of the **Renaissance**.

The revival these paintings celebrate was a response to the religious, social, economic, and political crises discussed in the previous chapter. Italians, and later Europeans, generally found themselves drawn to imitate Roman literature, ethics, and politics. The wisdom of antiquity seemed to offer an opportunity to perfect the theological ideas about moral and political life current in the earlier Middle Ages. Further, Renaissance writers were convinced that all knowledge, pagan and Christian, ancient and modern, could be combined into a single, uniform view of the world.

Renaissance Italians wrote of themselves and their contemporaries as having "revived" arts, "rescued" painting, and "rediscovered" classical authors. They even coined the phrases "Dark Ages" and "Middle Ages" to describe the period that separated the Roman Empire from their own times. They believed that their society saw a new age, a rebirth of culture. And, to this day, we use the French word for "rebirth," *renaissance*, to describe the period of intense creativity and change that began in Italy in the fourteenth century and then extended to all of Europe.

This view comes to us primarily from the work of the nineteenth-century Swiss historian Jacob Burckhardt. In his book, *The Civilization of the Renaissance in Italy* (1860), he argued that Italians were the first individuals to recognize the state as a moral structure free from the restraints of religious or philosophical traditions. Burckhardt believed that people are entirely free. Their success or failure depends on personal qualities of creative brilliance, rather than on family status, religion, or guild membership. Burckhardt thought he saw, in Renaissance Italy, the first signs of the romantic individualism and nationalism that characterized the modern world.

In fact, as brilliant as Renaissance writers and artists were, they do not represent a radical shift from the ideas or values of medieval culture. As we have seen, there were no "Dark Ages." Although the culture of Renaissance Europe was in many aspects new and innovative, it had close ties both to the ideas of the High Middle Ages and to traditional Christian values.

How, then, should we characterize the Renaissance in Europe? The Renaissance was an important cultural movement that aimed to reform and renew by imitating what the

FOCUS QUESTIONS

- How did Italians use classical values to deal with cultural and political issues?

- What was "new" about Renaissance art?

- In what ways did humanism outside Italy differ from Italian humanism?

- How did European rulers use Renaissance art and culture?

 This icon will direct you to additional materials on the website: www .cengage.com/history/ noble/westciv6e.

e See our interactive eBook for map and primary source activities.

Renaissance A word that has come to define any period of intense creativity. In this case, it refers specifically to a cultural movement based on imitating classical culture.

reformers believed were classical and early Christian traditions in art, education, religion, and political life. Italians, and then other Europeans, came to believe that the social and moral values, as well as the literature, of classical Greece and Rome offered the best formula for changing their own society for the better. This enthusiasm for a past culture became the vehicle for changes in literature, education, and art that established cultural standards that were to hold for the next five hundred years.

HUMANISM AND CULTURE IN ITALY, 1300–1500

How did Italians use classical values to deal with cultural and political issues?

Italians turned to models from classical antiquity in their attempts to deal with current issues of cultural, political, and educational reform. A group of scholars, who came to be known as humanists, began to argue the superiority of the literature, history, and politics of the past. As humanists discovered more about ancient culture, they were able to understand more clearly the historical context in which Roman and Greek writers and thinkers lived. And by the early sixteenth century, their debates on learning, civic duty, and the classical legacy had led them to a new vision of the past and a new appreciation of the nature of politics.

The Emergence of Humanism

humanism Western European literary and cultural movement, which emphasized the superiority of Greek and Roman literature and especially its values of personal and public morality.

Humanism initially held greater appeal in Italy than elsewhere in Europe because the culture in central and northern Italy was significantly more secular and more urban than the culture of much of the rest of Europe. Members of the clergy were less likely to dominate government and education in Italy. Quite the reverse: Boards dominated by laymen had built and were administering the great urban churches of Italy. Religious hospitals and charities were often reorganized and centralized under government control. Italy was the most urbanized region of Europe. Even the powerful Italian aristocracy tended to live at least part of the year in towns and conform to urban social and legal practices.

Differences between Italy and northern Europe are also apparent in the structure of local education. In northern Europe, education was organized to provide clergy for local churches. In the towns of Italy, education was much more likely to be supervised by town governments to provide training in accounting, arithmetic, and the composition of business letters. Public grammar masters taught these basics, and numerous private masters and individual tutors were prepared to teach all subjects. Giovanni Villani, a fourteenth-century merchant and historian, described Florence in 1338 as a city of nearly 100,000 people, in which perhaps as many as 10,000 young girls and boys were completing elementary education and 1,000 were continuing their studies to prepare for careers in commerce. Compared with education in the towns of northern Europe, education in Villani's Florence seems broad-based and practical.

Logic and Scholastic philosophy (see page 275) dominated university education in northern Europe in the fourteenth and fifteenth centuries but had less influence in Italy, where education focused on the practical issues of town life rather than on theological speculation. Educated Italians of this period were interested in the *studia humanitatis*, which we now call humanism. By *humanism*, Italians meant rhetoric and literature—the arts of persuasion. Poetry, history, letter writing, and oratory, based on standardized forms and aesthetic values, consciously borrowed from ancient Greece and Rome were the center of intellectual life. In general, fourteenth-century Italians were suspicious of ideological or moral programs based on philosophical arguments or religious assumptions about human nature.

By 1300, it was usual for towns to celebrate the feast days of their patron saints as major political, as well as religious, festivals. And town governments often supervised the construction and expansion of cathedrals, churches, and hospitals as signs of their wealth and prestige.

Literature of the early fourteenth century tended to emphasize the culture of towns. The most famous and most innovative work of the fourteenth century, *The Decameron* by Giovanni Boccaccio (1313–1375), pondered moral and ethical issues, but in the lively context of Italian town life. Boccaccio (bo-KAH-cho) hoped the colorful and irreverent descriptions of contemporary

Italians, which make his *Decameron* a classic of European literature, would also lead individuals to understand both the essence of human nature and the folly of human desires. The plot involves a group of privileged young people who abandon friends and family during the plague of 1348 to go into the country. There, on successive days, they mixed feasting, dancing, and song with one hundred tales of love, intrigue, and gaiety. With its mix of traditional and contemporary images, Boccaccio's book spawned numerous imitators in Italy and elsewhere.

Like Boccaccio, the majority of educated Italians in the early fourteenth century were not particularly captivated by thoughts of ancient Rome. Italian historians chose to write the histories of their hometowns. Most, including Giovanni Villani of Florence, were convinced that their towns could rival ancient Rome. Theirs was a practical world in which most intellectuals were men trained in notarial arts—the everyday skills of oratory, letter writing, and the recording of legal documents.

Petrarch and Early Humanism

The first Italians who looked back consciously to the literary and historical examples of ancient Rome were a group of northern Italian lawyers and notaries who imitated Roman authors. These practical men found Roman history and literature more stimulating and useful than medieval philosophy. Writers, such as Albertino Mussato of Padua (1262-1329), adopted classical styles in their poetry and histories. Mussato used his play *The Ecerinis* (1315) to tell of the fall of Can Grande della Scala, the tyrannical ruler of Verona (d. 1329), and to warn his neighbors of the dangers of tyranny. From its earliest, the classical revival in Italy was tied to issues of moral and political reform.

This largely emotional fascination for the ancient world was transformed into a literary movement for reform by **Francesco Petrarch** (1304-1374), who popularized the idea of mixing classical moral and literary ideas with the concerns of the fourteenth century. Petrarch was the son of an exiled Florentine notary living at the papal court in Avignon. Repelled by the urban violence and wars he had experienced on his return to Italy, Petrarch was highly critical of his contemporaries: "I never liked this age," he once confessed. He criticized the papacy in Avignon, calling it the "Babylonian Captivity" (see pages 290-291); he supported an attempt to resurrect a republican government in Rome; and he believed that imitation of the actions, values, and culture of the ancient Romans was the only way to reform his sorry world.

Petrarch believed that an age of darkness—he coined the expression "Dark Ages"—separated the Roman world from his own time and that the separation could be overcome only through a study and reconstruction of classical values: "Once the darkness has been broken, our descendants will perhaps be able to return to the pure, pristine radiance."[1] Petrarch's program, and, in many respects, the entire Renaissance, involved, first of all, a reconstruction of classical culture; then, a careful study and imitation of the classical heritage; and finally, a series of moral and cultural changes that went beyond the mere copying of ancient values and styles.

Petrarch labored throughout his life to reconstruct the history and literature of Rome. He learned to read and write classical Latin. In the 1330s, he discovered a number of classical works, including orations and letters by Cicero, the great philosopher, statesman, and opponent of Julius Caesar (see pages 134-135). Cicero's letters to his friend Atticus were filled with gossip, questions about politics in Rome, and complaints about his forced withdrawal from public life. They create the portrait of an individual who was much more complex than the austere philosopher of medieval legend.

Petrarch's humanism was not worldly or secular; he was and remained a committed Christian. He recognized the tension between the Christian present and pagan antiquity. He wrote a dialogue,

CHRONOLOGY

1304-1314	Giotto paints Arena Chapel in Padua
1345	Petrarch discovers Cicero's letters to Atticus
1348-1350	Boccaccio, *The Decameron*
1393-1400	Chaucer, *The Canterbury Tales*
1401	Ghiberti wins competition to cast baptistery doors, Florence
1405	Christine de Pizan, *The Book of the City of the Ladies*
1427	Unveiling of Masaccio's *Trinity*
1434	Van Eyck, *The Arnolfini Wedding*
1440	Valla, *On the Donation of Constantine*
1440s	Vitterino establishes Villa Giocosa in Mantua
1450s	Gutenberg begins printing with movable metal type
1460	Gonzaga invites Mantegna to Mantua
1475	Pope Sixtus IV orders construction of Sistine Chapel
1494	Dürer begins first trip to Venice
1501	Michelangelo, *David*
1511	Erasmus, *The Praise of Folly*
1513	Machiavelli, *The Prince*
1516	More, *Utopia*
1528	Castiglione, *The Book of the Courtier*

Francesco Petrarch
Influential poet, biographer, and humanist who strongly advocated imitation of the literary and moral values of the leading Greek and Roman writers.

Petrarch Responds to His Critics

Many traditional philosophers and theologians criticized humanists as "pagans" because of their lack of interest in logic and theology and their love of non-Christian writers. In this letter defending humanistic studies, Petrarch explains the value of Cicero's work to Christians.

[Cicero] points out the miraculously coherent structure and disposition of the body, sense and limbs, and finally reason and sedulous activity. ... And all this he does merely to lead us to this conclusion: whatever we behold with our eyes or perceive with our intellect is made by God for the well-being of man and governed by divine providence and counsel.... [In response to his critics who argued for the superiority of philosophy he adds:] I have read all of Aristotle's moral books. Some of them I have also heard commented on.... Sometimes I have become more learned through them when I went home, but not better, not so good as I ought to be; and I often complained to myself, occasionally to others too, that by no facts was the promise fulfilled which the philosopher makes at the beginning of the first book of his *Ethics*, namely, that "we learn this part of philosophy not with the purpose of gaining knowledge but of becoming better." I see virtue, and all that is peculiar to vice as well as to virtue, egregiously defined and distinguished by him and treated with penetrating insight. When I learn all this, I know a little bit more than I knew before, but mind and will remain the same as they were, and I myself remain the same.... However, what is the use of knowing what virtue is if it is not loved when known? What is the use of knowing sin if it is not abhorred when it is known? However,

everyone who has become thoroughly familiar with our Latin authors knows that they stamp and drive deep into the heart the sharpest and most ardent stings of speech by which those who stick to the ground [are] lifted up to the highest thoughts and to honest desire....

Cicero, read with a pious and modest attitude, ... was profitable to everybody, so far as eloquence is concerned, to many others as regards living. This was especially true in [Saint] Augustine's case.... I confess, I admire Cicero as much or even more than all whoever wrote a line in any nation. ... If to admire Cicero means to be a Ciceronian, I am a Ciceronian. I admire him so much that I wonder at people who do not admire him.... However, when we come to think or speak of religion, that is, of supreme truth and true happiness, and of eternal salvation, then I am certainly not a Ciceronian, or a Platonist, but a Christian. I even feel sure that Cicero himself would have been a Christian if he had been able to see Christ and to comprehend His doctrine.

QUESTIONS

1. Why is Cicero a valuable author to study?
2. Why does Petrarch believe Cicero is superior to Aristotle?
3. Does it seem that Petrarch sees any limits to the moral value of Cicero?

Source: From *The Renaissance Philosophy of Man,* ed. Ernst Cassirer, Paul Oskar Kristeller and John H. Randall, pp. 86, 103–04, 114–115. Reprinted by permission of the publisher, the University of Chicago Press.

The Secret, reflecting his own ambivalence. Did his devotion to reading and imitating classical authors involve a rejection of traditional Christian values? "My wishes fluctuate and my desires conflict, and in their struggle they tear me apart," he confessed.[2] Yet, he prized the beauty and moral value of ancient learning. He wrote *The Lives of Illustrious Men*, biographies of men from antiquity whose thoughts and actions he deemed worthy of emulation. To spread humanistic values, he issued collections of his poems, written in Italian, and his letters, written in classically inspired Latin. He believed that study and memorization of the writings of classical authors could lead to the internalization of the ideas and values expressed in those works, just as a honeybee drinks nectar to create honey. He argued that ancient moralists were superior to Scholastic philosophers, whose work ended with the determination of truth, or correct responses. "The true moral philosophers and useful teachers of the virtues," he concluded, "are those whose first and last intention is to make hearer and reader good, those who do not merely teach what virtue and vice are but sow into our hearts love of the best ... and hatred of the worst."[3] (See the feature, "The Written Record: Petrarch Responds to His Critics.")

civic humanism
An ideology, popular with the political leaders of Florence, that emphasized Rome's classical republican virtues of duty and public service.

Humanistic Studies

Petrarch's program of humanistic studies became especially popular with the wealthy oligarchy who dominated political life in Florence. The Florentine chancellor Coluccio Salutati (1331–1406), and a generation of young intellectuals who formed his circle, evolved an ideology of **civic humanism**.

Civic humanists wrote letters, orations, and histories praising their city's classical virtues and history. In the process, they gave a practical and public meaning to the Petrarchan program. Civic humanists argued, as had Cicero, that there was a moral and ethical value intrinsic to public life. In a letter to a friend, Salutati wrote that public life is "something holy and holier than idleness in [religious] solitude." To another he added, "The active life you flee is to be followed both as an exercise in virtue and because of the necessity of brotherly love."[4]

More than Petrarch himself, civic humanists desired to create and inspire men of virtue who could take the lead in government and protect their fellow citizens from lawlessness and tyranny. In the early years of the fifteenth century, civic humanists applauded Florence for remaining a republic of free citizens. Florence remained free of a lord, unlike Milan whose government was dominated by the Viscontis (see page 345). In his *Panegyric on the City of Florence* (ca. 1405), Leonardo Bruni (ca. 1370–1444) recalled the history of the Roman Republic and suggested that Florence could re-create the best qualities of the Roman state. To civic humanists, the study of Rome and its virtues was the key to the continued prosperity of Florence and similar Italian republics.

One of Petrarch's most enthusiastic followers was Guarino of Verona (1374–1460), who became the leading advocate of educational reform in Renaissance Italy. After spending five years in Constantinople learning Greek and collecting classical manuscripts, he became the most successful teacher and translator of Greek literature in Italy. Greek studies had been advanced by Manuel Chrysoloras (1350–1415), who, after his arrival from Constantinople in 1397, taught Greek for three years in Florence. Chrysoloras was later joined by other Greek intellectuals, especially after the fall of Constantinople to the Turks in 1453. Guarino built on this interest in Greek culture.

EDUCATIONAL REFORM

Guarino emphasized careful study of grammar and memorization of large bodies of classical history and poetry. He was convinced that through a profound understanding of Greek and Latin literature and a careful imitation of the style of the great authors, a person could come to exhibit the moral and ethical values for which Cicero, Seneca, and Plutarch were justly famous. Although it is unclear whether Guarino's style of education produced such results, it did provide a thorough training in literature and oratory. In an age that admired the ability to speak and write persuasively, the new style of humanistic education pioneered by Guarino spread quickly throughout Europe. The elegy spoken at Guarino's funeral sums up Italian views of humanistic education, as well as the contribution of Guarino himself: "No one was considered noble, as leading a blameless life, unless he had followed Guarino's courses."

Guarino's example was widely followed. One of his early students, Vittorino da Feltre (1378–1446), was appointed tutor at the Gonzaga court of Mantua. Like Guarino, he emphasized close literary study and careful imitation of classical authors. But the school he founded, the Villa Giocosa (jo-KO-sa), was innovative because he advocated games and exercises, as well as formal study. In addition, Vittorino required that bright young boys from poor families be included among the seventy affluent students normally resident in his school. Vittorino was so renowned that noblemen from across Italy sent their sons to be educated at the Villa Giocosa.

Since Italians viewed humanistic education as a preparation for public life, it was not necessary for laborers, women, or others without political power. Leonardo Bruni of Florence once composed a curriculum for a young woman to follow. He emphasized literature and moral philosophy, but, he cautioned, there was no reason to study rhetoric: "For why should the subtleties of . . . rhetorical conundrums consume the powers of a woman, who never sees the forum? . . . The contests of the forum, like those of warfare and battle, are the sphere of men."[5] To what extent did women participate in the cultural and artistic movements of the fourteenth and fifteenth centuries? Many assumed that women were intellectually and morally weaker than men. And Bruni saw a limited value to humanistic education for women, but his views were not unopposed.

THE LIMITS OF HUMANISM

During the fifteenth century, many women did learn to read and even to write. Religious women and wives of merchants read educational and spiritual literature. Some women needed to write in order to manage the economic and political interests of their families. Alessandra Macinghi-Strozzi (ma-CHIN-ghee STROT-zi) of Florence (1407–1471), for example, wrote numerous letters to her sons in exile, describing her efforts to find spouses for her children and to influence the government to end their banishments. Her letters, in fact, demonstrate the subtle, indirect power women used to influence politics.

Private Reading   Robert Campin's painting of Saint Barbara of 1438 shows a typical Flemish interior with a woman reading. It was not unusual for well-to-do women to read even if they could not write.   (Museo de Prado/Institut Amatller d'Art Hispanic)

Women acted with care because many men were suspicious of literate women. Just how suspicious is evident in the career of Isotta Nogarola of Verona (b. 1418), one of a number of fifteenth- and sixteenth-century Italian women whose literary abilities equaled those of male humanists. Isotta quickly became known as a gifted writer, but men's response to her work was mixed. One anonymous critic suggested that it was unnatural for a woman to have such scholarly interests and accused her of equally unnatural sexual interests. Guarino of Verona himself wrote warning her that if she was truly to be educated, she must put off female sensibilities and find "a man within the woman."[6]

The problem for humanistically educated women was that, as Bruni observed, society provided no acceptable public role for them. A noblewoman, such as Isabella d'Este (DES-tay) (see page 345), wife of the duke of Mantua, might gather humanists and painters around her at court, but it was not generally believed that women themselves could create literary works of true merit. When women tried, they were usually rebuffed and urged to reject the values of civic humanism and to hold instead to traditional Christian virtues of rejection of the world. In other words, a woman who had literary or cultural interests was expected to enter a convent. That was a friend's advice to Isotta Nogarola. It was wrong, he said, "that a virgin should consider marriage, or even think about that liberty of lascivious morals."[7] Throughout the fifteenth and early sixteenth centuries, some women in Italy and elsewhere in Europe learned classical languages and philosophy, but they became rarer as time passed. The virtues of humanism were public virtues, and Europeans of the Renaissance remained uncomfortable with the idea that women might act directly and publicly.

The Transformation of Humanism

The fascination with education based on ancient authorities was heightened by the discovery in 1416, in the Monastery of Saint Gall in Switzerland, of a complete manuscript of Quintilian's *Institutes of Oratory*, a first-century treatise on the proper education for a young Roman patrician. The document was found by Poggio Bracciolini (PO-joe bra-cho-LEE-nee) (1380–1459), who had been part of the humanist circle in Florence. The discovery was hardly accidental. Like Petrarch, the humanists of the fifteenth century scoured Europe for ancient texts to read and study. In searching out the knowledge of the past, these fifteenth-century humanists made a series of discoveries that changed their understanding of language, philosophy, and religion. Their desire to imitate led to a profound transformation of knowledge.

A Florentine antiquary, Niccolò Niccoli (1364–1437), coordinated and paid for much of this pursuit of "lost" manuscripts. A wealthy bachelor, Niccolò spent the fortune he had inherited from his father by acquiring ancient statuary, reliefs, and, most of all, books. When he died, his collection of more than eight hundred volumes of Latin and Greek texts became the foundation of the humanist library housed in the Monastery of San Marco in Florence. Niccolò had specified that all his books "should be accessible to everyone," and humanists from across Italy and the rest of Europe came to Florence to study his literary treasures. Niccolò's library prompted Pope Nicholas V (r. 1447–1455) to begin the collection that is now the Apostolic Library of the Vatican in Rome. The Vatican library became a lending library, serving the humanist community in Rome. Similar collections were assembled in Venice, Milan, and Urbino. The Greek and Latin sources preserved in these libraries allowed humanists to study classical languages in a way not possible before.

The career of Lorenzo Valla (1407–1457) illustrates the transformation that took place in the fifteenth century, as humanism swept Europe. Valla was born near Rome and received a traditional human-istic education in Greek and Latin studies. He spent the rest of his life at universities and courts lecturing on philosophy and literature. Valla's studies had led him to understand that languages change with time—that they, too, have a life and a history. In 1440, he published a work called *On the Falsely Believed and Forged Donation of Constantine.*

The donation purported to record the gift by the emperor Constantine (r. 311–337) of juris-diction over Rome and the western half of the empire to the pope when the imperial capital was moved to Constantinople (see pages 170–172). In the High and late Middle Ages, the papacy used the document to defend its right to political dominion in central Italy. The donation had long been criticized by legal theorists, who argued that Constantine had no right to make it. Valla went further and attacked the legitimacy of the document itself. Because of its language and form, he argued, it could not have been written at the time of Constantine: Valla was correct; the *Donation* was an eighth-century forgery.

> Through his [the writer's] babbling, he reveals his most impudent forgery himself.... Where he deals with the gifts he says "a diadem ... made of pure gold and precious jew-els." The ignoramus did not know that the diadem was [like a turban and] made of cloth, probably silk.... He thinks it had to be made of gold, since nowadays kings usually wear a circle of gold set with jewels.[8]

Valla later turned his attention to the New Testament. Jerome (331–420) had put together the Vulgate edition of the Bible in an attempt to create a single accepted Latin version of the Hebrew Bible and the New Testament (see page 193). In 1444, Valla completed his *Annotations on the New Testament.* In this work, he used his training in classical languages to correct Jerome's stan-dard Latin text and to show numerous instances of mistranslations. His annotations on the New

LORENZO VALLA AND HISTORICAL PERSPECTIVE

On the Falsely Believed and Forged Donation of Constantine This work demonstrated that an important papal claim to political rule of central Italy was based on an eighth-century forgery.

The Donation of Constantine Pope Julius II commissioned Raphael to include this painting of Constantine's purported gift in the Stanze, the papal apartments in the Vatican. The classical and imperial images were meant to emphasize that the Church was the heir to Roman imperial authority. (Scala/Art Resource, NY)

Testament were of critical importance to humanists outside Italy and were highly influential during the Protestant Reformation.

RENAISSANCE PHILOSOPHY

Like Valla, many other humanists anticipated that literary studies would lead eventually to philosophy. In 1456, a young Florentine began studying Greek with just such a change in mind. Supported by the Medici rulers of Florence, Marsilio Ficino (1433–1499) began a daunting project: to translate the works of Plato into Latin and to interpret Plato in light of Christian doctrine and tradition.

Ficino believed that Platonism, like Christianity, demonstrated the dignity of humanity. He wrote that everything in creation was connected along a continuum ranging from the lowliest matter to the person of God. The human soul was located at the midpoint of this hierarchy and was a bridge between the material world and God. True wisdom, and especially experience of the divine, could be gained only through contemplation and love. According to Ficino, logic and scientific observation did not lead to true understanding. Humans, he observed, know logically only what they can define in human language; individuals can, however, love things, such as God, that they are not fully able to comprehend.

Ficino's belief in the dignity of man was shared by Giovanni Pico della Mirandola (mi-RAHN-do-la) (1463–1494), who proposed to debate, with other philosophers, nine hundred theses dealing with the nature of man, the origins of knowledge, and the uses of philosophy. Pico extended Ficino's idea of the hierarchy of being, arguing that humans surpassed even the angels in dignity. Angels held a fixed position in the hierarchy, just below God. In contrast, humans could move either up or down in the hierarchy, depending on the extent to which they embraced spiritual or worldly interests. Pico further believed that he had proved that all philosophies contain at least some truth. He was one of the first humanists to learn Hebrew and to argue that divine wisdom could be found in Jewish as well as Christian and pagan mystical literature.

THE UNITY OF KNOWLEDGE

Pico's ideas were shared by other humanists, who contended that an original, unified, divine illumination—a "Pristine Theology," they called it—preceded even Plato and Aristotle. These humanists found theological truth in what they believed was ancient Egyptian, Greek, and Jewish magic. Ficino himself popularized the *Corpus Hermeticum* (the Hermetic collection), an amalgam of magical texts of the first century A.D. that was thought mistakenly to be the work of an Egyptian magician, Hermes Trismegistos. Humanists assumed Hermes wrote during the age of Moses and Pythagoras. Like many mystical writings of the first and second centuries, Hermetic texts explained how the mind could influence and be influenced by the material and celestial worlds.

Along with exploring Hermetic magic, many humanists of the fifteenth and sixteenth centuries investigated astrology and alchemy. All three systems posit the existence of a direct, reciprocal connection between the cosmos and the natural world. In the late medieval and Renaissance world, astrological and alchemical theories seemed reasonable. By the late fifteenth century, many humanists assumed that personality was profoundly affected by the stars and that the heavens were not silent regarding human affairs. It was not by accident that, for a century or more after 1500, astrologers were official or unofficial members of most European courts.

Interest in alchemy was equally widespread, though more controversial. Alchemists believed that everything was made of a primary material and that, therefore, it was possible to transmute one substance into another. The most popular variation, and the one most exploited by hucksters and frauds, was the belief that base metals could be turned into gold. The hopes of most alchemists, however, were more profound. They were convinced that they could unlock the secrets of the entire cosmos. On a personal and religious, as well as on a material level, practitioners hoped to make the impure pure. The interest in understanding and manipulating nature that lay at the heart of Hermetic magic, astrology, and alchemy was an important stimulus to scientific investigations and, ultimately, to the rise of modern scientific thought.

Humanism and Political Thought

The humanists' plan to rediscover classical sources meshed well with their political interests. Petrarch and the civic humanists believed that rulers, whether in a republic or a principality, should exhibit all the classical and Christian virtues of faith, hope, love, prudence, temperance, fortitude, and justice. A virtuous ruler would be loved as well as obeyed. The civic humanists viewed governments and laws as essentially unchanging and static. They believed that when change does occur, it most likely happens by chance—that is, because of fortune (the Roman goddess Fortuna). Humanists believed that the only protection against chance is true virtue, for the virtuous would never be dominated by fortune. Thus, beginning with Petrarch, humanists advised rulers to love their subjects, to be generous with their possessions, and to maintain the rule of law. Humanistic tracts of the fourteenth and fifteenth centuries were full of classical and Christian examples of virtuous actions by moral rulers.

The French invasions of Italy in 1494 (see page 301), and the warfare that followed, called into question many of the humanists' assumptions about the lessons and virtues of classical civilization. Francesco Guicciardini (gwih-char-DEE-nee) (1483–1540), a Florentine patrician who had served in papal armies, suggested that, contrary to humanistic hopes, history held no clear lessons. Unless the causes of separate events were identical down to the smallest detail, he said, the results could be radically different. An even more thorough critique was offered by Guicciardini's friend and fellow Florentine, **Niccolò Machiavelli** (1469–1527). In a series of writings, Machiavelli developed what he believed was a new science of politics. He wrote *Discourses on Livy*, a treatise on military organization, a history of Florence, and even a Renaissance play titled *The Mandrake Root*. He is best remembered, however, for *The Prince* (1513), a small tract numbering fewer than a hundred pages.

Machiavelli felt that his contemporaries paid too little heed to the lessons to be learned from history. Thus, in his discourses on Livy he comments on Roman government, the role of religion, and the nature of political virtue, emphasizing the sophisticated Roman analysis of political and military situations. A shortcoming more serious than ignorance of history, Machiavelli believed, was his contemporaries' ignorance of the true motivations for people's actions. His play, *The Mandrake Root*, is a comedy about the ruses used to seduce a young woman. In truth, however, none of the characters is fooled. All of them, from the wife to her husband, realize what is happening but use the seduction to their own advantage. In the play, Machiavelli implicitly challenges the humanistic assumption that educated individuals will naturally choose virtue over vice. He explicitly criticizes these same assumptions in *The Prince*. Machiavelli holds the contrary view: that individuals are much more likely to respond to fear and that power rather than morality makes for good government.

Machiavelli's use of the Italian word *virtù* led him to be vilified as amoral. Machiavelli deliberately chose a word that meant both "manliness" or "ability" and "virtue as a moral quality." Earlier humanists had restricted *virtù* to the second meaning, using the word to refer to upright qualities such as prudence, generosity, and bravery. Machiavelli tried to show that, in some situations, these "virtues" could have violent, even evil, consequences. If, for example, a prince was so magnanimous in giving away his wealth that he was forced to raise taxes, his subjects might come to hate him. Conversely, a prince who, through cruelty to the enemies of his state, brought peace and stability to his subjects might be obeyed and perhaps even loved. A virtuous ruler must be mindful of the goals to be achieved—that is what Machiavelli really meant by the phrase often translated as "the ends justify the means."

Like Guicciardini, Machiavelli rejected earlier humanistic assumptions that one needed merely to imitate the great leaders of the past. Governing is a process that requires different skills at different times, he warned: "The man who adapts his course of action to the nature of the times will succeed and, likewise, the man who sets his course of action out of tune with the times will come to grief."[9] The abilities that enable a prince to gain power may not be the abilities that will allow him to maintain it.

With the writings of Machiavelli, humanistic ideas of intellectual, moral, and political reform came to maturation. Petrarch and the early humanists believed fully in the powers of classical wisdom to transform society. Machiavelli and his contemporaries admitted the importance of classical wisdom, but also recognized the ambiguity of any simplistic application of classical learning to contemporary life.

Niccolò Machiavelli
A government functionary and political theorist in Florence, whose most famous work, *The Prince*, emphasized that the successful ruler must anticipate and adapt to change.

SECTION SUMMARY

- The culture of Italy was more urban and less clerical than the rest of Europe.

- Francesco Petrarch popularized cultural movements that attempted to use Roman learning to change moral values and public behavior in Europe.

- Because women lacked a role in public life, their relationship to the humanistic movement was limited.

- By the end of the fifteenth century, humanists had developed a sense of historical change.

- Political crisis in Italy led Machiavelli to challenge the assumptions about morality and public life.

PAINTING AND THE ARTS, 1250–1550

What was "new" about Renaissance art?

Townspeople and artists in Renaissance Italy shared the humanists' perception of the importance of classical antiquity. Filippo Villani (d. 1405), a wealthy Florentine from an important business family, wrote that artists had recently "reawakened a lifeless and almost extinct art." In the middle of the fifteenth century, the sculptor Lorenzo Ghiberti concluded that, with the rise of Christianity, "not only statues and paintings [were destroyed], but the books and commentaries and handbooks and rules on which men relied for their training." Italian writers and painters themselves believed that the recovery of past literary and artistic practices was essential if society was to recover from the "barbarism" that they believed characterized the recent past.

The Renaissance of the arts is traditionally divided into three periods. In the early Renaissance, artists imitated nature; in the middle period, they rediscovered classical ideas of proportion; in the High Renaissance, artists were "superior to nature but also to the artists of the ancient world," according to the artist and architect Giorgio Vasari (1511–1574), who wrote a famous history of the eminent artists of his day.

Early Renaissance Art

The first stirrings of the new styles can be found in the late thirteenth century. The greatest innovator of that era was Giotto di Bondone of Florence (ca. 1266–1337). Although Giotto's background was modest, his fellow citizens, popes, and patrons throughout Italy quickly recognized his skill. He

Giotto's Naturalism
Later painters praised the naturalistic emotion of Giotto's painting. In this detail from the Arena Chapel, Giotto portrays the kiss of Judas, one of the most dramatic moments in Christian history. (Scala/Art Resource, NY)

traveled as far south as Rome and as far north as Padua, painting churches and chapels. According to later artists and commentators, Giotto broke with the prevailing stiff, highly symbolic style and introduced lifelike portrayals of living persons. He produced paintings of dramatic situations, showing events located in specific times and places. The frescoes of the Arena Chapel in Padua (1304–1314), for example, recount episodes in the life of Christ. In a series of scenes leading from Christ's birth to his crucifixion, Giotto situates his actors in towns and countryside in what appears to be actual space. Even Michelangelo, the master of the High Renaissance, studied Giotto's painting. Giotto was in such demand throughout Italy that his native Florence gave him a public appointment, so that he would be required by law to remain in the city.

Early in the fifteenth century, Florentine artists devised new ways to represent nature that surpassed even the innovations of Giotto. The revolutionary nature of these artistic developments is evident from the careers of Lorenzo Ghiberti (gi-BER-tee) (1378–1455), Filippo Brunelleschi (broon-eh-LES-key) (1377–1446), and Masaccio (1401–ca. 1428). Their sculpture, architecture, and painting began an ongoing series of experiments with the representation of space through **linear perspective**. Perspective is a system for representing three-dimensional objects on a two-dimensional plane. It is based on two observations: (1) as parallel lines recede into the distance, they seem to converge; and (2) a geometric relationship regulates the relative sizes of objects at various distances from the viewer. Painters of the Renaissance literally found themselves looking at their world from a new perspective.

In 1401, Ghiberti won a commission to design door panels for the baptistery of San Giovanni in Florence. He was to spend much of the rest of his life working on two sets of bronze doors on which were recorded the stories of the New Testament (the north doors) and the Old Testament (the east doors). Ghiberti used the new techniques of linear perspective to create a sense of space into which he placed his classically inspired figures. Later, in the sixteenth century, Michelangelo remarked that the east doors were worthy to be the "Doors of Paradise," and so they have been known ever since.

In the competition for the baptistery commission, Ghiberti had beaten the young Filippo Brunelleschi, who, as a result, gave up sculpture for architecture and later left Florence to study in Rome. While in Rome, he is said to have visited and measured surviving examples of classical architecture—the artistic equivalent of humanistic literary research. According to Vasari, he was capable of "visualizing Rome as it was before the fall." Brunelleschi's debt to Rome is evident in his masterpiece, Florence's foundling hospital. Built as a combination of hemispheres and cubes and resembling a Greek stoa or an arcaded Roman basilica, the long, low structure is an example of how profoundly different Renaissance architecture was from the towering Gothic of the Middle Ages. But his experience in Rome was also critical to his famous plan for constructing a dome over the Cathedral of Santa Maria del Fiore in Florence. The Florentines were replacing their old cathedral with a vast new one. But until Brunelleschi, no one had been able to design a dome to cover the 180-foot space created by the vast new nave. He designed mutually supporting internal and external domes that were stronger and lighter than a single dome would have been.

In the first decade of the fifteenth century, many commentators believed that painting would never be as innovative as either sculpture or architecture. They knew of no classical models that had survived for imitation. Yet, the possibilities in painting became apparent in 1427 with the unveiling of Masaccio's *Trinity* in the Florentine Church of Santa Maria Novella. Masaccio (ma-SAH-cho) built on revolutionary experiments in linear perspective to create a painting in which a flat wall seems to become a recessed chapel. The space created is filled with the images of Christ crucified, the Father, and the Holy Spirit.

The Doors of Paradise   Ghiberti worked on panels for the baptistery from 1401 to 1453. In his representations of scenes from the Old Testament, he combined a love of ancient statuary with the new Florentine interest in linear perspective. (Baptistery of San Giovanni, Florence/ Scala/Art Resource, NY)

linear perspective
A revolutionary technique developed by early-fifteenth-century Florentine painters for representing three-dimensional objects on a two-dimensional plane.

In the middle years of the fifteenth century, artists came to terms with the innovations of the earlier period. In the second half of the fifteenth century, however, artists such as the Florentine Sandro Botticelli (bot-ti-CHEL-ee) (1445–1510) added a profound understanding of classical symbolism to the technical innovations of Masaccio and Brunelleschi. Botticelli's famous *Primavera* (*Spring*, 1478), painted for a member of the Medici family, is filled with Neo-Platonic symbolism concerning truth, beauty, and the virtues of humanity.

High Renaissance Art

The high point in the development of Renaissance art came at the beginning of the sixteenth century. Artists in Venice learned perspective from the Florentines and added their own tradition of subtle coloring in oils. The works of Italian artists were admired well beyond the borders of Italy. Even Sultan Mehmed II of Constantinople valued Italian painters. (See the feature, "The Global Record: Gentile Bellini Travels to Meet the Turkish Sultan.") Italian painters, goldsmiths, and architects continued to work in the Ottoman Empire through the sixteenth century.

The work of two Florentines, **Leonardo da Vinci** (1452–1519) and Michelangelo Buonarroti (1475–1564), best exemplifies the sophisticated heights that art achieved early in the sixteenth century. Leonardo, the bastard son of a notary, was raised in the village of Vinci outside of Florence. Cut off from the humanistic milieu of the city, he desired, above all else, to prove that his artistry was the equal of his formally schooled social superiors. In his notebooks, he confessed, "I am fully conscious that, not being a literary man, certain presumptuous persons will think they may reasonably blame me, alleging that I am not a man of letters."[10] But he defended his lack of classical education by arguing that all the best writing, like the best painting and invention, is based on the close observation of nature. Close observation and scientific analysis made Leonardo's work uniquely creative in all these fields. Leonardo is famous for his plans, sometimes prophetic, for bridges, fortresses, submarines, and airships. In painting, he developed chiaroscuro, a technique for using light and dark in pictorial representation, and showed aerial perspective. He painted horizons as muted, shaded zones rather than with sharp lines. It was Leonardo's analytical observation that had the greatest influence on his contemporaries.

Michelangelo, however, was widely hailed as the capstone of Renaissance art. In the words of a contemporary, "He alone has triumphed over ancient artists, modern artists and over Nature itself." In his career, we can follow the rise of Renaissance artists from the ranks of mere craftsmen to honored creators, courtiers who were the equals of the humanists—in fact, Michelangelo shared Petrarch's concern for reform and renewal in Italian society. We can also discern the synthesis of the artistic and intellectual transformations of the Renaissance with a profound religious sensitivity.

The importance of Michelangelo's contribution is obvious in two of his most important works: the statue *David* in Florence and his commissions in the **Sistine Chapel** of the Vatican in Rome. From his youth, Michelangelo had studied and imitated antique sculpture, to the point that some of his creations were thought by many actually to be antiquities. He used his understanding of classical art in *David* (1501). Florentines recalled David's defeat of the giant Goliath, saving Israel from almost certain conquest by the Philistines. *David* thus became a symbol of the youthful Florentine republic struggling to maintain its freedom against great odds. As Vasari noted, "Just as David had protected his people and governed them justly, so whoever ruled Florence should vigorously defend the city and govern it with justice."[11]

Michelangelo was a committed republican and Florentine, but he spent much of his life working in Rome on a series of papal commissions. In 1508, he was called by Pope Julius II (r. 1503–1513) to work on the ceiling of the Sistine Chapel. Michelangelo spent four years decorating the ceiling with hundreds of figures and with nine scenes from the Book of

Leonardo da Vinci A famous painter, engineer, and scientist who rejected arguments and ideas based on imitation of the ancients. Rather, he advocated careful study of the natural world.

Sistine Chapel The chapel at the Vatican Palace, containing Michelangelo's magnificent paintings of the Creation and Last Judgment; it captures the cultural, religious, and ideological program of the papacy.

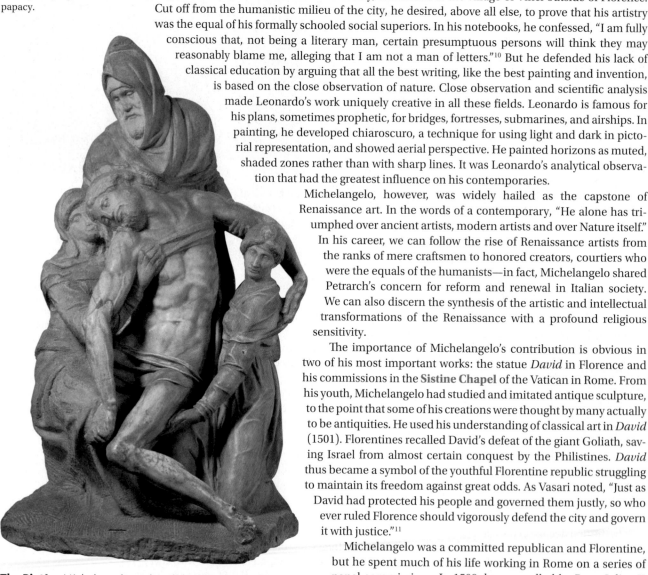

The Pietà Michelangelo sculpted three versions of Mary holding the crucified Jesus. This late, unfinished work reveals Michelangelo's desire to show the suffering of Christ. (Scala/Art Resource, NY)

Gentile Bellini Travels to Meet the Turkish Sultan

Giovanni and Gentile Bellini were two of the lead-ing Renaissance artists in Venice. Their fame spread throughout the Mediterranean and resulted in this unusual cultural meeting in 1479. A portrait of the emperor Mehmed II by Gentile now hangs in the National Gallery in London.

Some portraits having been taken to Turkey to the Grand Turk [the sultan] by an ambassador, that emperor was so struck with astonishment that, although the Mohammedan laws prohibit pictures, he accepted them with great goodwill, praising the work without end, and what is more, requesting that the master himself be sent to him. But the Senate, considering that Giovanni could ill support the hardships, resolved to send Gentile his brother, and he was conveyed safely in their galleys to Constantinople, where being presented to Mehmed [II], he was received with much kindness as an unusual visitor. He presented a beautiful picture to the prince, who admired it much, and could not persuade himself to believe that a mortal man had in him so much of the divinity as to be able to express the things of nature in such a lively manner. Gentile painted the Emperor Mehmed himself from life so well that it was considered a miracle, and the emperor, having seen many specimens of his art, asked Gentile if he had the courage to paint himself; and Gentile having answered "Yes," before many days were over he finished a lifelike portrait by means of a mirror, and brought it to the monarch, whose astonishment was so great that he would have it a divine spirit dwelt in him. And had not this art been forbidden by the law of the Turks, the

emperor would never have let him go. But either from fear that people would murmur, or from some other cause, he sent for him one day, and having thanked him, and given him great praise, he bade him to ask whatever he would and it should be granted him without fail. Gentile modestly asked for nothing more than that he would graciously give him a letter of recommendation to the Senate and Lords of Venice. His request was granted in as fervent words as possible, and then, loaded with gifts and honors, and with the dignity of a cavalier, he was sent away. Among the other gifts was a chain of gold of two hundred and fifty crowns weight, worked in the Turkish manner. So, leaving Constantinople, he came safely to Venice, where he was received by his brother Giovanni and the whole city with joy, every one rejoicing in the honors which Mehmed had paid him. When the Doge and Lords [of Venice] saw the letters of the emperor, they ordered that a provision of two hundred crowns a year should be paid him all the rest of his life.

QUESTIONS

1. What seems to be the role of Renaissance art and artists in Venetian and Turkish diplomacy?

2. What does Bellini's trip to Constantinople suggest about relations between the Turks and Christians?

Source: *Stories of the Italian Renaissance from Vasari*, arranged and translated by E. L. Seeley (London and New York, 1908), pp. 135–137.

Genesis, including the famous *Creation of Adam*. In the late 1530s, at the request of Pope Clement VII (r. 1523–1534), he completed *The Last Judgment*, which covers the wall above the altar. In that painting, the techniques of perspective and the conscious recognition of debts to classical culture recede into the background as the artist surrounds Christ in judgment with saints and sinners. In the hollow, hanging skin of flayed Saint Bartholomew we can detect a psychological self-portrait of an artist increasingly concerned with his own spiritual failings.

Michelangelo's self-portrait reminds us that the intellectual content of the artist's work is one of its most enduring traits. He was a Platonist who believed that the form and beauty of a statue are contained, buried, in the stone itself. The artist's job is to peel away excess material and reveal the beauty within. As he noted in one of his poems, sculpting is a process not unlike religious salvation:

Just as by carving . . . we set
Into hard mountain rock
A living figure
Which grows most where the stone is most removed;
In like manner, some good works . . .
Are concealed by the excess of my very flesh.[12]

Renaissance Art in the North

In the early fifteenth century, while Brunelleschi and Masaccio were revolutionizing the ways in which Italian artists viewed their world, artists north of the Alps, especially in Flanders, were making equally striking advances in the ways they painted and sculpted. Artistic innovation in northern Europe began with changes tied closely to the world of northern courts; only later did artists take up the styles of the Italian Renaissance. Northerners took Italian Renaissance art and fit it to a new environment.

Northern art of the late fourteenth and fifteenth centuries changed in two significant ways. In sculpture, the long, austere, unbroken vertical lines typical of Gothic sculpture gave way to a much more complex and emotional style. In painting, Flemish artists moved from ornate, vividly colored paintings to experiments with ways to create a sense of depth. Artists strove to paint and sculpt works that more faithfully represented reality. The sculptures of Claus Sluter (1350–1406), carved for a family chapel of the Burgundian dukes at Champmol, captured a lifelike drama unlike the previous Gothic sculpture. Court painters, such as Jan van Eyck (ca. 1390–1441), in miniatures, portraits, and altar paintings, also moved away from a highly formalized style to a careful representation of specific places. In van Eyck's portrait of the Italian banker and courtier Giovanni Arnolfini and his bride, the image of the painter is reflected in a small mirror behind the couple, and above the mirror is written, "Jan van Eyck was here, 1434." Whereas Italians of the early fifteenth century tried to re-create space through linear perspective, the Flemish used aerial perspective, softening colors and tones to give the illusion of depth.

The influence of Renaissance styles in the north of Europe dates from the reign of the French king Francis I (r. 1515–1547), when Italian artists in significant numbers traveled north. Francis invited Italian artists to his court—most notably Leonardo da Vinci, who spent his last years in France. The most influential of the Italian style creations in France was doubtless Francis's château Fontainebleau, whose decorations contained mythologies, histories, and allegories of the kind found in the Italian courts. Throughout the sixteenth century, Italianate buildings and paintings sprang up throughout Europe.

Perhaps the most famous artist who traveled to Italy, learned Italian techniques, and then transformed them to suit the environment of northern Europe was Albrecht Dürer of Nuremberg (1471–1528). Son of a well-known goldsmith, Dürer became a painter and toured France and Flanders, learning the techniques popular in northern Europe. Then, in 1494, he left Nuremberg on the first of two trips to Italy, during which he sketched Italian landscapes and studied the work of Italian artists, especially in Venice. What he learned in Italy, combined with the friendship of some of Germany's leading humanists, formed the basis of Dürer's works, which blended northern humanistic interests with the Italian techniques of composition and linear perspective. Dürer worked in charcoal, watercolors, and paints, but his influence was most widely spread through his numerous woodcuts covering classical and contemporary themes. His woodcut, *Whore of Babylon*, prepared in the context of the debate over the reform of the church, is based on sketches of Venetian prostitutes completed during his first visit to Italy.

Numerous other artists and engravers traveled south to admire and learn from the great works of Italian artists. The engravings they produced and distributed back home made the southern innovations available to those who would never set foot in Italy. In fact, some now lost or destroyed creations are known only through the copies engraved by northern artists eager to absorb Italian techniques.

Van Eyck: The Arnolfini Wedding   Careful observation of people and places was typical of the new art of both northern and southern Europe. Van Eyck seems to have re-created this scene to the smallest detail. His own image appears in the mirror on the wall.   (The National Gallery, London/Art Resource, NY)

Art and Patronage

The variety and vitality of art in the Renaissance depended, in large measure, on the economic prosperity of Europe's cities and towns. Because of banking, international trade, and even service as mercenaries, Italians, and particularly Florentines, had money to spend on arts and luxuries. Thus, the Italians of the Renaissance, whether as public or private patrons, could afford to use consumption of art as a form of competition for social and political status.

It was not just the elite who could afford art. Surprisingly, modest families bought small religious paintings, painted storage chests, and decorative arts. Moralists advised families to buy small paintings of the Virgin Mary or the baby Jesus. Families also bought small paintings of saints considered special to their town or family. Wealthy and modest families alike bought brightly decorated terra-cotta pitchers, platters, and plates. Decorative arts were a critical social marker for families at all levels. (See the feature, "The Visual Record: Renaissance Marriage Chests.") Thus, the market for art steadily increased in the fourteenth and fifteenth centuries, as did the number of shops and studios in which artists could be trained.

Artists in the modern world are accustomed to standing outside society as critics of conventional ideas. In the late Middle Ages and Renaissance, artists were not alienated commentators. In 1300, most art was religious in subject, and public display was its purpose. Throughout Europe, art fulfilled a devotional function. Painted crucifixes, altarpieces, and banners were often endowed as devotional or penitential objects. The Arena Chapel in Padua, with its frescoes by Giotto, was funded by a merchant anxious to pay for some of his sins.

In the late Middle Ages and Renaissance, numerous paintings and statues throughout Italy (and much of the rest of Europe) were revered for their miraculous powers. During plague, drought, and times of war people had recourse to the sacred power of the saints represented in these works of art. (See the feature, "The Visual Record: A Painting of the Plague" in Chapter 11, pages 306–307.) The construction of the great churches of the period was often a community project that lasted for decades, even centuries. The city council of Siena, for example, voted to rebuild its Gothic Cathedral of Saint Mary, saying that the Blessed Virgin "was, is and will be in the future the head of this city" and that through veneration of her "Siena may be protected from harm." Accordingly, although the subject of art was clearly and primarily religious, the message was bound up in civic values.

Portrait of a Black Man Albrecht Dürer sketched this portrait in the early sixteenth century, most likely in a commercial center such as Venice or Nuremberg. By that time, it was common to show one of the three Magi as black, but such depictions, unlike Dürer's drawing here, were rarely based on portrait studies. (Graphische Sammlung, Albertina, Vienna)

ART AND THE COMMUNE

The first burst of artistic creativity in the fourteenth century was paid for by public institutions. Communal governments built and decorated city halls to house government functionaries and to promote civic pride. Most towns placed a remarkable emphasis on the beauty of the work. Civic officials often named special commissions to consult with a variety of artists and architects before approving building projects. Governments, with an eye to the appearance of public areas, legislated the width of streets, height limits, and even the styles of dwelling façades.

Public art in Florence was often organized and supported by various guild organizations. Guild membership was a prerequisite for citizenship, so guildsmen set the tone in politics, as well as in the commercial life of the city. Most major guilds commissioned sculpture for the Chapel of Or San Michele. This was a famous shrine in the grain market (its painting of the Virgin Mary was popularly thought to have wonder-working powers). The room above the chapel eventually became the seat of the Guelf Party, the city's most powerful political organization. Guilds took responsibility for building and maintaining other structures in the city as well. Guildsmen took pride in creating a beautiful environment that would reflect not only on the city and its patron saint, but also on the power and influence of the guild itself.

INDIVIDUAL PATRONS

The princes who ruled outside the republics of Italy often had similarly precise messages that they wished to communicate. Renaissance popes embarked on a quite specific ideological program in the late fifteenth century to assert their dual roles as spiritual leaders of Christendom and temporal lords of a central Italian state (see pages 346–347). Rulers, such as the Este dukes of

Men and Women Playing Cards This fresco painted in the early fifteenth century in Milan is typical of the art used to decorate the homes of the wealthy. It depicts one of the pastimes of noble families. (Scala/Art Resource, NY)

Ferrara and the Sforza dukes of Milan, constructed castles within their cities or hunting lodges and villas in the countryside and adorned them with pictures of the hunt or murals of knights in combat—scenes that emphasized their noble virtues and their natural right to rule.

By the mid-fifteenth century, patrons of artworks in Florence and most other regions of Italy were more and more likely to be wealthy individuals. Many of the patrons who commissioned and oversaw artists were women. Women paid for the construction of convents and chapels. In many cases, their patronage can simply be understood as an extension of their families, but in many other cases, it was not. One woman who had lived for years as a concubine of a merchant in Florence used her dead lover's bequest to commission a painting titled *Christ and the Adulteress*, making clear that even women in her situation could hope for God's mercy.

Republics, in which all families were in principle equal, initially distrusted the pride and ambition implied by elaborate city palaces and rural villas. By the middle of the fifteenth century, however, such reserve was found in none but the most conservative republics, such as Venice and Lucca. Palaces, gardens, and villas became the settings in which the wealthy could entertain their peers, receive clients, and debate the political issues of the day. The public rooms of these palaces were decorated with portraits, gem collections, rare books, ceramics, and statuary. Many villas and palaces included private chapels. In the Medici palace in Florence, for example, the chapel is the setting for a painting of the Magi (the three wise men who came to worship the infant Jesus), in which the artist, Benozzo Gozzoli (1420–1498), used members of the Medici family as models for the portraits of the Magi and their entourage (see the painting on page 300). The Magi, known to be wise and virtuous rulers, were an apt symbol for the family that had come to dominate the city.

Artists at princely courts were expected to work for the glory of their lord. Often the genre of choice was the portrait. One of the most successful portraitists of the sixteenth century was Sofonisba Anguissola (1532–1625). Anguissola won renown as a prodigy because she was female and from a patrician family; one of her paintings was sent to Michelangelo, who forwarded it to the Medici in Florence. Since women would never be allowed to study anatomy, Anguissola concentrated her talents on portraits and detailed paintings of domestic life. Later, she was called to the Spanish court, where the king, queen, and their daughter sat for her. She continued to paint after her marriage and return to Italy. Even in her nineties, she welcomed painters from all parts of Europe to visit and discuss techniques of portraiture.

SECTION SUMMARY

- Renaissance painters were especially prized for their ability to depict particular events in realistic, natural seeming settings.

- Beginning with Brunelleschi, artists consciously searched for ancient models for their work.

- Northern artists were keenly aware of Italian art, but they contributed a realism based on contrasts of dramatic colors.

- The work of Michelangelo shows the combination of artistic skill with humanistic moral and philosophical values.

THE SPREAD OF THE RENAISSANCE, 1350–1536

In what ways did humanism outside Italy differ from Italian humanism?

By 1500, the Renaissance had spread from Italy to the rest of Europe. Well beyond the borders of the old Roman Empire, in Prague and Cracow, for example, one could find a renewed interest in classical ideas about art and literature. As information about the past and its relevance to contemporary life spread, however, the message was transformed in several important ways. Outside Italy, Rome and its history played a much less pivotal role. Humanists elsewhere in the West were interested more in religious than in political reform, and they responded to a number of important local interests. Yet, the Renaissance notion of renewal based on a deep understanding and imitation of the past remained at the center of the movement. The nature of the transformation will be clearer if we begin by considering the nature of vernacular literatures before the emergence of Renaissance humanism.

Vernacular Literatures

The humanistic movement was not simply a continuation of practical and literary movements. The extent of its innovation will be clearer if we look briefly at the vernacular literatures (that is, written in native languages, rather than Latin) of the fourteenth and fifteenth centuries.

As in Italy, fourteenth-century writers elsewhere were not immediately drawn to classical sources. Boccaccio's work, for example, influenced another vernacular writer, Geoffrey Chaucer (ca. 1343–1400), the son of a London burgher, who served as a diplomat, courtier, and member of Parliament. Chaucer's most famous work, *The Canterbury Tales*, consists of stories told by a group of thirty pilgrims who left the London suburbs on a pilgrimage to the shrine of Saint Thomas Becket at Canterbury Cathedral. The narrators and the stories themselves describe a variety of moral and social types, creating an acute, sometimes comic, portrait of English life. The Wife of Bath is typical of Chaucer's pilgrims: "She was a worthy woman all her life, husbands at the churchdoor she had five." After describing her own marriages she observes that marriage is a proper way to achieve moral perfection, but it can be so only, she asserts, if the woman is master!

Although Chaucer's characters present an ironic view of the good and evil that characterize society, Chaucer's contemporary, William Langland (ca. 1330–1400), took a decidedly more serious view of the ills of English life. Whereas Boccaccio and Chaucer all told realistic tales about life as it truly seemed to be, Langland used the traditional allegorical language (that is, symbolic language in which a place or person represents an idea) of medieval Europe. In *Piers Plowman*, Langland writes of people caught between the "Valley of Death" and the "Tower of Truth." He describes the seven deadly sins that threaten all of society and follows with an exhortation to do

Renaissance Marriage Chests

The image here shows a marriage procession, including a servant carrying a large chest, or cassone. The picture is self-referential, since it was painted on the front of just such a cassone. We know that the painter of this image was Lo Scheggia (lo-SKED-ja) (1406–1486), the younger brother of Masaccio, and that he was recording a popular story of a marriage between the Bardi and Buondelmonte families of Florence. Lo Scheggia's work exhibits many of the characteristics we associate with Renaissance style. But historians often want to evaluate more than just painting technique. Historians of material culture are interested in the objects themselves and in the meanings that contemporaries gave to the possession and exhibition of them. To understand this, we need to know when and where cassoni were produced, why individuals prized them, and what the study of this image from a cassone can tell us about life in Renaissance Italy.

These highly practical chests were used by all but the poorest members of society. In houses that lacked closets, cabinets, and other kinds of storage space, everything was kept in wooden chests. Larger chests were used to store clothing, bedding, jewelry, and even weapons. Smaller chests were used for money, account books, and documents. Many of these chests had secret compartments where, for example, a businessman might keep his most sensitive papers. The most important chests made up the furnishings of the master of the house's bedroom. In a Renaissance palace the master's bedroom was also the room where he met with important allies and family members and conducted his most private business.

Cassoni took on new meaning between the late fourteenth and early sixteenth centuries. During that time, it was common for a groom to commission a matched set of chests: one for himself and the second to hold the fine clothes and jewelry that were part of his wife's dowry. These chests were decorated inside and out with scenes from classical mythology, medieval romances, and other popular stories. Classical Roman figures, such as Lucretia, who sacrificed her life to maintain her virtue, were common subjects. Some chests celebrated the virtues of chastity or fortitude—virtues thought to be essential in a proper wife. Thus, cassoni came to represent the taste, wealth, and social status of the families involved.

With these thoughts in mind, let us look closely at Lo Scheggia's cassone painting. The first thing we should notice is the procession at the left of the picture. We see a man accompanying a woman dressed in black into a house. The two are followed by others leading a horse (a sign of nobility) and carrying bedclothes and the chest. The procession testifies to the very public completion of the marriage process, which often stretched over months, if not years. It began with an engagement, followed by a promise of marriage, then a symbolic exchange of rings and physical consummation of the marriage, usually at the bride's home. The marriage was finalized by a procession to the groom's home. This procession celebrated publicly the alliance between the two families, as well as their standing in the community. Everyone noted carefully what and how much was carried in the procession, which was an indication of the size of the bride's dowry. The decoration of the marriage chest(s) in some way reflected the families involved.

What does the cassone image by Lo Scheggia indicate? The bride is the key to the story. Typically, a wealthy bride wore bright new clothes and jewelry, but this bride is dressed in black. The image tells a story not unlike that of Romeo and Juliet. The families of the bride and groom, Lionora de' Bardi and Ippolito Buondelmonte, had been

better. Both Chaucer and Langland expected that their audiences would immediately recognize commonly held ideas and values.

Despite the persistence of old forms of literature, new vernacular styles arose, although they still dealt with traditional values and ideas. Letters like those of the Paston family in England or Alessandra Macinghi-Strozzi in Italy described day-to-day affairs of business, politics, and family life. Letters dictated and sent by Saint Catherine of Siena and Angela of Foligno offered advice to the troubled. Small books of moral or spiritual writings were especially popular among women readers in the fourteenth and fifteenth centuries, among them *The Mirror for Simple Souls* by Marguerite of Porete (d. 1310). Though Marguerite was ultimately executed as a heretic, her work continued to circulate anonymously. Her frank descriptions of love, including God's love for humans, inspired many other writers in the fourteenth and fifteenth centuries. Less erotic, but equally riveting, was the memoir of Margery Kempe, an alewife from England, who left her husband and family, dressed in white (symbolic of virginity), and joined other pilgrims on trips to Spain, Italy, and Jerusalem.

One of the most unusual of the new vernacular writers was Christine de Pizan (1369–1430), the daughter of an Italian physician at the court of Charles V of France. When the deaths of her father and husband left her with responsibility for her children and little money, she turned to writing. From 1389 until her death, she lived and wrote at the French court. She is perhaps best known for *The Book of the City of the Ladies* (1405). In it, she added her own voice to what is known

Lo Scheggia: The Bardi-Buondelmonte Wedding (Alberto Bruschi di Grassina Collection, Florence/Bridgeman Art Library International)

enemies for generations. Despite this fact, the two were in love. We can read the tale of their love in three scenes from right to left. In the first scene on the right, Ippolito is caught in Lionora's house. He refuses to declare his love for her because he wants to protect her reputation. In the middle scene, Lionora, dressed as a widow, interrupts Ippolito's trial and declares her love for him. By dressing as a widow, she symbolically declares that they have already made their wedding vows and are, in fact, married. The authorities accept her declaration, and in the final scene on the left, the marriage is made public. Ippolito leads Lionora in a marriage procession, complete with wedding chest, to their new home. According to tradition, their marriage ended the feud between the two families.

We do not know who commissioned this chest. Nonetheless, we can now step back and speculate a bit about what Florentines might have noticed when they viewed the procession in which this cassone was carried through the streets of Florence. The image of the wedding couple and the servants carrying expensive dowry items, as well as the chest itself, testifies to the importance of the families involved. In a community such as Florence, where certain families were at the center of politics and public life, this image no doubt reminded those watching the procession of the power of prominent families and the critical role of marriage alliances in maintaining civic peace.

QUESTIONS

1. Look carefully at the image. Can you identify what seems most significant in the procession of the bride and groom?

2. How would this particular image influence the meaning that observers might give to the procession of the bride and groom?

as the *querelle des femmes*, the "argument over women." Christine wrote to counter the prevalent opinions of women as inherently inferior to men and incapable of learning or moral judgments. She argued that the problem was education: "If it were customary to send daughters to school like sons, and if they were then taught the natural sciences, they would learn as thoroughly and understand the subtleties of all the arts and sciences as well as sons." Christine described, in her book, an ideal city of ladies in which prudence, justice, and reason would protect women from ignorant male critics.

All these vernacular writings built on popular tales and sayings as well as on traditional moral and religious writings. Unlike the early humanists, the vernacular writers saw little need for new cultural and intellectual models.

The Impact of Printing

The spread of humanism beyond Italy was aided greatly by the invention of printing. In the fifteenth century, the desire to own and to read complete texts of classical works was widespread, but the number of copies was severely limited. Manuscripts required time and money to hand-copy, collate, and check each new copy. Poggio Bracciolini's letters are filled with complaints about the time and expense of reproducing the classical manuscripts he had discovered. One copy he had commissioned was so inaccurate and illegible as to be nearly unusable. Traveling to repositories and libraries was often easier than creating a personal library. It was rarely possible for someone who read a manuscript once to obtain a complete copy to compare with other works.

The invention of printing with movable lead type changed things dramatically. Although block printing had long been known in China, it was only in the late fourteenth century that it became a popular way to produce playing cards and small woodcuts in Europe. In China, an entire page would be carved on a single wooden block. **Johann Gutenberg** developed molds by which single letters or individual words could be cast in metal. Metal fonts could produce many more copies before they had to be recast. And further, they could be reused to print different pages. Between 180 and 200 copies of the so-called Gutenberg Bible were printed in 1452 and 1453. It was followed shortly by editions of the Psalms. By 1470, German printing techniques had spread to Italy, the Low Countries, France, and England. It has been estimated that, by 1500, a thousand presses were operating in 265 towns (see **MAP 12.1**). The output of the early presses was extremely varied, ranging from small devotional books and other popular and profitable literature to complete editions of classical authors and their humanistic and theological texts.

Johann Gutenberg
German inventor of movable metal type. His innovations led to the publication of the first printed book in Europe, the Gutenberg Bible, in the 1450s.

🌐 MAP 12.1—The Spread of Printing

Printing technology moved rapidly along major trade routes to the most populous and prosperous areas of Europe. The technology was rapidly adopted in peripheral areas as well as in highly literate centers such as the Low Countries, the Rhine Valley, and northern Italy.

Printing allowed for a dramatic expansion of libraries. Early humanists had to strive to create a library of several hundred volumes. The Venetian printer Aldus Manutius (1450–1515) himself printed and distributed over 120,000 volumes!

Printing allowed for the creation of agreed-upon standard editions of works in law, theology, philosophy, and science. Scholars in different parts of the European world could feel fairly confident that they and their colleagues were analyzing identical texts. Similarly, producing accurate medical and herbal diagrams, maps, and even reproductions of art and architecture was easier. Multiple copies of texts also made possible the study of rare and esoteric literary, philosophical, and scientific works. An unexpected result of the print revolution was the rise of the printshop as a center of culture and communication. The printers Aldus Manutius in Venice and Johannes Froben (d. 1527) in Basel were humanists. Both invited humanists to work in their shops editing their texts and correcting the proofs before printing. Printshops became a natural gathering place for clerics and laymen. Thus, they were natural sources of humanist ideas and later, in the sixteenth century, of Protestant religious programs.

Humanism Outside Italy

As the influence of the humanist movement extended beyond Italy, the interests of the humanists changed. Although a strong religious strain infused Italian humanism, public life lay at the center of Italian programs of education and reform. Outside Italy, however, moral and religious reform formed the heart of the movement. Northern humanists wanted to renew Christian life and reinvigorate the church. Critics of the church complained that the clergy were wealthy and ignorant and that the laity were uneducated and superstitious. To amend those failings, northern humanists were involved in building educational institutions, in unearthing and publishing texts by Church Fathers, and in chronicling local customs and history. The works of the two best-known humanists, Thomas More and Desiderius Erasmus, present a sharp critique of contemporary behavior and, in the case of Erasmus, a call to a new sense of piety. The religious views of Erasmus were so influential that northern humanism has generally come to be known as "Christian humanism."

The intellectual environment into which humanism spread from Italy had changed significantly since the thirteenth century. The universities of Paris and Oxford retained the status they had acquired earlier but found themselves competing with a host of new foundations. Like Paris, almost all had theological faculties dominated by scholastically trained theologians. Nevertheless, the new foundations often had chairs of rhetoric, or "eloquence," which left considerable scope for those who advocated humanistic learning. These new universities, from Cracow (1367) to Uppsala in Sweden (1477), also reflected the increased national feeling in various regions of Europe. The earliest university in the lands of the German Empire, the Charles University in Prague (1348), was founded at the request of Emperor Charles IV, whose court was in Prague. The foundation of a new university at Poszony (1465) by Johannes Vitéz was part of a cultural flowering of the Hungarian court at Buda. A supporter of King Matthias Corvinus, Vitéz corresponded with Italian humanists, collected manuscripts, and tried to recruit humanist teachers to come to Buda. The universities in Vienna (1365), Aix (1409), Louvain (1425), and numerous other cities owed their foundations to the pride and ambition of local leaders.

HUMANISM AND UNIVERSITIES

The humanists associated with the new universities were often educated in Italy, but they brought a new perspective to their work. Humanists in Sweden wrote histories of the Goths, celebrating the contributions of Germans to European culture. Polish humanists wrote similarly, in one case trying to define where in eastern Europe one could draw the line between Europe and Asia.

Humanists on faculties of law at French universities used humanistic techniques of historical and linguistic study. Italian-trained French lawyers introduced what came to be called the "Gallican style" of jurisprudence. Because legal ideas, like language, changed over time, they argued that Roman law had to be studied as a historically created system and not as an abstract and unchanging structure. Humanists, like Guillaume Budé (1468–1540), moved from the study of law to considerations of Roman coinage, religion, and economic life in order to better understand the formation of Roman law. The desire to understand the law led other humanist-legists to add the study of society in ancient Gaul to their work on Rome, and then to examine the law of other societies as well.

The new universities often became centers of linguistic studies. Humanistic interest in language inspired the foundation of "trilingual" colleges in Spain, France, and the Low Countries to foster serious study of Hebrew, Greek, and Latin. Like Italian humanists, other humanists believed that knowledge of languages would allow students to understand more clearly the truths of Christianity. Typical of this movement was the archbishop of Toledo, Francisco Jiménez de Cisneros (1436–1517), who founded the University of Alcalá in 1508 with chairs of Latin, Greek, and Hebrew. He began the publication of a vast new edition of the Bible, called the "Polyglot ('many tongued') Bible" (1522) because it had parallel columns in Latin, Greek, and, where appropriate, Hebrew. Unlike Valla, Jiménez intended his translations not to challenge the Vulgate but merely to clarify its meaning. The university and the Bible were part of an effort to complete the conversion of Muslims and Jews and to reform religious practices among the old Christians.

To these humanists, the discovery and publication of early Christian authors seemed critical to any reform within the church. Jacques Lefèvre d'Étaples (le-FEV-ra du-TAHP-le) (1455–1536) of France was one of the most famous and influential of these humanistic editors of early Christian texts. After 1500, he concentrated on editing the texts of the early Church Fathers. The true spirit of Christianity, he believed, would be most clear in the works and lives of those who had lived closest to the age of the apostles. Christian humanists, inspired by Lefèvre, became key players in the later Reformation movements in France.

Tensions between the humanists and the advocates of Scholastic methods broke out over the cultural and linguistic studies that formed the heart of the humanist program. Taking to heart the humanistic belief that all philosophies and religions, not just Christianity, contained universal moral and spiritual truths, Johannes Reuchlin (RYE-klin) (1455–1522) of Württemberg embarked on a study of the Jewish Cabala. Johannes Pfefferkorn, a Dominican priest and recent convert from Judaism, attacked Reuchlin's use of Jewish traditions in the study of Christian theology. Sides were quickly drawn. The theological faculties of the German universities generally supported Pfefferkorn. The humanists supported Reuchlin. In his own defense, Reuchlin issued *The Letters of Illustrious Men*, a volume of correspondence he had received in support of his position. This work gave rise to one of the great satires of the Renaissance, *The Letters of Obscure Men* (1516), written by anonymous authors and purporting to be letters from various narrow-minded Scholastics in defense of Pfefferkorn. Although the debate arose over the validity of Hebraic studies for Christian theology, and not over humanistic ideas of reform or wisdom, it indicates the division between the humanists and much of the Scholastic community. Many people initially misunderstood the early controversies of the Protestant Reformation as a continuation of the conflicts between humanists and Scholastic theologians over the uses of Hebrew learning.

Humanists as Critics

Thomas More Well-known humanist and chancellor of England under Henry VIII. His best-known work, *Utopia*, describes a fictional land of peace and harmony that has outlawed private property.

Desiderius Erasmus Prominent Dutch humanist who is best known for his satire *The Praise of Folly*.

The careers of two humanists in particular exemplify the strength—and the limits—of the humanistic movement outside Italy: Sir **Thomas More** (1478–1535) of London and **Desiderius Erasmus** (1466–1536) of Rotterdam. Their careers developed along very different paths. More was educated at St. Anthony's School in London and became a lawyer. He translated Lucan and wrote a humanistic history of Richard III while pursuing his public career. Erasmus, on the other hand, was born the illegitimate son of a priest in the Low Countries. Forced by relatives into a monastery, he disliked the conservative piety and authoritarian discipline of traditional monastic life. Once allowed out of the monastery to serve as an episcopal secretary, he never returned. He made his way as an author and editor.

More is most famous for his work *Utopia* (1516), the description of an ideal society located on the island of Utopia (literally, "nowhere") in the newly explored oceans. This powerful and contradictory work is written in two parts. Book I is a debate over the moral value of public service between Morus, a well-intentioned but practical politician, and Hythloday, a widely traveled idealist. Morus tries to make the bureaucrat's argument about working for change from within the system. Hythloday rejects the argument out of hand. Thomas More himself seems to have been unsure, at that time, about the virtues of public service. He was of two minds, and the debate between Morus and Hythloday reflects his indecision. As part of his critique of injustice and immoral governments in Europe, Hythloday describes in Book II the commonwealth of Utopia, in which there is no private property but strict equality of possessions, and, as a result, harmony, tolerance, and little or no violence.

Since the publication of *Utopia*, debates have raged about whether More, or anyone, could ever really hope to live in such a society. Some scholars have questioned how seriously More took this work—he seems to have written the initial sections merely to amuse friends. Yet, whatever More's intentions, Utopia's society of equality, cooperation, and acceptance continues to inspire social commentators.

Ironically, More, like his creation Morus, soon found himself trying to work for justice within precisely the sort of autocratic court that Hythloday criticized. Not long after the completion of *Utopia*, More entered the service of King Henry VIII (r. 1509–1547), eventually serving as chancellor of England. As a staunch Catholic and royal official, More never acted on utopian principles of peace and toleration. He was, in fact, responsible for the persecution of English Protestants in the years before the king's break with Rome (see pages 395–396). He implied that society could be reformed, yet, in the period after 1521, his humanism and his vision of utopian justice and tolerance had no influence on his own public life.

Unlike More, who was drawn to the power of king and pope, Erasmus always avoided working for authorities. Often called the "Prince of Humanists," he was easily the best-known humanist of the early sixteenth century. He lived and taught in France, England, Italy, and Switzerland. Of all the humanists, it was Erasmus who most benefited from the printing revolution. The printer Aldus Manutius invited him to live and work in Venice, and he spent the last productive years of his life at Johannes Froben's press in Basel.

DESIDERIUS ERASMUS

Over a long career, Erasmus brought out repeated editions of works designed to educate Christians. His *Adages*, first published in 1500, was a collection of proverbs from Greek and Roman sources. The work was immensely popular, and Erasmus repeatedly issued expanded editions. He tried to present Greek and Roman wisdom that would illuminate everyday problems. *The Colloquies* was a collection of popular stories. Designed as primers for students, they presented moral lessons, even as they taught good language. His ironic *The Praise of Folly* (1511) was dedicated to Thomas More. An oration by Folly in praise of folly, it is satire of a type unknown since antiquity. Folly's catalog of vices includes everyone from the ignoramus to the scholar. But more seriously, Erasmus believed, as Saint Paul had said, that Christians must be "fools for Christ." In effect, human existence is folly. Erasmus's *Folly* first made an observation that Shakespeare would refine and make famous: "Now the whole life of mortal men, what is it but a sort of play in which … [each person] plays his own part until the director gives him his cue to leave the stage."[13]

Erasmus's greatest contributions to European intellectual life were his edition of and commentaries on the New Testament. His was a critical edition of the Greek text and a Latin translation independent of the fourth-century Latin Vulgate of Jerome. Unlike Jiménez, Erasmus corrected parts of the Vulgate. He rejected the authority of tradition, saying, "The sin of corruption is greater, and the need for careful revision by scholars is greater also, where the source of corruption was ignorance."[14] What was revolutionary in his edition was his commentary, which emphasized the literal and historical recounting of human experiences. Erasmus's Bible was the basis of later vernacular translations of Scripture during the Reformation.

Underlying Erasmus's scholarly output was what he called his "Philosophy of Christ." Erasmus was convinced that the true essence of Christianity was to be found in the life and actions of Christ. Reasonable, self-reliant, truly Christian people did not need superstitious rituals or magic. In his *Colloquies*, he tells of a terrified priest who, during a shipwreck, promised everything to the Virgin Mary if only she would save him from drowning. But, Erasmus observed, it would have been more practical to start swimming!

Erasmus believed that a humanistic combination of classical and Christian wisdom could wipe away violence, superstition, and ignorance. Yet, his philosophy of Christ, based on faith in the goodness and educability of the individual, was swamped in the 1520s and 1530s by the sectarian claims of both Protestants and Catholics. Although Erasmus's New Testament was influential in the Reformation, his calls for reforms based on tolerance and reason were not.

SECTION SUMMARY

- Vernacular literatures of northern Europe emphasized religious and moral themes drawn from daily life.

- The development of printing using movable type made books more widely available. Humanists in northern Europe were more closely linked to university life and less tied to ideas of Roman public life.

- Thomas More and Desiderius Erasmus used their humanistic learning to develop a sophisticated critique of contemporary life.

POLITICS AND RENAISSANCE CULTURE

How did European rulers use Renaissance art and culture?

The educational reforms of the humanists and the innovations in the arts between 1300 and 1550 provided an opportunity for rulers and popes alike to use culture to define and celebrate their authority. Art, literature, and politics merged in the brilliant life of the Renaissance Italian courts, both secular and papal. To understand fully the Renaissance and its importance in the history of Europe, we need to examine the uses of culture by governments, specifically investigating the transformation of European ideas about service at court. We will take as a model the politics and cultural life at one noble court: the court of the Gonzaga family of Mantua. Then, we will see how the Renaissance papacy melded the secular and religious aspects of art, culture, and politics in its glittering court in Rome. Finally, we will discuss the development of the idea of the Renaissance gentleman and courtier made famous by Baldassare Castiglione (ka-stee-lee-OH-nay), who was reared at the Gonzaga court.

The Elaboration of the Court

The courts of northern Italy recruited artists and humanists inspired by classical civilization, and they closely imitated many of the values and new styles that were developing in the courts of northern Europe, such as the court of Burgundy. Throughout Europe, attendance at court became increasingly important to members of the nobility as a source of revenue and influence. Kings and the great territorial lords were equally interested in drawing people to their courts as a way to influence and control the noble and the powerful.

Rulers in most parts of Europe instituted monarchical orders of knighthood to reward allies and followers. The most famous in the English-speaking world was the Order of the Garter, founded in 1349 by King Edward III. The orders were but one of the innovations in the organization of the court during the fourteenth and fifteenth centuries. The numbers of cooks, servants, huntsmen, musicians, and artists employed at court jumped dramatically in the late Middle Ages. In this expansion, the papal court was a model for the rest of Europe. The popes at Avignon, in the fourteenth century, already had households of nearly six hundred persons. If all the bureaucrats, merchants, local officials, and visitors who continually swarmed around the elaborate papal court were also counted, the number grew even larger.

Courts were becoming theaters built around a series of widely understood signs and images that the ruler could manipulate. Culture was meant to reflect the reputation of the ruler. On important political or personal occasions, rulers organized jousts or tournaments around themes drawn from mythology. The dukes of Milan indicated the relative status of courtiers by inviting them to participate in particular hunts or jousts. They similarly organized their courtiers during feasts or elaborate entries into the towns and cities of their realms.

The late fourteenth and fifteenth centuries were periods of growth in the political and bureaucratic power of European rulers. The increasingly elaborate and sumptuous courts were one of the tools that rulers used to create a unified culture and ideology. At the court of the Gonzagas in Mantua, one of the most widely known of the fifteenth-century courts, the manipulation of Renaissance culture for political purposes was most complete.

The Court of Mantua

The city of Mantua, with perhaps 25,000 inhabitants in 1500, was small compared with Milan or Venice—the two cities with which it was most commonly allied. Located in a rich farming region near the Po River, Mantua did not have a large merchant or manufacturing class. Most Mantuans were involved in agriculture and regional trade in foodstuffs. The town had been a typical medieval Italian city-state until its government was overthrown by the noble Bonacolsi family in the thirteenth century. The Bonacolsis, in turn, were ousted in a palace coup in 1328 by their former comrades, the Gonzagas, who ruled the city until 1627.

The Gonzagas faced problems typical of many of the ruling families in northern Italy. The state they were creating was relatively small, their right to rule was not very widely recognized, and their control over the area was weak. The first step for the Gonzagas was to construct fortresses and fortified towns that could withstand foreign enemies. The second step was to gain recognition of their right to rule. In 1329, they were named imperial vicars, or representatives in the region. Later, in 1432, they bought the title "marquis" from the emperor Sigismund for the relatively low price of £12,000—equivalent to a year's pay for their courtiers. By 1500, they had exchanged that title for the more prestigious "duke."

Presiding over a strategic area between the Milanese and Venetian states, the Gonzagas maintained themselves through astute diplomatic connections with other Italian and European courts and through service as well-paid mercenaries in the Italian wars of the fifteenth and sixteenth centuries.

The family's reputation was enhanced by Gianfrancesco (jan-fran-CHES-ko) (d. 1444) and Lodovico, who brought the Renaissance and the new court style to Mantua. By 1500, as many as eight hundred or more nobles, cooks, maids, and horsemen may have gathered in the court. Critics called them idlers, "who have no other function but to cater to the tastes of the Duke." It was under the tutelage of the Gonzagas that Vittorino da Feltre created his educational experiment in Villa Giocosa, which drew noble pupils from throughout Italy. It would be hard to overestimate the value for the Gonzagas of a school that attracted sons of the dukes of Urbino, Ferrara, and Milan and of numerous lesser nobles. The family also called many artists to Mantua. Lodovico invited Antonio Pisano, called Pisanello (ca. 1415–1456), probably the most famous court artist of the fifteenth century. Pisanello created a series of frescoes on Arthurian themes for the Gonzaga palace. In these frescoes, Lodovico is portrayed as a hero of King Arthur's Round Table.

The Gonzagas are best known for their patronage of art with classical themes. The Florentine writer and architect Leon Battista Alberti (1404–1472) redesigned the façade of the Church of Sant'Andrea for the Gonzagas, in the form of a Roman triumphal arch. The church, which long had been associated with the family, became a monument to the Gonzaga court, just as the Arch of Constantine in Rome had celebrated imperial power a thousand years earlier. In the 1460s, Lodovico summoned Andrea Mantegna (1441–1506) to his court. Trained in Padua and Venice, Mantegna was, at that time, the leading painter in northern Italy. His masterwork is the *Camera degli Sposi* (literally, "the room of the spouses"), completed in 1474. It features family portraits of Lodovico Gonzaga and his family, framed in imitations of Roman imperial portrait medallions. One scene shows Lodovico welcoming his son, a newly appointed cardinal, back from Rome. Lodovico even included the portrait of the Holy Roman emperor who had never been to Mantua but was related to Lodovico's wife, Barbara of Brandenburg. As Mantegna finished the work, diplomats and rulers throughout Italy carefully monitored it—proof to all of the new status of the Gonzagas.

The Gonzaga court, like most others, was both public and private. On the one hand, finances for the city, appointments to public offices, and important political decisions were made by the men who dominated the court. On the other hand, as the prince's domestic setting, it was a place where women were expected to be seen and could exert their influence. Women were thus actively involved in creating the ideology of the court. Through the patronage of classical paintings, often with moral and political messages, wives of princes helped make the court better known and more widely accepted throughout Italy and Europe.

The arrival at court of Isabella d'Este (1494–1539), as the wife of Francesco Gonzaga, marked the high point of the Renaissance in Mantua. Isabella had received a classical education at Ferrara and maintained an interest in art, architecture, and music all her life. Isabella was also an accomplished musician, playing a variety of string and keyboard instruments. She and others of the Gonzaga family recruited Flemish and Italian musicians to their court. By the end of the sixteenth century, Mantua was one of the most important musical centers of Europe. As a patron of the arts, she knew what she wanted. Isabella used the general interest in the cultural life of Mantua as a way to increase contacts with the Italian and European powers. She used these informal cultural connections to further the family's political and diplomatic goals.

In the fourteenth century, Petrarch had complained that however enjoyable feasting in Mantua might be, the place was dusty, plagued by mosquitoes, and overrun with frogs. By the end of the fifteenth century, the Gonzagas had transformed their city and secured a prominent place for themselves on the Italian, and the European, stage.

The Renaissance Papacy

The issues of power and how it is displayed had religious as well as secular dimensions. After its fourteenth- and fifteenth-century struggles over jurisdiction, the papacy found itself reduced, in many respects, to the status of an Italian Renaissance court. But popes still needed to defend their primacy within the church from conciliarists, who had argued that all Christians, including the pope, were bound to obey the commands of general councils. The ideological focus of the revived papacy was Rome.

THE TRANSFORMATION OF ROME　　The first step in the creation of a new Rome was taken by Pope Nicholas V (r. 1446–1455), a cleric who had spent many years in the cultural environment of Renaissance Florence. Hoping to restore Rome and its church to their former glory, Nicholas and his successors patronized the arts, established a lively court culture, and sponsored numerous building projects. Nicholas was an avid collector of ancient manuscripts that seemed to demonstrate the intellectual and religious primacy of Rome. He invited numerous artists and intellectuals to the papal court, including Leon Battista Alberti. He based his treatise, *On Architecture* (1452), on his research in topography and reading done in Rome. This was the most important work on architecture produced during the Renaissance. It was probably under Alberti's influence that Nicholas embarked on a series of ambitious urban renewal projects in Rome, which included bridges, roads, and a rebuilt Saint Peter's Basilica.

The transformation of Rome had an ideological purpose. As one orator proclaimed, "Illuminated by the light of faith and Christian truth, [Rome] is destined to be the firmament of religion . . . , the secure haven for Christians."[15] Thus, the papal response to critics was to note that Rome and its government were central to political and religious life in Christendom. By reviving

Giving of the Keys to Saint Peter　　Pietro Perugino's painting of Saint Peter receiving from Christ the keys to "bind and loose" on earth and in heaven illustrates the basis of papal claims to authority within the Christian church. This is the central message of the decorative plan of the Sistine Chapel. (Scala/Art Resource, NY)

the style and organization of classical antiquity, the church sought to link papal Rome to a magnificent imperial tradition, reaching back to Augustus and even to Alexander the Great. To papal supporters, only one authority could rule the church. Early tradition and the continuity of the city itself, they assumed, demonstrated papal primacy.

THE SISTINE CHAPEL

One particular monument in Rome captures most vividly the cultural, religious, and ideological program of the papacy: the Sistine Chapel in the Vatican Palace. The chapel is best known for the decoration of the ceiling by the Florentine artist Michelangelo (see pages 332–333) and for the striking images in his painting of the Last Judgment. The chapel, however, was commissioned by Pope Sixtus IV in 1475. It was to be an audience chamber in which an enthroned pope could meet the representatives of other states. In addition, it was expected that the college of cardinals would gather in the chapel for the election of new popes.

The decorations done before Michelangelo painted the ceiling reflect the intellectual and ideological values that Sixtus hoped to transmit to the ambassadors and churchmen who entered the chapel. Along the lower sidewalls are portraits of earlier popes, a feature typical of early Roman churches. More ideologically significant, however, are two cycles of paintings of the lives of Moses and Christ, drawing parallels between them. To execute the scenes, Sixtus called to Rome some of the greatest artists of the late fifteenth century: Sandro Botticelli, Domenico Ghirlandaio, Luca Signorelli, and Pietro Perugino. The works illustrate the continuity of the Old Testament and New Testament and emphasize the importance of obedience to the authority of God. The meaning is most obvious in Perugino's painting of Saint Peter receiving the keys to the Kingdom of Heaven from Christ. The allusion is to Matthew 16:18: "Thou art Peter and upon this rock I shall build my church." The keys are the symbol of the claim of the pope, as successor to Saint Peter, to have the power to bind and loose sinners and their punishments. Directly across from Perugino's painting is Botticelli's *The Judgment of Corah*, which portrays the story of the opponent who challenged the leadership of Moses and Aaron while the Israelites wandered in the wilderness. Corah and his supporters, according to Numbers 16:33, fell live into Hell. Various popes recalled the fate of Corah and the rebels. The pope was bound to oppose the council, Pope Eugenius argued, "to save the people entrusted to his care, lest together with those who hold the power of the council above that of the papacy they suffer a punishment even more dire than that which befell Corah."[16] The meaning of the painting and the entire chapel could not be clearer.

The effects of Renaissance revival were profound. Rome grew from a modest population of about 17,000 in 1400 to 35,000 in 1450. By 1517, the city had a population of over 85,000, five times its population at the end of the Great Schism. The papal program was a success. Rome was transformed from a provincial town to a major European capital, perhaps the most important artistic and cultural center of the sixteenth century. Visitors to the Sistine Chapel, like visitors to the papal city itself, were expected to leave with a profound sense of the antiquity of the papal office and of the continuity of papal exercise of religious authority. Because the building and decorating were being completed as the Protestant Reformation was beginning in Germany, some historians have criticized the expense of the political and cultural program undertaken by the Renaissance popes. But to contemporaries on the scene, the work was a logical and necessary attempt to strengthen the church's standing in Christendom.

Castiglione and the European Gentleman

Renaissance ideas did not just spread in intellectual circles. They also were part of the transformation of the medieval knight into the early modern "gentleman." In 1528, Baldassare Castiglione (1478–1529) published *The Book of the Courtier*. The work, which describes the ideal behavior of a courtier, was based on Castiglione's own distinguished career serving in Italian courts. Set at the court of Urbino, the book chronicles a series of fictional discussions over the course of four nights in March 1507. Among the participants are the duchess of Urbino, Elizabeth Gonzaga; Emilia Pia, her lady-in-waiting; and a group of humanists, men of action, and courtiers. In four evenings, members of the circle try to describe the perfect gentleman of court. In the process, they debate the nature of nobility, humor, women, and love.

Castiglione describes, in many respects, a typical gathering at court, and the discourses reflect contemporary views of relations between men and women. The wives of princes were

Federigo da Montefeltro's Studiolo The duchy of Urbino was a showpiece of Renaissance court life and was the eventual locale for Castiglione's *Book of the Courtier*. It owed much of its fame to Duke Federigo da Montefeltro. Federigo's study is decorated with an expensive inlaid wooden design. Its illusion of great space and the expense of its construction were meant to celebrate Federigo's wealth and power. (Scala/Art Resource, NY)

expected to be organizers of life at court but also paragons of domestic virtues. Women were expected to manage the household and even the financial interests if her husband was away. Noble and elite women also played an important, but indirect, role in political and diplomatic negotiations. Women communicated informally ideas and information that could not be passed in public dispatches. But even powerful women had to be careful about public appearances. In Castiglione's book, for example, the women organize the discussion, and the men discuss. Although the women direct and influence the talk by jokes and short interventions, they cannot afford to dominate the debate. As Emilia Pia explains, "[women] must be more circumspect, and more careful not to give occasion for evil being said of them ... for a woman has not so many ways of defending herself against false calumnies as a man has."[17] Thus, in debate, as in politics and diplomacy, the influence of women was most effective when it was indirect.

The topics of such discussions were not randomly chosen. Castiglione explains that he wished "to describe the form of courtiership most appropriate for a gentleman living at the courts of princes." Castiglione's popularity was based on his deliberate joining of humanistic ideas and traditional chivalric values. Although his topic is the court with all its trappings, he tells his readers that his models for the discussion were Latin and Greek dialogues, especially those of Cicero and Plato. As a Platonist, he believed that all truly noble gentlemen have an inborn quality of "grace." It has to be brought out, however, just as Michelangelo freed his figures from stone.

What struck Castiglione's readers most was his advice about behavior. Francesco Guicciardini of Florence once remarked, "When I was young, I used to scoff at knowing how to play, dance, and sing, and other such frivolities. ... I have nevertheless seen from experience that these ornaments and accomplishments lend dignity and reputation even to men of good rank."[18] Guicciardini's comment underlines the value that readers found in Castiglione's work. Grace may be inbred, but it must be brought to the attention of those who control the court. Courtiers should, first of all, study the military arts. They have to fight, but only on occasions when their prowess will be noticed. Castiglione adds practical advice about how to dress, talk, and participate in music and dancing: Never leap about wildly when dancing as peasants might, but dance only with an air of dignity and decorum. Castiglione further urges the courtier to be careful in dress: the French are "overdressed"; the Italians too quickly adopt the most recent and colorful styles. Bowing to the political, as well as social realities of Spanish domination of Italy, Castiglione advises black or dark colors, which "reflect the sobriety of the Spaniards, since external appearances often bear witness to what is within."

According to Castiglione, the courtier must take pains "to earn that universal regard which everyone covets." Too much imitation and obvious study, however, lead to affectation. Castiglione counsels courtiers to carry themselves with a certain diffidence or unstudied naturalness (*sprezzatura*) covering their artifice. Accomplished courtiers should exhibit "that graceful and nonchalant spontaneity (as it is often called) ... so that those who are watching them imagine that they couldn't and wouldn't even know how to make a mistake." Thus, Castiglione's courtier must walk a fine line between clearly imitated and apparently natural grace.

Castiglione's book was an immediate success and widely followed even by those who claimed to have rejected it. By 1561, it was available in Spanish, French, and English translations. The reasons are not difficult to guess. It was critical for the courtier "to win for himself the mind and favour of the prince," and even those who disliked music, dancing, and light conversation learned Castiglione's arts "to open the way to the favour of princes." Many of the courtly arts that Castiglione preached had been traditional for centuries. Yet, Castiglione's humanistic explanations and emphasis on form, control, and fashion had never seemed so essential as they did to the cultured gentlemen of the courts of the Renaissance and early modern Europe.

SECTION SUMMARY

- Rulers found Renaissance art and culture to be convenient vehicles to explain or justify political power.

- The Gonzaga rulers of Mantua followed a conscious policy of recruiting famous artists to work at their court.

- The papacy used art and culture to explain and justify their predominance in Rome and the Christian church.

- Castiglione's dialogue on behavior at court became a European bestseller because of its explanation of how to succeed at court.

CHAPTER SUMMARY

The Renaissance was a broad cultural movement that began in Italy in response to a series of crises in the early fourteenth century. It was a cultural and ideological movement based on the assumption that study and imitation of the past was the best method for reform and innovation in the future. The impulse for change arose from the belief, shared by thinkers from Petrarch to Machiavelli, that a great deal could be learned from study of the Roman past. This was the basis for humanistic innovations in language, history, and politics. Even revolutionary thinkers, such as Lorenzo Valla and Niccolò Machiavelli, began with the study of classical literature and history.

The same transformation is evident among the artists. Early in the fifteenth century, Florentines who experimented with perspective were intent on recovering lost Roman knowledge, and Michelangelo was praised not only for mastering, but also for surpassing, Roman norms. Similar trends were evident in northern Europe, where artists like Albrecht Dürer combined their understanding of Italian art with northern ideas. Throughout Europe, art was an important component of religious and political culture.

FOCUS QUESTIONS

- How did Italians use classical values to deal with cultural and political issues?

- What was "new" about Renaissance art?

- In what ways did humanism outside Italy differ from Italian humanism?

- How did European rulers use Renaissance art and culture?

Humanistic studies outside of Italy were less tied to public life. Moral and spiritual issues were more important. Yet, the same movement from imitation to transformation is evident. Erasmus and More valued humanistic learning from Italy, but in *The Praise of Folly* and *Utopia*, the use of past ideas and models was neither simple nor direct. Both authors, however, shared with Italian humanists the idea that humanistic values could lead to a transformation of individuals and society as a whole.

The integration of art, literature, and public life was most evident in the ways that governments used art. The Gonzaga court and the papacy clearly recognized the value of artistic and literary works as vehicles for explaining and justifying power and influence. The beauty of Mantegna's painting and the power of Michelangelo's frescoes do not obscure their messages about power and authority.

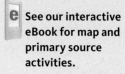 **This icon will direct you to additional materials on the website: www .cengage.com/history/ noble/westciv6e.**

KEY TERMS

Renaissance (p. 321)
humanism (p. 322)
Francesco Petrarch
  (p. 323)
civic humanism
  (p. 324)

***On the Falsely Believed
  and Forged Donation
  of Constantine*** (p. 327)
Niccolò Machiavelli
  (p. 329)
linear perspective (p. 331)

Leonardo da Vinci (p. 332)
Sistine Chapel (p. 332)
Johann Gutenberg (p. 340)
Thomas More (p. 342)
Desiderius Erasmus (p. 342)

See our interactive eBook for map and primary source activities.

NOTES

1. Quoted in J. B. Trapp, ed., *Background to the English Renaissance* (London: Gray-Mills Publishing, 1974), p. 11.

2. Quoted in N. Mann, *Petrarch* (Oxford: Oxford University Press), p. 67.

3. Petrarch, "On His Own Ignorance and That of Many Others," in *The Renaissance Philosophy of Man*, ed. Ernst Cassirer, Paul Oskar Kristeller, and John H. Randall (Chicago: University of Chicago Press, 1948), p. 105.

4. Quoted in Benjamin G. Kohl and Ronald G. Witt, *The Earthly Republic* (Philadelphia: University of Pennsylvania Press, 1978), p. 11.

5. Quoted in M. L. King, *Women of the Renaissance* (Chicago: University of Chicago Press, 1991), p. 194.

6. Quoted ibid., p. 222.

7. Quoted ibid., p. 198.

8. K. R. Bartlett, *The Civilization of the Italian Renaissance* (Lexington, Mass.: D. C. Heath, 1992), p. 314.

9. Quoted ibid., p. 160.

10. Quoted in *The Notebooks of Leonardo da Vinci*, ed. J. P. Richter, vol. 1 (New York: Dover, 1883 and 1970), p. 14.

11. Giorgio Vasari, *The Lives of the Artists*, trans. George Bull (Baltimore: Penguin, 1965), p. 338.

12. Julia Bondanella and Mark Musa, eds., *The Italian Renaissance Reader* (New York: Meridian Books, 1987), p. 377.

13. Quoted in A. Rabil, Jr., *Renaissance Humanism: Foundations, Forms, and Legacy*, vol. 2 (Philadelphia: University of Pennsylvania Press, 1988), p. 236.

14. Quoted ibid., p. 229.

15. Raffaele Brandolini, quoted in Charles L. Stinger, *The Renaissance in Rome* (Bloomington: Indiana University Press, 1985), p. 156.

16. Quoted in Leopold D. Ettlinger, *The Sistine Chapel Before Michelangelo* (Oxford: Oxford University Press, 1965), p. 105.

17. Quoted in R. M. San Juan, "The Court Lady's Dilemma: Isabella d'Este and Art Collecting in the Renaissance," *Oxford Art Journal* 14 (1991): 71.

18. Quoted in R. W. Hanning and D. Rosand, eds., *Castiglione: The Ideal and the Real in Renaissance Cultur*e (New Haven, Conn.: Yale University Press, 1983), p. 17.

CHAPTER OUTLINE

Hernán Cortés   Cortés—here shown with Doña Marina—is greeted by local leaders during the march to Tenochtitlán.   (Trans. no. V/C 31[2]. Courtesy Department of Library Sciences, American Museum of Natural History)

European Overseas Expansion to 1600

Hernán Cortés's (kor-TEZ) march in 1519 through the Valley of Mexico toward Tenochtitlán (teh-NOCK-tit-lan), the Aztec capital, was recorded not only in Spaniards' journals, but also by local witnesses. In the native portrayal shown here, an elegantly garbed Mexica leader brings food and supplies to Cortés. Behind the adventurer are his own Spanish soldiers and his native allies. Many native peoples saw the Spanish as their defenders against the Aztecs, their harsh, recently arrived overlords. The woman standing next to Cortés is Malintzin, who later adopted the Spanish name Doña Marina. She was an Aztec noblewoman, traded by her stepfather to the Maya, and eventually given to Cortés. As a translator and interpreter, she was an essential ally during the conquest of Mexico.

The image, with its baskets of bread, meats, and fodder, is part of a pictograph telling the story of Cortés in the Nahuatl (na-HWAT-luh) language of the Mexica peoples. The arrival of the Spanish began a cultural exchange between the Spanish and the peoples of the Americas that was more complex than anyone initially imagined. The picture captures the contradictory aspects of European contact with Asia and the Americas. Europeans called it discovery, but they were encountering sophisticated, fully functioning political and cultural worlds. Doña Marina's presence also reminds us of a more general truth—that without allies, pilots, and interpreters among the native peoples, Europeans would have been lost both in the New World and in the Old.

Cortés's meeting with the Mexica peoples was part of a program of European overseas expansion that began in the last decade of the fifteenth century and would eventually carry Europeans to every part of the world. It would change how Europeans thought of themselves and how they understood their own connections to the rest of the world. Their expansion unified the "Old World" continents of Asia, Africa, and Europe with a "New World"—the Americas and the islands of the Pacific.

Those who focus on the transfer of European religion and culture view exploration and settlement as marking the creation of a new world with new values. However, the descendants of the native peoples who greeted the newly arriving Europeans—the Amerindians and the Aborigines, Maori, and Polynesians of the Pacific islands—remind us that the outsiders invaded another world. Their arrival brought modern warfare and epidemic diseases that virtually destroyed indigenous cultures.

Spain sent its explorers west because the Portuguese already controlled the eastern routes to Asia around the African coast and because certain technological innovations made long open-sea voyages possible. Thus, the story includes national competition, the development of navigational techniques, and strategic choices.

FOCUS QUESTIONS

- What did Europeans know about the wider world in the Middle Ages?
- How did the Portuguese exploit their new connection to the East?
- Why did the Spanish choose to sail west in their attempt to find Asia?
- How did the Spanish conquer and control the new world they entered?
- What changes did European expansion bring to the Old World and the New?

 This icon will direct you to additional materials on the website: www .cengage.com/history/ noble/westciv6e.

See our interactive eBook for map and primary source activities.

Finally, the Europeans overthrew the great empires of the Aztecs and the Inca, but the transfer of European culture was never as complete as the Europeans thought or expected. As our image suggests, the language and customs of the conquered peoples, blanketed by European language and law, survived, though the lands colonized by the Europeans would never again be as they had been before their encounter with the Old World.

THE EUROPEAN BACKGROUND, 1250–1492

What did Europeans know about the wider world in the Middle Ages?

By 1400, Europeans already had a long history of connections with Africa and Asia. They regularly traded with Arabs in North Africa, traveled through the Muslim lands on the eastern edge of the Mediterranean, and eventually reached India, China, and beyond. After 1400, however, Europeans developed the desire and the ability to travel overseas to distant lands in Africa and Asia. Three critical factors behind the exploratory voyages of the fifteenth and early sixteenth centuries were technology, curiosity and interest, and geographic knowledge. A series of technological innovations made sailing far out into the ocean less risky and more predictable than it had been. The writings of classical geographers, myths and traditional tales, and merchants' accounts of their travels fueled popular interest in the East and made ocean routes to the East seem safe and reasonable alternatives to overland travel.

Early Exploration and Cultural Interactions

Medieval Europeans knew there were lands to their west. Irish monks and Norse settlers traveled there. Indeed, by the late ninth century, Norse sailors, primarily Norwegians, had constructed boats combining oars and sails with strong-keeled hulls, which they used to travel to Iceland, Greenland, and eventually Vinland—the coast of Labrador and Newfoundland. The Norse traveled in families. A woman named Gudridr gave birth to a son in North America before returning to Iceland and eventually going on a pilgrimage to Rome. Although the settlements in North America and Greenland ultimately failed, the Norse were followed by English, French, and Spanish fishermen who regularly visited the rich fishing grounds off North America.

CONTACTS THROUGH TRADE The Greeks and Romans had cultivated contacts with the civilizations of Asia and Africa, and despite the nation-building focus of the Middle Ages, interest in the lands beyond Christendom had never been lost. In the thirteenth and fourteenth centuries, European economic and cultural contacts with these lands greatly increased. The rising volume of trade between Europe and North Africa brought with it information about the wealthy African kingdoms of the Niger Delta. The Mongols, in the thirteenth century, allowed European merchants and missionaries to travel along trade routes extending all the way to China, opening regions formerly closed to them by hostile Muslim governments.

Trade in the Mediterranean also kept Christians and Muslims, Europeans and North Africans, in close contact. Europeans sold textiles to Arab traders, who carried them across the Sahara to Timbuktu, where they were sold for gold bullion to residents of the ancient African kingdoms of Ghana and Mali, located just above the Niger River. European chroniclers recorded the pilgrimage to Mecca of Mansa Musa, the fabulously wealthy fourteenth-century emperor of Mali. Italian merchants tried unsuccessfully to trade directly with these African kingdoms, but Arab merchants prevented any permanent contact.

Europeans enjoyed more successful trade connections farther east. The discovery in London of a brass shard inscribed with a Japanese character attests to the breadth of connections in the early fourteenth century. Since the Roman period, the Mediterranean had been connected to Asia by the Silk Road, in reality, a network of roads that carried people, ideas, and commerce. In the Middle Ages, European access to the Silk Road had been restricted by local rulers. After the rise of the Mongols, Italian merchants regularly traveled east through Constantinople and on to India and China. By the fourteenth century, they knew how long travel to China might take and the probable expenses along the way. European intellectuals also maintained an interest in the lands beyond Christendom. They had read the late classical and early medieval authors who described Africa, the Indies, and China.

The work of the greatest of the classical geographers, Ptolemy (TOL-eh-mee) of Alexandria (ca. A.D. 127–145), was known only indirectly until the early fifteenth century, but medieval thinkers read avidly and speculated endlessly about the information contained in the works of authors from Late Antiquity. For instance, one author reported that snakes in Calabria, in isolated southern Italy, sucked milk from cows and that men in the right circumstances became wolves—the earliest mention of werewolves. By the twelfth century, fictitious reports circulated widely in the West of a wealthy Christian country in the East or possibly in Africa. Chroniclers, at that time, talked of Prester John, who some thought was a wealthy and powerful descendant of the Magi, the wise men from the East who Scripture says visited the baby Jesus. The legend of the kingdom of Prester John probably reflects some knowledge of the Christian groups living near the shrine of Saint Thomas in India or the Christian kingdom of Ethiopia. In the fifteenth century, European Christians looked to Prester John for aid against the rising Turkish empire.

GEOGRAPHIC KNOWLEDGE

Tales of geographic marvels are epitomized by *The Travels of Sir John Mandeville,* a book probably written in France, but purporting to be the observations of a knight from St. Albans, just north of London. Mandeville says that he left England in 1322 or 1323 and traveled to Constantinople, Jerusalem, Egypt, India, China, Persia, and Turkey. Sir John describes the islands of wonders, inhabited by dog-headed humans, one-eyed giants, headless men, and hermaphrodites. Less fantastically, Mandeville reports that the world could be, and in fact had been, circumnavigated.

More reliable information became available in the thirteenth century, largely because of the arrival of the Mongols. Jenghiz Khan (JEN-gus KAHN) and his descendants created an empire that reached from eastern Hungary to China (see page 252). This pax Mongolica, or area of Mongol-enforced peace, was a region in which striking racial and cultural differences were tolerated. In the 1240s and 1250s, a series of papal representatives traveled to the Mongol capital at Karakorum near Lake Baikal in Siberia. The letters of these papal ambassadors, who worked extensively to gain converts and allies for a crusade against the Turks, were widely read and greatly increased accurate knowledge about Asia. Other missionaries and diplomats journeyed to the Mongol court, and some continued farther east to India and China. By the early fourteenth century, the church had established a bishop in Beijing.

CHRONOLOGY	
ca. 1400	Portuguese reach Azores
1444	Prince Henry "the Navigator" discovers Cape Verde Islands
1487	Dias becomes first European to sail around Cape of Good Hope
1492	Columbus reaches New World
1494	Treaty of Tordesillas
1497	Da Gama sails to India around Cape of Good Hope
	Cabot sights Newfoundland
1501	Vespucci concludes Columbus discovered a new continent
1507	Waldseemüller issues the first map showing "America"
1510	Portuguese capture Goa
1513	Balboa becomes first European to see Pacific Ocean
1519–1522	Magellan's expedition sails around the world
1519–1523	Cortés conquers the Aztecs, destroys Tenochtitlán
1533	Pizarro conquers Cuzco, the Inca capital
1534	Cartier discovers St. Lawrence River
1542	Charles V issues "New Laws"
1545	Spanish discover Potosí silver mines

Italian merchants followed closely on the heels of the churchmen and diplomats. The pax Mongolica offered the chance to trade directly in Asia and the adventure of visiting lands known only from travel literature. In 1262, Niccolo and Maffeo Polo embarked from Venice on their first trip to China. On a later journey, they took Niccolo's son, Marco (1255–1324). In all, they spent twenty-four years in China. Marco dictated an account of his travels to a Pisan as they both languished as prisoners of war in a Genoese jail in 1298. It is difficult to know how much of the text represents Marco's own observations and how much is chivalric invention by the Pisan. Some modern commentators have even speculated that Marco himself never traveled to China. His contemporaries, however, had no doubts. The book was an immediate success even among Venetians, who could have exposed any fraud. Christopher Columbus himself owned and extensively annotated a copy of Marco Polo's *Travels,* which combines a merchant's observations of ports, markets, and trade with an administrator's eye for people and organizations.

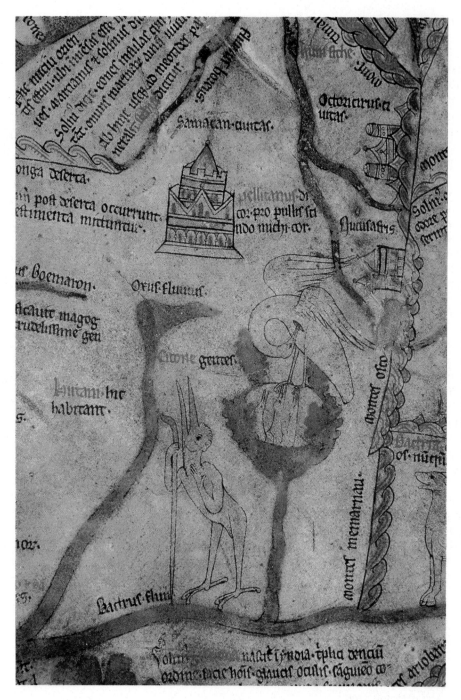

Hereford Mappa Mundi   Like other medieval illustrations of Eastern lands, this thirteenth-century map combines known fact with myth. The top section locates the city of Samarcand (modern-day Samarkand, Uzbekistan). At the bottom, next to a mythical bird-person, a pelican feeds its young with its own blood.   (The Dean and Chapter of Hereford and the Hereford Mappa Mundi Trust)

By 1300, a modest community of Italians had settled in China. By the late thirteenth and fourteenth centuries, Italian traders were traveling directly to the East in search of Asian silks, spices, pearls, and ivory. They, and other European merchants, could consult the *Handbook for Merchants* (1340), compiled by the Florentine Francesco Pegalotti (pey-gah-LOW-tee), which described the best roads, the most hospitable stopping points, and the appropriate freight animals for a trip to the East. Fragmentary reports of Europeans in the Spice Islands (also known as the Moluccas), Japan, and India indicate that many Europeans other than merchants traveled simply for the adventure of visiting new lands.

Navigational Innovations

The invention of several navigational aids in the fourteenth and fifteenth centuries made sailing in open waters easier and more predictable. Especially important was the fly compass, consisting of a magnetic needle attached to a paper disk (or "fly"). The simple compass had been invented in China and was known in Europe by the late twelfth century, but because it was not initially marked off in degrees, it was only a rudimentary aid to navigation. By 1500, astrolabes and other devices enabling sailors to use the positions of the sun and stars to assist in navigation had also become available. An astrolabe allowed sailors to measure the altitude of the polestar in the sky and thereby calculate the latitude, or distance north or south of the equator, at which their ship was sailing. Still, until the general adoption of charts marked with degrees of latitude, most navigators sailed by relying on the compass, experience, and instinct.

The most common Mediterranean ship of the late Middle Ages was a galley powered by a combination of sails and oars. Such a vessel was able to travel quickly and easily along the coast, but it was ill-suited for sailing the open seas. Throughout the Mediterranean, shipbuilders experimented with new designs, and during the fifteenth century, the Portuguese and Spanish perfected the caravel and adapted the European full-rigged ships. Large, square sails efficiently caught the wind and propelled these ships forward, and smaller triangular sails (lateens) allowed them to tack diagonally across a headwind, virtually sailing into the wind.

By the 1490s, the Portuguese and Spanish had developed the ships and techniques that would make long open-sea voyages possible. What remained was for Europeans, especially the Portuguese and Spanish, to conclude that such voyages were both necessary and profitable.

The Revolution in Geography

Sea routes to Asia seemed more important by the end of the fourteenth century. With the conversion of the Mongols to Islam, the breakdown of Mongol unity, and the subsequent rise of the Ottoman Turks, the highly integrated and unusually open trade network fell apart. The caravan routes across southern Russia, Persia, and Afghanistan were abruptly closed to Europeans. Western merchants once again became dependent on Muslim middlemen.

The reports of travelers, however, continued to circulate long after the trade routes shut down, contributing to a veritable revolution in geographic knowledge in the decades before the Portuguese and Spanish voyages.

In 1375, Abraham Cresques (KRESK), a Jewish mathematician from the Mediterranean island of Majorca, produced what has come to be known as the *Catalan World Atlas*. He combined the traditional medieval *mappa mundi* (world map) with a Mediterranean *portolan*. The mappa mundi often followed the O-T form—that is, a circle divided into three parts representing Europe, Africa, and Asia, the lands of the descendants of Noah. Jerusalem—the heart of Christendom—was always at the center of the map. What the map lacked in accuracy, it made up in symbolism. The portolan, in contrast, was entirely practical. Sailors valued it because of its accurate outline of coasts, complete with sailing instructions and reasonable portrayals of ports, islands, and shallows along with general compass readings. The *Catalan World Atlas* largely holds to the portolan tradition but has more correct representations of the lands surrounding the Mediterranean.

In the fifteenth century, following Ptolemy's suggestions, mapmakers began to divide their maps into squares, marking lines of longitude and latitude. This format made it possible to show, with some precision, the contours of various lands and the relationships between landmasses. Numerous maps of the world were produced in this period. The culmination of this cartography was a globe constructed for the city of Nuremberg in 1492, the very year Columbus set sail. From these increasingly accurate maps, it has become possible to document the first exploration of the Azores, the Cape Verde Islands, and the western coast of Africa.

After his voyages, Columbus observed that maps had been of no use to him. True enough. But without the accumulation of knowledge by travelers and the mingling of that knowledge with classical ideas about geography, it is doubtful whether Columbus or the Portuguese seaman Vasco da Gama would have undertaken—or could have found governments willing to support—the voyages that so dramatically changed the relations between Europe and the rest of the world.

SECTION SUMMARY

- Throughout the Middle Ages, Europe had indirect trade connections with Asia and Africa.

- In the fourteenth century, Italian merchants traveled widely in central and eastern Asia.

- Technological advances in ship design and navigation made it possible to sail far into the Atlantic.

- Restrictions on land routes between Europe and Asia made sailing to Asia a practical economic venture.

PORTUGUESE VOYAGES OF EXPLORATION, 1350–1515

How did the Portuguese exploit their new connection to the East?

Portugal, a tiny country on the edge of Europe, for a short time led the European overseas expansion. Portuguese sailors were the first Europeans to perfect the complex techniques of using the winds and currents of the South Atlantic, especially along the western coast of Africa (see **MAP 13.1**). As the Portuguese moved down the African coast, and later, as they tried to compete commercially in Asia, they adapted traditional Mediterranean cultural and commercial attitudes to fit the new environment in which they found themselves. In some areas, the Portuguese created networks of isolated naval and trading stations to control the movement of goods. In other areas, they attempted to create substantial colonies, inhabited by Portuguese settlers. In still other areas, they used slaves to produce commercial products for the international market. Spain and the other European states would use these same strategies in Asia and the New World as they expanded their economic and political interests overseas.

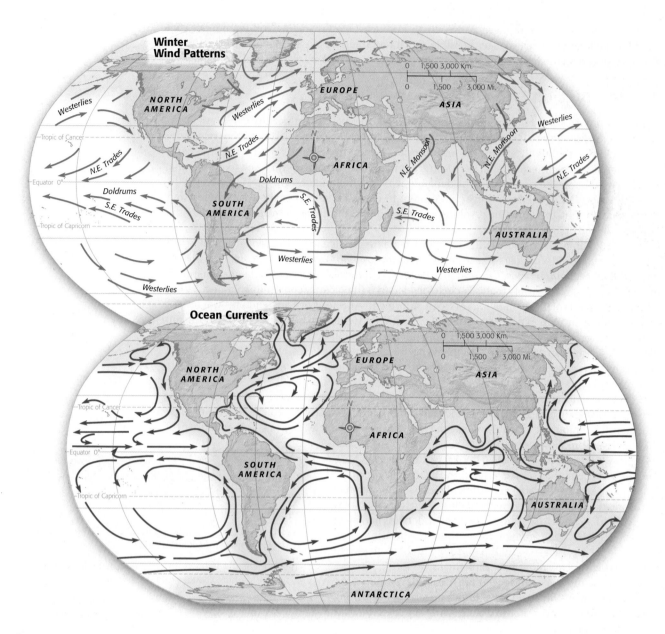

🌐 **MAP 13.1—Winds and Currents**
Winds and ocean currents move in giant clockwise and counterclockwise circles that limit the directions in which ships can sail efficiently. It was impossible, for example, for the explorers to sail directly south along the entire western coast of Africa.

The Early Voyages

Portugal, like other late medieval European states, hoped that exploration and expansion would lead to "gold and Christians." The search for Christians was accelerated in the fifteenth century by the growing power of the Ottoman Turks. Europeans increasingly desired an alliance with the mythical Christian kingdoms of the East to open a second front against the militant Turks. Further, rediscovering the "lost" Christians and the hope of reclaiming Jerusalem fed Christian expectations that they were living in the last days before Christ's return.

For the Portuguese, facing the Atlantic and insulated from a direct Turkish threat, the lure of gold was always mixed with their religious motives. The nearest source of gold was well known to late medieval Christians: the African kingdoms of the Niger Delta. The problem for European traders and their governments was that overland contacts with this wealthy region remained controlled by the Muslim merchants of North Africa. The Portuguese and Spanish hoped to break the monopoly by taking control of the North African coast or by means of a flanking movement along the western coast of Africa.

Actual exploration of the Atlantic had begun long before Europeans recognized the extent of the Turkish threat. By 1350, the Madeiras and the Canaries, groups of islands off the western coast of Africa, regularly were included on European maps. By about 1365, Portuguese, Spanish, and probably French sailors were visiting the Canary Islands. By 1400, the Azores (AY-zorz), a chain of islands one-third of the way across the Atlantic, were known and, from early in the fifteenth century, were routine ports of call for Portuguese ships (see **MAP 13.2**). These voyages were no mean feat, calling for sophisticated ocean sailing out of sight of land for weeks at a time.

In the second decade of the fifteenth century, the Portuguese expansion began in earnest with the capture of the Muslim port of Ceuta (say-OO-tuh) on the coast of Morocco. From then on, the Portuguese moved steadily down the western coast of Africa. They were led by **Prince Henry "the Navigator"** (1394–1460), the younger son of King John I (r. 1385–1433). Legend has it that Prince Henry founded a school for the study of geography and navigation at Sagres, on the southwestern coast of Portugal. Whether he did or not, contemporaries agreed that Prince Henry was intent on reaching the "River of Gold"—that is, the Gold Coast of Africa and the Niger Delta. To accomplish this, he sponsored a series of expeditions down the African coast, reaching Senegal and the Cape Verde Islands by 1444. The Portuguese quickly established trading stations in the region and soon were exporting gold and slaves to Lisbon.

The islands off the coast of Africa were uninhabited, except for the Canaries, which the Portuguese tried unsuccessfully to keep from the Spanish. Thus, the Portuguese could not merely plant trading communities within a larger population. As a result, by the early 1440s, the Portuguese were bringing sheep, seed, and peasants to these hitherto unoccupied islands, and the Crown was granting extensive lordships to encourage reluctant nobles to relocate to the Azores. The islanders survived largely by exporting sheep and grain to Iberia.

A significant transformation occurred on Madeira in the 1440s, when the Portuguese introduced sugar cane to the island. A great many workers were needed to cut the cane, and expensive mills and lengthy processing were required to extract and produce sugar. On Madeira, most of the work was done by Portuguese peasants. However, when the Portuguese extended sugar cultivation

Prince Henry "the Navigator" The prince who directed Portuguese exploration and colonization along the west coast of Africa.

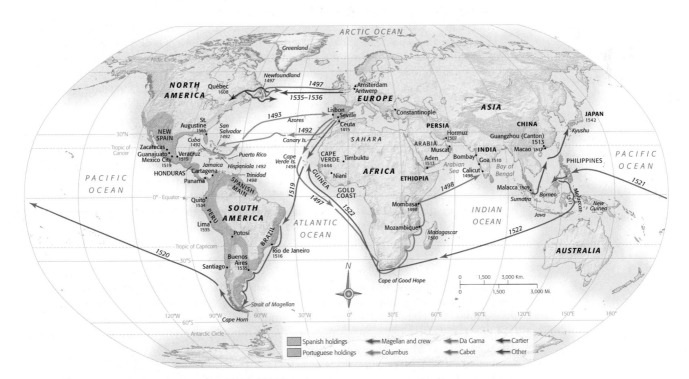

🌐 **MAP 13.2—World Exploration, 1492–1535**
The voyages of Columbus, da Gama, and Magellan charted the major sea-lanes that became essential for communication, trade, and warfare for the next three hundred years.

to the newly discovered and colonized Cape Verde Islands in the 1460s, they found that Portuguese peasants would not work voluntarily in the sultry equatorial climate. Soon, the Portuguese introduced slave-based farming to maximize production and profits.

Slaves, imported from the Black Sea areas, had been used in agriculture since the introduction of sugar cultivation into the Mediterranean in the thirteenth century. The Portuguese had been trading in slaves along the western coast of Africa since the 1440s—the date from which black slaves appear in Lisbon. African slaves, along with slaves from northern and eastern Europe, could be found in Italy and throughout the Mediterranean in the fifteenth century, most often as domestics or laborers in small enterprises. Not since Roman times, however, had slave-based industries developed on the scale of the Portuguese sugar plantations. Sugar production in the New World eventually would be modeled on a plantation system begun by the Portuguese on their island colonies in the Atlantic.

The Search for a Sea Route to Asia

Until the middle of the fifteenth century, the Niger Delta remained the focus of Portuguese interest. Only after securing control of the western coast of Africa did the Portuguese look seriously at sailing around Africa and discovering a sea route to Asia.

The fifteenth-century sailors who first tried to sail down the coast of Africa faced enormous difficulties. Water and wind currents tend to move in clockwise and counterclockwise circles, against which it is difficult for a sail-powered ship to make progress (see **MAP 13.1**). Winds near the equator generally blow from the east; farther north and south, the westerlies prevail. Some zones, in certain seasons, are pockets of stillness—called doldrums—with few breezes to propel ships. A navigator had to find winds and currents moving in the direction he wished to travel. Sailing directly from port to port was virtually impossible.

Knowledge of winds and currents allowed Bartholomeu Dias (1450?–1500) to explore the coast of southern Africa in 1487. He followed the traditional Portuguese routes until southeasterly winds forced him to sail south and west, almost to the Brazilian and Argentine coasts. Then, he was able to ride the westerlies well past the southern tip of Africa, where he turned north. On his return, he sighted what he called the "Cape of Storms," later renamed the "Cape of Good Hope" by the Portuguese king. Dias had perfected the techniques for searching out currents in the Southern Hemisphere and opened the way to India.

Vasco da Gama Pioneering Portuguese trader, whose voyage to East Africa and India began the four-hundred-year presence of the Portuguese in the Indian Ocean.

A decade after Dias's return from the Cape of Good Hope, **Vasco da Gama** (1460?–1524) set sail on a voyage that would take him to Calicut on the western coast of India (see **MAP 13.2**). Using the information gathered from countless navigators, travelers, and even spies sent into East Africa, da Gama set sail in 1497, with four square-rigged, armed caravels and over 170 men. He had been provided with maps and reports that indicated what he might expect to find along the eastern coast of Africa. He also carried textiles and metal utensils, merchandise of the type usually traded along the western coast of Africa. This was a trading mission and, in no sense, a voyage of discovery.

Da Gama followed established routes beyond the Cape of Good Hope and into the Indian Ocean. He traveled up the coast until he reached Malindi in Mozambique, where he secured an Arab pilot who taught him the route to Calicut. Although the goods the Portuguese traders presented were not appropriate for the sophisticated Asian market, da Gama did manage to collect a cargo of Indian spices, which he brought back to Portugal, arriving in 1499. From that pioneering voyage until the Portuguese lost their last colonies in the twentieth century (Goa, 1961; Mozambique, 1975), Portugal remained a presence in the Indian Ocean.

The Portuguese in Asia

Muslims predominated in the Indian Ocean, but in fact, a mixture of ethnic and religious groups—including Muslims, Hindus, Chinese, Jains, and Nestorian Christians—participated in the movement of cottons, silks, and spices throughout the region. There were numerous small traders, as well as prosperous long-distance merchants with connections reaching into central Asia, Africa, and China.

Less than a century before Vasco da Gama's arrival, the Chinese seaman Zheng He (JUNG HUH) made a series of voyages into the Indian Ocean. In 1405, he led a huge armada of 317 ships and over 27,000 sailors on an expedition designed to expand the trade and political influence of Ming China. He would make six subsequent trips before a new emperor, intent on concentrating his resources on China's internal development, ended the ventures. With the retreat of the Chinese, trade returned to its previous patterns.

The hodgepodge of trade reflected the political situation. Vasco da Gama's arrival coincided with the rise of the Moguls, Muslim descendants of Jenghiz Khan. By 1530, they had gained control of most of northern India, and during the sixteenth century, their influence increased in the south. The wealth and security of the Moguls depended on landed power. They generally left traders and trading ports to themselves. Throughout the sixteenth century, the Moguls remained tolerant of India's religious, cultural, and economic diversity. Neither Muslim nor Hindu powers initially considered the Portuguese an unusual threat.

Asians may not have worried much about the Portuguese because, at first, there were so few of them. Vasco da Gama arrived with only three ships. And the subsequent fleet of Pedro Alvares Cabral carried only fifteen hundred men. In the 1630s, after more than a century of emigration, probably no more than ten thousand Portuguese were scattered from modern Indonesia to the east coast of Africa. In addition to government officials, Portuguese settlers were likely to be petty traders, local merchants, and poorly paid mercenaries.

The Portuguese faced a number of problems as they attempted to compete in Eastern markets. There were very few of them and the trade goods they brought with them had little value in sophisticated, highly developed Asian markets. In most cases, they bought spices, textiles, and dyes with gold and silver brought from mines in central Europe and the New World. They could not profit from the India trade by competing with the indigenous traders. In response, they created a seaborne **trading-post empire**—an empire based on control of trade rather than on colonization. It was, in fact, a model that fit well with their crusading experience in North Africa and their desire to push back Muslim control.

Despite disadvantages, Portugal's commercial empire succeeded, thanks especially to fortified, strategically placed naval bases. As early as Vasco da Gama's second expedition in 1502, the Portuguese bombarded Calicut and defeated an Arab fleet off the coast of India. This encounter set the stage for Portugal's most important imperial strategist, Alfonso d'Albuquerque (1453–1515), governor-general of Portuguese colonies in India. He convinced the monarchy that the key to dominance in the region was the creation of fortified naval bases commanding the Bay of Bengal and thereby controlling access to the coveted Spice Islands. (See the feature, "The Written Record: Albuquerque Defends the Portuguese Empire.") By 1600, the Portuguese had built a network of naval bases that reached from Mozambique and Mombasa on the east coast of Africa to Goa on the west coast of India and the island of Macao off southeastern China (see **MAP 13.2**).

The Portuguese established a royal trading firm, the Casa da India, to manage the booming market in cinnamon, ginger, cloves, mace, and a variety of peppers. Although their control was far from total, the Portuguese did become significant exporters of spices to Europe. More significant was the creation of the Portuguese Estado da India, or India office, to oversee Portuguese naval forces, administer ports, and regulate maritime trade. Under the Portuguese system, all merchants were expected to acquire export licenses and to ship products through Portuguese ports. Though a vigorous and highly profitable local trade remained out of Portuguese control, Asians still often found it more convenient to cooperate than to resist, and most agreed to pay for export licenses and trade through Portuguese ports. They even found it expedient to ship in European-style vessels and to use Portuguese as the language of commerce.

Portuguese in India This watercolor by a Portuguese traveler shows the varied peoples and customs and the great wealth to be found in India. Europeans were fascinated by all that seemed different from their own world. (Biblioteca Casanatense, Rome. Photo: Humberto Nicoletti Serra)

trading-post empire A system developed by the Portuguese to allow them to use fortified naval bases to dominate commerce in the Indian Ocean.

SECTION SUMMARY

- The Portuguese were especially interested in trade with the West African kingdoms along the Gold Coast.

- The Portuguese developed complex navigational techniques that allowed them to sail around the tip of Africa and into the Indian Ocean.

- Before the arrival of the Portuguese, the Muslim Mogul Empire left seaborne trade under the control of various ethnic and religious groups.

- The Portuguese established a trading-post empire that allowed them to dominate trade in the Indian Ocean.

Albuquerque Defends the Portuguese Empire

In this letter of 1512, to the king of Portugal, Alfonso d'Albuquerque, the governor-general of Portugal's colonies in India, informs the king of conditions in the East, explains his strategy, and defends himself against his critics.

The first time the Muslims entered Goa, we killed one of their captains. They were greatly grieved by the [Portuguese] capture of Goa and there is great fear of Your Highness among them. You must reduce the power of [the Muslim] rulers, take their coastal territories from them and build good fortresses in their principal places. Otherwise you will not be able to set India on the right path and you will always have to have a large body of troops there to keep it pacified. Any alliance which you may agree with one or other Indian king or lord must be secured, Sire, because otherwise you may be certain that, the moment your back is turned, they will at once become your enemies.

What I am describing has now become quite usual among them. In India there is not the same punctiliousness as in Portugal about keeping truth, friendship and trust, for nobody here has any of these qualities. Therefore, Sire, put your faith in good fortresses and order them to be built; gain control over India in time and do not place any confidence in the friendship of the kings and lords of this region because you did not arrive here with a just cause to gain domination of their trade with blandishments and peace treaties. Do not let anybody in Portugal make you think that this is a very hard thing to achieve and that, once achieved, it will place you under great obligation. I tell you this, Sire, because I am still in India and I would like people to sell their property and take part in this enterprise that is so much to your advantage, so great, so lucrative and so valuable....

In a place where there is merchandise to be had and the Muslim traders will not let us have precious stones or spices by fair dealing, and we want to take these foods by force, then we must fight the Muslims for them. If, on the other hand, they see us with a large body of troops, they do us honor, and no thought of deceit or trickery enters their heads. They exchange their goods for ours without fighting and they will abandon the delusion that they will expel us from India.

QUESTIONS

1. Why does Albuquerque believe that fortresses are essential to a Portuguese presence in India?
2. What Portuguese reaction does Albuquerque fear?

Source: T. F. Earle and J. Villiers, eds., *Albuquerque: Caesar of the East*, p. 109. Copyright © 1990 by Aris and Phillips. Reprinted by permission of the publisher.

SPANISH VOYAGES OF EXPLORATION, 1492–1522

Why did the Spanish choose to sail west in their attempt to find Asia?

Spanish overseas expansion seems a logical continuation of the centuries-long Reconquista (see pages 249–250). In 1492, just before Columbus set sail, Castile was finally able to conquer the last Muslim kingdom of Granada and unify all of Iberia, with the exception of Portugal, under a single monarchy. Initially, in 1479, the Spanish kingdoms had agreed to leave the exploration and colonization of the African coast to the Portuguese, yet, they watched nervously as the Portuguese expanded their African contacts. Portuguese successes led Castilians to concentrate their efforts on what came to be called the "Enterprise of the Indies"—that is, the conquest and settlement of Central and South America.

The sailing and exploring necessary to compete with the Portuguese produced critical information about ocean winds and currents and facilitated later voyages. They also established the basic approaches that the Spanish would follow in their exploration, conquest, and colonization of the lands where they dropped anchor.

The Role of Columbus

The story of the enterprise begins with Christopher Columbus (1451–1506), a brilliant seaman, courtier, and self-promoter who has become a symbol of European expansion. Columbus, however, was not a bold pioneer who fearlessly did what no others could conceive of doing. He benefited from long-standing interests in the world beyond European shores.

Columbus was born into a modest family in Genoa and spent his early years in travel and in the service of the Castilian and Portuguese crowns. His vision seems to have been thoroughly traditional and medieval. He knew the medieval geographic speculations inherited from Arab, and ultimately Classical Greek, sources. Medieval seafarers did not fear a flat earth; rather, the concern was whether a ship could cover the vast distances necessary to sail west to Asia. Studying information in *Imago Mundi* (*Image of the World,* 1410), by the French philosopher Pierre d'Ailly (die-YEE) (1350–1420), Columbus convinced himself that the distance between Europe and Asia was much less than it actually is. D'Ailly's estimate put the east coast of Asia within easy reach of the western edge of Europe. "This sea is navigable in a few days if the wind is favorable," d'Ailly concluded.

Columbus's own study convinced him that the distance from the west coast of Europe to the east coast of Asia was about 5,000 miles, instead of the actual 12,000. Columbus's reading of traditional sources put Japan in the approximate location of the Virgin Islands. (It is not surprising that Columbus remained convinced that the Bahamas were islands just off the coast of Asia.) When Amerindians told him of Cuba, he concluded that it "must be Japan according to the indications that these people give of its size and wealth."[1]

On the basis of first-century descriptions, Columbus assured Spanish authorities that King Solomon's mines were only a short distance west of his newly discovered islands. In addition to finding the gold of Solomon, Columbus expected that by sailing farther west he could fulfill a series of medieval prophecies that would lead to the conversion of the whole world to Christianity. This conversion, he believed, would shortly precede the Second Coming of Christ. In Columbus's own view, then, his voyages were epochal not because they were ushering in a newer, more secular world, but because they signaled the fulfillment of Christian history.

Columbus's enthusiasm for the venture was only partially shared by the Spanish monarchs, Ferdinand and Isabella. Vasco da Gama had been well supplied with a flotilla of large ships and a crew of over 170 men, but Columbus sailed in 1492 with three small vessels and a crew of 90. Da Gama carried extra supplies and materials for trade and letters for the rulers he knew he would meet. Columbus had nothing similar in his sea chest. His commission did authorize him as "Admiral of Spain" to take possession of all he should find, but royal expectations do not seem to have been great.

Yet, on October 12, about ten days later than he had expected, Columbus reached landfall on what he assumed were small islands in the Japanese chain. He had actually landed in the Bahamas. Because Columbus announced to the world that he had arrived in the Indies, the indigenous peoples have since been called "Indians" and the islands are called the "West Indies."

Columbus reported to the Spanish monarchs that the inhabitants on the islands were friendly and open to the new arrivals. He described a primitive, naked people eager, he believed, to learn of Christianity and European ways. Indeed, the Tainos, or Arawaks, whom he had misidentified, did live simple, uncomplicated lives. The islands easily produced sweet potatoes, maize, beans, and squash, which, along with fish, provided an abundant diet. Initially, these people shared their food and knowledge with the newcomers, who they seem to have thought were sky-visitors.

The Spanish, for their part, praised the Tainos. The visitors generally believed that they had discovered a compliant, virtuous people who, if converted, would be exemplars of Christian virtues to Europeans. Columbus himself observed:

> They are very gentle and do not know what evil is; nor do they kill others, nor steal; and they are without weapons. They say very quickly any prayer that we tell them to say, and they make the sign of the cross, †. So your Highnesses ought to resolve to make them Christians.[2]

The Spanish authorities changed their opinion quickly. The settlers Columbus left at his fortress set an unfortunate example. They seized food stocks, kidnapped women, and embarked on a frenzied search for gold. Those who did not kill one another were killed by enraged Tainos.

During succeeding voyages, Columbus struggled to make his discoveries the financial windfall he had promised the monarchs. He was utterly unable to administer this vast new land. He quickly lost control of the colonists and was forced to allow the vicious exploitation of the island population. He and other Spanish settlers claimed larger and larger portions of the land and required the Indians to work it. Islands that easily supported a population of perhaps a million natives could not support those indigenous peoples and the Spanish newcomers and still provide exports to Spain. Scholars have estimated that the native population of the islands may have fallen to little more than thirty thousand by 1520, largely because of diseases (see pages 375–376). By the middle of the sixteenth century, the native population had virtually disappeared.

Columbus remained convinced that he would find vast fortunes just over the horizon. However, he found neither the great quantities of gold he promised nor a sea passage to Asia. With the islands in revolt and his explorations seemingly going nowhere, the Spanish monarchs stripped Columbus of his titles and commands. Once, he was returned to Spain in chains. Even after his final transatlantic trip, he continued to insist that he had finally found either the Ganges (GAN-jeez) River of India or one of the rivers that according to the Hebrew Bible flow out of the earthly paradise. Although Columbus died in 1506, rich and honored for his discoveries, he never did gain all the power and wealth he had expected. He remained frustrated and embittered by the Crown's refusal to support one more voyage, during which he expected to find the mainland of Asia.

In 1501, after sailing along the coast of Brazil, the Florentine geographer Amerigo Vespucci (1451–1512) drew the obvious conclusion from the information collected by Columbus's explorations. He argued that Columbus had discovered a new continent unknown to the classical world. These claims were accepted by the German mapmaker Martin Waldseemüller (vald-SAY-mill-er), who, in 1507, honored Amerigo's claim by publishing the first map showing "America."

Columbus's Successors

Columbus's explorations set off a debate over which nations had the right to be involved in trade and expansion. Portuguese claims were based on a papal bull of 1481, issued by Pope Sixtus IV (r. 1471–1484), that granted Portugal rights to all lands south of the Canaries and west of Africa. After Columbus's return, the Spaniards lobbied one of Sixtus's successors, Alexander VI (r. 1492–1503), whose family, the Borgias, was from the kingdom of Aragon. In a series of bulls, Pope Alexander allowed the Spanish to claim all lands lying 400 miles or more west of the Azores. Finally, in the **Treaty of Tordesillas** (tor-day-SEE-yas) (1494), Spain and Portugal agreed that the line of demarcation between their two areas should be drawn 1,480 miles west of the Azores. The treaty was signed just six years before Pedro Alvares Cabral (1467–1520) discovered the coast of Brazil. Thus, the Spanish unwittingly granted the Portuguese rights to Brazil.

Adventurers and explorers worried little about the legal niceties of exploration. Even as Columbus lay dying in 1506, others, some without royal permission, sailed up and down the eastern coasts of North and South America. Amerigo Vespucci traveled on Spanish vessels as far as Argentina, while Spanish explorers sailed among the islands of the Caribbean and along the coast of the Yucatán Peninsula. Vasco Nuñez de Balboa (1475–1519) crossed the Isthmus of Panama in 1513 and found the Pacific Ocean exactly where the natives living in the region said it would be.

The most important of the explorations that Columbus inspired was the voyage undertaken by **Ferdinand Magellan** in 1519 (see **MAP 13.2**). Although his motives are unclear, Magellan (1480?–1521) may have planned to complete Columbus's dream of sailing to the Indies. By the 1510s, mariners and others understood that the Americas were a new and hitherto unknown land, but they did not know what lay beyond them or what distance separated the Americas from the Spice Islands of Asia. After sailing along the well-known coastal regions of South America, Magellan continued south, charting currents and looking for a passage into the Pacific. Late in 1520, he beat his way through the dangerous straits (now the Strait of Magellan) separating Tierra del Fuego (ti-AIR-ah del foo-WAY-go) from the mainland. These turbulent waters marked the boundary of the Atlantic and Pacific Oceans. It took almost four months to travel from the straits to the Philippines. The crew suffered greatly from scurvy and a shortage of water and, at times, had to eat the rats aboard ship to survive. One crew member reported, "We ate biscuit, which was no longer biscuit, but powder of biscuit swarming with worms, for they had eaten the good."[3]

Treaty of Tordesillas

A treaty negotiated between Spain and Portugal dividing the newly explored lands in the New World and the Old. All New World lands except Brazil were given to the Spanish.

FERDINAND MAGELLAN

Ferdinand Magellan

The Spanish explorer who established the routes by which ships could sail around the world.

Nevertheless, Magellan managed to reach the Philippines by March 1521. A month later, he was killed by natives.

Spanish survivors, in two remaining ships, continued west, reaching the Moluccas, or Spice Islands, where they traded merchandise that they had carried along for a small cargo of cloves. A single surviving ship continued around Africa and back to Spain, landing with a crew of 15 at Cádiz in September 1522, after a voyage of three years and the loss of four ships and 245 men. Magellan completed and confirmed the knowledge of wind and ocean currents that European sailors had been accumulating. One of his sailors wrote of him, "More accurately than any man in the world did he understand sea charts and navigation."[4] The way was now open for the vast expansion of Europeans and European culture into all parts of the world.

Although the pope seemingly divided the non-European world between the Spanish and the Portuguese, Spanish adventurers were not the only ones to follow in Columbus's wake. The French and the English never accepted the pope's right to determine rights of exploration. They did, however, concentrate their explorations farther north. Building on a tradition of fishing off the coast of Newfoundland, English sailors under the command of John Cabot (1450?–1499?) sighted Newfoundland in 1497, and later voyages explored the coast as far south as New England. Cabot initiated an intense period of English venturing that would lead to an unsuccessful attempt to found a colony on Roanoke Island in 1587 and eventually to a permanent settlement at Jamestown in 1607. French expeditions followed Cabot to the north. In 1534, Jacques Cartier (kar-ti-YAY) (1491–1557) received a royal commission to look for a northern passage to the East. He was the first European to sail up the St. Lawrence River and began the process of exploration and trading that would lead to a permanent presence in Canada beginning in the early seventeenth century. But British and French settlements in the New World came later. The sixteenth century belonged to the Spanish.

ENGLISH AND FRENCH EXPLORERS

SECTION SUMMARY

- Columbus was a brilliant seaman whose exploration was based on geographic knowledge accumulated in the previous centuries.

- The frenzied Spanish search for wealth destroyed the economies of the island peoples.

- Magellan's voyage around the world completed the geographic knowledge necessary for commerce connecting Europe, Asia, and the New World.

- It was only with the writings of Amerigo Vespucci that most Europeans accepted the idea that Columbus had sailed to a previously unknown continent.

SPAIN'S COLONIAL EMPIRE, 1492–1600

How did the Spanish conquer and control the new world they entered?

Spanish penetration of the New World was a far cry from the model of the Portuguese in Asia. The Spaniards established no complex network of trade and commerce, and no strong states opposed their interests. A trading-post empire could not have worked in the New World. To succeed, the Spaniards needed to colonize and reorganize the lands they had found.

Between 1492 and 1600, almost 200,000 Spaniards immigrated to the New World. "New Spain," as they called these newly claimed lands, was neither the old society transported across the ocean nor an Amerindian society with a thin veneer of Spanish and European culture. To understand the history of New Spain, it is essential to grasp what it replaced, and how: The Spaniards overthrew two major civilizations and created new institutions in the wake of conquest. The whole story is not conquest and extermination—many of the Spanish attempted to secure fair treatment for the indigenous peoples who were now part of the Spanish Empire.

The Americas Before the European Invasion

The Spaniards, and later their European peers, entered a world vastly different from their own. It was a world formed by two momentous events—one geological, the other anthropological. The first was the creation of the continents of North and South America. The Americas, along with Africa and the Eurasian landmass, were once part of a single supercontinent. The breakup of this supercontinent left the Americas, Africa, and Eurasia free to evolve in dramatically different ways. The continental breakup occurred millions of years ago, long before the appearance of human beings and many other forms of mammalian life.

The second momentous event was the peopling of the Americas. Some migrants may have come over the seas. Most, though, arrived thanks to a temporary rejoining of the Americas to the Eurasian landmass by land and ice bridges that allowed Asians to cross over what is now the Bering Strait to the Americas in the period between 40,000 and 15,000 B.C. Their timing had a great impact. They arrived in the Americas long before the beginnings of the Neolithic agricultural revolution, which involved the domestication of numerous plants and animals. The agricultural revolution in the Americas occurred around 3000 B.C., perhaps six thousand years after similar developments in the Old World. The peoples of the Americas created complex societies, but those societies lacked large domesticated meat or pack animals (the llama was the largest), iron, other hard metals, and the wheel.

Nonetheless, by the time of Columbus's arrival, relatively populous societies were living throughout North and South America. Population estimates for the two continents range from 30 million to 100 million—50 million seems the most commonly accepted figure. North America saw the development of complex Mound Builder societies in the East and along the Mississippi River and pueblo societies in the deserts of the American Southwest. In Central and South America, there may have been 350 tribal or clan groups concentrated around fifteen or more cultural centers. But the greatest powers in the Amerindian world were the **Aztecs** in central and coastal Mexico and the **Inca** in the mountains of Peru.

Aztecs People who dominated the Valley of Mexico from the fourteenth to the sixteenth centuries and whose empire was destroyed by Cortés.

Inca A mountain empire that flourished in Peru. It was conquered for Spain by Pizarro.

THE AZTECS

When the collection of tribes, now known as the "Aztec" (or Mexica) peoples, appeared in central Mexico in the early fourteenth century, they found an already flourishing civilization concentrated around the cities and towns dotting the Valley of Mexico. The Aztecs conquered and united the many Nahuatl-speaking groups living in the valley, forming a confederation centered in Tenochtitlán, a city of perhaps 200,000 people built on an island in Lake Texcoco (see **MAP 13.3**). In early-sixteenth-century Europe, only London, Constantinople, and Naples would have been as large as the Aztec capital. It literally rose out of the water of Lake Texcoco. Only Venice could have equaled the sight. The whole valley supported an unusually high population of about a million. Using canals along the edge of the lake and other canals in Tenochtitlán itself, merchants easily moved food, textiles, gold and silver ornaments, jewels, and ceremonial feathered capes into the city markets. Spaniards later estimated that fifty thousand or more people shopped in the city on market days.

Religion was integral to the Aztecs' understanding of their empire. They believed that the world was finite and that they lived in the last of five empires. It was only regular human sacrifice to Huitzilopochtli (wheat-zeel-oh-POSHT-lee) that allowed the world to continue: The hearts of victims were necessary to sustain their god, to ensure that the sun would rise each morning. Thus, life for the Aztecs required a relentless parade of death.

Tenochtitlán The Aztec capital was built on an island. Its central temples and markets were connected to the rest of the city and the suburbs on the lakeshore by numerous canals. The city and its surrounding market gardens seemed to the Spanish to be floating on water. (The Newberry Library, Chicago)

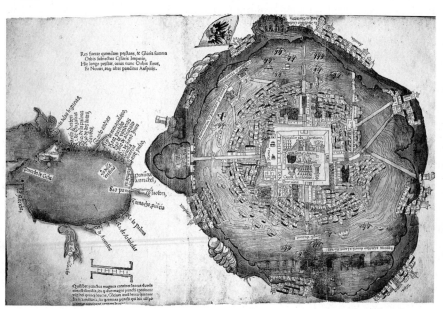

Tenochtitlán was the center of an imperial culture based on tribute. Towns and villages under Aztec control owed ongoing allotments of food and precious metals to the Aztecs. To emphasize that Aztec power and dominance were complete, the Aztecs not only collected vast quantities of maize, beans, squash, and textiles, but demanded payment in everything down to centipedes and snakes. The most chilling tribute, however, was in humans for sacrifice. When the wars of expansion that had provided prisoners came to an end, the Aztecs and their neighbors fought "flower wars"—highly ritualized battles to provide prisoners to be sacrificed. Five thousand victims

Map legend:

- Aztec Empire in 1519
- *MIXE*　Selected Native American peoples
- ⊛　Capital city
- ▲　Mountain
- ←　Route of Cortés, 1518–1519

VALLEY OF MEXICO, 1519

🌐 Map 13.3—Mexico and Central America

The Valley of Mexico was a populous region of scattered towns, most of which were part of the Aztec Empire. As Cortés marched inland from Vera Cruz toward the valley, he passed through lands that for generations had been in an almost constant state of war with the Aztecs.

were sacrificed at the coronation of Moctezuma II (r. 1502–1520) in 1502. Even more, reportedly twenty thousand, were sacrificed at the dedication of the great temple of Huitzilopochtli in Tenochtitlán.

Aztec society maintained a perpetual state of war with the peoples beyond the mountains that ringed the Valley of Mexico—especially the people along the Caribbean coast. Given this constant state of war, plus the heavy burdens in tribute placed on the near by subject cities, it is no wonder that the Aztecs were obsessed by the contingencies of life. At the end of each calendar cycle of fifty-two years, all fires in the empire were extinguished until fire-priests ascertained that the world would continue. And the Aztec world did continue until August 1523 (see page 369).

THE INCA

The other great Amerindian empire of the fifteenth century, the empire of the Inca, was also of recent origin. During the fifteenth century, the Inca formed efficient armies and expanded their control beyond the central highlands of Peru. Fifteen thousand miles of roads and a sophisticated administrative system allowed the Inca to create a state that extended from modern-day Ecuador to Chile (see **Map 13.4**). As they expanded, they demanded political control and tribute, but seem to have been tolerant of local traditions and language. The Inca perfected systems of irrigation and bridge-building, initiated by earlier inhabitants of the region. The empire, centered on the city of Cuzco high in the mountains of Peru, was able to sustain a population that may have reached 10 million by the end of the fifteenth century.

Human sacrifice, though not unknown to the Inca people, was not an essential part of their religious life. Their state was unsettled, however, by increasingly harsh tax exactions. Under the Inca system, the title Sapa Inca, or "Emperor," was inherited by the eldest son of the ruler's principal wife. The ruler's wealth, however, was retained by the rest of his family, who maintained the court as if the ruler still lived. Thus, each new ruler needed money to finance the creation of an entirely new court, and taxes were not only high but continuously climbing.

Both great Amerindian empires, despite their brilliance, rested on uneasy conquests. Subject groups would be willing allies for any invader.

The Spanish Conquests

Hernán Cortés The Spanish commander who conquered the Aztec Empire with a tiny force of Spaniards, reinforced by numerous Indian allies.

Doña Marina An enslaved Mexica noblewoman who served as translator and guide for Cortés.

Hernán Cortés (1485–1546) was ambitious to make something of himself in the New World. Of a poor but aristocratic background, from the Extremadura region of southwestern Spain, he had gone to the West Indies in 1504 to seek his fortune in the service of the governor of Cuba. The governor gave him a commission to lead an expeditionary force to investigate reports of a wealthy and prosperous mainland Indian civilization. From the beginning, Spanish authorities seem to have distrusted Cortés's aims. In fact, he departed hastily from Cuba to evade formal notification that the governor had revoked his commission because of insubordination.

Cortés landed in Mexico at the site of the city he would name Vera Cruz ("True Cross") early in 1519, with a tiny command of five hundred men, sixteen horses, eleven ships, and a few pieces of artillery. Aided by a devastating outbreak of smallpox and Amerindian peoples happy to shake off Aztec control, Cortés and his troops managed to destroy the network of city-states dominated by the Aztecs of Tenochtitlán in two years and lay claim to the Valley of Mexico for the king of Spain. The manner in which Cortés explained and justified his mission can serve as a model against which to measure the adventures of other sixteenth-century Europeans in the Americas.

Cortés, like Machiavelli (see page 329), believed in the power of truly able leaders (men of *virtù*) to overcome chance through bold acts. Even so, an attempt to capture a city of 200,000 with an army of 500 appears more foolhardy than bold. Cortés seems to have attempted it simply because he found himself with very little choice. With his commission revoked by the governor of Cuba, Cortés arrived on the mainland as a rebel against both the governor of Cuba and the king of Spain. He burned his ships in Vera Cruz harbor, making clear to all his men that there was no turning back. Much of what he did and said concerning the great Aztec Empire was an attempt to justify his initial act of insubordination and win back royal support. He quickly found allies among native groups who, for their own reasons, wished to see the Aztec Empire destroyed. The allied forces moved toward Tenochtitlán.

Cortés was greatly aided by fortune in the form of Malintzin, a Mexica woman who, after her conversion to Christianity, called herself **Doña Marina** (ca. 1501–1550). Malintzin was Cortés's interpreter and, later, his mistress. Without her, one of Cortés's followers recalled, "we could not have understood the language of New Spain and Mexico." Her story illustrates many of the complex interactions at play in sixteenth-century Mexico. Born a noble Aztec, she was sold by her stepfather and mother, ending up in the hands of the Maya. They gave her, along with twenty other women, to Cortés. Knowing both the Maya and Mexica languages, and quickly learning Spanish, she was the one person who could mediate between Spaniard and native. After bearing Cortés

🌐 **MAP 13.4—The Inca Empire**

The Inca Empire was accessible from Spanish strongholds in Mexico only by sea. Spanish exploration and domination brought the destruction of Inca mountain citadels and the transfer of administrative power to the new Spanish city of Lima on the coast.

a son, she finished her life in Spain as the wife of a Spanish gentleman. Like many of the natives, who felt no affection for the Aztecs of Tenochtitlán, she did not find it difficult to aid the Spaniards.

Despite the help of Malintzin and Spaniards who had previously lived with the natives, the meeting of Aztecs and Spaniards demonstrated the breadth of the chasm separating the Old World and the New. At first, the Aztec king Moctezuma was unconcerned about the coming of the Spaniards. Later, he seems to have attempted to buy them off. And finally, he and his successors fought desperately to drive them out of Tenochtitlán. The Aztecs' indecision was caused in large part by the fact that in neither words nor gestures did the two groups speak the same language. Hearing that the Spaniards were on the march, Moctezuma sent ambassadors bearing gold, silver, and other costly gifts, which they presented in a most humble fashion to the Spaniards. To a modern ear, the gifts sound like (and have often been interpreted to be) desperate attempts to buy off the invaders. To Cortés, or any European or Asian resident of the Old World, such gifts were a sign of submission. But to Moctezuma, and most Amerindians, the giving of gifts with great humility by otherwise powerful and proud people could be a show of status, power, and wealth. Seen in that light, Moctezuma's lavish gifts and apparent humility were probably meant to demonstrate the superiority of his civilization, and Cortés's acceptance of the gifts indicated to the Aztecs, at least, a recognition of Spanish inferior status.

Spaniards later explained that the Aztecs believed that Quetzalcoatl, the serpent-god symbolically conquered by Huitzilopochtli, had traveled to the east, promising one day to return and reclaim his lands, thus ending Aztec rule. The Spaniards believed that Moctezuma's ambivalence toward them was rooted in his belief in that myth.

The story does not hold up in light of the evidence, the myth of the return of Quetzalcoatl was first recorded in Spanish, not Mexica, sources long after the conquest. In truth, neither Cortés nor historians can satisfactorily explain, in Western terms, Moctezuma's initial response to the Spaniards. Cortés took the Aztec leader captive in 1521 and began what would be a two-year battle to take control of the capital and its empire. Although weakened by the arrival of smallpox and other virulent Old World diseases, the Aztecs continued to fight, even as more and more of the subject peoples joined the Spanish besiegers. The Spaniards cut off food and water to Tenochtitlán, but still the Aztecs fought.

Different understandings of the rules of war, different traditions of diplomacy, and different cultures prevented the Aztecs and Cortés from reaching any understanding. Warfare in pre-conquest America was highly ritualized. Armies captured enemies either to enslave them or to sacrifice them in one of the temples. The Spaniards, to Aztec eyes, killed indiscriminately and needlessly on the battlefield. Cortés later complained of the Aztecs' refusal to negotiate: "We showed them more signs of peace than have ever been shown to a vanquished people." It was a conflict that neither side could resolve in any other way; thus, by August 1523, Cortés and his allies had destroyed completely the garden city of Tenochtitlán.

Aztec Warrior This watercolor, by a Mexican artist who was trained in European painting, depicts a pre-Aztec ruler. The dress and the stone-edged sword would have been typical of the Aztecs, too. (Bibliothèque nationale de France)

LATER CONQUESTS

Cortés's recurring insubordination was an unfortunate model. His own lieutenants later rebelled against his control and attempted to create their own governments as they searched for riches and El Dorado, a mythical city of gold. Later adventurers marched throughout the North American Southwest and Central and South America, following rumors of hidden riches. Using private armies and torturing native peoples, veterans of Cortés's army and newly arrived speculators hoped to find wealth that would allow them to live like nobles on their return to Spain.

Francisco Pizarro (1470–1541) was the most successful of the private adventurers. Poor and illegitimate at birth, he arrived in the Americas ambitious for riches and power. After serving in Balboa's army, participating in several slaving expeditions, and helping to found Panama City, Pizarro was prosperous but still not wealthy. Rumors of Inca wealth filtered through to Central America. Pizarro and two partners resolved in 1530 to lead an expedition down the west coast of South America in search of the Inca capital. Benefiting from disorganization, caused by a smallpox epidemic and ensuing civil war, Pizarro was able to find local sympathizers.

Like Cortés, he used numerous Indian allies in his most important battles. Aided by Amerindians, eager to throw off Inca domination, he captured and executed the Sapa Inca and conquered the capital of Cuzco by 1533. He later built a new capital on the coast at Lima (see **Map 13.4**), from which he worked to extend his control over all of the old Inca Empire. Pizarro and his Spanish partners seized vast amounts of gold and silver from the Inca. The Spanish eventually found silver mines at Potosí (po-to-SEE), which would be a critical source of revenue for the Spanish monarchy. Resistance to Spanish rule continued into the 1570s, when the last of the independent Inca strongholds was finally destroyed.

Colonial Organization

The Spanish crown needed to create a colonial government that could control the actions of its headstrong adventurers and create an orderly economy. Although the Spaniards proclaimed that they would "give to those strange lands the form of our own [land]," the resulting political and economic organization of the new Spanish possessions was a curious mixture of old and new.

The head of the administration was the monarchy. As early as the reigns of Ferdinand and Isabella, Spanish monarchs had tried to curb the excesses of the explorers and conquerors who traveled in their name. Isabella initially opposed the enslavement of Amerindians and any slave trade in the new lands. Further, the monarchs promoted a broad-based debate about the rights of Amerindians and the nature of religious conversion. It was royal policy that native rights, even the right not to become Christian, were to be protected. Mexicans had to accept missionaries, but they did not have to convert. Royal control, however, was limited by the sheer distance between the court and the new provinces. On average, it took the Spanish fleet two years to complete a round-trip voyage. It could easily take two years for a royal response to a question to arrive at its destination. Things moved so slowly that as one viceroy ruefully noted, "If death came from Madrid, we should all live to a very old age." Given the difficulties of communication, the powers of local administrators had to be very broad.

Council of the Indies An administrative body established in 1524 to oversee commerce and administration in Spain's colonial possessions.

By 1535, Spanish colonial administration was firmly established in the form it would retain for the next two hundred years. The king created the **Council of the Indies**, located at court, eventually in Madrid, which saw to all legal and administrative issues pertaining to the new possessions. The new territories themselves were eventually divided into the viceroyalty of New Spain (primarily Central America and part of Venezuela) and the viceroyalty of Peru.

In New Spain, royal administrators created Indian municipalities, or districts, in which Spaniards had no formal right to live or work. Government in these municipalities remained largely in the hands of pre-conquest native elites. Throughout the sixteenth century, official documents in these communities continued to be written in Nahuatl, the Aztec language. These native communities were, however, fragile. Colonists and local administrators often interfered in the hope of gaining control. (See the feature, "The Global Record: An Inca Nobleman Defends His Civilization.")

encomienda A royal protectorship granted with the obligation to protect and Christianize the people. Instead, natives became virtual slaves.

The Colonial Economy

The problem that most plagued the government was the conquerors' desire for laborers to work on the lands and in the mines that they had seized. From Columbus's first visit, the Spanish adopted a system of forced labor developed in Spain. A colonist called an *encomendero* (en-co-men-DARE-o) was offered a grant, or *encomienda* (en-co-mi-EN-da), of a certain number

An Inca Nobleman Defends His Civilization

Felipe Guaman Poma was born into a noble Inca family with a long history of service first to the Inca kings and later to the Spanish administrators. Although Guaman Poma became a Christian and adapted to Spanish rule, he appealed to the king of Spain in 1613 to intervene on behalf of the Indian peoples. In this section he describes the evils he has seen and suggests how the king could remedy them.

The aforementioned priests . . . do not act like the blessed priests of Saint Peter. . . . Rather, they give themselves over to greed for silver, clothing, and things of the world. . . . [They] ask for Indians to carry to market their wine, peppers, coca, and maize. Some have Indians bring mountain wine and coca down from the high plains to the hot lowlands. Being highland people, they die from fever and chills. . . . [They] have thread spun and woven, oppressing the widows and unmarried women, making them work without pay. . . . And in this [dealing with the priests] the Indian women become notorious whores. . . . [The priests] clamor to involve themselves too much in judicial matters. . . . As a result they enter into disputes and initiate petitions and are bad examples for the pueblo [i.e., village]. . . . They treat them so imperiously and thereby destroy the Indians of this kingdom.

The ancient [Andean] priests . . . acted devoutly and gave good example, as with the virgins and nuns of the temples. And so the rest [of the Indians] submitted to their justice and law. They were Christians in everything but their idolatry.

Because of such damage and so many complaints lodged against them, these fathers and pastors should be appointed on an interim basis—for a year at a time if he is good; and if he is not, may he not remain a single day. He should be at least fifty years old because a child's or a young man's follies are not good. . . . They should be proven and tested for academic preparation as well as for humility, charity, love and fear of God and justice, and for knowledge of the Quechua [or] Aymara languages of the Indians, needed to reach them, confess them, and preach the Gospel and sermons [to them].

They should be examined by the reverend fathers . . . who are great scholars and preachers in the world. Those [who pass the examinations] should be sent to Your Lordship and to the head viceroy for appointment as interim pastors, posting a guaranteed bond. With this they will lose their arrogance; they will obey your lordship.

In the time of the conquest of a province there was only one priest in charge of instruction; . . . he demanded no silver and only enough to eat. Thus these first ones were exemplary saints. They . . . did not pretend to be a bishop or a magistrate. Thus [the people] converted to God giving themselves over to peace and to the royal Crown.

QUESTIONS

1. What are the complaints about the behavior of Christian priests? What do these complaints imply about the place of a priest in a village?

2. What role does Guaman Poma expect priests to play in a village?

3. What are the benefits Guaman Poma expects villagers to receive from Spanish administrators?

Source: Kenneth Mills and William B. Taylor, eds., *Colonial Latin America: A Documentary History.* Copyright 2002 by Scholarly Resources, Inc. Reprinted by permission of Scholarly Resources, Inc.

of people or tribes who were required to work under his direction. The Spanish government expected that the encomendero was to be a protector of the conquered peoples, someone who would Christianize and civilize them. In theory, Indians who voluntarily agreed to listen to missionaries or to convert to Christianity could not be put under the control of an encomendero. If natives refused to hear the missionaries, however, the Spaniards believed they had the right of conquest. In many areas, encomenderos allowed life to continue as it had, simply collecting traditional payments that the pre-conquest elites had claimed. In other cases, where the subject peoples were forced into mining districts, the conditions were brutal. The treatment of native peoples was "more unjust and cruel," one reformer concluded, "than Pharaoh's oppression of the Jews."

The pressures exerted by the encomenderos were worsened by the precipitous fall in the indigenous population. Old World diseases, such as smallpox and measles, swept through peoples with no previous exposure to them (see pages 375–376). In central Mexico, where we know most about population changes, the pre-conquest population was at least 10 million to 12 million and may have been twice that. By the mid-sixteenth century, the native population may have declined to just over 6 million, and it probably plunged to less than 1 million early in the seventeenth century, before beginning to grow again.

A large population was essential to the Spanish and the Portuguese. The Caribbean islands and Brazil were ideal for the production of sugar—a commercial crop in great demand

Guaxtepec Map　This detail from a map from 1580 shows the mixture of Spanish and Mexica that represents the ideal impact of Charles V's New Laws. The map shows a native village, but with a monastery at the center. The map is explained with Spanish captions and Nahuatl pictographic symbols.　(Relación Geográfica map of Guaxtepec, Nettie Lee Benson Latin American Collection, the University of Texas Libraries)

throughout Europe. At first, plantations and mines were worked by Amerindians, but when their numbers shrank, the Spanish and Portuguese imported large numbers of slaves from Africa.

Africans had participated in the initial stages of the conquest. (See the feature, "The Visual Record: The Mulattos of Esmeraldas.") Some had lived in Spain and become Christian; indeed, Amerindians called them "black whitemen." Most Africans, however, were enslaved laborers. African slaves were in Cuba by 1518; they labored in the mines of Honduras by the 1540s. After the 1560s, the Portuguese began mass importations of African slaves into Brazil to work on the sugar plantations. It has been estimated that 62,500 slaves were brought into Spanish America and 50,000 into Brazil during the sixteenth century. By 1810, when the movement to abolish the slave trade began to gather momentum, almost 10 million Africans had been involuntarily transported to the New World to work the fields and mines on which the colonial economy depended.

The conquerors had hoped to find vast quantities of wealth that they could take back to the Old World. In the viceroyalty of Mexico, the search for El Dorado remained largely unsuccessful. The discovery, in 1545, of the silver mines at Potosí in Peru, however, fulfilled the Spaniards' wildest dreams. Between 1550 and 1650, the Spanish probably sent back to Spain 181 tons of gold and 16,000 tons of silver, one-fifth of which was paid directly into the royal treasury.

The flood of silver and gold did have a significant impact on the Continent. The treasure represents one-quarter of the income of King Philip II of Spain in the 1560s and made him the richest monarch in Europe. The New World bonanza funded Spanish opposition to the Protestant Reformation and Spain's attempts to influence the politics of most of its neighbors. And the Spanish coins, the *reales* (re-AL-es) and *reales a ocho* (re-AL-es a O-cho) (the "pieces of eight" prized by English pirates), became the common coin of European traders and even Muslim and Hindu traders in the Indian Ocean. In a world with limited commercial credit, the Spanish treasure was critical for a truly integrated system of world trade.

The Debate Over Indian Rights

To most conquerors, the ruthless pursuit of wealth and power needs little justification, but the more thoughtful among the Spaniards were uneasy. "Tell me," demanded Friar Antonio Montesinos (mon-teh-SEE-nos) in 1511, "by what right or justice do you hold these Indians in such cruel and horrible slavery? By what right do you wage such detestable wars on these people who lived idly and peacefully in their own lands?"[5]

Initially, the conquerors claimed the right to wage a just war of conquest if Amerindians refused to allow missionaries to live and work among them. Later, on the basis of reports of human sacrifice and cannibalism, written by Columbus and other early explorers, Europeans concluded that the inhabitants of the New World rejected basic natural laws. Juan Gines de Sepulveda (HWAN HE-nays de se-PUL-ve-da), chaplain of King Charles I of Spain, argued that the idolatry and cannibalism of the Indians made them, in Aristotle's terms, natural slaves—"barbarous and inhuman peoples abhorring all civil life, customs and virtue." People lacking "civil life" and "virtue" clearly could not be allowed self-government. Other writers commented that nakedness and cannibalism were both signs of the lack of "civility" among the Amerindians. Sepulveda implied that Indians were merely "humanlike," not necessarily human.

Franciscan and Dominican missionaries were especially vocal opponents of views such as Sepulveda's. Missionaries initially argued that Indians were innocents and ideal subjects for conversion to the simple piety of Christ and his first apostles. In their eyes, Indians were like children who could be converted and led by example and, where necessary, by stern discipline. The simple faith of the newly Christian native peoples was to be an example, the missionaries believed, for the lax believers of old Europe. These mendicants saw themselves as advocates for Indians; they desired to protect the natives from the depredations of the Spanish conquerors and the corruptions of European civilization.

The most eloquent defender of Indian rights was **Bartolomé de Las Casas** (1474–1566), a former encomendero who became a Dominican missionary and eventually bishop of Chiapas in southern Mexico. Las Casas passionately condemned the violence and brutality of the Spanish conquests. In a famous debate with Sepulveda, Las Casas rejected the "humanlike" argument. "All races of the world are men," he declared. All are evolving along a historical continuum. It was wrong, he added, to dismiss any culture or society as outside or beyond natural law. Like all other peoples, Indians had reason. That being the case, even the most brutal could be civilized and Christianized, but by conversion, not coercion. In the view of Las Casas, the argument for natural slavery was indefensible.

Bartolomé de Las Casas A former encomendero and the first bishop of Chiapas who passionately defended Indian rights and urged the passage of laws abolishing Indian slavery.

King Charles accepted Las Casas's criticisms of the colonial administration. In 1542, he issued "New Laws," aimed at ending the virtual independence of the most adventurous encomenderos. He further abolished Indian slavery and greatly restricted the transfer of encomiendas. We should have no illusion, however, that these measures reflected a modern acceptance of cultural pluralism. The very mendicants who protected the Indians assumed that Westernization and Christianization would quickly follow mercy. When it did not, as during revolts in the 1560s, the mendicants themselves sometimes reacted with a puzzled sense of anger, frustration, and betrayal.

SECTION SUMMARY

- Before the arrival of the Spanish, the Aztecs and Inca were large empires that dominated surrounding tribes and clans.

- Cortés found ready allies among the peoples dominated by the two empires.

- The conquest of Mexico set off a Spanish expansion, barely under the control of the Crown.

- The Crown eventually attempted to protect Amerindians by restricting encomiendas, outlawing Indian slavery, and forming Indian-controlled communities.

The Mulattos of Esmeraldas

This painting, which is entitled *Los Mulatos de Esmeraldas*, is the earliest known signed colonial portrait, dating back to 1599. It was commissioned by Juan del Barrio de Sepúlveda, judge of the Audiencia of Quito. He sent it to the Spanish king in Madrid, where the painting still resides. The artist who painted this very European-styled painting was an Amerindian named Andrés Sánchez Galque who had trained with a Spanish Dominican. The resulting work is a striking mix of native and Spanish cultures and leads a historian to ask, "What does this image suggest about colonial Latin America?"

It demonstrates, first of all, how quickly even isolated areas became integrated into a complex international culture. In the center of the painting stands Don Francisco de Arobe, the head of one of two important Afro-Indian clans that dominated the region since the middle of the sixteenth century. He is flanked by his two sons, Don Petro (on his right) and Don Domingo (on his left). Don Francisco is of mixed ancestry—his father was African, his mother an enslaved Nicaraguan. The parents had escaped into the wild region of Esmeraldas, an isolated coastal area northwest of Quito (see **Map 13.2**). It was an area that the Spanish imagined was filled with gold and perhaps, as its name seemed to imply, emeralds. It was also an area that various missionaries and private adventurers attempted to control in the name of the Crown. They were convinced that had they subdued Esmeraldas, their reward would have been treasure and political power.

In the half-century before this portrait was painted, the mulatto groups had variously negotiated with, helped, and avoided the Spanish. Clan leaders regularly promised to become Christian, to give food to the explorers, and to help in the search for gold and other treasures. Throughout the sixteenth century, they regularly and successfully resisted incorporation into the empire. The leader of one clan had offered allegiance to the Spanish if they would name him governor "over your subjects and vassals and natives." And

so, it is no doubt significant that the Spanish named Don Francisco governor. It was, in fact, his peaceful submission to the Audiencia that occasioned this surprising work. All this makes the portrait fascinating, but ambiguous. Are the three, as some have suggested, "trophies, stuffed and mounted on a wall of blue" or perhaps crafty diplomats who preferred "Renaissance dissimulation to . . . rebellion?"*

The three figures have struck a pose typical in Renaissance portraits. Don Francisco looks directly at the viewer, while his sons look only at him. The three are wearing Spanish cloaks and ruffled collars, over what is probably a South American poncho, but the design of the material suggests it is European or Asian in origin. What is most striking is the gold jewelry—earrings and noseplugs. These very likely were scavenged from burial mounds left in the region by earlier native peoples. Spanish visitors to Esmeraldas often commented on the gold jewelry of the mulattos. The mulatto clans often used promises of gold to mesmerize the adventurers who came. The three also are wearing shell necklaces—a tradition among coastal peoples reaching back perhaps a millennium. And finally, they are carrying spears, probably a combination of local wood and imported steel tips.

But how to interpret the image? The first thing a historian must do is acknowledge that we cannot know for sure the thoughts of the painter, the patron, or the three who posed. But we can line up the visual evidence that might lead us to a tentative conclusion. First, notice the interesting mix of dress. The three men doubtless would not have worn so many layers of clothing at home, along the steamy seacoast. Are the Spanish additions indications that Don Barrio, the judge of the Audiencia in Quito, dressed them to look more subdued, Spanish, and civilized? All three are addressed as "don," an honorific title that indicates both Christian conversion and elevated social status. But if that is the case, why are there no crosses, no signs of deference? They continue wear their coastal shells and their gold

THE COLUMBIAN EXCHANGE

What changes did European expansion bring to the Old World and the New?

Columbian Exchange
A term used to describe the blending of cultures between the Old World and the New. Columbus, and others who followed, brought plants, animals, and diseases that transformed North and South America.

The conquerors, adventurers, and traders who completed the expansion, begun by the voyages of Christopher Columbus and Vasco da Gama, profoundly altered the Old World and the New. A system of world trade had been in place before 1492, but now, as the Spanish proclaimed, Europe, and especially Spain, were at the center of economic and political life. As the Spanish and other Europeans moved throughout the world, they carried with them religions, ideas, people, plants, animals, and diseases—forever uniting the Old World and the New. This blending of cultures is known as the **Columbian Exchange**.

The Mulattos of Esmeraldas (Institut Amatller d'Art Hispanic)

jewelry taken from sites still unknown to the Spanish. Their hats are in their hands, perhaps a sign of respect or submission, but their eyes are not downcast or submissive. Don Francisco looks directly at the viewer and all three hold their spears. They may now be Spanish subjects, but Don Francisco does have the look of a governor.

In the end, it may be that Don Francisco and Judge Barrio would not have agreed on what the painting signified. But the ambiguity of the portrait does demonstrate to subsequent historians the extent to which understanding the Spanish role in Latin America requires more than simply ideas of conquest, domination, or rebellion. Identities may have been transformed, but persons like Don Francisco seem to be more than just obedient subjects.

QUESTIONS

1. Look at the portrait and try to identify those items that seem native or Spanish.

2. Can you find indications of either submission or independence in the portraits?

---

* The first conclusion is from Kenneth Mills and William B. Taylor, eds., *Colonial Latin America: A Documentary History* (Wilmington, Del.: SR Books, 2002), p. 160; the second from Kris Lane, *Quito, 1599* (Albuquerque: University of New Mexico Press, 2002), p. 33.

Disease

Columbus, and those who followed him, brought not only people to the New World, but also numerous Old World diseases. "Virgin-soil" epidemics—that is, epidemics of previously unknown diseases—are invariably fierce. Although the New World may have passed syphilis to Spain, from which it quickly spread throughout the Old World, diseases transferred from the Old World to the New were much more virulent than syphilis. Smallpox spread from Cuba to Mexico as early as 1519. It was soon followed by diphtheria, measles, trachoma, whooping cough, chickenpox, bubonic plague, malaria, typhoid fever, cholera, yellow fever, scarlet fever, amoebic dysentery, influenza, and some varieties of tuberculosis. Disease served as the silent ally of the conquerors. At critical points during the conquest of Tenochtitlán, smallpox was raging in the Aztec population. The disease later moved along traditional trade networks, often arriving in parts of North and South America decades before the Old World adventurers appeared. An

Sye figur anzaigt uns das volck und insel die gefunden ist durch den christenlichen Künig zu Portigal oder von seinen underthonen.Die leüt sind also nacket hübsch.braun wolgestalt von leib.ir heübter. halß.arm.scham.füß.frawen und mann ain wenig mit federn bedeckt. Auch haben die mann in iren angesichten und brust vil edel gestain . Es hat auch nyemann nichtes sunder sind alle ding gemain. Unnd die mann haben dt weyber welche in gefallen.es sey mütter.schwester oder freünde.darinn haben sy kain underschayd. Sy streyten auch mit einander. Sy essen auch ainander selbs die erschlagen werden.und hencken das selbig fl.isch in den rauch.Sy werden alt hundert und fünftzig iar. Und haben kain regiment.

Images of the New World   A mix of fact and fiction characterized many early images of the New World. The text below this illustration claims that these natives share everything, even wives; that they are cannibals; and that they have no government. The woodcut seems to justify Spanish domination.   (Spencer Collection, New York Public Library/Art Resource, NY)

epidemic shortly before Pizarro's expedition to Peru carried off the Sapa Inca and may have contributed to the unrest and civil war that worked to the advantage of the invaders.

Lacking sources, historians cannot trace accurately the movement of epidemic diseases or their effects on New World populations, yet many archaeologists and historians remain convinced that Old World diseases moved north from Mexico and ravaged and disrupted Amerindian populations in eastern North America long before the arrival of European immigrants. In most of the New World, 90 percent or more of the native population was destroyed by wave after wave of previously unknown afflictions. Explorers and colonists did not enter an empty land but rather an *emptied* one.

It was at least partially because of disease that both the Spanish and the Portuguese needed to import large numbers of African slaves to work their plantations and mines. With the settlement of southeastern North America, commercial agriculture was extended to include the production of tobacco and later cotton. As a result of the needs of plantation economies and the labor shortages caused by epidemics, African slaves were brought in by the thousands, then hundreds of thousands. In the Caribbean and along the coasts of Central and South America, the Africans created an African Caribbean or African American culture that amalgamated African, European, and American civilizations.

Plants and Animals

The impact of Old World peoples on native populations was immediately evident to all parties. However, scholars have recently argued that the importation of plants and animals had an even more profound effect than the arrival of Europeans. The changes that began in 1492 created "Neo-Europes" in what are now Canada, the United States, Mexico, Argentina, Australia, and New Zealand. The flora and fauna of the Old World, accustomed to a relatively harsh, competitive environment, found ideal conditions in the new lands. Like the rabbits that overran the Canary Islands and eventually Australia, Old World plants and animals multiplied, driving out many New World species.

The most important meat and dairy animals in the New World today—cattle, sheep, goats, and pigs—are imports from the Old World. Sailors initially brought pigs or goats aboard ship because they were easily transportable sources of protein. When let loose on the Caribbean islands, they quickly took over. The spread of horses through what is now Mexico, Brazil, Argentina, the United States, and Canada was equally dramatic. To the list of domesticated animals can be added donkeys, dogs, cats, and chickens. The changes these animals brought were profound. Cattle, pigs, and chickens quickly became staples of the New World diet. Horses enabled Amerindians and Europeans to travel across and settle the vast plains of both North and South America.

Gardening in Spanish Mexico This closed Spanish-style garden is a mix of the old and the new. Workers use both a Spanish hoe and an indigenous spade to cultivate new plants introduced by the Spanish. (Biblioteca Nacional, Madrid/Institut Amatller d'Art Hispanic)

The flora of the New World was equally changed. Even contemporaries noted how Old World plants flourished in the New. By 1555, European clover was widely distributed in Mexico—Aztecs called it "Castilian grass." Other Old World grasses, as well as weeds such as dandelions, quickly followed. Domesticated plants, including apples, peaches, and artichokes, spread rapidly and naturally in the hospitable new environment. The Old World also provided new and widely grown small grains such as oats, barley, and wheat. Early in the twentieth century, it was estimated that only one-quarter of the grasses found on the broad prairies of the Argentine pampas were native before the arrival of Columbus.

The exchange went both ways. Crops from the New World also had an effect on the Old. By the seventeenth century, maize (or American corn), potatoes, sweet potatoes, and many varieties of beans had significantly altered the diets of Europe and Asia. New crops supported the dramatic population growth that invigorated Italy, Ireland, and Scandinavia. With the addition of the tomato in the nineteenth century, much of the modern European diet became dependent on New World foods. The new plants and new animals, as well as the social and political changes initiated by the Europeans, pulled the Old World and the New more closely together.

Culture

One reason for the accommodation between the Old World and the New was that the Europeans and Amerindians tended to interpret conquest and cultural transformation in the same way. The peoples living in the Valley of Mexico believed that their conquest was fated by the gods and that their new masters would bring in new gods. The Spaniards' beliefs were strikingly similar, based on the revelation of divine will and the omnipotence of the Christian God. Cortés, by whitewashing former Aztec temples and converting native priests into white-clad Christian priests, was in a way fulfilling the Aztecs' expectations about the nature of conquest.

Acculturation was also facilitated by the Spanish tendency to place churches and shrines at the sites of former Aztec temples. The shrine of the Virgin of Guadalupe (gwa-da-LOO-peh) (on the northern edge of modern Mexico City), for example, was located on the site of the temple of the goddess Tonantzin (to-NAN-tzin), an Aztec fertility-goddess of childbirth and midwives. The shrine of Guadalupe is a perfect example of the complex mixture of cultures. The shrine initially appealed to *creoles*—people of mixed Spanish and Mexican descent. In the seventeenth century and after, it came to symbolize the connection of poor Mexicans to Christianity and was a religious rallying point for resisting state injustices.

The colonists tended to view their domination of the New World as a divine vindication of their own culture and civilization. During the sixteenth century, they set about remaking the world they had found. In the century after the conquest of Mexico, Spaniards founded 190 new cities in the Americas. Lima, Bogota, and many others were proudly modeled on and compared with the cities of Spain. In 1573, King Philip II (r. 1556–1598) established ordinances requiring all new cities to be laid out on a uniform grid with a main plaza, market, and religious center. In these cities, religious orders founded colleges for basic education, much like the universities they had organized in the Old World. In 1551, a century before English colonists founded Harvard University in Massachusetts, the Crown authorized the first universities in the New World. The universities in Mexico City and Lima mirrored the great Spanish university in Salamanca, teaching law and theology to the colonial elites. Colonists attempted to re-create in all essentials the society of Spain.

The experience of the Spanish and Portuguese in the sixteenth century seemed confirmed by the later experiences of the French and English in the seventeenth century. In seventeenth-century New England, the English Puritan John Winthrop concluded, "For the natives, they are nearly all dead of smallpox, so as the Lord hath cleared our title to what we possess."[6] A seventeenth-century French observer came to a similar conclusion: "Touching these savages, there is a thing that I cannot omit to remark to you, it is that it appears visibly that God wishes that they yield their place to new peoples."[7] Political philosophers believed that in the absence of evidence that the indigenous peoples were improving the land, the rights to that land passed to those who would make the best use of it. Thus, colonists believed that they had divine and legal sanction to take and to remake these new lands in a European image.

SECTION SUMMARY

- Old World diseases, introduced into the New World, destroyed perhaps 90 percent of the indigenous population.

- Thousands of enslaved Africans were brought to the New World to replace the lost population.

- Old World plants and animals transformed the economy of the New World.

- The cult of the Virgin of Guadalupe shows how religious practices of the Old World were influenced by New World religious practices.

CHAPTER SUMMARY

As we have seen, there was never a time when Europeans were unaware of or unconcerned about the outside world. In addition to traditional geographical knowledge, reaching back to the classical world, Europeans had valuable trade contacts via Muslim traders with both Africa and Asia. Further, in the thirteenth century, Italian merchants and adventurers began making regular trips through central Asia to China and even to Japan.

Yet, the expansion begun by the Portuguese along the coast of Africa and then on to India began a fateful transformation of European economic, political, and cultural influence. The Portuguese voyages were almost never adventures of discovery. By rumor and careful reading, explorers had ideas about what they would find. Nonetheless, they were faced with challenges that led them to adapt their Mediterranean and European ways of organization. The Portuguese developed a trading-post system to control trade in Asia.

Portuguese control of the African coast seemed to foreclose Spanish connections to Asian markets. Yet, based on a misunderstanding of classical texts, Columbus convinced the Spanish that the shortest route to Asia involved sailing west. Although Columbus never acknowledged it, by early in the sixteenth century, the Spanish knew that he had found a world unknown to the Old World.

In the wake of savage conquest and exploitation by adventurers, the Spanish developed a system of law and administration that transformed the world they had found. In the New World, even as the Spanish conquered peoples and changed

FOCUS QUESTIONS

- What did Europeans know about the wider world in the Middle Ages?

- How did the Portuguese exploit their new connection to the East?

- Why did the Spanish choose to sail west in their attempt to find Asia?

- How did the Spanish conquer and control the new world they entered?

- What changes did European expansion bring to the Old World and the New?

their languages, governments, and religions, many aspects of Amerindian culture survived in the local Indian municipalities.

The meeting of the Old World and the New brought unexpected changes to both. The old empires of the Americas were replaced by a Spanish colonial government. They brought with them foods, livestock, religion, and traditional European culture. They also brought diseases that decimated populations and transformed economies.

Modern historians have made us very aware of what was lost during the violent and tragic conquests that were part of European expansion. It is impossible to say whether the economic and technical benefits of the amalgamation of the Old World and the New outweigh the costs. Even those who celebrate the transformation of the New World would probably agree with the conclusions of a Native American in the Pacific Northwest: "I am not sorry the missionaries came. But I wish they had known how to let their news change people's lives from the inside, without imposing their culture over our ways."[8]

KEY TERMS

Prince Henry "the Navigator" (p. 359)

Vasco da Gama (p. 360)

trading-post empire (p. 361)

Treaty of Tordesillas (p. 364)

Ferdinand Magellan (p. 364)

Aztecs (p. 366)

Inca (p. 366)

Hernán Cortés (p. 368)

Doña Marina (p. 368)

Council of the Indies (p. 370)

encomienda (p. 370)

Bartolomé de Las Casas (p. 373)

Columbian Exchange (p. 374)

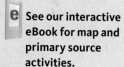 **This icon will direct you to additional materials on the website: www .cengage.com/history/ noble/westciv6e.**

e See our interactive eBook for map and primary source activities.

NOTES

1. Quoted in William D. Phillips, Jr., and Carla Rahn Phillips, *The Worlds of Christopher Columbus* (Cambridge: Cambridge University Press, 1992), p. 163.

2. Quoted ibid., p. 166.

3. Quoted in J. H. Parry, ed., *The European Reconnaissance: Selected Documents* (New York: Harper & Row, 1968), p. 242.

4. Quoted in Alfred W. Crosby, *Ecological Imperialism: The Biological Expansion of Europe, 900–1900* (Cambridge: Cambridge University Press, 1986), p. 125.

5. Quoted in Mark A. Burkholder and Lyman L. Johnson, *Colonial Latin America* (Oxford: Oxford University Press, 1990), p. 29.

6. Quoted in Crosby, p. 208.

7. Quoted ibid., p. 215.

8. Quoted in Maria Parker Pascua, "Ozette: A Makah Village in 1491," *National Geographic* (October 1991), p. 53.

14

CHAPTER OUTLINE

The Reformation Movements, ca. 1517–1545

The Empire of Charles V (R. 1519–1556)

The English Reformation, 1520–1603

France, Scandinavia, and Eastern Europe, 1523–1560

The Late Reformation, ca. 1545–1600

El Greco: The Burial of the Count de Orgaz This traditional chapel painting shows the close connection between the earthly and celestial realms in traditional Catholic Christianity. (Institut Amatller d'Art Hispanic)

The Age of the Reformation

El Greco's *The Burial of the Count de Orgaz* encapsulates the hopes and contradictions of the age of the Reformation. El Greco ("the Greek") first learned to paint on the island of Crete, then studied and worked in Venice and Rome before settling in Spain. This painting expresses the medieval Christian understanding of a good death. We see a saintly knight surrounded by clergy and witnesses as his soul (in the form of a cloud-wrapped body) is commended to Christ. But El Greco (1541–1614) painted during a period of social, political, and religious turmoil, when medieval assumptions about the unity of the Christian world and the nature of salvation were being challenged by religious reformers and their political supporters.

If we look more closely at the painting, we can see what Catholic Christians wished to emphasize. The two figures are Saint Stephen, the first Christian martyr, and Saint Augustine, perhaps the most important of the early Church Fathers. They represent the continuity of the Christian tradition. But just as important is the heavenly hierarchy of saints and angels reaching from the count upward to Christ. At the very top are Saint John and Saint Mary, who are interceding with Christ for the count's soul. The hierarchy of saints and intercessors so vividly painted by El Greco represents one of the clearest differences between the two contending visions of Christian life and society. Most reformers rejected the idea that salvation depended on the intervention of others, no matter how saintly. Salvation was a simpler process. The hierarchy of saints and angels depicted by El Greco seemed unnecessary.

The crisis of the Reformation began with a challenge to the religious authority of the papacy. Debates over the power and status of the church that raged during this period, however, did not occur in a political vacuum. Support for the old church was an issue of state that profoundly affected the exercise of political authority in the Holy Roman Empire. In England and Scandinavia, by contrast, monarchs viewed the church as a threat to strong royal government, and reformers soon found themselves with royal patrons. Elsewhere, especially in eastern Europe, no strong central governments existed to enforce religious unity, and so a variety of Christian traditions coexisted.

By the second half of the sixteenth century, political and religious leaders concentrated their energies on a process of theological definition and institutionalization that led to the formation of the major Christian religious denominations we know today. They created Roman Catholic, Anglican, Reformed (Calvinist), and Lutheran churches as clearly defined confessions, with formally prescribed religious beliefs and practices.

An important aspect of the reform movement was the emphasis on individual belief and religious participation. Far from freeing the individual, however, the Christian churches of the late sixteenth century all emphasized correct doctrine and orderliness in personal

FOCUS QUESTIONS

- Why did the reformers feel it was necessary to establish entirely new churches outside the Roman Catholic Church?

- What political factors limited Charles V's ability to respond to the religious crisis?

- Why did the English monarchs take the lead in efforts to reform the English church?

- How did ideas of church reform influence social and political developments in the rest of Europe?

- How did Catholic and Protestant Christians differ from each other by the end of the Reformation?

 This icon will direct you to additional materials on the website: www.cengage.com/history/noble/westciv6e.

 See our interactive eBook for map and primary source activities.

behavior. Although early Protestants rejected a system that they accused of oppressing the individual, the institutions that replaced the old church developed their own traditions of control. The increased moral discipline advocated by churches accompanied and even fostered the expansion of state power that would characterize the late sixteenth and seventeenth centuries.

THE REFORMATION MOVEMENTS, CA. 1517–1545

Why did the reformers feel it was necessary to establish entirely new churches outside the Roman Catholic Church?

Martin Luther   German theologian and religious reformer who began the Protestant Reformation in 1517 by questioning, and finally discarding, Catholic teaching about penance and salvation.

In 1517, **Martin Luther**, a little-known professor of theology in eastern Germany, launched a protest against practices in the late medieval church. Luther's criticisms struck a responsive chord with many of his contemporaries and led to calls for reform across much of Europe. All the reformers, even the most radical, shared with Luther a sense that the essential sacramental and priestly powers claimed by the late medieval church were illegitimate. These reformers initially had no intention of forming a new church; they simply wanted to return Christianity to what they believed was its earlier, purer form. Although their various protests resulted in the creation of separate and well-defined religious traditions, the differences among the reformers became clear only in the second half of the sixteenth century. Thus, it is appropriate to speak of "Reformation movements" rather than a unified Protestant Reformation.

The Late Medieval Context

In the flourishing religious life of the late Middle Ages, questions of an individual's salvation and personal relationship to God and to the Christian community remained at the heart of religious practice and theological speculation. Christians believed in a holy covenant in which God would save those who, by means of the church's sacraments and through penitential and charitable acts, were partners in their own salvation. Foremost among the penitential acts was the feeding of "Christ's Poor," especially on important feast days. The pious constructed and supported hospices for travelers and hospitals for the sick. Christians went on pilgrimages to shrines, such as the tomb of Saint Thomas Becket in Canterbury or the Church of Saint James of Compostela in Spain. They also endowed chapels, called chantry chapels, where prayers would be offered for their own souls. To moralists, work itself was, in some sense, a penitential and ennobling act.

POPULAR RELIGION   The most common religious practice of the late Middle Ages was participation in religious brotherhoods. Urban brotherhoods were usually organized around a craft guild or neighborhood; rural brotherhoods were more likely to include an entire village or parish. Members vowed to attend monthly meetings, to participate in processions on feast days, and to maintain peaceful and charitable relations with fellow members.

The most typical religious feast was that of *Corpus Christi* (the "Body of Christ"). The feast celebrated and venerated the sacrament of the mass and the ritual by which the bread offered to the laity became the actual body of Christ. Corpus Christi was popular with the church hierarchy because it emphasized the role of the priest in the central ritual of Christianity. The laity, however, equated Corpus Christi with the body of citizens who made up the civic community. Thus, religious identity seemed to be at the very heart of social identity. The most revered saint in the late Middle Ages, however, was the Virgin Mary, the mother of Jesus. The most popular new pilgrimage shrines in the north of Europe were dedicated to the Virgin. It was she, townspeople believed, who protected them from invasion, plague, and natural disasters. In such a society, it was impossible to distinguish between religion and society, church and state.

WOMEN AND RELIGION   Women played a prominent role in late medieval religious life. Holy women who claimed any sort of moral standing often did so because of visions or prophetic gifts, such as knowledge of future events or discernment of the status of souls in Purgatory. The Italian Blessed Angela of Foligno (fo-LIN-yo) (ca. 1248–1309) had several visions and became the object of a large circle of devoted followers. She was typical of a number of late medieval religious women who, on the death of a spouse, turned to religion. They tended to gather "families" around them, people whom they described as their spiritual "fathers" or "children." They offered moral counsel and boldly warned businessmen and politicians of the dangers of lying and sharp dealings.

In the late Middle Ages, religious houses for women probably outnumbered those for men. For unmarried or unmarriageable (because of poverty or disabilities) daughters, convents provided an economical, safe, and controlled environment. Moralists denounced the dumping of women in convents: "They give [unmarriageable daughters] to a convent, as if they were the scum and vomit of the world," Saint Bernardino of Siena (1380–1444) complained. The general public, however, believed that well-run communities of religious women promoted the spiritual and physical health of the general community. In a society in which women were not allowed to control their own property and, except among the nobility, lacked a visible role in political and intellectual life, a religious vocation may have had a compelling appeal. At the least, it permitted women to define their own religious and social relationships. Well-to-do or aristocratic parents also appreciated the fact that the traditional gift that accompanied a daughter entering a religious house was much smaller than a dowry.

Some women declined to join convents, which required vows of chastity and obedience to a Rule and close male supervision. They could be found among the many pilgrims who visited local shrines, the great churches of Rome, or even the holy city of Jerusalem. Many other women chose to live as anchoresses, or recluses, in closed cells beside churches and hospitals or in rooms in private homes. Men and women traveled from all parts of England seeking the counsel of the Blessed Julian of Norwich (d. after 1413), who lived in a tiny cell built into the wall of a parish church. The most controversial group of religious women was the Beguines, who lived in communities without taking formal vows and often with minimal connections to the local church hierarchy. By the early fifteenth century, Beguines were suspect because clerics believed that these independent women rejected traditional religious cloistering and the moral leadership of male clergy; consequently, it was thought, they were particularly susceptible to heresy.

A more conservative movement for renewal in the church was the Brothers and Sisters of the Common Life, founded by the Dutchman Geert Groote (HIRT HROW-ta) (1340–1384). A popular preacher and reformer, Groote gathered male and female followers into quasi-monastic communities at Deventer in the Low Countries. Members followed a strict, conservative spirituality that has come to be known as the *devotio moderna*, or "modern devotion." Although they called themselves "modern," their piety was traditional. They advocated the contrary ideals of fourteenth-century religious life: broader participation by the laity and strict control by clerical authorities.

Religious life in the late medieval period was broadly based and vigorous. Theologians, laypeople, and popular preachers could take heart that they were furthering their own salvation and that of their neighbors. Thus, the Reformation of the sixteenth century involved more than simple moral reform.

CHRONOLOGY

1513–1517	Fifth Lateran Council meets to consider reform of the Catholic Church
1517	Luther makes public his "Ninety-five Theses"
1518	Zwingli is appointed people's priest of Zurich
1520	Pope Leo X condemns Luther's teachings
1521	Luther appears at the Diet of Worms
1524–1525	Peasant revolts in Germany
1527	Imperial troops sack Rome
1530	Melanchthon composes the Augsburg Confession summarizing Lutheran belief
1534	Calvin flees Paris Loyola founds the Society of Jesus
1535	Anabaptist community of Münster is destroyed
1536	Calvin arrives in Geneva and publishes *Institutes of the Christian Religion*
1545–1563	Council of Trent meets to reform Catholic Church
1555	Emperor Charles V accepts the Peace of Augsburg
1559	Parliament passes Elizabethan Act of Supremacy and Act of Uniformity

Martin Luther and the New Theology

Martin Luther (1483–1546) eventually challenged many of the assumptions of late medieval Christians. He seemed to burst onto the scene in 1517, when he objected to the way in which papal indulgences—that is, the remission of penalties owed for sins—were being bought and sold in the archbishopric of Magdeburg. Luther's father, a miner from the small town of Mansfeld,

Crowning with Thorns   Late medieval Christians meditated on Christ's sufferings and preferred images like this one, painted by Jörg Breu, that shows a tortured Christ living in their own time.
(Courtesy, Augustiner Chorherrenstift, Herzogenburg. Photo: Fotostudio Wurst Erich)

had hoped that his son would take a degree in law and become a wealthy and prestigious lawyer. Luther chose instead to enter a monastery and eventually become a priest.

JUSTIFICATION BY FAITH

justification by faith
Luther's doctrine that Christians can be saved only by grace, a free gift of God and independent of any penitential or charitable acts.

Luther recalled having been troubled throughout his life by a sense of his own sinfulness and unworthiness. According to late medieval theology, the life of a Christian was a continuing cycle of sin, confession, contrition, and penance. Luther came to believe that the church's requirement that believers achieve salvation by means of confession, contrition, and penance made too great a demand on the faithful. Instead, Luther said, citing the New Testament, salvation (or justification) was God's gift to the faithful. Luther's belief is known as **justification by faith**. Acts of charity were important products resulting from God's love, but in Luther's opinion, they were not necessary for salvation. In Luther's theology, the acts of piety so typical of the medieval church were quite unnecessary for salvation because Christ's sacrifice had brought justification once and for all. Justification came entirely from God and was independent of human works.

Luther also attacked the place of the priesthood in the sacramental life of the church and, by extension, the power and authority a church might claim in public life. Priests, in Luther's view, were not mediators between God and individual Christians. John Wyclif and Jan Hus (see page 293) had argued against the spiritual authority of unworthy priests. Luther, however, challenged the role of all clergy, and of the institutional church itself, in the attainment of salvation. Thus, he argued for a "priesthood of all believers."

CONTROVERSY OVER INDULGENCES

In the years before 1517, Luther's views on salvation and his reservations about the traditional ways of teaching theology attracted little interest outside his own university. Matters changed, however, when he questioned the sale of indulgences, rewards for pilgrimages or for noteworthy acts of charity or sacrifice. The papacy frequently authorized the sale of indulgences to pay various expenses. Unscrupulous priests often left the impression that purchase of an indulgence freed a soul from Purgatory. After getting no response to his initial complaints, Luther posted his "Ninety-five Theses" on the door of the Wittenberg Castle church, the usual way to announce topics for theological debates. His text created a firestorm, when it was quickly translated and printed throughout German-speaking lands. His charges against the sale of indulgences encapsulated German feelings about unworthy priests and economic abuses by the clergy. Luther was acclaimed as the spokesman of the German people. (See the feature, "The Written Record: Martin Luther's Address to the Christian Nobility of the German Nation.")

Responding to the crisis in Germany, Pope Leo X (r. 1513–1521) condemned Luther's teachings in 1520 and gave him sixty days to recant. Luther refused to do so and publicly burned the papal letter. In 1521, Emperor **Charles V** called an imperial diet, or parliament, at Worms to deal with the religious crisis. Charles demanded that Luther submit to papal authority. Luther, however, countered that religious decisions must be based on personal experience and conscience informed by a study of Scripture. Luther's refusal became a ringing statement conscience, when a later editor added the famous, "Here I stand. I can do no other, may God help me."

The emperor and his allies stayed firmly in the papal camp, and the excommunicated Luther was placed under an imperial ban—that is, declared an outlaw. As Luther left the Diet of Worms, friendly princes took him to Wartburg Castle in Saxony, where they could protect him. During a year of isolation at Wartburg, Luther used Erasmus's edition of the Greek New Testament as the basis of a translation of the New Testament into German, which became an influential literary as well as religious work.

Charles V   Holy Roman emperor and King Charles I of Spain. His empire included Spain, Italy, the Low Countries, Germany, and the New World.

The Reformation of the Communities

Luther challenged the authority of the clerical hierarchy and called on laypeople to take responsibility for their own salvation. His ideas spread rapidly in the towns and countryside of Germany because he and his followers took advantage of the new technology of printing. (See the feature, "The Visual Record: A Reformation Woodcut.") Perhaps 300,000 copies of his early tracts were published in the first years of the protest. Luther's claim that the Scriptures must be the basis of all life and his appeal to the judgment of the laity made sense to the men and women in towns and villages, where councils of local people were accustomed to making decisions based on ideas of the common good.

The impact of Luther's ideas quickly became evident. If the active intercession of the clergy was not necessary for the salvation of individuals, then, according to Luther's followers, there was no reason for the clergy to remain unmarried and celibate, nor for men and women to cloister themselves in monasteries and convents. Because Luther's followers believed that penitential acts were not prerequisites for salvation, they tended to set aside the veneration of saints and give up pilgrimages to the shrines and holy places all over Europe.

Many historians have referred to the spread of these reform ideas as the "Reformation of the Common Man." Where Luther's own reform was individual and doctrinal, the reformation in towns and villages was led by the people and contained a strong communal sense. The message seems to have spread especially quickly among artisan and mercantile groups, which put pressure on town governments to press for reform. Agitation was often riotous. One resident of Augsburg exposed himself during a church service to protest what he believed was an evil and idolatrous service. Women on both sides of the reform stepped away from traditional ideas about male and female roles. One reformer demanded to be judged "not according to the standards of a woman, but according to the standards of one . . . filled with the Holy Sprit."[1] Women, like Katherine Zell of Strasbourg, who married a former priest dedicated their lives to the social and moral work of community reform. They became strong moral voices in the turbulent struggles in their communities. Other women wrote tracts advocating reform or defending the old order, and still others used shovels and rakes to defend religious values.

The process of reform in Zurich is instructive. **Huldrych Zwingli** (SVING-lee) (1484–1531), son of a rural official, received a university education and became a typical late medieval country priest, right down to his publicly acknowledged mistress. Yet, after experiences as a military chaplain and an acquaintance with the humanist writings of Erasmus, Zwingli began to preach

Huldrych Zwingli   Town preacher of Zurich and leading reformer in Switzerland and southwest Germany. He emphasized the role of the godly community in the process of individual salvation.

Martin Luther's Address to the Christian Nobility of the German Nation

Luther wrote this tract to the rulers of Germany to explain the nature of his conflict with the church over ecclesiastical authority. In this excerpt, he outlines his disagreements with the system of clerical status and immunities that had grown throughout the Middle Ages.

The Romanists have very cleverly built three walls around themselves. In the first place, when pressed by the temporal power, they have made decrees and declared that the temporal power had no jurisdiction over them, but that on the contrary, the spiritual power is above the temporal. In the second place, when the attempt is made to reprove them with the Scriptures, they raise the objection that only the Pope may interpret the Scriptures. In the third place if threatened with a council, their story is that no one may summon a council but the Pope.

Let us begin by attacking the first wall. It is pure invention that the Pope, bishops, priests, and monks are called the spiritual estate while princes, lords, craftsmen, and peasants are the temporal estate. This is indeed a piece of deceit and hypocrisy: all Christians are truly of the spiritual estate. The Pope or bishop anoints, shaves heads, ordains, consecrates, and prescribes garb different from that of the laity, but he can never make a man into a Christian or into a spiritual man by so doing. He might well make a man into a hypocrite or a humbug and a blockhead, but never a Christian or a spiritual man. Therefore a priest in Christendom is nothing else but an officeholder. As long as he holds his office, he takes precedence; where he is deposed, he is a peasant or a townsman like anybody else.

The second wall is still more loosely built and less substantial. The Romanists want to be the only masters of Holy Scripture, although they never learn a thing from the Bible their life long. Besides, if we are all priests, and all have one faith, one gospel, one sacrament, why should we not also have the power to test and judge what is right or wrong in matters of faith?

The third wall falls of itself, when the first two are down. When the Pope acts contrary to the Scriptures, it is our duty to stand by the Scriptures and to reprove him and to constrain him, according to the word of Christ. The Romanists have no basis in Scripture for their claim that the Pope alone has the right to call or to confirm a council. This is just their own ruling, and it is only valid so long as it is not harmful to Christendom or contrary to the laws of God.

QUESTIONS

1. What are the ideas that Luther claims the papacy uses to protect itself from criticism?

2. Under what conditions does Luther allow that church authorities may make rules?

Source: Martin Luther, "Three Treatises," in *The American Edition of Luther's Works* (Philadelphia: Fortress Press, 1970), pp. 10–22. Copyright © 1943 Muhlenberg Press. Used by permission of Augsburg Fortress.

strongly biblical sermons. In 1522, he defended a group of laymen in Zurich, who protested by breaking the required Lenten fast. Later in the same year, he requested episcopal permission to marry. Early in 1523, he led a group of reformers in a public debate over the nature of the church. The city council declared in favor of the reformers, and Zurich became in effect a Protestant city.

Unlike Luther, Zwingli believed that reform should be a communal movement—that town governments should take the lead in bringing reform to the community. Zwingli explained that the moral regeneration of individuals was an essential part of God's salvation. In the years following 1523, the reformers restructured church services, abolishing the mass. They also removed religious images from churches and suppressed monastic institutions.

The reform message spread from towns into the countryside, but often with effects that the reformers did not expect or desire. Luther thought his message was a spiritual and theological one. Many peasants and modest artisans, however, believed that Luther's message of biblical freedom carried material, as well as theological, meaning.

In many parts of Germany, landlords and local governments had increased their claims for rents and services from villagers and peasants. Their tenants and subjects, however, argued that new tithes and taxes not only upset tradition, but violated the Word of God. Their demands that landlords and magistrates give up human ordinances and follow "Godly Law" soon turned violent. Peasants, miners, and villagers in 1524 and 1525 participated in a series of uprisings that began on the borderlands between Switzerland and Germany and spread throughout southwestern Germany, upper Austria, and even northern Italy. Bands of peasants and villagers, perhaps a total of 300,000 in the empire, revolted against their seigneurial lords or even their territorial overlords.

Luther initially counseled landlords and princes to redress the just grievances. As reports of riots and increased violence continued to reach Wittenberg, however, Luther condemned the rebels as "mad dogs" and urged that they be suppressed. Territorial princes and large cities quickly raised armies to meet the threat. The peasants were defeated and destroyed in a series of battles in April 1525. A townsman of Zurich noted the result, "Many came to a great hatred of the preachers, where before they would have bitten off their feet for the Gospel."[2]

John Calvin and the Reformed Tradition

The revolts of 1524 and 1525 demonstrated the mixed messages traveling under the rubric "true" or "biblical" religion. In the 1530s, the theological arguments of the reformers began to take on a greater clarity, mostly because of the Franco-Swiss reformer **John Calvin** (1509–1564). Calvin received a humanistic education in Paris and became a lawyer before coming under the influence of reform-minded thinkers in France. In 1534, he fled from Paris, as royal pressures against reformers increased. He arrived in Geneva in 1536, where he would remain, except for a short exile, until the end of his life.

The heart of Calvin's appeal lay in his formal theological writings. In 1536, he published the first of many editions of the *Institutes of the Christian Religion*, which was to become the summa of Reformed theology. Here he outlined his understanding of how only some were predestined to salvation. And, he added, there were ways to tell who was and who was not to be saved.

Like Luther, Calvin viewed salvation as a mysterious gift from God. Yet, Calvin differed from Luther in a crucial aspect. Salvation was by grace, but it was part of progressive sanctification. This was a critical difference, for Luther did not believe that human behavior could be transformed. We are, he said, "simultaneously justified and sinners." By contrast, Calvin believed that there could be no salvation "if we do not also live a holy life." Thus, the religious behavior of the individual and the community was evidence of justification. As a result, Calvin believed that it was the church's duty to promote moral progress. Public officials were to be "vicars of God." They had the power to lead and correct both the faithful and the unregenerate sinners who lived in Christian communities. In his years in Geneva, Calvin tried to create a "Christian Commonwealth," but Geneva was far from a theocracy.

Elders—the true leaders of the Genevan church—were selected from the patriciate who dominated the civil government of the city. Thus, it makes as much sense to speak of a church

John Calvin A Franco-Swiss theologian whose *Institutes of the Christian Religion* was the key text of Reformed theology. He stressed the absolute power of God.

Iconoclasm Calvinists believed that Christians had to live in communities in which "true religion" was practiced. Iconoclasts (image smashers) cleansed churches of all paintings and statuary that might lead people back to the worship of idols—that is, the medieval cult of saints. This illustration shows just how organized iconoclasm really was. (Calvinists destroying statues in the Catholic Churches, 1566 (engraving), Flemish School, (16th century)/Private Collection/ The Bridgeman Art Library)

A Reformation Woodcut

Erhard Schön's 1533 woodcut, "There Is No Greater Treasure Here on Earth Than an Obedient Wife Who Desires Honor," and other broadsheets like it, informed and amused Europeans of all walks of life in the late fifteenth and sixteenth centuries. Schön's image of a henpecked husband and his wife followed by others would have been instantly recognizable to most people. Accompanying texts clarified the message implied in the woodcut itself. But how may we, centuries later, "read" this message? How does the modern historian analyze Schön's broadsheet to investigate popular ideas about social roles, religion, and politics? What do this and similar broadsheets tell us about popular responses to the social and religious tumults of the sixteenth century?

Look at the simple and clear lines of the woodcut. They give a clue about the popularity of broadsheets. They were cheap and easy to produce and were printed on inexpensive paper. Artists would sketch an image that an artisan would later carve onto a block. A printer could produce a thousand or more copies from a single block. Even famous artists, such as Albrecht Dürer (see pages 334–335), sold highly profitable prints on religious, political, and cultural themes.

Almost anyone could afford broadsheets. Laborers and modest merchants decorated their houses with pictures on popular themes. In the middle of the fifteenth century, before the Reformation, most images were of saints. It was widely believed, for example, that anyone who looked at an image of Saint Christopher would not die on that day.

During the political and religious unrest of the sixteenth century, artists increasingly produced images that referred to the debates over religion. Schön himself made his living in Nuremberg producing and selling woodcuts. He and other artists in the city were closely tuned to the attitudes of the local population. One popular image was titled "The Roman Clergy's Procession into Hell."

Schön's "Obedient Wife" reflects a fear shared by both Protestants and Catholics: the rebellious nature of women. Evidence suggests that women in the late fifteenth and sixteenth centuries may have been marrying at a later age and thus were likely to be more independent-minded than their younger sisters. The ranks of single women were swollen by widows and by former nuns who had left convents and liberated themselves from male supervision. Thus, it was not difficult for men in the sixteenth century to spot women who seemed dangerously free from male control.

Let us turn again to the woodcut, to see what worried villagers and townspeople and how Schön depicted their fears. Notice the henpecked husband. He is harnessed to a cart carrying laundry. Both the harness and the laundry were popular images associated with women's duties. During popular festivals, German villagers often harnessed unmarried women to a plow to signify that they were shirking their duty by not marrying and raising children. Doing the laundry was popularly thought to be the first household chore that a powerful wife would force on her weak-kneed husband. Countless other images show women, whip in hand, supervising foolish husbands as they pound diapers with a laundry flail. "Woe is me," says the poor man, all this because "I took a wife." As if the message were not clear enough, look at what the woman carries in her left hand: his purse, his sword, and his pants. (The question "Who wears the pants in the family?" was as familiar then as it is now.) But the woman responds that he is in this position not because of marriage but because he has been carousing: "If you will not work to support me, then you must wash, spin, and draw the cart."*

The figures following the cart are commenting on the situation. The young journeyman is asking the maiden at his side, "What do you say about this?" She responds coyly, "I have no desire for such power." The woman dressed as a fool counsels the young man never to marry and thus to avoid anxiety and suffering. But an old man, identified as "the wise man," closes the procession and ends the debate. "Do not listen to this foolish woman," he counsels. "God determines how your life together will be, so stay with her in love and suffering and always be patient."

If we think about this woodcut's images and text, we can understand the contrary hopes and fears in sixteenth-century Germany. Like the young woman, the Christian wife was expected to eschew power either inside or outside the home. Martin Luther concluded that "the

governed by the town as a town dominated by the church. The elders actively intervened in education, charity, and attempts to regulate prostitution. Consistories, or church courts, made up of preachers and community elders who enforced moral and religious values, became one of the most important characteristics of Reformed (Calvinist) communities.

Reformed churchmen reacted promptly and harshly to events that seemed to threaten their vision of the Christian community. The most famous episode involved the capture, trial, and execution of Michael Servetus (1511–1553), a Spanish physician and radical theologian who rejected traditional doctrines such as the Trinity and specifically criticized many of Calvin's teachings in the *Institutes*. After corresponding with Servetus for a time, Calvin remarked that

"There Is No Greater Treasure Here on Earth Than an Obedient Wife Who Desires Honor,"
Erhard Schön   (Schlossmuseum, Gotha)

husband is the head of the wife even as Christ is head of the Church. Therefore as the Church is subject to Christ, so let wives be subject to their husbands in everything" (Ephesians 5:23–24). Authority was to be in the hands of husbands and fathers. But if the good wife was required to avoid power, the good husband was expected to follow Luther's precepts for the Christian family. As the wise old man observes, the husband must be a loving and forgiving master.

Schön's woodcut and others similar to it should remind you of the "argument over women" discussed in Chapter 12 (see 338–339). The words of the wise man and the young maid bring to mind Christine de Pizan's *Book of the City of the Ladies* when they urge love and understanding, but their hopefulness is undercut by the power and immediacy of the image. As the broadsheet clearly demonstrates,

suspicion of women characterized even the most simple literature of Reformation Europe.

QUESTIONS

1. What conclusion might a viewer draw about women from thinking about the three women pictured in this woodcut?

2. How does the image of the godly marriage differ in this woodcut and the picture of the holy household (see page 405)?

*Keith Moxey, *Peasants, Warriors and Wives: Popular Imagery in the Reformation* (Chicago: University of Chicago Press, 1989), pp. 108–109; includes a translation of portions of the text in the broadsheet.

if Servetus were in Geneva, "I would not suffer him to get out alive." After living in various parts of Europe, Servetus eventually did come anonymously to Geneva. He was recognized and arrested. Calvin was as good as his word. After a public debate and trial, Servetus was burned at the stake for blaspheming the Trinity and the Christian religion. Calvin's condemnation of Servetus was all too typical of Christians in the sixteenth century. Lutherans, Calvinists, and Catholics all believed that protection of true religion required harsh measures against the ignorant, the immoral, and the unorthodox. All too few would have agreed with the humanist reformer Sebastian Castellio that "To burn a heretic is not to defend a doctrine, but to burn a man."[3]

The Radical Reform of the Anabaptists

Anabaptists Radical reformers in Germany and Switzerland who emphasized that baptism should only be of adults and that Christians should separate themselves into communities of the "truly redeemed."

Michael Servetus was but one of a number who felt Luther, Zwingli, and Calvin had not gone far enough. Called **Anabaptists** (or "rebaptizers" because of their rejection of infant baptism) or simply "radicals," they tended to take biblical commands more literally than the mainline reformers. More interested in behavior and community standards than in learned theological arguments, they believed that only adults should be baptized, and then, only after confession of sin. In their view, Christians should live apart in communities of the truly redeemed. Thus, civil oaths or public office were a compromise with "the Abomination," that is, unreformed civil society.

Radicals, such as the revolutionaries who took control of the northern German city of Münster, rejected infant baptism, adopted polygamy, and proclaimed a new "Kingdom of Righteousness." The reformers of Münster instituted the new kingdom in the city by rebaptizing those who joined their cause and expelling those who opposed them. They abolished private property rights and instituted new laws concerning morality and behavior. Leadership in the city eventually passed to a tailor, Jan of Leiden (d. 1535), who proclaimed himself the new messiah and lord of the world. After a sixteen-month siege, the bishop of Münster and his allies recaptured the city in 1535. Besieging forces massacred men, women, and children. Jan of Leiden was captured and executed by mutilation with red-hot tongs.

In the wake of the siege of Münster, leaders, such as Menno Simons (1495–1561), who founded the Mennonites, and Jakob Hutter (d. 1536), who founded the Hutterian Brethren, or Hutterites, rejected their predecessors' violent attempts to establish truly holy cities. To varying degrees, they also rejected connections with civil society, military service, and even civil courts. They did, however, believe that their own communities were exclusively of the elect. They tended to close themselves off from outsiders and enforce a strict discipline over their members. The elders of these communities were empowered to excommunicate or "shun" those who violated the groups' precepts. Anabaptist communities have proved unusually durable. Hutterite and Mennonite communities continue to exist in western Europe, North America, and parts of the former Soviet Union.

Like Luther, all of the early reformers appealed to the authority of the Bible in their attacks on church tradition. Yet, in the villages and towns of Germany and Switzerland, many radicals were prepared to move far beyond the positions Luther had advocated. When they did so, Luther found himself in the odd position of appealing for vigorous action by the very imperial authorities whose previous inaction had allowed his own protest to survive.

SECTION SUMMARY

- Women played an important role in popular religious observance in the Middle Ages.

- Luther's religious ideas challenged the late medieval church's understanding of sin and salvation rather than immoral behavior.

- The key to Luther's theology was his emphasis on the role of grace and biblical authority.

- Calvin's religious reforms centered on the role of the Reformed community in enforcing religious discipline.

- Radical reformers and Anabaptists formed small, tightly controlled communities suspicious of the outside world.

THE EMPIRE OF CHARLES V (R. 1519–1556)

What political factors limited Charles V's ability to respond to the religious crisis?

Luther believed that secular authorities should be neutral in religious matters. In his eyes, the success of the early Reformation was simply God's will:

[W]hile I slept or drank Wittenberg beer with my friends, the Word [of God] so greatly weakened the Papacy that no prince or emperor ever inflicted such losses on it.[4]

Luther's belief in the Word of God was absolute, yet, he must have known, even as he drank his beer, that the Holy Roman emperor could have crushed the reform movements if he had been able to enforce imperial decrees. But attempts to resolve religious conflict became entangled with the need to hold together the family lands of the Habsburg emperor. The eventual religious settlement required a constitutional compromise that preserved the virtual autonomy of the great princes of Germany. Charles had dreamed of using his imperial office to restore and maintain the political and religious unity of Europe. The realities of sixteenth-century Europe, however, made nobles afraid of the emperor, even when he tried to preserve the unity of the church.

Imperial Challenges

Emperor Charles V (r. 1519–1556) was the beneficiary of a series of marriages that, in the words of his courtiers, seemed to re-create the empire of Charlemagne. From his father, Philip of Habsburg, he inherited claims to Austria, the imperial crown, and Burgundian lands that included the Low Countries and the county of Burgundy. Through his mother, Joanna, the daughter of Ferdinand and Isabella of Spain, Charles became heir to the kingdoms of Castile, Aragon, Sicily, Naples, and Spanish America (see **MAP 14.1**). By 1506, he was duke in the Burgundian lands; in 1516, he became king of Aragon and Castile; and in 1519, he was elected Holy Roman emperor. Every government in Europe had to deal with one part or another of Charles's empire. His chancellor enthused, "[God] has set you on the way towards a world monarchy, towards the gathering of all Christendom under a single shepherd."

Charles seems sincerely to have desired such a world monarchy, but he faced challenges in each of the areas under his control. Between 1517 and 1522, when religious reform was making dramatic advances in Germany, many of the most important towns of Spain were in open rebellion against the Crown. In Castile, for example, grandees, townspeople, and peasants had many complaints. But most of all, they objected that too many of his officials were foreigners whom he had brought with him from his home in Flanders. Protests festered in the towns and villages of Castile and finally broke out into a revolt called the *Comunero* (townsmen's or citizens') movement. Charles's forces eventually took control of the situation, and by 1522, he had crushed the Comuneros. However, in the critical years between 1522 and 1530, he was careful to spend much of his time in his Spanish kingdoms.

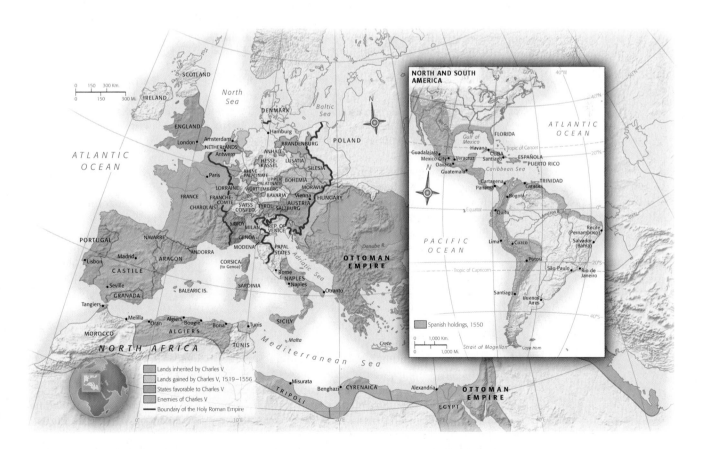

🌐 **MAP 14.1—The Global Empire of Charles V.**
Religious and political change were profoundly affected by the complexity of the empire of Charles V. German calls for reform had to be understood in the context of an immense empire.

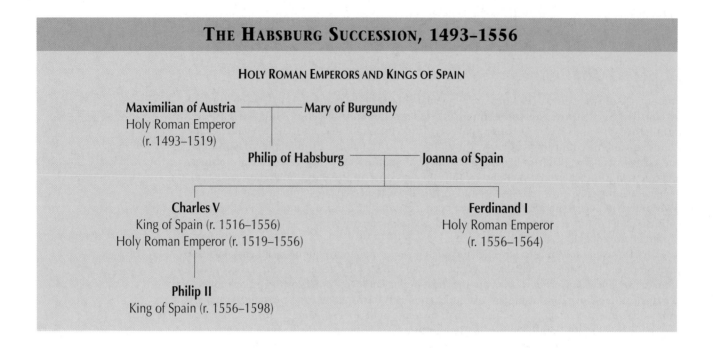

THE HABSBURG SUCCESSION, 1493–1556

HOLY ROMAN EMPERORS AND KINGS OF SPAIN

Maximilian of Austria
Holy Roman Emperor
(r. 1493–1519)
— Mary of Burgundy

Philip of Habsburg — Joanna of Spain

Charles V
King of Spain (r. 1516–1556)
Holy Roman Emperor (r. 1519–1556)

Ferdinand I
Holy Roman Emperor
(r. 1556–1564)

Philip II
King of Spain (r. 1556–1598)

Charles's claims in Italy, as well as in the Pyrenees and the Low Countries, brought him into direct conflict with the Valois kings of France. In the critical 1520s, the Habsburgs and the Valois fought a series of wars (see page 301). Charles dramatically defeated the French at Pavia in northern Italy in 1525, sacked and occupied Rome in 1527, and became the dominant power in Italian politics. The Habsburg-Valois Wars, however, dragged on until, in exhaustion, the French king Henry II (r. 1547–1559) and the Spanish king Philip II (r. 1556–1598) signed the Treaty of Cateau-Cambrésis in 1559.

Charles was not the only ruler to claim the title "emperor" and a tradition of authority reaching back to the Roman Empire. After the conquest of Constantinople in 1453, the sultan of the Ottoman Turks often referred to himself as "the Emperor." After consolidating control of Constantinople and the Balkans, Turkish armies under the command of the emperor Suleiman (r. 1520–1566), known as "the Magnificent," resumed their expansion to the north and west. After capturing Belgrade, Turkish forces soundly defeated a Hungarian army at the Battle of Mohács in 1526. Charles appealed for unity within Christendom against the threat. Even Martin Luther agreed that Christians should unite during invasion.

Suleiman's army besieged Vienna in 1529 before being forced to retreat. The Turks also deployed a navy in the Mediterranean and, with French encouragement, began a series of raids along the coasts of Italy and Spain. The Turkish fleet remained a threat throughout the sixteenth century. The reign of Suleiman marked the permanent entry of Turkey into the European military and diplomatic system. Turkish pressure was yet another reason Charles was unable to deal with German Protestants in a direct and uncompromising way. (See the feature, "The Global Record: Duels Among Europeans and Turks.")

German Politics

The political configuration of Germany had an ongoing influence on the course of religious reform. In 1500, Germany was much less centralized than France or England. Indeed, the empire lacked a unified legal system, and the emperor himself had only one vote on the imperial council. In many respects, political centralization and innovation were characteristics of individual territories, not of the empire as a whole. The power of the emperor depended on his relations with the towns and princes of Germany.

In the first years after Luther issued his "Ninety-five Theses," he was defended by the elector Frederick of Saxony, who held a key vote in Charles's quest for election as Holy Roman emperor. As long as Frederick protected Luther, imperial officials had to proceed against the reformer with caution. When Luther was outlawed by the imperial Diet of Worms in 1521, Frederick and many

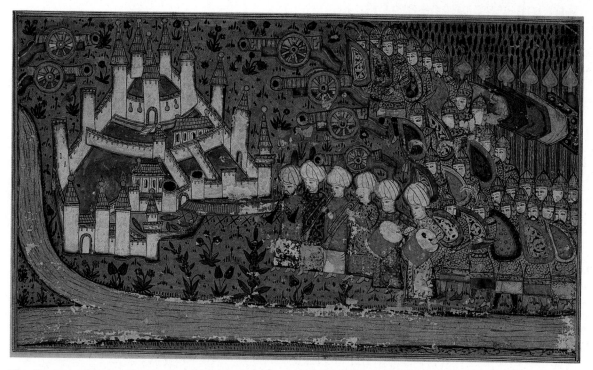

The Capture of Belgrade, 1521   During the sixteenth century, Ottoman Turks dominated the Balkans militarily and were a significant force in European diplomacy. They were masters of coordinated attacks combining artillery and infantry.   (Österreichische Nationalbibliothek)

other princes and towns refused to enforce the edict against him and his followers unless their own grievances against the emperor and their complaints about the church were taken up at the same time. At the Diet of Speyer in 1526, delegates passed a resolution empowering princes and towns to settle religious matters in their territories as they saw it. In effect, this resolution legitimated the reform in territories where authorities chose to follow the new teachings and presaged the final religious settlement in Germany.

German authorities took advantage of the emperor's relative powerlessness and made choices reflecting a complex of religious, political, and diplomatic issues. Some rulers acted in ways that were even more consciously cynical and self-serving. The grand master of the religious order of the Teutonic Knights, Albrecht von Hohenzollern (1490–1568), who controlled the duchy of Prussia, renounced his monastic vows and secularized the order's estates (that is, he transferred them from church to private ownership), which then became East Prussia, hereditary lands of the Hohenzollern family. In other territories, rulers managed to claim the properties of suppressed religious orders. In the autonomous towns, many decisions about religion were often made with one eye on the choices made by neighbors and competitors.

Some rulers found their personal reservations about Luther reinforced by their fears of popular unrest. Luther's call for decisions based on personal conscience seemed to the dukes of Bavaria, for example, to repudiate princely authority and even to provoke anarchy. In the confused and fluid situation of the 1520s and 1530s, imperial interests were never the primary issue.

The Religious Settlement

With the fading of the Turkish threat on Vienna in 1529, Charles V renewed his pressure on the German principalities at a meeting of the imperial diet at Augsburg in 1530. It was for this diet that Philipp Melanchthon (1497–1560), Luther's closest adviser, prepared the **Augsburg Confession**, which would become the basic statement of the Lutheran faith. Melanchthon hoped that the document would form the basis of compromise with Catholic powers, but that possibility was rejected out of hand by the imperial party. Charles aimed to end the reform movement and enforce bans on Luther's teachings.

Augsburg Confession
Document, written by Philipp Melanchthon, that became the most widely accepted statement of the Lutheran faith.

Duels Among Europeans and Turks

Augier Ghislain de Busbecq (1522–1592), a Flemish diplomat in the service of Ferdinand I of Austria (who became Emperor Ferdinand I after the abdication of Charles V), was twice sent to Constantinople as ambassador. Understanding the Turks and their interests was critical for the Germans as attacks by the Turks in eastern Europe prevented the empire from either suppressing the German Protestants or pressing German claims against the French. The following selection is part of a letter written from Constantinople in 1560. In it Busbecq discusses violence among the Turks. He contrasts Turkish political and individual control with the Europeans' desire for a violent defense of personal honor. Duels were an increasing problem in sixteenth-century Europe.

The mention I made a while ago of matters in the confines of Hungary, gives me occasion to tell you, what the Turks think of duels, which among Christians are accounted a singular badge of personal valor. There was one Arstambey, a sanjack [district official], who lived on the frontier of Hungary, who was very much famed as a robust person [Arsta signifies a lion in Turkish]. He was an expert with the bow; no man brandished his sword with more strength; none was more terrible to his enemy. Not far from his district there also dwelt one Ulybey, also a sanjack, who was jealous of the same praise. And this jealousy (initiated perhaps by other occasions) at length occasioned hatred and many bloody combats between them. It happened thus, Ulybey was called to Constantinople, upon what occasion I know not. When he arrived there, the Pashas [governors] had asked many questions of him in the Divan [court] concerning other matters. At last they demanded how it was that he and Arstambey came to fall out. To put his own cause in the

best light, he said that once Arstambey had laid an ambush and wounded him treacherously. Which he said Arstambey need not have done, if he would have shown himself worthy of the name he bears because Ulybey often challenged him to fight hand to hand and never refused to meet him on the field. The Pashas, taking great offense, replied, "How dare you challenge a fellow soldier to a duel? What? Was there no Christian to fight with? Do both of you eat your emperor's bread? And yet, you attempt to take one another's life? What precedent did you have for this? Don't you know that whichever of you had died, the emperor would have lost a subject?" Whereupon, by their command, he was carried off to prison where he lay pining for many months. And at last, with difficulty, he was released, but with the loss of his reputation.

It is quite different among us Christians. Our people will draw their swords many times against each other before they ever come in sight of a public enemy, and unfortunately, they count it a brave and honorable thing to do. What should one do in such a case? Vice has usurped the seat of virtue and that which is worthy of punishment is counted noble and glorious.

QUESTIONS

1. How did Turkish officials understand the significance of private violence?

2. What most distinguishes the Turkish empire from Christendom?

Source: *The Four Epistles of A.G. Busbequius Concerning His Embassy to Turkey* (London: J. Taylor & J. Wyat, 1694), pp. 196–198.

Religious reform and political resistance to imperial power, however, remained closely connected. In the religious Peace of Augsburg of 1555, the emperor formally acknowledged the principle that sovereign princes could choose the religion to be practiced in their territories— *cuius regio, eius religio* ("whose territory, his religion"). There were limits, however: Leaders had only two choices—remain under papal authority or adopt the Augsburg Confession outlined by Melanchthon. Reformed churches associated with Zwingli or Calvin were not legally recognized (see **MAP 14.2**).

Shortly after the settlement, Charles abdicated his Spanish and imperial titles. Exhausted by years of political and religious struggle, he ceded the imperial crown to his brother, Ferdinand (r. 1556–1564). He transferred his possessions in the Low Countries, Spain, Italy, and the New World to his son, Philip II (r. 1556–1598). Charles had believed his courtiers when they had compared his empire to that of the ancient Romans. He had accepted that his duty as emperor was to unite Christendom under one law and one church. But in no part of his empire did he ever command the authority that would have allowed him to unite his lands politically, let alone to reestablish religious unity. Following his abdication, Charles retired to a monastery in Spain, where he died in 1558.

SECTION SUMMARY

- Charles V united under his personal rule Germany, the Low Countries, Spain, most of Italy, and Latin America.

- Political control in the area of Charles's empire was just weak enough that Charles was never able to act effectively against Luther and his allies.

- Throughout the sixteenth century, the Ottoman Turks were a major threat to the western European powers.

- The religious Peace of Augsburg (1555) recognized the political and religious autonomy of the independent princes and towns.

🌐 **MAP 14.2—Catholics and Protestants in 1555**

At the time of the Peace of Augsburg, Christendom in western Europe was divided into three major groups. Lutheran influence was largely confined to parts of Germany and Scandinavia, while Calvinist influence was strong in Switzerland, Scotland, the Low Countries, and parts of France. Most of the West remained within the Roman Catholic Church.

THE ENGLISH REFORMATION, 1520–1603

Why did the English monarchs take the lead in efforts to reform the English church?

The Reformation in England is often called a monarchical Reformation. In contrast with Germany, where reform occurred in spite of imperial opposition, in England, the Crown instituted the reform. As in Germany, however, institutional change in the church followed from both secular issues and reform ideas. In England, an initially hostile monarch began to tolerate reform when he perceived the papacy as an unbiblical, tyrannical force blocking essential state policy. And by the middle of the sixteenth century, it was royal interest in compromise that brought a settlement that left England a curious hybrid of reformed and traditional religious practices.

Henry VIII and the Monarchical Reformation

England had close economic ties to Germany. Reformers from Wittenberg and other Protestant towns influenced English merchants from London who traded and traveled on the Continent. One reformer, William Tyndale (ca. 1494–1536), served as a bridge between the Continent and England. He had a humanistic education in classical languages and began working on an English translation of the Bible in the 1520s. Forced by the church hierarchy to flee London, he visited Luther in Wittenberg, before settling in Antwerp, where he completed his English New Testament. By 1526, copies of his translation and his religious tracts flooded England. By the 1520s, Lutheran influence was noticeable in London and Cambridge. There is still debate about just how strong this early influence was. To some extent, the ground may have been prepared for the reformers by the few surviving Lollards (see page 293), who tended to be literate and were an ideal market for Tyndale's English Bible and his numerous reformist tracts. But religious brotherhoods, lay piety, and traditional forms of penance remained an important part of religious life. If reform was to succeed, it required support from the king.

Henry VIII (r. 1509–1547) began his reign as a popular and powerful king. Handsome, athletic, and artistic, he seemed to be the ideal ruler. At first, he was quite hostile to Luther's reform ideas. He wrote *Defense of the Seven Sacraments*, which earned him the title "Defender of the Faith" from a grateful Pope Leo X. Throughout his life, Henry remained suspicious of many Protestant ideas, but he led the initial phase of the break with the papacy because of his political problems with the highly orthodox Holy Roman emperor Charles V. The first phase of the English Reformation was thus monarchical.

Henry VII had initiated closer relations with Spain when he married his eldest son, Arthur, Prince of Wales, to Ferdinand of Aragon's daughter, Catherine. After Arthur's death, the future Henry VIII was married to his brother's widow in 1509. **Henry VIII** later tried to further the Anglo-imperial alliance when he arranged a treaty by which the emperor Charles V, who was Catherine of Aragon's nephew, agreed to marry Henry's daughter, Mary Tudor. But by the late 1520s, the Anglo-imperial alliance fell apart when Charles, responding to Spanish pressures, renounced the proposed marriage and instead married a Portuguese princess.

Henry VIII King of England who broke with the church over the issue of his divorce. In the end, Henry claimed that, as king, he was the head of the Church in England.

DIVORCE

Henry's relations with Charles were further hampered by what the English called "the King's Great Matter"—that is, his determination to divorce Catherine. Recalling the unrest of the Wars of the Roses (see page 311), Henry believed that he needed a son to ensure that the Tudors could maintain control of the English crown. By 1527, Henry and Catherine had a daughter, Mary, but no living sons. Henry became convinced that he remained without a male heir because, by biblical standards, he had committed incest by marrying his brother's widow. As Leviticus 20:21 says, "If a man takes his brother's wife, it is impurity; they shall remain childless." Henry desired an annulment. Unfortunately for him, Leo X's successor, Pope Clement VII (r. 1523–1534), was a virtual prisoner of imperial troops who had recently sacked Rome and taken control of most of Italy. As long as Charles supported Catherine of Aragon and his forces occupied Rome, a papal annulment was out of the question.

The king's advisers quickly divided into two camps. Sir Thomas More, humanist writer (see pages 342–343), royal chancellor and staunch Catholic, urged the king to continue his policy of negotiation with the papacy and his efforts to destroy the growing Protestant party. Until his resignation in 1532, More led royal authorities in a vigorous campaign against the dissemination of the newly translated Tyndale Bible and against the spread of Protestant ideas. More was opposed and eventually ousted by a radical party of Protestants led by Thomas Cranmer (1489–1556) and Thomas Cromwell (1485?–1540), who saw in the king's desire for a divorce an effective wedge to pry Henry out of the papal camp. Cromwell, who eventually replaced More as chancellor, advised the king that the marriage problem could be solved by the English clergy without papal interference.

MONARCHICAL REFORMATION

Act of Supremacy Act of the English Parliament, during the Protestant Reformation, that finalized the break with the Catholic Church by declaring the king to be head of the Church of England. Henry VIII required a public oath supporting the act, which Sir Thomas More refused to take; More was then executed for treason.

Between 1532 and 1535, Henry and Parliament took a number of steps that effectively left the king in control of the church in England. In 1533, Parliament ruled that appeals of cases concerning wills, marriages, and ecclesiastical grants had to be heard in England. In May, an English court annulled the king's marriage to Catherine. Four months later, Henry's new queen, Anne Boleyn, gave birth to a daughter, Elizabeth.

After the split, the king began to seize church properties. Parliamentary action culminated in the passage of the **Act of Supremacy** in 1534, which declared the king to be "the Protector and only Supreme Head of the Church and the Clergy of England." Henry meant to enforce his control by requiring a public oath supporting the act. Sir Thomas More refused to take the oath and was arrested, tried, and executed for treason.

Cromwell and Cranmer had hoped to use "the King's Great Matter" as a way to begin a Lutheran-style reform of the church. But, Henry remained suspicious of religious change. Between 1534 and Henry's death in 1547, neither the Protestant nor the Catholic party was able

Reform of the Old Church   This woodcut shows the Protestant understanding of the reforms of Edward VI, the removal of Catholic paraphernalia, and Edward's patronage of the Bible and Holy Communion.   (Courtesy, Brown University Library)

The Ninth Booke containing the Actes and thinges done in the Reigne of King Edward the sixt.

to gain the upper hand at court or at Canterbury. Substantive changes in the English church would be made by Henry's children.

Reform and Counter-Reform Under Edward and Mary

Prince Edward, Henry's only surviving son in 1547, was born to Henry's third wife, Jane Seymour. He was only 10 years old when his father died. By chance, Edward Seymour, who was Prince Edward's uncle, and the Protestant faction were in favor at the time of Henry's death. Seymour was named duke of Somerset and Lord Protector of the young King Edward VI (r. 1547–1553). Under Somerset, the Protestants were able to make significant changes in religious life in England. Edward completed the "dissolution of the monasteries"—the process of confiscating properties belonging to chapels and shrines—that his father had begun. In an act of great symbolic meaning, priests were legally allowed to marry. Finally, Archbishop Cranmer introduced the first edition of the English *Book of Common Prayer* in 1549. The publication updated some late medieval English prayers and combined them with liturgical and theological ideas taken from Luther, Zwingli, and Calvin. In its beautifully expressive English, it provided the laity with a primer on how to combine English religious traditions with reform theology. If Edward had not died of tuberculosis in 1553, England's reform would have looked very much like the movement in Switzerland and southern Germany.

Protestant reformers attempted to prevent Mary Tudor (r. 1553–1558), Henry's Catholic daughter, from claiming the throne, but Mary and the Catholic party quickly took control of the court and the church. Mary immediately declared previous reform decrees to be void. Cardinal Reginald Pole (1500–1558), who had advocated reform within the Catholic Church, became the center of the Catholic restoration party in Mary's England. Pole rooted out Protestants within the church. More than eight hundred gentlemen, clerics, and students fled England for Protestant havens on the Continent. Some officials, including Cranmer, chose to remain and paid with their lives. In all, three hundred Protestants, mostly artisans and laborers, were tried and executed by church courts, earning the queen her nickname, "Bloody Mary."

The policies of the queen brought about an abrupt change in official policy. Many parishes quickly and easily returned to traditional Roman religious practices. Statues were removed from hiding and restored to places of honor in churches and chapels. In many others, there was an uneasy amalgam of traditional and reformed. Although conclusive evidence is lacking, the queen's initial successes may indicate that the Reformation was not broadly supported by the people. In fact, a Catholic reform led by Mary might have succeeded had the queen not died after little more than six years on the throne. At her death, the issue of the reform in England was far from certain.

SECTION SUMMARY

- England's Reformation was monarchical because it was shaped and directed by the cultural and political needs and attitudes of the monarchs.

- Cranmer's *Book of Common Prayer* organized and introduced into England the ideas of the continental Reformation.

- Queen Mary might have succeeded in restoring much of traditional church practice had she not died after just a short reign.

FRANCE, SCANDINAVIA, AND EASTERN EUROPE, 1523–1560

How did ideas of church reform influence social and political developments in the rest of Europe?

In England and in the empire of Charles V, the success of the new religious reforms depended greatly on the political situation. It would be naive to conclude, as Luther claimed, that "the Word did everything." Yet, this complex religious reform movement cannot be reduced to the politics of kings and princes. The issues will be clearer if we survey politics and reform in the rest of Europe, noting whether and to what extent the new ideas took root (see **Map 14.2**). In France, for example, the widespread, popular support of the old religion limited the options of the country's political leaders. Similarly, in northern Europe, religious reform was an issue of both popular feeling and royal politics.

France

Luther's work, and later the ideas of the urban reformers of southwestern Germany and Switzerland, passed quickly into France. Geneva is in a French-speaking area, close to the French border. Perhaps because of France's proximity to the Calvinists in French-speaking Switzerland or because of the clarity and power of Calvin's *Institutes*, French Protestants, known as Huguenots, were tied more closely to the Calvinists of Geneva than to the Lutherans of Germany.

At the height of the Reformation's popularity, Protestants probably represented no more than 10 percent of the total population of France. Protestants seem to have comprised a diverse mix that included two of the three most important noble families at court: the Bourbon and Montmorency families. Clerics interested in moral reform and artisans who worked at new trades, such as the printing industry, also made up a significant portion of the converts. Perhaps reflecting the numerous printers and merchants in their numbers, Protestants tended to be of higher than average literacy. They were particularly well represented in towns and probably constituted a majority in the southern and western towns of La Rochelle, Montpellier, and Nîmes. Paris was the one part of the realm in which they had little influence, and this may have been their undoing.

The conservative theologians of the Sorbonne in Paris were some of Luther's earliest opponents. They complained that many masters at the University of Paris were "Lutheran." But as in Germany, there was no clear understanding of who or what a Lutheran was. The Sorbonne theologians were also suspicious of a number of "pre-reformers," including the humanistic editor Jacques Lefèvre d'Étaples (1455–1536; see page 342), who, late in life, had come to an understanding of justification quite like Luther's. Others were clerics intent on religious reform within the traditional structures. Unlike Luther and the French Protestants, these pre-reformers did not challenge the priests' relationship to the sacraments. They were interested in the piety and behavior of churchmen. They never challenged the role of the clergy in salvation. King Francis's own sister, Margaret of Angoulême (1492–1549), gathered a group of religious persons, including several reformers, at her court. However, Margaret herself urged that theology be left to scholars; she believed that the laity should stick to simple pieties. Like Margaret, most French Christians had no clear sense that Protestant teachings required a complete break with medieval Christian traditions.

Like other monarchs, Francis I (r. 1515–1547) largely interpreted religious issues in the context of royal interests. Primarily engaged in the seemingly intractable wars with the Habsburgs, Francis generally ignored religious questions. He was not initially opposed to what seemed to be moral reform within the church. His own view was that the king's duty was to preserve order and prevent scandal, and at first, carrying out that duty meant protecting reformers whom the conservative militants persecuted. The king feared disorder more than he feared religious reform.

On October 18, 1534, however, Francis's attitude changed when he and all Paris awoke to find the city littered with anti-Catholic placards containing, in the words of the writers, "true articles on the horrible, great and insufferable abuses of the Papal Mass." The "Affair of the Placards" changed Francis's ideas about the sources of disorder. Opposition to traditional religious practices became more difficult and more dangerous. John Calvin himself was forced to leave Paris, and eventually

The Great Cauldron   In dramatic images, this French woodcut shows the Protestant expectation that the Bible carried down by the Holy Spirit will overturn the whole cauldron of false images and errors that supported the old church.   (Bibliothèque nationale de France)

France, because he feared persecution. Between 1534 and 1560, some ten thousand Protestants fled France, many joining Calvin in Geneva.

By the middle of the sixteenth century, it was clear that neither Protestant nor Catholic factions would be able to control religious and political life in France. Francis I died in 1547, and the stage was set for a series of destructive factional struggles over religion and political power that would continue for the rest of the century (see Chapter 15).

Scandinavia

All of Scandinavia became Lutheran. Initial influences drifted north from Germany, carried by Hanseatic merchants and students who had studied at the universities of northern Germany. Yet, the reform in Sweden and Denmark, even more than in England, was monarchical. In both Scandinavian kingdoms, the kings began with an attack on the temporal rights and properties of the church. Changes in liturgy and practice came later, as reformers gained royal protection.

In Sweden, the establishment of a strong monarch required concern for religious reform. Gustav Vasa, a leading noble, was able to secure the loyalty of most of the Swedes and in 1523, he was elected king of Sweden. Gustav's motto was "All power is of God." Like Henry VIII of

England, Gustav (r. 1523–1560) moved carefully in an attempt to retain the loyalty of as many groups as possible. Although he never formally adopted a national confession of faith, the Swedish church and state gradually took on a more Lutheran character. In an effort to secure royal finances, the Riksdag, or parliament, passed the Västerås Ordinances, which secularized ecclesiastical lands and authorized the preaching of the "Pure Word of God." Olaus Petri (1493–1552), Sweden's principal reform preacher, was installed by royal order in the Cathedral of Stockholm.

In Denmark, the reformers also moved cautiously. Frederick I (r. 1523–1533) and his son, Christian III (r. 1534–1559), continued the policy of secularization and control that Christian I had initiated. Danish kings seemed interested in reform as a diplomatic means of attack on the Roman church. The kings tended to support reformers as a way to attack the political power of the bishops. In 1538, the Danes finally accepted the Augsburg Confession, which was becoming the most widely accepted exposition of Lutheran belief. The transformation of practice proceeded slowly over the next decades.

In the frontier regions of Scandinavia—Finland, Iceland, and Norway—the reform was undertaken as a matter of royal policy. Initially, only a handful of local reformers introduced and proselytized the new theology and practice. In many regions, resistance to the Reformation continued for several generations. One valley, hidden in the mountains of western Norway, continued to follow the old religion for three centuries after its contacts with Rome had been severed.

Eastern Europe

In some respects, there was less opposition to the expansion of Protestantism in eastern Europe. The result was the creation of a unique religious culture. The church hierarchy was not in a position to enforce orthodoxy. Some Christian rulers were indifferent to religious debates, as were the Muslim Ottoman Turks, who controlled much of eastern Hungary and what is now Romania. Other rulers whose societies already contained Orthodox and Catholic Christians, as well as Muslims and Jews, offered toleration because they could ill afford to alienate any portion of their subject populations.

Protestant ideas initially passed through the German communities of Poland and the trading towns along the Baltic coast. But in the 1540s, Calvinist ideas spread quickly among the Polish nobles, especially those at the royal court. Given the power and influence of some of the noble families, Catholics were unable to suppress the various secret Calvinist congregations. During the first half of the sixteenth century, Protestantism became so well established in Poland that it could not be rooted out. Throughout the sixteenth century, Protestantism remained one of the rallying points for those Polish nobles opposed to the expansion of royal power.

Much was the same in Hungary and Transylvania. Among German colonists, Magyars, and ethnic Romanians, many individuals were interested first in Luther's message and later in Reformed theology. The situation was exacerbated after the Turkish victory at Mohács in 1526, which destroyed the traditional political and religious elite of Hungary. Because no one could hope to enforce uniformity, some cities adopted a moderate Lutheran theology, and others followed a Calvinist confession. In 1568, the Estates (representative assemblies) of Transylvania had decreed that four religions were to be tolerated—Catholic, Lutheran, Reformed (Calvinist), and Unitarian. Further, when various radical groups migrated from the west in search of toleration, they were able to create their own communities in Slavic and Magyar areas.

The Reformation was to have virtually no influence farther to the east, in Russia. The Orthodox Church in Russia was much more firmly under government control than was the church in the West. The Russian church followed the traditions of the Greek church, and Western arguments over justification made little sense in Orthodox churches. Given the historic suspicion of the Orthodox churches toward Rome, the Russians were more tolerant of contacts with the Protestants of northern Europe, but there would be no theological innovation or reform in sixteenth-century Russia.

SECTION SUMMARY

- Widespread support for traditional religious practices in France limited the spread of reformed ideas.

- Francis I tolerated religious dissent until it seemed that religious strife might lead to civil unrest.

- In Scandinavia, religious change was fostered by monarchs who wished to reduce the influence of the church in public life.

- Religious toleration was much more common in eastern Europe, where many rulers declined to support one religious movement over another.

THE LATE REFORMATION, CA. 1545–1600

How did Catholic and Protestant Christians differ from each other by the end of the Reformation?

In the first half of the sixteenth century, Catholics applied the term *Lutheran* to anyone critical of the papacy. As was clear from countless debates and attempts at compromise, there was real confusion about what Luther had meant. In parts of Germany by the late 1520s and across Europe by the 1550s, political and religious leaders attempted to explain to the people just what *Lutheran, Reformed (Calvinist),* and *Catholic* had come to mean. It was only in the second half of the sixteenth century that these terms came to have any clarity. After the middle of the sixteenth century, it was true that along with theological and political changes, the Reformation represented a broad cultural movement.

The profound changes that began in the sixteenth century continued into the seventeenth. Central governments supported religious authorities who desired religious uniformity and control over individual Christians. In all parts of Europe, religious behavior changed. Both Protestants and Catholics became more concerned with the personal rather than the communal aspects of Christianity. After the sixteenth century, the nature of Christianity and its place in public life, whether in Protestant or in Catholic countries, differed profoundly from Christianity in the Middle Ages.

Catholic Reform, 1512–1600

Historians commonly speak of both a movement for traditional reform and renewal within the Catholic Church, and a "Counter-Reformation," which was a direct response to and rejection of the theological positions championed by the Protestants. It is certainly true that one can categorize certain acts as clearly challenging the Protestants. However, to do so is to miss the point that the energetic actions of the Roman Catholic Church during the sixteenth century both affirmed traditional teachings and created new institutions better fitted to the early modern world.

The idea of purer, earlier church practices to which the "modern" church should return had been a commonplace for centuries. In 1512, five years before Luther made his public protests, Pope Julius II (r. 1503–1513) convened another ecumenical council, the Fifth Lateran Council (1513–1517), which was expected to look into the problems of nonresident clergy, multiple benefices, and a host of other issues. This tradition of moral reform was especially strong in Spain, Portugal, and Italy, lands whose political rulers were either indifferent or opposed to Protestant reforms.

In the wake of the sack of Rome by imperial troops in 1527, one Roman cardinal, Bishop Gian Matteo Giberti (ji-BARE-ti) of Verona (1495–1543), returned to his diocese and began a thoroughgoing reform. He conducted visitations of the churches and other religious institutions in Verona, preached tirelessly, worked hard to raise the educational level of his clergy, and required that priests live within their parishes. Giberti believed that morally rigorous traditional reform

Marian Shrine   Shrines, such as this one in Regensburg dedicated to the Virgin Mary, remained important centers of Catholic piety. As we see here, shrines drew large crowds made up of individuals and religious groups who came in search of spiritual and physical healing.   (Foto Marburg/Art Resource, NY)

and renewal could counter the malaise he perceived. Other reforming bishops could be found throughout Catholic Europe.

THE ROLE OF MUSIC AND MYSTICISM

New religious foundations sprang up to renew the church. Members of the new orders set out to change the church through example. The Florentine Filippo Neri (1515–1595) founded the Oratorian order, so named because of the monks' habit of leading the laity in prayer services. Filippo was joined in his work by Giovanni Palestrina (ca. 1525–1594), who composed music for the modest, but moving, prayer gatherings in Rome. Palestrina's music combined medieval plainchants with newer styles of polyphony, creating complex harmonies without obscuring the words and meaning of the text. The popularity of the Oratorians and their services can be measured in part by the fact that oratories, small chapels modeled on those favored by Filippo, remain to this day important centers of musical life in the city of Rome.

The Catholic reform of the sixteenth century, however, was better known for its mystical theology than for its music. In Italy and France, but especially in Spain, a profusion of reformers chose to reform the church through austere prayer and contemplative devotions. Teresa of Avila (1515–1582), who belonged to a wealthy converso family (see page 317), led a movement to reform the lax practices within the religious houses of Spain. Famed for her rigorous religious life, her trances, and her raptures, Teresa animated a movement to reform the order of Carmelite nuns in Spain. Because of her writings about her mystical experiences, she was named a "Doctor of the Church," a title reserved for the greatest of the church's theologians.

JESUITS

Society of Jesus (Jesuits) Religious group founded in 1534 by Ignatius Loyola; they were famed for their role in the Catholic Counter-Reformation.

Ignatius Loyola A Spanish nobleman and founder of the Society of Jesus. Loyola's order vowed absolute authority to the papacy.

The most important of the new religious orders was the **Society of Jesus**, or Jesuits, founded in 1534 by **Ignatius Loyola** (1491–1556). He initially meant to organize a missionary order directed at converting the Muslims. The structure of his order reflected his military experience. It had a well-defined chain of command, leading to the general of the order and then to the pope. To educate and discipline the members, Loyola composed *Spiritual Exercises*, emphasizing the importance of obedience. He encouraged his followers to understand their own attitudes, beliefs, and even lives as less important than the papacy and the Roman church. If the church commands it, he concluded, "I will believe that the white object I see is black." He prohibited Jesuits from holding any ecclesiastical office that might compromise their autonomy. After papal approval of the order in 1540, the Jesuits directed their activities primarily to education in Catholic areas and reconversion of Protestants.

Throughout Europe, Jesuits gained fame for their work as educators of the laity and as spiritual advisers to the political leaders of Catholic Europe. In the late sixteenth and early seventeenth centuries, they were responsible for a number of famous conversions, including that of Christina (1626–1689), the Lutheran queen of Sweden, who abdicated her throne in 1654 and spent the rest of her life in Rome. Jesuits were especially successful in bringing many parts of the Holy Roman Empire back into communion with the papacy. They have rightly been called the vanguard of the Catholic reform movement.

CATHOLIC REFORM

Index of Prohibited Books A list of books banned by the Roman Catholic Church because of moral or doctrinal error. It was thought that this would inhibit the spread of Protestant ideas.

Catholic reformers were convinced that one of the reasons for the success of the Protestants was that faithful Christians had no clear guide to orthodox teachings. The first Catholic response to the reformers was to try to separate ideas they held to be correct from those they held to be incorrect. Successive popes made public lists of books and ideas that they considered to be in error. The lists were combined into the *Index of Prohibited Books* in 1559. The climate of suspicion was such that the works of humanists, such as Erasmus, were prohibited alongside the works of Protestants, such as Martin Luther. In times of religious tensions, the *Index* could be vigorously enforced. In Italy, for example, no editions of the Holy Bible in Italian translation were published in the late sixteenth and seventeenth centuries. In general, however, the *Index* could not prevent the circulation of books and ideas. It was finally suppressed in 1966.

COUNCIL OF TRENT

During the first half of the sixteenth century, Catholics joined Protestants in calls for an ecumenical council that all believed would solve the problems dogging the Christian church. But in the unsettled political and diplomatic atmosphere that lasted into the 1540s, it was impossible to find any agreement about where or when a universal council should meet. Finally, in 1545, at a time when the hostilities between the Valois and Habsburgs had cooled, Pope Paul III (r. 1534–1549) was able to convene an ecumenical council in the city of Trent, a German imperial city located on the Italian side of the Alps.

The **Council of Trent** marked and defined Roman Catholicism for the next four hundred years. Reformers within the Catholic Church hoped that it would be possible to create a broadly based reform party within the church and that the council would define theological positions acceptable to the Protestants, making reunion possible.

The Council of Trent sat in three sessions between 1545 and 1563. The initial debates were clearly meant to mark the boundaries between Protestant heresy and the orthodox positions of the Catholic Church. In response to the Protestant emphasis on Scripture alone, the council affirmed that Scripture has to be interpreted in the context of Church tradition. Delegates rejected the humanists' work on the text of the Bible, declaring that the Latin Vulgate edition compiled by Jerome in the late fourth century was the authorized text. In response to the widely held Protestant belief that salvation came through faith alone, the council declared that good works were not merely the outcome of faith but prerequisites to salvation. The council rejected Protestant positions on the sacraments, the giving of wine to the laity during Holy Communion, the marriage of clergy, and the granting of indulgences.

To assume that the council's decrees were merely negative, however, is to ignore the many ways in which the decrees of the council were an essential part of the creation of the Roman Catholic Church that would function for the next four centuries. The delegates at Trent generally felt that the real cause behind the Protestant movement was the lack of leadership and supervision within the church. Many of the acts of the council dealt with that issue.

First, the council affirmed apostolic succession—the idea that the authority of a bishop is transmitted through a succession of bishops, ultimately leading back through the popes to Saint Peter. Thus, the council underlined the ultimate authority of the pope in administrative, as well as theological, matters. The council ordered that local bishops should reside in their dioceses; that they should establish seminaries to see to the education of parish clergy; and that, through regular visitation and supervision, they should make certain that the laity participated in the sacramental life of the church. In the final sessions of the council, the nature of the Roman Catholic Church was summed up in the Creed of Pius IV, which, like the Lutheran Augsburg Confession, expressed the basic position of the church.

A Mystical Reformer   Saint Teresa of Avila came from a converso family. She believed that renewal within the Christian church would come through mysticism, prayer, and a return to traditional religious practices. She founded a reformed Carmelite order of nuns to further religious renewal in Spain.   (Institut Amatller d'Art Hispanic)

Council of Trent   An ecumenical council of the Roman Catholic Church called to both respond to the Protestant challenge and institute reforms in the Catholic Church. Its decrees established the basic tenets of Roman Catholicism for the next four hundred years.

Confessionalization

The labors of the Jesuits and the deliberations of the Council of Trent at midcentury proved that reconciliation between the Protestant reformers and the Catholic Church was not possible. Signs of the separation include the flight of important Protestant religious leaders from Italy in the late 1540s and the wholesale migration of Protestant communities from Modena, Lucca, and other Italian towns to France, England, and Switzerland. These actions signify the beginnings of the theological, political, and social separation of "Protestant" and "Catholic" in European society. Further, the states of Europe saw themselves as the enforcers of religious uniformity within their territories. It is from this time forward that denominational differences become clearer.

The theological separation was marked in a number of concrete and symbolic ways. Churches in which both bread and wine were distributed to the laity during the sacrament of Holy Communion passed from Catholic to Protestant. Churches in which the altar was moved forward to face the congregation but the statuary was retained were likely to be Lutheran. Churches in which statues were destroyed and all other forms of art were removed were likely to be Reformed (Calvinist), for Calvin had advised that "only those things are to be sculpted or painted which the eye is capable of seeing; let not God's majesty, which is far above the perception of the eyes, be debased through unseemly representations."[5] Even matters such as singing differentiated the churches. Although the Calvinist tradition tended to believe that music, like art, drew the Christian away from consideration of the Word, Luther believed that "next to the Word of God, music deserves the highest praise." Lutherans emphasized congregational singing and the use of music within the worship service. Countless pastors in the sixteenth and seventeenth centuries followed Luther in composing hymns and even theoretical tracts on music. This tradition would reach its zenith in the church music of Johann Sebastian Bach (1685–1750), most of whose choral works were composed to be part of the normal worship service.

Music had played an important role in Catholic services since well before the Reformation. It was really architecture that distinguished Catholic churches from Protestant churches in the late sixteenth and seventeenth centuries. In Rome, the great religious orders built new churches in the baroque style (see page 437). Baroque artists and architects absorbed all the classical lessons of the Renaissance and then went beyond them, sometimes deliberately violating them. Baroque art celebrates the supernatural, the ways in which God is not bound by the laws of nature. Whereas Renaissance art was meant to depict nature, baroque paintings and sculpture seem to defy gravity. The work celebrates the supernatural power and splendor of the papacy. This drama and power are clear in the construction of the Jesuit Church of the Gesù (jeh-ZOO) in Rome and, even more so, in Gianlorenzo Bernini's (1598–1680) throne of Saint Peter, made for Saint Peter's Basilica in the Vatican. The construction of baroque churches, first in Spain and Italy, but especially in the Catholic parts of Germany, created yet another boundary between an austere Protestantism and a visual and mystical Catholicism.

The Regulation of Religious Life

Because of the continuing religious confusion and political disorder brought on by the reforms, churchmen, like state officials, were intent on maintaining religious order within their territories by requiring what they understood to be the practice of true Christianity. In an ironic twist, both Protestant and Catholic authorities followed much the same program. In both camps, regulation of religion became a governmental concern. Religious regulation and state power grew at the same time. This true religion was much less a public and communal religion than medieval Christianity had been. In the age of confessionalization, theologians—both Protestant and Catholic—became preoccupied with the moral status and interior life of individuals. Sexual sins and gluttony now seemed more dangerous than economic sins, such as avarice and usury. Even penance was understood less as a "restitution" that would reintegrate the individual into the Christian community, than as a process of coming to true contrition for one's sins.

All of the major religious groups in the late sixteenth century emphasized education, right doctrine, and social control. In Catholic areas, it was hoped that a renewed emphasis on private confession by the laity would lead to a proper understanding of doctrine. During this period, Charles Borromeo, archbishop of Milan (1538–1584), introduced the private confessional box, which isolated priest and penitent from the prying ears of the community. This allowed confessors the time and opportunity to instruct individual consciences with care. As early as the 1520s, some Lutheran princes had begun visitations to ensure that the laity understood basic doctrine.

Churchmen in both Protestant and Catholic areas used catechisms—handbooks containing instruction for the laity. The first and most famous was by Luther himself. Luther's *Small Catechism* includes the Lord's Prayer, Ten Commandments, and Apostles' Creed, along with simple, clear explanations of what they mean. More than Catholic rulers, Protestant rulers used church courts to enforce discipline within the community. Churchmen began to criticize semi-religious popular celebrations, such as May Day, harvest feasts, and the Feast of Fools, whose origins lay in popular myths and practices that preceded Christianity. Such observances were now scorned for encouraging superstition and mocking the social and political order with, for example, parodies of ignorant clergy and foolish magistrates.

Religious authorities were also concerned by what seemed to be out-of-control mysticism and dangerous religious practices, especially among women. The impact of the Reformation on the status of women has often been debated. The Protestant position is that the Reformation freed women from the cloistered control of traditional convents. Further, the Protestant attack on state-controlled prostitution reduced one of the basest forms of exploitation. To the realists who argued that young, unmarried men would always need sexual outlets, Luther replied that

The Holy Household　One of the most popular ideas among Protestants was that true religion should be taught and preserved in the Christian family, presided over by the father. The detail in this painting shows not only the interior of a Flemish home, but also the role of the father and the symbolic importance of meals eaten together.　(The Shakespeare Birthplace Trust)

one cannot merely substitute one evil practice for another. Critics of the Reformation counter that a convent was one of very few organizations that a woman could administer and direct. Women who took religious vows, Catholics point out, could engage in intellectual and religious pursuits similar to those enjoyed by men. The destruction of religious houses for women, Catholics argue, destroyed one of the few alternatives that women had to life in an authoritarian, patriarchal society.

In fact, in the late sixteenth and early seventeenth centuries, both Protestant and Catholic authorities viewed with suspicion any signs of religious independence by women. In the first years of the Reformation, some women did leave convents, eager to participate in the reform of the church. They wrote tracts concerning the morality of the clergy. And, for a time, women served as deacons in some Reformed (Calvinist) churches. Yet, like the female witches discussed in Chapter 15, these religious women seemed somehow dangerous. Lutheran and Calvinist theologians argued that a woman's religious vocation should be in the Christian care and education of her family. And even the most famous of the sixteenth- and seventeenth-century female Catholic mystics were greeted with distrust and some hostility. Religious women in Catholic convents were required to subordinate their mysticism to the guidance they received from male spiritual advisers. Calvinist theologians exhibited similar suspicions toward the theological and spiritual insights of Protestant women. For the laity, in general, and for women, in particular, the late Reformation brought increased control by religious authorities.

SECTION SUMMARY

- Catholic reform emphasizing moral reform and renewed piety had begun before Luther's protests.

- The Council of Trent defined Catholic doctrine for the next four hundred years.

- During the second half of the sixteenth century, Protestant and Catholic churches became more clearly differentiated by architecture and ritual.

- Both traditions emphasized personal discipline and self-control, which became an important part of the early modern state.

CHAPTER SUMMARY

D uring the age of the Reformation, Europe experienced a number of profound shocks. The medieval assumption of a unified Christendom in the West was shattered. No longer could Europeans assume that, at heart, they held similar views of the world and the place of individuals in it. Charles V had begun his reign with hopes for one law, one faith, and one empire. He ended it by dividing his empire and retiring to a monastery.

FOCUS QUESTIONS

- Why did the reformers feel it was necessary to establish entirely new churches outside the Roman Catholic Church?

- What political factors limited Charles V's ability to respond to the religious crisis?

- Why did the English monarchs take the lead in efforts to reform the English church?

- How did ideas of church reform influence social and political developments in the rest of Europe?

- How did Catholic and Protestant Christians differ from each other by the end of the Reformation?

The Protestant challenge did not simply attack the institutional structure or the moral lapses as previous heretical movements had done. The early Protestant reformers rejected the penitential system that was at the heart of the medieval church. Peasants and artisans argued that Luther's message of Christian freedom liberated them from both economic and spiritual oppression. Both Protestant and peasant claimed all authority must rest on Holy Scripture. They rejected the traditions of the late Middle Ages.

Emperor Charles V was opposed to Luther and wanted to maintain the unity of the church and of his empire. But he faced almost continuous problems in one part or another of his empire. Both the French and the Turks did all they could to reduce his power. Consequently, even after years of struggle, he was forced, in the religious Peace of Augsburg, to accept the principle that the towns and regional principalities had the right to accept either traditional Catholic worship or the new Lutheran reform.

In England, on the other hand, the monarchy was powerful enough that Henry VIII was able to shift religious debate and declare himself the head of the Church in England. But Henry's children were alternately Protestant, Catholic, and Protestant again. The result in England was a church that maintained certain aspects of traditional Catholic Christianity, even as it allowed a married clergy and accepted other Protestant reforms.

Monarchies and republics throughout Europe came to view religious institutions and religious choices as matters of state. In Scandinavia, monarchs seemed to have favored the Lutherans as a way to weaken the power of the Catholic clergy. While in France, Francis I was willing to allow some Protestant protests, until it seemed that religious unrest threatened public order. At that point, he began to suppress Protestant worship, acknowledging the fact that France had largely remained Catholic. Much of the rest of eastern Europe followed no clear pattern. When faced with theological challenges and cries for moral reform, governments reacted in ways that offered religious change and bolstered the claims of secular authorities.

By the second half of the sixteenth century, Protestants and Catholics had largely adopted patterns that made clear which religion was favored. Calvinist churches were spare; Catholic churches, ornate; and Lutheran churches, filled with varieties of music.

As a part of their reform movements, both Protestant and Catholic governments redoubled their efforts to regulate religion and moral life. In Catholic countries, the church hierarchy extended its control over the religious life of the laity. Thus, both Reformation and Counter-Reformation brought about a significant strengthening of religious and secular authorities.

 This icon will direct you to additional materials on the website: www .cengage.com/history/ noble/westciv6e.

KEY TERMS

Martin Luther (p. 382)

justification by faith (p. 384)

Charles V (p. 385)

Huldrych Zwingli (p. 385)

John Calvin (p. 387)

Anabaptists (p. 390)

Augsburg Confession (p. 393)

Henry VIII (p. 396)

Act of Supremacy (p. 396)

Society of Jesus (p. 402)

Ignatius Loyola (p. 402)

Index of Prohibited Books (p. 402)

Council of Trent (p. 403)

NOTES

1. Quoted in Merry Wiesner-Hanks, "Women and Religious Change," in *The Cambrdige History of Christianity, volume 6 Reform and Expansion 1500–1660* (Cambridge: Cambridge University Press, 2007), p467.

2. Quoted in Robert W. Scribner, *The German Reformation* (London: Macmillan, 1986), p. 32.

3. Quoted in Carter Lindberg, *The European Reformations* (New York: Blackwell Publishers, 1996), p. 269.

4. Quoted in Euan Cameron, *The European Reformation* (Oxford: Clarendon Press, 1991), pp. 106–107.

5. Quoted in Lindberg, p. 375.

e See our interactive eBook for map and primary source activities.

CHAPTER OUTLINE

The Saint Bartholomew's Day Massacre   (The Art Archive/Musée des Beaux Arts Lausanne/Gianni Dagli Orti/Picture Desk)

Europe in the Age of Religious Wars, 1560–1648

Three well-dressed gentlemen stand over a mutilated body; one of them holds up the severed head. Elsewhere, sword-wielding men engage in indiscriminate slaughter, even of babies. Corpses are piled up in the background. This painting memorializes the grisly events of August 24, 1572. A band of Catholic noblemen, accompanied by the personal guard of the king of France, had hunted down a hundred Protestant nobles, asleep in their lodgings in and around the royal palace, and murdered them in cold blood. The king and his counselors had planned the murders as a preemptive strike because they feared that other Protestant nobles were gathering an army outside Paris. But the calculated attack became a massacre when ordinary Parisians, overwhelmingly Catholic and believing they were acting in the king's name, turned on their neighbors. About three thousand Protestants were slain in Paris over the next three days.

This massacre came to be called the Saint Bartholomew's Day Massacre for the Catholic saint on whose feast day it fell. Though horrible in its scope, the slaughter was not unusual in the deadly combination of religious and political antagonisms it reflected. Religious conflicts were, by definition, intractable political conflicts, since virtually every religious group felt that all others were heretics who could not be tolerated and must be eliminated. Rulers of all faiths looked to divine authority and religious institutions to uphold their power.

In the decades after 1560, existing political tensions led to instability and violence, especially when newly reinforced by religious differences. Royal governments continued to consolidate authority, but resistance to royal power by provinces, nobles, or towns accustomed to independence now might have a religious sanction. Warfare over these issues had consumed the Holy Roman Empire in the first half of the sixteenth century. The conflict now spilled over into France and the Netherlands and threatened to erupt in England. In the early seventeenth century, the Holy Roman Empire once again was wracked by a war simultaneously religious and political in origin. Regardless of its roots, warfare itself had become more destructive than ever before thanks to innovations in military technology and campaign tactics. Tensions everywhere were also worsened by economic changes, especially soaring prices and unemployment. The political and religious struggles of the era took place against a background of increasing want, and economic distress was often expressed in both political and religious terms.

FOCUS QUESTIONS

- What circumstances permitted Spain's ambitious policies and to what degree were they successful?

- What conditions led to civil war in France? How did religious and political conflict develop differently in England?

- Why did war erupt again within the Holy Roman Empire and what was the significance of the conflict?

- What caused the economic stresses of these decades and how did ordinary people cope with them?

- In what ways do the literature and art of this period reflect the political, social, and religious conflicts of the age?

This icon will direct you to additional materials on the website: www.cengage.com/history/noble/westciv6e.

See our interactive eBook for map and primary source activities.

A period of tension, even extraordinary violence, in political and social life, the era of the late sixteenth and early seventeenth centuries was also distinguished by great creativity in some areas of cultural and intellectual life. The plays of Shakespeare, for example, mirrored the passions, but also reflected on the dilemmas of the day and helped to analyze Europeans' circumstances with a new degree of sophistication.

IMPERIAL SPAIN AND THE LIMITS OF ROYAL POWER

What circumstances permitted Spain's ambitious policies and to what degree were they successful?

Philip II King of Spain (r. 1556–1598), son of Charles V who ruled Spain at the height of its influence.

To contemporary observers, no political fact of the late sixteenth century was more obvious than the ascendancy of Spain. **Philip II** (r. 1556–1598) ruled Spanish conquests in the New World, as well as wealthy territories in Europe, including the Netherlands and parts of Italy. Yet imperial Spain did not escape the political, social, and religious turmoil of the era. Explosive combinations of religious dissent and political disaffection led to revolt against Spain in the Netherlands. This conflict revealed the endemic tensions of sixteenth-century political life: nobles, towns, and provinces trying to safeguard remnants of medieval autonomy against efforts at greater centralization—with the added complications of economic strain and religious division. The revolt also demonstrated the material limits of royal power, since even with treasure from American conquests pouring in, Philip could, at times, barely afford to keep armies in the field. As American silver dwindled in the seventeenth century, Philip's successors faced severe financial and political strains, even in their Spanish domains.

The Revolt of the Netherlands

Philip's power stemmed in part from the far-flung territories he inherited from his father, the Habsburg king of Spain and Holy Roman emperor Charles V: Spain, the Low Countries (the Netherlands), the duchy of Milan, the kingdom of Naples, the conquered lands in the Americas, and the Philippine Islands in Asia. (Control of Charles's Austrian lands had passed to his brother, Ferdinand, Philip's uncle; see **MAP 15.1**.) Treasure fleets bearing silver from the New World began to reach Spain regularly during Philip's reign. Spain was now the engine powering a trading economy unlike any that had existed in Europe before. To supply its colonies, Spain needed timber and other shipbuilding materials from the hinterlands of the Baltic Sea. Grain from the Baltic fed the urban populations of Spain (where wool was the principal cash crop) and the Netherlands, while the Netherlands, in turn, was a source of finished goods, such as cloth. The major exchange point for all of these goods was the city of Antwerp in the Netherlands, the leading trading center of all of Europe by 1550.

The Netherlands were the jewel among Philip's European possessions. These seventeen provinces (constituting mostly the modern nations of Belgium and the Netherlands) had been centers of trade and manufacture since the twelfth century. In the fourteenth and fifteenth centuries, they had enjoyed political importance and a period of cultural innovation under the control of the dukes of Burgundy. Like his father, Philip was, technically, the ruler of each province separately—that is, he was count of Flanders, duke of Brabant, and so forth. (See **MAP 15.2**.) By Philip's reign, a sort of federal system of government had evolved to accommodate the various centers of power. Each province had an assembly (Estates) in which representatives of leading nobility and towns authorized taxation, but each also acknowledged a central administration in Brussels that represented Philip. Heading the council of state in Brussels was a governor-general, Philip's half sister, Margaret of Parma.

BACKGROUND TO THE REVOLT

Philip's clumsy efforts to adjust this distribution of power in his favor pushed his subjects in the Netherlands into revolt. Born and raised in Spain, Philip had little real familiarity with the densely populated, linguistically diverse Netherlands, and he never visited there after 1559. Early in his reign, tensions in the Netherlands arose over taxation and Spanish insistence on maintaining tight control. Bad harvests and disruptions of trade, caused by wars in the Baltic region in the 1560s, depressed the Netherlands' economy and made it difficult for the provinces to pay the taxes Spain demanded. When the Peace of Cateau-Cambrésis (kahtoe kam-bray-SEE) of 1559 brought an end to the long struggle between the Habsburgs and the Valois (val-WAH) kings of France, the people of the Netherlands had reason to hope for lower taxes and reduced levels of Spanish control, yet neither was forthcoming. Indeed, Philip named to the council of state in Brussels officials who were Spaniards themselves or had close ties to the Spanish court, bypassing local nobles who had fought for Philip and his father before 1559.

Philip only added to the discontent by unleashing an invigorated repression of heresy. Unlike his father, Philip directed the hunt for heretics, not just at lower-class dissenters, but also at well-to-do Calvinists—followers of the French Protestant religious reformer John Calvin—whose numbers were considerable. Punishment for heresy now included confiscation of family property along with execution of the individual. By 1565, town councils in the Netherlands routinely refused to enforce Philip's religious policies, believing that their prosperity—as well as their personal security—depended on restraint in the prosecution of heresy. Leading nobles also stopped enforcing the policies on their estates.

Encouraged by greater tolerance, Protestants began to hold open-air meetings and attract new converts in many towns. In a series of actions called the "iconoclastic fury," Calvinist townsfolk around the provinces stripped Catholic churches of the relics and statues they believed idolatrous. At the same time, reflecting the economic strain of these years, some townsfolk rioted to protest the price of bread. One prominent nobleman warned Philip, "All trade has come to a standstill, so that there are 100,000 men begging for their bread who used to earn it . . . which is [important] since poverty can force people to do things which otherwise they would never think of doing."[1]

CHRONOLOGY

1556–1598	Reign of Philip II
1558–1603	Reign of Elizabeth I
1559	Act of Supremacy (England)
1562–1598	Religious wars in France
1565	Netherlands city councils and nobility ignore Philip II's law against heresy
1566	Calvinist "iconoclastic fury" begins in the Netherlands
1567	Duke of Alba arrives in the Netherlands
1571	Defeat of Turkish navy at Lepanto
1576	Sack of Antwerp
1579	Union of Utrecht
1588	Defeat of Spanish Armada
1589–1610	Reign of Henry IV
1598	Edict of Nantes (France)
1609	Truce between Spain and the Netherlands declared
1618–1648	Thirty Years' War
1620	Catholic victory at Battle of White Mountain
1621	Truce between Spain and the Netherlands expires; war between Spain and the Netherlands begins
1629	Peace of Alais
1631	Swedes under Gustav Adolf defeat imperial forces
1635	Peace of Prague
1640–1653	"Long Parliament" in session in England
1648	Peace of Westphalia

THE PROVINCES REVOLT

In early 1567, armed Calvinist insurgents seized two towns in the southern Netherlands in hopes of stirring a general revolt that would secure freedom of worship. Margaret of Parma quelled the uprisings by rallying city governments and loyal nobles, now fearful for their own property and power. But by then, far away in Spain, a decision had been made to send in the Spanish duke of Alba with an army of ten thousand men.

When Alba arrived in August 1567, he repeated every mistake of Spanish policy that had triggered rebellion in the first place. He billeted troops in friendly cities, established new courts to try rebels, arrested thousands of people, executed about a thousand rebels (including Catholics as well as prominent Protestants), and imposed heavy taxes to support his army.

Margaret of Parma resigned in disgust and left the Netherlands. Protestants from rebellious towns escaped into exile, where they were joined by nobles who had been declared traitors for resisting Alba's policies. The most important of these was William of Nassau (NAS-saw), prince of Orange (1533–1584), whose lands outside the Netherlands, in France and the Holy Roman Empire, lay beyond Spanish reach and so could be used to finance continued warfare against Spain. A significant community with military capability began to grow in exile.

In 1572, ships of exiled Calvinist privateers, known as the "Sea Beggars," began preying on Spanish shipping and coastal fortresses from bases in the northern provinces. These provinces,

🌐 **MAP 15.1—The Spanish Habsburgs and Europe, ca. 1556**

Philip II's control of territories in northern Italy permitted the overland access of Spanish troops to the Netherlands and heightened the Spanish threat to France. Lands bordering the western Mediterranean made the sea a natural sphere of Spanish influence as well. Habsburg lands in central Europe were controlled after 1556 by Charles V's brother Ferdinand and his descendants.

increasingly Calvinist, became the center of opposition to the Spanish, who concentrated their efforts against rebellion in the wealthier southern provinces. Occasionally, the French and English lent aid to the rebels.

The war in the Netherlands was a showcase for the new and costly technology of warfare in this period. Many towns were (or came to be, as a consequence of the revolt) equipped with "bastions," newly designed walled defenses that could resist artillery fire; such cities could not be taken by storm. Where bastions had been built, military campaigns consisted of grueling sieges, skirmishes in surrounding areas for control of supplies, and occasional pitched battles between besiegers and forces attempting to break the siege. Vast numbers of men were required, both for effective besieging forces and for garrisoning the many fortresses that controlled the countryside and defended access to major towns.

In an attempt to supply the Netherlands with veteran troops and materiel from Spain and Spanish territories in Italy, the Spanish developed the "Spanish Road," an innovative string of supply depots where provisions could be gathered in advance of troops marching to the Netherlands (see **MAP 15.1**). Maintaining its large armies, however, taxed Spain's resources

The City of Antwerp   Antwerp, in the southern Netherlands, was the point of sale for
Portuguese spices brought around Africa from India; the selling and transshipping center for
Baltic goods, including timber, fur, and grain; and the source for manufactured goods such as
cloth.   (Musées royaux des Beaux-Arts de Belgique)

to the breaking point. Even with American silver at hand, Philip could, at times, barely afford
to keep armies in the field. Inevitably, large numbers of troops also exhausted the countryside, and both soldiers and civilians suffered great privations. On occasion, Spanish troops
reacted violently to difficult conditions and to delayed pay (American treasure dwindled badly
between 1572 and 1578). In 1576, they sacked the hitherto loyal city of Antwerp and massacred about eight thousand people. Bitterly remembered as the "Spanish Fury," the massacre
prompted leaders in the southern provinces to raise their own armies to protect themselves
against the Spanish. Late in 1576, they concluded an alliance with William of Orange and the
northern rebels.

The alliance between northern and southern provinces did not last. The provinces were increasingly divided by religion, and their differences were skillfully exploited by Philip's new commander, Margaret of Parma's son Alexander Farnese (far-NAY-zee), duke of Parma. With silver
from America filling the king's coffers again, Parma wooed the Catholic elites of the southern
provinces back into loyalty to Philip, in return for promises to respect their provincial liberties
and safeguard their property from troops.

**FORMATION OF THE
UNITED PROVINCES**

In 1579, the northern provinces united in a defensive alliance, the Union of Utrecht
(OO-trekt), against the increasingly unified south. Parma's forces could not push beyond the
natural barrier of rivers that bisect the Low Countries (see **MAP 15.2**), particularly as Spain
diverted money to conflicts with England in 1588 and France after 1589. In 1609, a truce was
finally concluded between Spain and the northern provinces. This truce did not formally recognize the "United Provinces" as an independent entity, though in fact they were. The modern

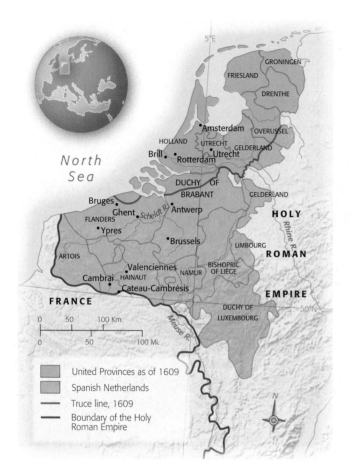

🌐 **MAP 15.2—The Netherlands, 1559–1609**
The seventeen provinces of the Netherlands were strikingly diverse politically, economically, and culturally.

nations of Belgium (the southern Spanish provinces) and the Netherlands are the distant result of this truce.

The independent **United Provinces** (usually called, simply, the Netherlands) was a fragile state, an accident of warfare at first. But commercial prosperity began to emerge as its greatest strength. Much of the economic activity of Antwerp had shifted north to Amsterdam in the province of Holland because of fighting in the south and a naval blockade of Antwerp by rebel ships. Philip's policies had created a new enemy nation and had enriched it at his expense.

In addition, the revolt of the Netherlands lured Spain into wider war, particularly against England. Spain and England had a common foe in France and common economic interests, and Philip had married Mary Tudor, the Catholic queen of England (r. 1553–1558). Even after Mary's death and the accession of her Protestant half sister, Queen Elizabeth (r. 1558–1603), Spanish-English relations remained cordial. Relations started to sour, however, when Elizabeth began tolerating the use of English ports by the rebel Sea Beggars and authorizing attacks by English privateers on Spanish treasure fleets. In response, Spain supported Catholic resistance to Elizabeth within England, including plots to replace her on the throne with

United Provinces The seven northern provinces of the Low Countries that successfully revolted against Spanish rule in the late sixteenth century and became the modern nation of the Netherlands.

her Catholic cousin, Mary, Queen of Scots. Greater Spanish success in the Netherlands, raids by the Spanish and English on each other's shipping, and Elizabeth's execution of Mary in 1587 prompted Philip to order an invasion of England. A fleet (*armada*) of Spanish warships sailed in 1588.

"The enterprise of England," as the plan was called in Spain, represented an astounding logistical effort. The **Armada** was supposed to clear the English Channel of English ships in order to permit an invading force—troops under Parma in the Netherlands—to cross on barges. The sheer number of ships required—about 130—meant that some, inevitably, were slower supply ships, or vessels designed for the more protected waters of the Mediterranean. The English also had the advantage in arms, since they had better long-range artillery and better-trained gunners. Spain's Armada was defeated by the English and by bad weather that dispersed much of the fleet. The invasion failed and fewer than half of the 130-ship Armada ever made it back to Spain.

Armada Massive fleet of Spanish warships sent against England by Philip II but defeated by the English navy and bad weather in 1588. The tactics used by the English helped set the future course of naval warfare.

Successes at Home and Around the Mediterranean

Despite his overseas empire and his preoccupation with the Netherlands, many of Philip's interests still centered on the Mediterranean. In his kingdoms of Spain and their Mediterranean sphere of interest, Philip made his power felt more effectively, though not without effort.

Philip's father, Charles V, had tried to secure the western Mediterranean against the Ottoman Turks and their client states along the African coast, but it was under Philip that the Turkish challenge in the western Mediterranean receded. The Spanish allied temporarily with the papacy and Venice—both were concerned with Turkish naval power in the Mediterranean—and their combined navies inflicted a massive defeat on the Turkish navy at Lepanto, off the coast of Greece, in October 1571 (see **MAP 15.1**). The Turks remained the leading power in the eastern Mediterranean,

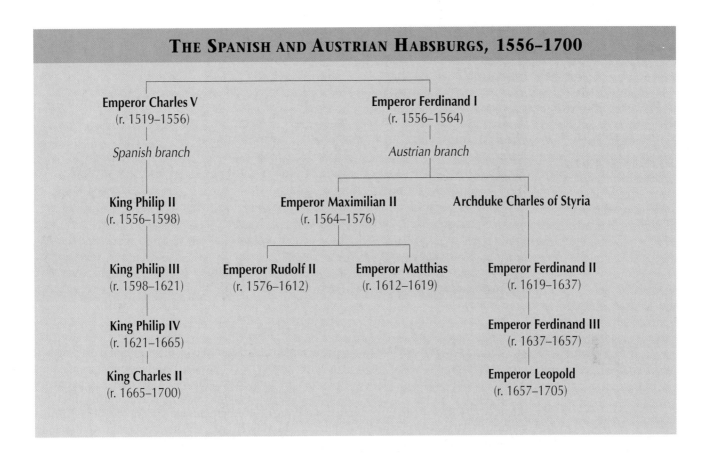

THE SPANISH AND AUSTRIAN HABSBURGS, 1556–1700

Emperor Charles V
(r. 1519–1556)

Spanish branch

Emperor Ferdinand I
(r. 1556–1564)

Austrian branch

King Philip II
(r. 1556–1598)

Emperor Maximilian II
(r. 1564–1576)

Archduke Charles of Styria

King Philip III
(r. 1598–1621)

Emperor Rudolf II
(r. 1576–1612)

Emperor Matthias
(r. 1612–1619)

Emperor Ferdinand II
(r. 1619–1637)

King Philip IV
(r. 1621–1665)

Emperor Ferdinand III
(r. 1637–1657)

King Charles II
(r. 1665–1700)

Emperor Leopold
(r. 1657–1705)

but their ability to threaten Spain and Spanish possessions in the West was over.

To Philip and his advisers, the Turks represented a potential internal threat as well, since it was feared that they might incite rebellion among his Muslim subjects. These were the nominally Christian descendants of the Muslims of Granada, who had been conquered by the Spanish in 1492. Called moriscos, they had been forced to convert to Christianity in 1504 or be expelled from Spain. Yet, no serious effort had been made to teach them Christian beliefs in their own language (Arabic), and they had not been assimilated into Spanish society. Philip inaugurated a new wave of persecution and provoked a massive rebellion by the moriscos that began on Christmas Day in 1568. The revolt took two years to suppress. After it was crushed, the moriscos of Granada were forcibly exiled and dispersed farther north in Spain.

Philip II in 1583   Dressed in the austere black in fashion at the Spanish court, Philip holds a rosary and wears the Order of the Golden Fleece, an order of knighthood, around his neck. Though conscientious to a fault, Philip was a rigid, unimaginative man ill-suited to meet the challenges he faced.   (Philip II of Spain (1527–98) 1565 (oil on canvas), Anguissola, Sofonisba (c. 1532–1625)/Prado, Madrid, Spain /The Bridgeman Art Library)

The Battle of Lepanto   On October 7, 1571, vessels of the Holy League (Spain, Venice, and the papacy) defeated the Ottoman fleet off the coast of Greece. Lepanto was the last great battle between galleys—the oared warships that had dominated Mediterranean waters since ancient times.   (Courtesy, National Maritime Museum)

Philip's power in each of his Spanish kingdoms was limited by the traditional privileges of towns, nobility, and clergy. In Aragon, for example, he could raise revenues only by appealing to local assemblies, the Cortes (core-TEZ). Philip made inroads into Aragonese independence by the end of his reign, however, because noble feuds and peasant rebellions during the 1580s provided an excuse to send in veteran troops from the Netherlands campaigns to establish firmer control. Philip was successful, in the long run, in Aragon, as he had not been in the Netherlands, because he used adequate force but tempered it afterward with constitutional changes that were cleverly moderate. He cemented the peace by appearing in Aragon in person, in the words of a contemporary, "like a rainbow at the end of a storm."[2]

In Castile, the arid kingdom in the center of the Iberian Peninsula, the king was able to levy taxes more easily, but only because of concessions that gave nobles undisputed authority over their peasants. Philip established his permanent capital, Madrid, and his principal residence, the Escorial, there. The Spanish Empire became more and more Castilian as the reign progressed, with royal advisers and counselors increasingly drawn only from the Castilian elite. Yet, the rural economy of Castile was stunted by the dual oppression of landholders and royal tax collectors.

Philip also invaded and annexed Portugal in 1580, temporarily unifying the Iberian Peninsula. The annexation was ensured by force but had been preceded by careful negotiation to guarantee that Philip's claim to the throne—through his mother—would find some support within the country. When Philip died in 1598, he was old and ill, a man for whom daily life had become a painful burden. His Armada had been crushed; the Netherlands had slipped through his fingers. Yet, he had been more successful, by his own standards, in other regions that he ruled.

Spain in Decline, 1600–1648

Spain steadily lost ground economically and strategically after the turn of the century. Imports of silver declined. The American mines were exhausted, and the natives forced to work in them were decimated by European diseases and brutal treatment. Spain's economic health was also threatened by the very success of its colonies: Local industries in the Americas began to produce goods formerly obtained from Spain. Also, Spanish colonists could now buy, from English, French, and Dutch traders, many of the goods they needed. Often, these competitors' goods were cheaper than Spanish ones. Spanish productivity was low and prices were high because of the inflationary effects of the influx of American silver.

Spain renewed hostilities with the United Provinces in 1621, after the truce of 1609 had expired. Philip IV (r. 1621–1665) also aided his Habsburg cousins in the Thirty Years' War in the Holy Roman Empire (see page 428). Squeezed for troops and revenue for these commitments, other Spanish territories revolted. The uprisings reflected both economic distress and unresolved issues of regional autonomy. Castile bore the brunt of the financial support of the state. When Philip IV's chief minister tried to distribute the burdens more equitably among the various regions of Spain, rebellions broke out in Catalonia and Portugal.

In Catalonia, a province of the kingdom of Aragon, Spain resumed control only in 1652, after years of fighting and promises to respect Catalan liberties. In Portugal, a war of independence began in 1640, launched by a popular revolt against Spanish policies. The Spanish government tried to restore order with troops under the command of a leading Portuguese prince, John, duke of Braganza. The duke, however, was the nearest living relative to the last king of Portugal, and he seized this opportunity to claim the crown of Portugal for himself. Although war dragged on until 1668, the Portuguese, under John IV (r. 1640–1656), succeeded in winning independence from Spain. In 1647, upheaval would shake Spain's Italian possessions of Sicily and Naples. By mid-century, Spain had lost its position as the preeminent state in Europe.

SECTION SUMMARY

- Spain was the most powerful state in Europe in the second half of the sixteenth century because it controlled territory in Italy and in the Netherlands, as well as colonies in the Americas.

- The prosperous Netherlands revolted against Spanish control for political, economic, and religious reasons.

- The invention of new kinds of fortifications increased the cost and destructiveness of the war.

- The northern provinces within the Netherlands, called the United Provinces, won independence from Spanish control by 1609.

- Spain attempted, but failed, to invade England with the Armada.

- The Spanish state weakened economically and politically in the seventeenth century as its income from colonies declined.

RELIGIOUS AND POLITICAL CONFLICT IN FRANCE AND ENGLAND

What conditions led to civil war in France? How did religious and political conflict develop differently in England?

In the second half of the sixteenth century, France was convulsed by civil war that had both religious and political causes. A fragile peace was achieved by 1598, but the kingdom was still divided by religion and by military and political challenges to royal authority. England, in contrast, was spared political and religious upheaval in the second half of the century, in part because of the talents and long life of its ruler, Elizabeth I. But in the seventeenth century, religious dissent and political opposition combined to dramatically threaten royal power.

The French Religious Wars, 1562–1598

Civil war wracked France from 1562 until 1598. As in the Netherlands, the conflicts in France had religious and political origins and international consequences. The French monarch, like Philip, was unable to monopolize military power. In 1559, the king of France, Henry II (r. 1547–1559), had concluded the Peace of Cateau-Cambrésis with Philip II, ending the Habsburg-Valois Wars, but died in July of that year from wounds suffered at a tournament held to celebrate the new treaty. His death was a political disaster. Great noble families vied for influence over his young sons, Francis II (r. 1559–1560) and Charles IX (r. 1560-1574). The queen mother, Catherine de' Medici (day MAY-di-chi) (1519–1589), worked carefully and intelligently to balance the nobles' interests. But it proved impossible to keep the conflicts among the great courtiers from boiling over into civil war.

In France, as elsewhere, noble conflict invariably had a violent component. Noblemen carried swords and daggers and were accompanied by armed entourages. Provincial land holdings, together with the royal offices they enjoyed, afforded enough resources to support private warfare, and the nobles assumed the right to wage it.

In addition, religious tension was rising throughout France. Public preaching by and secret meetings of Protestants (known as **Huguenots** in France) were causing unrest in towns. At court,

BACKGROUND TO CIVIL WAR

Huguenots French Protestants, followers of the teachings of John Calvin.

Le Maſsacre fait a Vaſsy le premier iour de Mars. 1562.

A. La grange ou l'on preſchoit ou eſtoyent enuiron 1200 perſonnes.
B. Monſieur de Guiſe qui commandoit.
C. Le Miniſtre dedans la Chaire priant Dieu.
D. Le Miniſtre ſe cuydant ſauuer eſt bleſſé en pluſieurs lieux

& euſt eſté tué ſi l'eſpee ne fuſt rompue en deux.
E. Le Cardinal de Guyſe appuyé ſur l; cimentiere de la paroiſſe.
F. Le toiſt que les gens du preſche rompent pour eux ſauuer,
G. Pluſieurs qui ſe iettans ſur la muraille de la ville ſe ſauuent

aux champs,
H. Pluſieurs qui ſe cuydans ſauuer ſui le toiſt ſont harque, bouſés.
I. Le trone des poures arraché,
k. Les trompetes qui ſonnerent par deux diuerſes fois,

Massacre at Vassy This contemporary engraving by two Protestant artists depicts the Duke of Guise (*center left*) and his men coldly butchering Huguenot worshipers at Vassy. In a Catholic version of the event, the Protestants were killed by gunfire after pelting Guise's men with rocks when they tried to disperse the worshipers. (HIP/Art Resource, NY)

members of leading noble families—including the Bourbons, princes of royal blood—had converted to Protestantism and worshiped openly in their rooms in the palace. In 1561, Catherine convened a national religious council to reconcile the two faiths. When it failed, she chose provisional religious toleration as the only practical course and issued a limited edict of toleration of Huguenots (HEW-guh-nots) in the name of the king in January 1562.

The edict solved nothing. Ignoring its restrictions, Protestants armed themselves, while townspeople of both faiths insulted and attacked one another at worship sites and religious festivals. In March 1562, the armed retainers of a Catholic duke killed a few dozen Protestants gathered in worship at Vassy (vah-SEE), near one of the duke's estates. The killing, bringing the military power of the nobility to bear on the broader problem of religious division, sparked the first of six civil wars.

DECADES OF CIVIL WAR In some ways, the initial conflict in 1562 was decisive. The Protestant army lost the principal pitched battle of the war in December. This defeat reduced the appeal of the Protestant movement to nobles. The limited rights granted by the peace edict in 1563 made it difficult for Protestants in towns—where the vast majority of them lived—to worship. But if the Huguenots were not powerful enough to win, neither were they weak enough to be decisively beaten.

The turning point most obvious to contemporaries came a decade later. The Protestant faction, still represented at court by the Bourbon princes and their allies, pressed the king for war against Spain to aid Protestant rebels in the Netherlands. Opposed to another war against Spain and alarmed by rumors of Huguenot armies massing outside Paris, Charles IX (r. 1560–1574) and his mother authorized royal guards to murder the Protestant leaders on August 24, 1572—Saint Bartholomew's Day. These murders touched off a massacre of Protestants throughout Paris and, once news from Paris had spread, throughout the kingdom.

The Saint Bartholomew's Day Massacre revealed the degree to which religious differences had strained the fabric of community life. Neighbor murdered neighbor in an effort to rid the community of heretical pollution; bodies of the dead were mutilated. Gathered in the south of France, the remaining Huguenot forces vowed "never [to] trust those who have so often and so treacherously broken faith and the public peace."[3] Huguenot writers published tracts arguing that royal power was by nature limited and that rebellion was justified against tyrants who overstepped their legitimate authority.

Many Catholics also renounced reconciliation. Some noblemen formed a Catholic league to fight in place of the weakened monarchy. Charles's successor, his brother Henry III (r. 1574–1589), was forced to cooperate with first one of the warring parties and then another. In December 1588, he resorted to murdering two leaders of the ultra-Catholic faction; in turn, he was murdered by a priest in early 1589.

The new king was the Bourbon prince Henry of Navarre, who became Henry IV (r. 1589–1610). He was a Protestant, and he had to fight for his throne. He faced Catholic armies now subsidized by Philip II of Spain, an extremist Catholic city government in Paris, and subjects who were tired of war but mainly Catholic. Given these obstacles, the politically astute Henry agreed to convert to Catholicism.

After his conversion in 1593, many of Henry's subjects believed that only rallying to the monarchy could save France from chaos. In any case, nobles were increasingly inclined to cooperate with the Crown. Service to a successful king was honorable and a source of patronage; Henry was personally esteemed because he was a talented general and brave, gregarious, and charming. The nobility forced the citizens of Paris and other cities to accept Henry's authority. The civil war period thus proved to be an important phase in the accommodation of the nobility to the power of the state.

In April 1598, Henry granted toleration for the Huguenot minority in a royal edict proclaimed in the city of Nantes (NAHNT). The **Edict of Nantes** was primarily a repetition of provisions from the most generous edicts that had ended the various civil wars. Nobles were allowed to practice the Protestant faith on their estates; townspeople were granted more limited rights to worship in selected towns in each region. Protestants were also guaranteed rights of self-defense—specifically, the right to maintain garrisons in about two hundred towns. About half of these garrisons would be paid for by the Crown.

The problem was that the Edict of Nantes, like any royal edict, could be revoked by the king at any time. Moreover, the provision allowing Protestants to keep garrisoned towns reflected concessions to Protestant aristocrats, who could support their followers by paid garrison duty. It also reflected the assumption that living peacefully amid religious diversity might prove to be impossible. Thus, although Henry IV ended the French religious wars, he had not solved the problem of religious and political division within France.

Edict of Nantes   1598 edict of Henry IV, granting France's Protestants (Huguenots) the right to practice their faith and maintain defensive garrisons.

The Consolidation of Royal Authority in France, 1598–1643

During Henry IV's reign, France began to recover from the long years of civil war. Population and productivity began to grow; the Crown increased royal revenue by nibbling away at traditional local self-government and control of taxation.

Yet, Henry's regime was stable only in comparison with the preceding years of civil war. The power of the great nobility had not been definitively broken. Also, the king had agreed to a measure, known as the *paulette* (named for the functionary who first administered it), that allowed royal officeholders to own their offices and to pass on those offices to their heirs in return for the payment of an annual fee. The paulette was primarily a device to raise revenue after decades of civil war, but it also helped cement the loyalty of royal bureaucrats at a critical time, particularly that of the royal judges of the supreme law court, the Parlement of Paris, who had recently agreed to register the Edict of Nantes only under duress. However, the paulette made royal officeholders largely immune from royal control, since their posts were now in effect property, like the landed property of the traditional nobility.

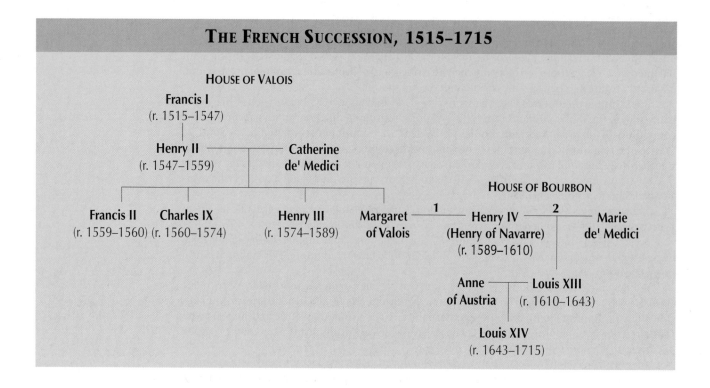

THE FRENCH SUCCESSION, 1515–1715

HOUSE OF VALOIS

Francis I
(r. 1515–1547)

Henry II ——— Catherine
(r. 1547–1559)   de' Medici

HOUSE OF BOURBON

Francis II   Charles IX   Henry III   Margaret ——1—— Henry IV ——2—— Marie
(r. 1559–1560) (r. 1560–1574) (r. 1574–1589) of Valois   (Henry of Navarre)   de' Medici
                                                            (r. 1589–1610)

Anne ——— Louis XIII
of Austria   (r. 1610–1643)

Louis XIV
(r. 1643–1715)

In 1610, a fanatical Catholic assassinated Henry IV. Henry's death brought his 9-year-old son, Louis XIII (r. 1610–1643), to the throne with Louis's mother, Marie de' Medici, initially serving as regent. Within four years, Louis faced a major rebellion by his Huguenot subjects in southwestern France. Huguenots felt that Louis's policies, including his recent marriage to a Spanish princess, meant that royal support for toleration was wavering. The war persisted, on and off, for eight years, as the French royal troops, like the Spanish in the Netherlands, had difficulty breaching the defenses of even small fortress towns held by the Protestants. The main Huguenot stronghold was the well-fortified port city of La Rochelle, which had grown wealthy from European and overseas trade. Not until the king took the city, after a siege lasting more than a year, did the Protestants accept a peace on royal terms.

The Peace of Alais (ah-LAY) (1629) reaffirmed the policy of religious toleration but rescinded the Protestants' military and political privileges. It was a political triumph for the Crown because it deprived French Protestants of the means for further rebellion, while reinforcing their dependence on the Crown for religious toleration. Most of the remaining great noble leaders began to convert to Catholicism.

The Peace of Alais was also a personal triumph for the king's leading minister, who crafted the treaty and had directed the bloody siege that made it possible. Armand-Jean du Plessis (1585–1642), Cardinal Richelieu (RISH-el-yiuh), came from a provincial noble family and rose in the service of the queen mother. He was admired and feared for his skill in the political game of seeking and bestowing patronage—a crucial skill in an age when elites received offices and honors through carefully cultivated relationships at court. He and the king—whose sensitive temperament Richelieu handled adeptly—formed a lasting partnership that had a decisive impact, not only on French policy, but also on the entire shape of the French state.

Richelieu favored an aggressive foreign policy to counter what he believed still to be the greatest external threat to the French crown: the Spanish Habsburgs. After war resumed between the Netherlands and Spain in 1621 (see page 428), Richelieu attacked Spanish possessions in Italy, superintended large-scale fighting against Spain in the Netherlands itself, and subsidized Swedish and German Protestant armies fighting the Habsburgs in Germany.

Richelieu's policies were opposed by many French people, who saw taxes double, then triple, in just a few years. Many courtiers and provincial elites favored keeping the peace with Spain, a fellow Catholic state, and objected to alliances with German Protestants. They were also alarmed by the revolts that accompanied the peasants' distress. Their own status was also directly threatened by Richelieu's monopoly of royal patronage and by his creation of new offices, which undermined their power. In 1632, for example, Richelieu created the office of *intendant*. Intendants had wide powers for defense and administration in the provinces that overrode the established bureaucracy.

By 1640, Richelieu's ambitious foreign policy seemed to be bearing fruit. The French had won territory along their northern and eastern borders by their successes against Habsburg forces. But when Richelieu and Louis XIII died within five months of each other, in December 1642 and May 1643, Louis XIII was succeeded by his 5-year-old son, and the warrior-nobility, as well as royal bureaucrats, would waste little time before challenging the Crown's new authority.

Precarious Stability in England: The Reign of Elizabeth I, 1558–1603

England experienced no civil wars during the second half of the sixteenth century, but religious dissent challenged the stability of the monarchy. In **Elizabeth I** (r. 1558–1603), England—in stark contrast to France—possessed an able and long-lived ruler. Elizabeth was well educated in the humanistic tradition and was already an adroit politician at the age of 25, when she acceded to the throne at the death of her Catholic half sister, Mary Tudor (r. 1553–1558).

Elizabeth faced the urgent problem of effecting a religious settlement. Her father, Henry VIII (r. 1509–1547), had broken away from the Catholic Church for political reasons but had retained many Catholic doctrines and practices. A Calvinist-inspired Protestantism had been prescribed for the Church of England by the advisers of Henry's successor, Elizabeth's young half brother, Edward VI (r. 1547–1553). True Catholicism, such as her half sister Mary had tried to reimpose, was out of the question. The Roman church had never recognized Henry VIII's self-made divorce from Mary's mother and thus regarded Elizabeth as a bastard with no right to the throne.

Elizabeth reimposed royal control over the church and made limited concessions to accommodate the beliefs of a wide range of her subjects. In 1559, Parliament passed a new Act of Supremacy, which restored the monarch as head of the Church of England. Elizabeth dealt with opposition to the act by arresting bishops and lords whose votes would have blocked its passage by Parliament. The official prayer book, in use in Edward's day, was revised to include elements of both traditional and radical Protestant interpretations of Communion. But church liturgy, clerical vestments, and, above all, the hierarchical structure of the clergy closely resembled Catholic practices. The Act of Uniformity, also passed in 1559, required all worship to be conducted according to the new prayer book. Although uniformity was required in worship, Elizabeth was careful, in her words, not to "shine beacons into her subjects' souls."

Catholicism continued to be practiced, especially by otherwise loyal nobility and gentry in the north of England, who worshiped privately on their estates. But priests returning from exile beginning in the 1570s, most newly imbued with the proselytizing zeal of the Counter-Reformation (the Catholic response to the Protestant Reformation), practiced it more visibly and were zealously prosecuted for their boldness. In the last twenty years of Elizabeth's reign, approximately 180 Catholics were executed for treason, two-thirds of them priests. (By 1585, being a Catholic priest in itself was a crime.)

In the long run, the greater threat to the English crown came from the most radical Protestants in the realm, known (by their enemies initially) as **Puritans**. Puritanism was a broad movement for reform of church practice along familiar Protestant lines: an emphasis on Bible reading, preaching, and private scrutiny of conscience; a de-emphasis on institutional ritual and clerical authority. Most Puritans had accepted Elizabeth's religious compromise because they had no choice, but grew increasingly alienated by her insistence on clerical authority and her refusal to change any elements of the original religious settlement. A significant Presbyterian underground movement began to form among them. Presbyterians wanted to dismantle the episcopacy—the hierarchy of priests and bishops—and to govern the church instead with councils, called "presbyteries," that included lay members of the congregation. Laws were passed late in the queen's reign to enable the Crown to prosecute

Elizabeth I Able and long-lived ruler who firmly established Protestantism in England and defended the nation against the Spanish Armada, but who bequeathed financial, religious, and political problems to her successors.

Puritans Radical Protestants in late-sixteenth- and seventeenth-century England who became a majority in Parliament during the reign of Charles I and led opposition to the king.

more easily, and even to force into exile, anyone who attended "nonconformist" (non-Anglican) services.

The greatest challenge Elizabeth faced from Puritans came in Parliament, where they were well represented by many literate gentry. Parliament met only when called by the monarch. In theory, members could merely voice opinions and complaints; they could not initiate legislation and prescribe policy. However, only Parliament could vote taxes. Further, since it had in effect helped constitute royal authority by means of the two Acts of Supremacy, Parliament's merely advisory role had been expanded by the monarchy itself. During Elizabeth's reign, Puritans capitalized on Parliament's enlarged scope, using meetings to press for further religious reform. In 1586, they went so far as to introduce bills calling for an end to the episcopacy and the Anglican prayer book. Elizabeth had to resort to imprisoning one Puritan leader to end debate on the issue and on Parliament's right to address it.

Also during Elizabeth's reign, efforts at English expansion in the New World began, in the form of unsuccessful attempts at colonization and successful raids on Spanish possessions. However, the main focus of her foreign policy remained Europe itself. Elizabeth, like all her forebears, felt her interests tightly linked to the independence of the Netherlands, whose towns were a major outlet for English wool. Philip II's aggressive policy in the Netherlands increasingly alarmed her, especially in view of France's weakness. She began to send small sums of money to the rebels and allowed their ships access to southern English ports, from which they could raid Spanish-held towns on the Netherlands' coast. In 1585, in the wake of the duke of Parma's successes against the rebellions, she committed troops to help the rebels.

Her decision was a reaction, not only to the threat of a single continental power dominating the Netherlands, but also to the threat of Catholicism. From 1579 to 1583, the Spanish had helped the Irish fight English domination and were involved in several plots to replace Elizabeth with her Catholic cousin, Mary, Queen of Scots. These threats occurred as the return of Catholic exiles to England peaked. The victory over the Spanish Armada in 1588 was quite rightly celebrated, for it ended any Catholic threat to Elizabeth's rule.

The success against the Armada has tended to overshadow other aspects of Elizabeth's foreign policy, particularly with regard to Ireland. Since the twelfth century, an Anglo-Irish state, dominated by transplanted English families, had been loosely supervised from England, but most of

Elizabeth I: The Armada Portrait   Both serene and resolute, Elizabeth is flanked by "before" and "after" glimpses of the Spanish fleet; her hand rests on the globe in a gesture of dominion that also memorializes the circumnavigation of the globe by her famous captain, Sir Francis Drake, some years before.   (Elizabeth I, Armada Portrait, c. 1588 (oil on panel), Gower, George (1540–96) (attr. to)/ Woburn Abbey, Bedfordshire, UK/The Bridgeman Art Library)

Ireland remained under the control of Gaelic chieftains. Just as Charles V and Philip II attempted to tighten their governing mechanisms in the Netherlands, so did Henry VIII's minister, Thomas Cromwell, streamline control of outlying areas such as Wales and Anglo-Ireland. Cromwell proposed that the whole of Ireland be brought under English control, partly by the established mechanism of feudal ties: The Irish chieftains were to pay homage as vassals to the king of England.

Under Elizabeth, this legalistic approach gave way to virtual conquest. Elizabeth's governor, Sir Henry Sidney, appointed in 1565, inaugurated a policy whereby Gaelic lords, by means of various technicalities, could be entirely dispossessed of their lands. Any Englishman capable of raising a private force could help enforce these dispossessions and settle his conquered lands as he saw fit. This policy provoked stiff Irish resistance, which was viewed as rebellion and provided the rationale for further military action, more confiscations of lands, and more new English settlers. Eventually the Irish, with Spanish assistance, mounted a major rebellion, consciously Catholic and aimed against the "heretic" queen. The rebellion gave the English an excuse for brutal suppression and massive transfers of lands to English control. The political domination of the Irish was complete with the defeat, in 1601, of the Gaelic chieftain Hugh O'Neill, lord of Tyrone, who had controlled most of the northern quarter of the island. Although the English were unable to impose Protestantism on the conquered Irish, to Elizabeth and her English subjects, the conquests in Ireland seemed as significant as the victory over the Spanish Armada.

The English enjoyed relative peace at home during Elizabeth's reign. However, her reign ended on a note of strain. The foreign involvements, particularly in Ireland, had been very expensive. Taxation granted by Parliament more than doubled during her reign, and local taxes further burdened the people. Price inflation related to government spending, social problems caused by returned unemployed soldiers, and a series of bad harvests heightened popular resentment against taxation. Despite her achievements, therefore, Elizabeth passed two problems on to her successors: unresolved religious tensions and financial instability. Elizabeth's successors would also find in Parliament an increasing focus of opposition to their policies.

Rising Tensions in England, 1603–1642

In 1603, Queen Elizabeth died, and James VI of Scotland, the Protestant son of Mary, Queen of Scots, ascended to the English throne as James I (r. 1603–1625). Tensions between Anglicans and Puritans were briefly quieted under James because of a plot, in 1605, by Catholic dissenters. The Gunpowder Plot, as it was called, was a conspiracy to blow up the palace housing both king and Parliament at Westminster. Protestants of all stripes again focused on their common enemy, Catholics—though only temporarily.

Financial problems were James's most pressing concern. Court life became more elaborate and an increasing drain on the monarchy's resources. James's extravagance was partly to blame, but so were pressures for patronage from courtiers. To the debts left from the Irish conflicts and wars with Spain, James added new expenses to defend the claims of his daughter and her husband, a German prince, to rule Bohemia (see page 427).

JAMES I

To raise revenue without Parliament's consent, James relied on sources of income that the Crown had enjoyed since medieval times: customs duties, wardship (the right to manage and liberally borrow from the estates of minor nobles), and the sale of monopolies, which conveyed the right to be sole agent for a particular kind of goods. James's increase of the number of monopolies for sale was widely resented. Merchants objected to the arbitrary restriction of production and trade; common people found that they could no longer afford certain ordinary goods, such as soap, under monopoly prices. Criticism of the court escalated, particularly by the nobility, as James indulged in extreme favoritism of certain courtiers. He even created a new noble title—baronet—which he sold to socially ambitious commoners.

When James summoned Parliament to ask for funds in 1621, Parliament used the occasion to protest court corruption and the king's financial measures. The members revived the medieval procedure of impeachment and removed two royal ministers from office. In 1624, still faced with expensive commitments to Protestants abroad, James again called Parliament, which voted new taxes but also openly debated the wisdom of the king's foreign policy.

Tensions between Crown and Parliament increased under James's son, Charles I (r. 1625–1649). Charles's foreign policy caused both financial strain and political opposition. Charles declared war on Spain and supported the Huguenot rebels in France. Many merchants opposed this

CHARLES I

Criticism of Monopolies Holders of royally granted monopolies were bitterly resented by English consumers and tradespeople alike, as this contemporary print reveals. The greedy beast pictured here controls even ordinary commodities such as pins, soap, and butter. (Courtesy of the Trustees of the British Museum)

aggressive foreign policy because it disrupted trade. In 1626, Parliament was dissolved without granting any monies, in order to stifle its objections to his policies. Instead, Charles levied a forced loan and imprisoned gentry who refused to lend money to the government.

Above all, Charles's religious policies caused controversy. Charles was personally inclined toward "high church" practices: an emphasis on ceremony and sacrament reminiscent of Catholic ritual. He also was a believer in Arminianism, a school of thought that rejected the Calvinist notion that God's grace cannot be earned, and hence emphasized the importance of the sacraments and the authority of the clergy. Charles's views put him on a collision course with gentry and aristocrats who leaned toward Puritanism.

Charles's views were supported by William Laud (1573–1645), archbishop of Canterbury from 1633, and thus leader of the Church of England. He tried to impose changes in worship, spread Arminian ideas, and censor opposing views. He also challenged the redistribution of church property, which had occurred in the Reformation of the sixteenth century, and thereby alienated the gentry on economic as well as religious grounds.

Charles's style of rule worsened religious, political, and economic tensions. Cold and intensely private, he lacked the charm and the political skills to disarm his opponents. His court was ruled by formal protocol, and access to the king was highly restricted—a serious problem in an age when proximity to the monarch was a guarantee of political power.

Revenue and religion dominated debate in the Parliament of 1628–1629, which Charles had called, once again, to get funds for his foreign wars. Parliament presented the king with a document called the Petition of Right, which protested his financial policies, as well as arbitrary imprisonment. (Seventeen members of Parliament had been imprisoned for refusing loans to the Crown.) Though couched conservatively as a restatement of customary practice, the petition, in fact, claimed a tradition of expanded parliamentary participation in government. Charles dissolved Parliament in March 1629, having decided that the money he might extract was not worth the risk.

For eleven years, Charles ruled without Parliament. When he was forced to summon it again in 1640, the kingdom was in crisis. Royal finances were in desperate straits, even though Charles had pressed collection of revenues far beyond traditional bounds.

1640: THE KINGDOM IN CRISIS

The immediate crisis and the reason for Charles's desperate need for money was a rebellion in Scotland. Like Philip II in the Netherlands, Charles tried to rule in Scotland through a small council of men who did not represent local elites. Worse, he also tried to force his "high church" practices on the Scots. The Scottish church had been more dramatically reshaped during the Reformation and now was largely Presbyterian in structure. The result of Charles's policies was riots and rebellion. Unable to suppress the revolt in a first campaign in 1639, Charles was forced to summon Parliament for funds to raise a more effective army.

But the Parliament that assembled in the spring of 1640 provided no help. Instead, members questioned the war with the Scots and other royal policies. Charles's political skills were far too limited for him to reestablish a workable relationship with Parliament under the circumstances. Charles dissolved this body, which is now known as the "Short Parliament," after just three weeks. Even more stinging than Charles's dissolution of the Parliament was the lack of respect he had shown the members: A number of them were harassed or arrested. Mistrust, fomented by the eleven years in which Charles had ruled without Parliament, thus increased.

Another humiliating defeat at the hands of the Scots, later in 1640, made summoning another Parliament imperative. Members of the "Long Parliament" (it sat from 1640 to 1653) took full advantage of the king's predicament. Charles was forced to agree not to dissolve or adjourn Parliament without the members' consent and to summon Parliament at least every three years. Parliament abolished many of the traditional revenues he had abused and impeached and removed from office his leading ministers, including Archbishop Laud. The royal commander deemed responsible for the Scottish fiasco, Thomas Wentworth, earl of Strafford, was executed without trial in May 1641.

The execution of Strafford shocked many aristocrats in the House of Lords (the upper house of Parliament), as well as some moderate members of the House of Commons. Meanwhile, Parliament began debating the perennially thorny religious question. A bare majority of members favored abolition of Anglican bishops as a first step in thoroughgoing religious reform. Working people in London, kept updated on the issues by the regular publication of parliamentary debates, demonstrated in support of that move. Moderate members of Parliament, in contrast, favored checking the king's power, but not upsetting the Elizabethan religious compromise.

An event that unified public and parliamentary opinion at a crucial time—a revolt against English rule in Ireland in October 1641—temporarily eclipsed these divisions over religious policy but did not diminish suspicion of the king. Fearing that Charles would use Irish soldiers against his English subjects, Parliament demanded that it control the army to put down the rebellion. In November, the Puritan majority introduced a document known as the "Grand Remonstrance," an appeal to the people and a long catalog of parliamentary grievances against the king. It passed by a narrow margin, further inflaming public opinion in London against Charles. The king's remaining support in Parliament eroded in January 1642, when he tried to arrest five members on charges of treason. The five escaped, and the stage was set for wider violence. The king withdrew from London, unsure he could defend himself there, and began to raise an army. In mid-1642, the kingdom stood at the brink of civil war.

SECTION SUMMARY

- France suffered through more than thirty years of civil war after 1562, caused by religious conflict, weak rulers, and powerful nobility.

- The French religious wars ended in the 1590s, when war-weary elites rallied behind the talented king Henry IV; Henry decreed religious toleration in the Edict of Nantes.

- After Henry, religious and political conflict broke out again, but the king's minister, Cardinal Richelieu, successfully reinforced royal authority.

- Elizabeth I of England weathered religious and political tensions at home and challenges from abroad during her long reign.

- James I and Charles I struggled with limited financial resources, unpopular policies, and religious division.

- Parliamentary resistance to Charles's authority and policies led England to a political crisis in 1640.

THE HOLY ROMAN EMPIRE AND THE THIRTY YEARS' WAR

Why did war erupt again within the Holy Roman Empire and what was the significance of the conflict?

The Holy Roman Empire enjoyed a period of comparative quiet after the Peace of Augsburg halted religious and political wars in 1555. The 1555 agreement had permitted rulers of the various states within the empire to impose either Catholicism or Lutheranism in their lands. By the early seventeenth century, however, fresh causes of instability brought about renewed fighting. One factor was the rise of Calvinism, for which no provision had been necessary in 1555. Also destabilizing was the attempt by the Austrian Habsburgs to reverse the successes of Protestantism, both in their own lands and in the empire at large, and to solidify their control of their own diverse territories. The result was a devastating conflict known as the **Thirty Years' War** (1618–1648).

Like conflicts elsewhere in Europe, the Thirty Years' War reflected religious tensions, regionalism versus centralizing forces, and dynastic and strategic rivalries between rulers. As a result of the war, the empire was eclipsed as a political unit by the regional powers that composed it.

Thirty Years' War Destructive war (1618–1648) involving most European countries but fought in Germany, resulting from religious tensions, regionalism versus centralizing forces, and dynastic and strategic rivalries between rulers.

Fragile Peace in the Holy Roman Empire, 1556–1618

The Austrian Habsburgs ruled over a diverse group of territories in the Holy Roman Empire, as well as northwestern Hungary. On his abdication in 1556, Emperor Charles V granted the Habsburg lands in the Holy Roman Empire to his brother, Ferdinand (see the chart on page 415), who was duly crowned emperor when Charles died in 1558.

🌐 **Map 15.3—Europe During the Thirty Years' War, 1618–1648**
The Thirty Years' War was fought largely within the borders of the Holy Roman Empire.
It was the result of conflicts within the empire as well as the meddling of neighbors for
their own strategic advantages.

Though largely contiguous, Ferdinand's territories comprised independent duchies
and kingdoms. In addition to the Habsburgs' ancestral lands (separate territories more or
less equivalent to modern Austria in extent), Ferdinand also ruled the non-German lands of
Bohemia (the core of the modern Czech Republic) and Hungary (see **Map 15.3**). Both kingdoms
bestowed their crowns by election and had chosen Ferdinand, the first Habsburg to rule them,

in separate elections in the 1520s and 1530s. Most of Hungary was now under Ottoman control, but the kingdom of Bohemia, with its rich capital, Prague, was a wealthy center of population and culture.

Unlike the Netherlands, each of these linguistically and culturally diverse lands was still governed by its own distinct institutions. Moreover, unlike their Spanish cousins, the Austrian Habsburgs made no attempt to impose religious uniformity in the late sixteenth century. Ferdinand was Catholic but tolerant of reform efforts within the church. Both he and his son, Maximilian II (r. 1564–1576), believed that an eventual reunion of the Catholic and Protestant faiths might be possible. During his reign, Maximilian worked to keep religious peace in the empire as a whole and granted limited rights of worship to Protestant subjects in the Habsburgs' own lands. Catholicism and many varieties of Protestantism flourished side by side in Maximilian's domains, particularly in Hungary and, especially, Bohemia, which had experienced a religious reform movement under Jan Hus in the fifteenth century.

Maximilian's son, Rudolf II (r. 1576–1612), shared the religious style of his father and grandfather. He patronized education and the arts and sponsored the work of scientists. Yet, Rudolf was a weak leader politically and was challenged by his brother and ambitious cousins for control both of Habsburg lands and of the empire itself. Meanwhile, the resurgence of Catholicism in the wake of the Council of Trent (1545–1563) had begun to shift the religious balance. Members of the Jesuit order arrived in Habsburg lands in the reign of Maximilian. Tough-minded and well trained, they established Catholic schools and became confessors and preachers to the upper classes. Self-confident Catholicism emerged as a potent form of cultural identity among the German-speaking ruling classes, and thus, as a religious impetus to further political consolidation of all the Habsburg territories.

Resurgent Catholicism spread in the empire as a whole, too, and many Catholic princes believed they might now eliminate Protestantism, as their ancestors had failed to do. Like the English under Elizabeth, Habsburg subjects and peoples in the empire had enjoyed a period of calm in political and religious matters. Now, as in England, the stage was set for conflict of both kinds.

The Thirty Years' War, 1618–1648

The Thirty Years' War was touched off in 1618 by a revolt against Habsburg rule in the kingdom of Bohemia. Rudolf II had made Bohemia's bustling capital, Prague, his imperial capital. Its powerful Protestant community had wrested formal recognition of its right to worship from Rudolf and his younger brother, Matthias (r. 1612–1619).

Matthias was quickly succeeded by his cousin Ferdinand II (r. 1619–1637), who did not honor these agreements. Educated by the Jesuits, Ferdinand sincerely believed that reimposing Catholicism was his Christian duty; he once stated that he would "sooner beg than rule over heretics."[4] He would not tolerate the political independence of nobles and towns in Bohemia or the religious pluralism that independence defended. As Philip II had done in the Netherlands, Ferdinand appointed a council to govern in his name, which enforced unpopular policies, such as denying the right to build Protestant churches and barring non-Catholics from serving in government.

On May 23, 1618, delegates to a Protestant assembly that had unsuccessfully petitioned Ferdinand to honor his predecessors' earlier guarantees marched to the palace in Prague where his officials met. After a confrontation over their demands, the delegates "tried" the officials on the spot for treason and, literally, threw them out of the palace window. The incident became known as the "Defenestration of Prague" (from the Latin *fenestra*, or "window"). (The officials survived because they fell into a pile of garbage in the moat.) The rebels set up their own government.

This upstart Bohemian government officially deposed Ferdinand and elected a new Bohemian king in 1619: Frederick, the Protestant elector of the Palatinate. His election had implications for the Holy Roman Empire as a whole because his territories in west-central Germany, called the Lower and Upper Palatinate, conveyed the right to be one of the seven electors who chose the emperor.

The revolt in Bohemia set off a wider war because foreign rulers also felt their interests to be involved. The English king, James I, supported Frederick because Frederick was married to his daughter. Spain's supply routes north from Italy to the Netherlands passed next to Frederick's lands in western Germany. France's first interest was its rivalry with Spain; thus, France kept its

The Defenestration of Prague This contemporary print memorializes the events of May 23, 1618. Bohemian Protestants "tried" two imperial officials for violating agreements that safeguarded their religious liberties. The two officials and their secretary were thrown out of the windows of Prague castle. (Corbis)

eye on the border principalities that were strategically important to Spain and wanted to keep Protestant, as well as Catholic, princes within the empire strong enough to thwart Austrian Habsburg ambitions. Thus, from the outset, the war was a conflict not only over the Habsburgs' power in their own lands, but also over the balance of religious and political power in the empire and in Europe (see **Map 15.3**).

Ferdinand secured aid from Catholic princes, including his cousin, King Philip III (r. 1598–1621) of Spain, by promising them Frederick's lands in the Palatinate. By the fall of 1620, a Catholic army faced Bohemian rebels who had received little support as yet from fellow Protestants. The Battle of White Mountain, in November, was a complete Catholic victory.

Despite the rout, fighting did not end, but instead became more widespread. The 1609 truce between Spain and the Netherlands expired in 1621, and the nearby Lower Palatinate, now in Spanish hands, offered a staging point for Spanish forces and thus threatened the peace in that corner of the empire. Claiming to be a Protestant champion, the Protestant king of Denmark, Christian IV (r. 1588–1648), who was also duke of Holstein in northern Germany, entered the fight. He wanted to gain greater control over German Baltic seaports and to defend his northern German territories against any Catholic aggressors. Christian received little help from fellow Protestants, however. The Dutch were busy with Spain, the English were wary of fighting after Frederick's defeat, and Denmark's rival, the Swedes, were not interested in helping Danish ambitions in the Baltic.

Just as Protestant powers did not always support each other, neither did Catholic ones. When imperial forces defeated Denmark's armies in 1626, Catholic princes became alarmed at the possibility of greater imperial power in northern Germany. Led by the duke of Bavaria, they arranged a truce that resulted in Denmark's withdrawal from the fighting on relatively generous terms.

The Danish king's rival, Gustav Adolf, king of Sweden (r. 1611–1632), hoping to gain territory along the Baltic seacoast, now assumed the role of Protestant leader. Gustav Adolf was an innovative commander and his campaigns were capped by a victory over an imperial army at Breitenfeld, in Saxony, in 1631. However, the tide turned in favor of Ferdinand's forces when Gustav Adolf was killed in battle the following year; further imperial victories led to the Peace of Prague (1635), a general peace treaty favorable to Catholics.

The Peace of Prague brought only a temporary peace, however, because Ferdinand died shortly afterwards and French involvement increased now that other anti-Habsburg forces had been eclipsed. France seized imperial territory along its own eastern border and subsidized continued war within the empire by channeling monies to Protestant princes and mercenaries there. The fighting dragged on. By the end of the Thirty Years' War, order had disintegrated so completely in the wake of the marauding armies that both Catholic and Protestant rulers willingly allied with any power necessary, even religious enemies, to safeguard their states.

A comprehensive peace treaty became possible when France withdrew its sponsorship of the fighting in order to concentrate on its conflict with Spain, namely, the continued rivalry with the Spanish Habsburgs for control of territory along France's eastern and northern borders and in Italy. The French wanted only a workable balance of power in the empire, which had been achieved with a convincing defeat of imperial forces in 1645. Negotiations for peace began among war-weary states of the empire in 1643 and resulted in a group of agreements known as the **Peace of Westphalia** (west-FAIL-yuh) in 1648.

Peace of Westphalia
Treaty that ended the Thirty Years' War in 1648. The principalities within the Holy Roman Empire were recognized as virtually autonomous, severely weakening the power of the emperor.

The Effects of the War

The Thirty Years' War ruined the economy and decimated the population in many parts of the empire and had long-term political consequences for the empire as a whole. One reason for the war's devastation was a novel application of firepower to warfare that increased both the size of armies and their deadly force in battle. This was the use of volley fire, the arrangement of foot soldiers in parallel lines so that one line of men could fire while another reloaded. This tactic, pioneered in the Netherlands around the turn of the century, was refined by Gustav Adolf of Sweden. He amassed large numbers of troops and increased the rate of fire so that a virtually continuous barrage was maintained. He also used maneuverable field artillery to protect the massed infantry from cavalry charges.

Following Gustav Adolf's lead, armies of all the major states adopted these new offensive tactics. But defensive expertise—as in holding fortresses—also remained important, and pitched battles still tended to be part of sieges. The costs in resources and human life of this kind of warfare reached unheard-of dimensions. Compounding these effects of battle was the behavior of troops hired by enterprising mercenary generals, for whom loyalty to the princes who paid them took a back seat to personal advancement. They were contracted to provide and supply troops and thus were more willing than the princes would have been to allow armies to live "economically" on plunder. European states could field large armies but had not yet evolved the mechanisms fully to fund, and thus control, them. Popular printed literature and court drama both condemned the horrors of the war.

Where fighting had been concentrated, as in parts of Saxony, between one-third and one-half of the inhabitants of rural villages and major towns may have disappeared. Many starved, were caught in the fighting, or were killed by marauding soldiers. Some people migrated to other regions or joined the armies simply in order to survive.

The Peace of Westphalia was one of the most important outcomes of the war. The various individual treaties composing the Peace effectively put an end to religious war in the empire. Calvinism was recognized as a tolerated religion. The requirement that all subjects must follow their ruler's faith was retained, but some leeway was allowed for those who now found themselves under new rulers.

In political matters, the treaties reflected Swedish successes by granting them territory on the Baltic coast. France gained the important towns of Metz, Toul, and Verdun on its eastern border. Spain formally recognized the independence of the Netherlands. The son of Frederick, Protestant king of Bohemia, received back the smaller of the two Palatine territories that his father had held. The Upper Palatinate—as well as

The Horrors of War   The painter of this scene of soldiers plundering a farm in the Thirty Years' War was himself a veteran of Spanish campaigns in the Netherlands. The scene he depicts was commonplace in this era of poorly-supplied troops: soldiers loot a household, killing peasants who refused to hand over their own stores of food   (Soldiers Plundering a Farm during the Thirty Years' War, 1620 (oil on wood), Vrancx, Sebastian (1573–1647)/Deutsches Historisches Museum, Berlin, Germany/©DHM/The Bridgeman Art Library)

SECTION SUMMARY

- The Holy Roman Empire was relatively peaceful until destabilized by the spread of Calvinism and the ambition of the Austrian Habsburgs to extend their political and religious control within the empire.

- The Thirty Years' War started in Bohemia (modern Czech Republic) when local leaders challenged Habsburg policies.

- The Bohemian revolt led to a wider war because many rulers, inside and outside Germany, had a stake in the balance of religious and political power there.

- Large armies of mercenaries caused widespread devastation in certain areas of Germany.

- The Peace of Westphalia established a new balance of power between states within the Holy Roman Empire, but the empire itself declined as a political entity.

the right to be a new elector of the emperor—was given to the Catholic duke of Bavaria.

The most important political outcome of the peace, however, was a new balance of power in the empire. Most of the major Catholic and Protestant rulers extended their territories at the expense of smaller principalities and cities. The principalities within the empire were acknowledged, in the peace, to be virtually autonomous, both from the emperor and from one another. In addition, the constitution of the empire was changed to make it very difficult for one prince or a group of princes to disrupt the peace in their own interests. As a result, the agreements at Westphalia were the beginning of one hundred years of peace within the Holy Roman Empire.

Another outcome was that the Habsburgs, though weakened as emperors, were strengthened as rulers of their own hereditary lands on the eastern fringes of the empire. They moved their capital back to Vienna from Prague, and the government of their hereditary lands gained in importance as administration of the empire waned.

ECONOMIC CHANGE AND SOCIAL TENSIONS

What caused the economic stresses of these decades and how did ordinary people cope with them?

Religious strife disrupted the everyday lives of whole communities in the late sixteenth and early seventeenth centuries. Wars devastated many areas of western Europe and contributed to severe economic decline in parts of the Low Countries (the Netherlands), France, and the Holy Roman Empire. But other factors, most notably a steady rise in prices, also played a role in the dramatic economic and social changes of the century after 1550. Economic changes altered power relations in cities, in the countryside, and in the relationship of both to central governments. Ordinary people managed their economic difficulties in a variety of ways: they sought new sources of work; they protested against burdensome taxes; sometimes they found scapegoats for their distress among their neighbors.

Economic Transformation and Social Change

The most obvious economic change was an unrelenting rise in prices. Sixteenth-century observers attributed rising prices to the inflationary effects of the influx of silver from Spanish territories in the New World. Historians now believe that European causes may also have helped trigger this **price revolution**. Steady population growth caused a relative shortage of goods, particularly food, and the result was higher prices. Between 1550 and 1600, with local variations, the price of grain may have risen between 50 and 100 percent, and sometimes more, in cities throughout Europe. Wages did not keep pace with prices; historians estimate that wages lost between one-tenth and one-fourth of their value by the end of the century.

price revolution Steady rise in prices in the sixteenth and seventeenth centuries, resulting from population growth and the importation of precious metals from Spain's New World territories.

Wealth in the countryside was also becoming more stratified. Population growth caused many peasant farms to be subdivided for numerous children, creating tiny plots that could not support the families who lived on them. Countless peasants lost what lands they had to wealthy investors who lent them money to rent more land or to buy seed and tools and then reclaimed the land when the peasants failed to repay. Land rents rose because of high demand and some peasants were unable to rent land at all. To survive, they sought work as day laborers for rich landlords or more prosperous farmers. Many found their way to cities, where they swelled the ranks of the poor. In eastern Europe, peasants faced other dilemmas, for their lands had a different relationship to the wider European economy. The more densely urbanized western Europe, whose wealth controlled the patterns of trade, sought bulk goods, particularly grain, from eastern Germany,

Poland, and Lithuania. Thus, there was an economic incentive for landowners in eastern Europe to bind peasants to the land, just as the desire of their rulers for greater cooperation had granted the landlords more power. Serfdom now spread in eastern Europe, while precisely the opposite condition—a more mobile labor force—grew in the West.

The growth of markets around Europe and in Spanish possessions overseas, as well as population growth within Europe, had a marked effect on patterns of production and the lives of artisans. Production of cloth on a large scale for export, for example, now required large amounts of capital—much more than a typical guild craftsman could amass. Cloth production was increasingly controlled by new investor-producers with access to distant markets. These entrepreneurs bought up large amounts of wool and hired it out to be cleaned, spun into thread, and woven into cloth by wage laborers in urban workshops or by pieceworkers in their homes. Thousands of poor women and men in the countryside around towns supported their families in this way. In towns, guilds still regulated most trades but, as their share of production declined, they could not accommodate the numbers of artisans who sought to join them. Fewer and fewer apprentices and journeymen could expect to become master artisans. The masters began to treat apprentices virtually as wage laborers, at times, letting them go during slow periods.

Another consequence of the circumstances guild members faced was the effort to reduce competition at the expense of the artisans' own mothers, sisters, and daughters. Increasingly, widows were forbidden to continue their husbands' enterprises, though they headed from 10 to 15 percent of households in many trades. Women had traditionally practiced many trades, but rarely followed the formal progress from apprenticeship to master status, since they usually combined work of this kind with household production. Outright exclusion of women from guilds occurred as early as the thirteenth century, but now began regularly to appear in guild statutes. Town governments also restricted women's participation even in work they had long dominated, such as selling in markets. Working women thus began to have difficulty supporting themselves if single or widowed and difficulty supporting their children.

Profits from expanding production and trade and from higher land values made more capital available to wealthy urban or landholding families to invest in the countryside, by buying land outright on which to live like **gentry** or by making loans to desperate peasants. Enterprising landholders raised rents on farming and grazing land wherever they could, or they converted land to the production of wool, grain, and other cash crops destined for distant markets.

gentry   Class of wealthy, educated, and socially ambitious families in western Europe, especially England, whose political and economic power was greatly enhanced during the sixteenth century.

As a result, a stratum of wealthy, educated, and socially ambitious "new gentry," as these families were called in England, began to grow. Many of the men of these families were royal officeholders. Many bought titles of nobility or were granted nobility as a benefit of their offices. They often lent money to royal governments. The monumental expense of wars made becoming a lender to government, as well as to individuals, an attractive way to live off personal capital.

No one would have confused these up-and-coming gentry with warrior-aristocrats from old families, but the social distinctions between them are less important (to us) than what they had in common: legal privilege, the security of landownership, and a cooperative relationship with the monarchy. Monarchs deliberately favored the new gentry as counterweights to independent aristocrats.

City governments also changed character. Town councils became dominated by small numbers of privileged families, now more likely to live from landed wealth, like gentry, than from trade or manufacture. By the beginning of the seventeenth century, traditional guild control of government had been eliminated in many places. The long medieval tradition of towns serving as independent corporate bodies had come to an end.

Coping with Poverty and Violence

The common people of Europe did not submit passively to either the economic difficulties or the religious and political crises of their day. Whatever their religion, common people took the initiative in attacking members of other faiths to rid their communities of them. Heretics were considered to be spiritual pollution that might provoke God's wrath, and ordinary citizens believed that it was up to them to eliminate heretics if the state failed to do so.

Ordinary people fought in wars not only from conviction, but also from the need for self-defense and from economic choice. It was ordinary people who defended the walls of towns, dug siege works, and manned artillery batteries. Although nobles remained military leaders, armies consisted mostly of infantry made up of common people, not mounted knights. Women were part of armies, too. Much of the day-to-day work of finding food and firewood, cleaning guns, and repairing clothing was done by women looking after their husbands and lovers among the troops. Landless farm hands, day laborers, and out-of-work artisans joined armies because having work was attractive enough to outweigh the dangers of military life. Desertion was common; nothing more than the rumor that a soldier's home village was threatened might prompt a man to abandon his post. Battle-hardened troops could threaten their commanders, not only with desertion, but with mutiny. Occasionally, mutinies were brutally suppressed; more often, they were successful and troops received some of their back wages.

The devastation of religious war led to both peasant rebellions and urban uprisings. Peasants and townspeople rebelled because of high taxes and food shortages. Elites participated too; former soldiers, prosperous farmers, or even noble landlords whose economic fortunes were tied to peasant profits led some rural revolts. Rebels sometimes seized property—for example, they might distribute looted bread among themselves—and occasionally killed officials. Their protests rarely generated lasting political change and were usually brutally quashed.

Governments at all levels tried to cope with the increasing problem of poverty by changing the administration and scale of poor relief. In both Catholic and Protestant Europe, caring for the poor became more institutionalized and systematic, and more removed from religious impulses. Governments established public almshouses and poorhouses to dispense food or to care for orphans or the destitute in towns throughout Catholic and Protestant Europe. At first, these institutions reflected an optimistic vision of an ideal Christian community caring for its neediest members. But by 1600, the distribution of food was accompanied by attempts to distinguish "deserving" from "undeserving" poor, by an insistence that the poor work for their ration of food, and even by an effort to force the poor to live apart, in poorhouses.

A Beggar is Whipped Through the Streets In this sixteenth-century woodcut, probably made in England, a poor man is tied up and led through the streets of a town while being whipped on his bare back. The gallows in the distance, just outside the city gates, imply that the poor were now thought of as dangerous outlaws. ("A beggar is tied and whipped through the streets," c.1567 (woodcut) (b/w photo), English School, (16th century)/Private Collection/The Bridgeman Art Library)

These efforts were not uniformly successful. Although begging was outlawed by Catholic and Protestant city governments alike, it was never thoroughly suppressed. Catholic religious orders often resisted efforts at regulating their charitable work, even when they were imposed by Catholic governments. Nonetheless, the trend was clear. From viewing poverty as a fact of life and a lesson in Christian humility, European elites began to see it as a social problem and poor people as needing to be controlled.

The Hunt for Witches

Between approximately 1550 and 1650, Europe saw a dramatic increase in the persecution of women and men for witchcraft. Approximately one hundred thousand people were tried and about sixty thousand executed. The surge in witch-hunting was closely linked to communities' religious concerns and also to the social tensions that resulted from economic difficulties.

Certain types of witchcraft had long existed in Europe. So-called black magic of various kinds—one peasant casting a spell on another peasant's cow—had been common since the Middle Ages. The practice now seemed dangerous, especially to elites, who linked black magic to Devil worship. Catholic leaders and legal scholars began to advance such theories in the fifteenth century, and by the late sixteenth century, both Catholic and Protestant elites viewed a witch not only as someone who might cast harmful spells, but also as a heretic.

The impetus for most individual accusations of witchcraft came from within the communities where the "witch" lived—that is, from common people. Usually targeted were solitary or unpopular people whose difficult relationships with fellow villagers made them seem likely sources of evil. Often, such a person had practiced black magic (or had been suspected of doing so) for years, and the villagers took action only when faced with a community crisis, such as an epidemic.

Because they were often prompted by village disasters, individual accusations of witchcraft increased in this period in response to the crises that beset many communities. In addition, isolated accusations often started localized frenzies of active hunting for other witches. These more widespread hunts were driven, in part, by the anxieties of local elites about disorder and heresy and were facilitated by contemporary legal procedures that they applied. These procedures permitted lax rules of evidence and the use of torture to extract confessions. Torture or the threat of torture led most accused witches to "confess" and to name accomplices or other "witches." In this way, a single initial accusation could lead to dozens of prosecutions. In regions where procedures for appealing convictions were fragile or nonexistent, witch-hunts could expand with alarming speed and dozens of "witches" might be identified and executed before the whirlwind subsided. Aggressive hunts were common, for example, in the small principalities and imperial cities of the Holy Roman Empire, which were largely independent of higher political and judicial authority. (See the box, "The Written Record: A City Official Worries About Witch-Hunting.")

The majority of accused witches were women. Lacking legal, social, and political resources, women may have been more likely than men to use black magic for self-protection or advancement. Women's work often made them vulnerable to charges of witchcraft, since families' food supplies and routine medicines passed through women's hands. The deaths of young children or of domestic animals, such as a milk cow, were among the most common triggers for witchcraft accusation. The increase in poverty during the late sixteenth and early seventeenth centuries made poor women frequent targets of witch-hunts.

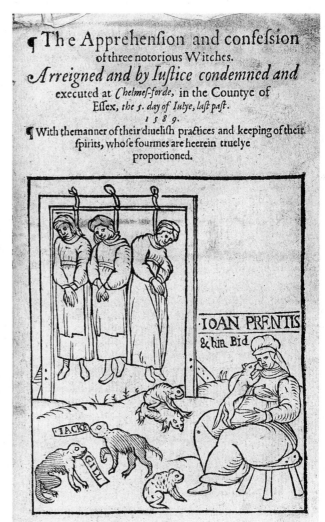

Publicizing Witch Trials Printed pamphlets, such as this one describing the execution of three women in Essex, England, spread the news of local "outbreaks" of witchcraft. One of the women, Joan Prentis, is also depicted surrounded by her animal familiars. The ferret in Joan's lap, the pamphlet relates, was the Devil himself in animal form. (Lambeth Palace Library)

A City Official Worries About Witch-Hunting

In this letter written to a friend in 1629, the chancellor to the prince-bishop of the German city of Würzburg describes the witch-hunt in his community.

As to the affair of the witches, which Your Grace thinks brought to an end before this, it has started up afresh, and no words can do justice to it. Ah, the woe and misery of it—there are still four hundred in the city, high and low, of every rank and sex, nay, even clerics, so strongly accused that they may be arrested at any hour. It is true that, of the people of my Gracious Prince here, some out of all the offices and faculties must be executed: clerics, elected councilors and doctors, city officials, court assessors several of whom Your Grace knows. There are law students to be arrested. The Prince-Bishop has over forty students who are soon to be pastors; among them thirteen or fourteen are said to be witches. A few days ago a Dean was arrested; two others who were summoned have fled.

The notary of our Church consistory, a very learned man, was yesterday arrested and put to the torture. In a word, a third part of the city is surely involved. The richest, most attractive, most prominent of the clergy are already executed. A week ago a maiden of nineteen was executed, of whom it is everywhere said that she was the fairest in the whole city, and was held by everybody a girl of singular modesty and purity. She will be followed by seven or eight others of the best and most attractive persons. . . . And thus many are put to death for renouncing God and being at the witch-dances, against whom nobody has ever else spoken a word.

To conclude this wretched matter, there are children of three or four years, to the number of three hundred, who are said to have had intercourse with the Devil. I have seen put to death children of seven, promising students of ten, twelve, fourteen and fifteen of the nobles—but I cannot and must not write more of this misery. There are persons of yet higher rank, whom you know, and would marvel to hear of, nay, would scarcely believe it; let justice be done. . . .

P.S. Though there are many wonderful and terrible things happening it is beyond doubt that, at a place called the Fraw-Rengberg, the Devil in person, with eight thousand of his followers, held an assembly and celebrated mass before them all, administering to his audience (that is, the witches) turnip-rinds and pairings in place of the Holy Eucharist. There took place not only foul but most horrible and hideous blasphemies, whereof I shudder to write. It is also true that they all vowed not to be enrolled in the Book of Life, but all agreed to be inscribed by a notary who is well known to me and my colleagues. We hope, too, that the book in which they are enrolled will yet be found, and there is no little search being made for it.

QUESTIONS

1. Which townspeople are victims of the witch-hunt?

2. Does the document reveal why the hunt is continuing? Who is in charge?

3. What is the author's attitude toward the events he describes? Does the chancellor believe that witchcraft exists?

Source: Alan C. Kors and Edward Peters, eds., *Witchcraft in Europe, 1100–1700: A Documentary History* (Philadelphia: University of Pennsylvania, 1972), pp. 251–252. Reprinted by permission of the University of Pennsylvania Press.

Both Christian dogma and humanistic writing portrayed women as morally weaker than men and thus more susceptible to the Devil's enticements. Writings on witchcraft described Devil worship in sexual terms, and the prosecution of witches had a voyeuristic, sexual dimension. The bodies of accused witches were searched for the "Devil's mark"—a blemish thought to be Satan's imprint. In some regions, women accounted for 80 percent of those prosecuted and executed. A dynamic of gender stereotyping was not always at work, however; in other regions, prosecutions were more evenly divided between men and women, and occasionally, men made up the majority of those accused.

The widespread witch-hunts virtually ended by the late seventeenth century, in part, because the intellectual energies of elites shifted from religious to scientific thought. The practice of witchcraft continued among common folk, although accusations of one neighbor by another never again reached the level of these crisis-ridden decades.

SECTION SUMMARY

- A price revolution caused a decline in the value of wages in the sixteenth century.

- Elites, particularly new gentry families, could grow rich by controlling increasingly scarce and valuable land.

- Economic hardship led common people to seek jobs in cities, join armies, and protest taxation.

- Persecutions for witchcraft dramatically increased between 1550 and 1650, reflecting both common people's search for scapegoats for their hard lives and elites' anxiety about controlling common people's religion.

WRITING, DRAMA, AND ART IN AN AGE OF UPHEAVAL

In what ways do the literature and art of this period reflect the political, social, and religious conflicts of the age?

Both imaginative literature and speculative writing, such as political theory, bear the stamp of their times. In the late sixteenth and early seventeenth centuries, political speculation concerned questions of the legitimacy of rulers and of the relationship of political power to divine authority—urgent problems in an age when religious division threatened the very foundations of states. Authors and rulers alike often relied on still-prevalent oral modes of communication to convey their ideas. Indeed, some of the greatest literature and some of the most effective political statements of the period were presented as drama and not conveyed in print. Nevertheless, literacy continued to spread and led to greater opportunities for knowledge and reflection. The medium of print became increasingly important to political life. In the visual arts, the dramatic impulse combined with religious purposes to create works that conveyed both power and emotion.

Literacy and Literature

Traditional oral culture changed slowly under the impact of the spread of printing, education, and literacy. Works of literature from the late sixteenth and early seventeenth centuries incorporate material from traditional folktales and reflect the coexistence of oral and literate culture. In *Don Quixote* (key-HO-tay), by Spain's Miguel de Cervantes (sair-VAHN-tayz) (1547–1616), the title character and his companion, Sancho Panza, have a long discussion about oral and literate traditions. The squire Panza speaks in the style that was customary in oral culture—a rather roundabout and repetitive style, which enabled the speaker and listener to remember what was said. Much of the richness of *Don Quixote* is due to the interweaving of prose styles and topical concerns from throughout Cervantes' culture—from the oral world of peasants to the refined world of court life. Yet, what enabled Cervantes to create this rich portrayal was his own highly developed literacy and the awareness of language that literacy made possible.

Much literature in this period stressed the value of education—particularly, by means of the humanist recovery of ancient wisdom, a new vision of what it meant to be a cultivated and disciplined man of the world. The French author Michel de Montaigne (1533–1592) was the epitome of the reflective gentleman. Montaigne (mon-TEN-yuh) was a judge in the parlement (law court) of Bordeaux. In 1570, he resigned from the court and retired to his small château, where he wrote his *Essais* (from which we derive the word *essays*), a collection of short reflections that were revolutionary in both form and content. Montaigne invented writing in the form of a sketch, an "attempt" (the literal meaning of *essai*) that enabled him to combine self-reflection with formal analysis.

Owing to the spread of printing, Montaigne had a virtually unparalleled opportunity to compare different events, values, and cultures through reading a wide variety of printed texts. His reflections range from the destructiveness of the French civil wars to the consequences of European exploration of the New World. Toward all of these events, Montaigne was able to achieve an analytic detachment remarkable for his day. For example, he noted ironically that Europeans labeled New World peoples "savages," yet, they committed seemingly endless and wanton violence against those "savages" and one another. (See the box "The Global Record: Montaigne Discusses Barbarity in the New World and the Old.") Montaigne's essays also reveal self-reflection—a distancing from himself. This distancing was also the result of literacy and leisure, which enabled him to enjoy long periods of solitude and reflection in the company of other solitary, book-bound voices. Montaigne's works mark the beginning of what we know as the "invention" of private life, in which an individual is defined more by internal character and personality traits than by social role.

The Great Age of Theater

The works of the great English poet and playwright William Shakespeare (1564–1616) are still compelling to us because of the profundity of the questions asked about love, honor, and political legitimacy; he asked these questions in terms appropriate to his own own day. One of his favorite

Montaigne Discusses Barbarity in the New World and the Old

n one of his most famous essays, the French jurist and essayist Michel de Montaigne (1533–1592) ironically compares the customs of Native Americans with the customs of his own society. Information about Native Americans came from published reports of European voyages and from news of individual Native Americans who had journeyed (usually forcibly) to Europe. Europeans' encounters with peoples in the New World gave Montaigne a vantage point from which to criticize his own society.

They have their wars with [other] nations, to which they go quite naked, with no other arms than bows or wooden spears. . . . It is astonishing that firmness they show in their combats, which never end but in slaughter and bloodshed; for, as to routs and terror, they know nothing of either.

Each man brings back as his trophy the head of the enemy he has killed. . . . After they have treated their prisoner well for a long time with all the hospitality they can think of . . . they kill him with their swords. This done, they roast him and eat him in common and send some pieces to their absent friends.

I am not sorry that we notice the barbarous horror of such acts, but am heartily sorry that . . . we should be so blind to our own. I think there is more barbarity . . . in tearing by tortures and the rack a body still full of feeling, in roasting a man bit by bit, having him bitten and mangled by dogs (as we have not only read but seen within fresh memory . . . among neighbors and fellow citizens, and what is worse, on the pretext of piety and religion).

Three of these men (were brought to France) . . . and [someone] wanted to know what they had found most amazing. . . . They said that in the first place they thought it very strange that so many grown men, bearded, strong and armed who were around the king . . . should submit to obey a child [the young French king]. . . . Second (they have a way in their language of speaking of men as halves of one another), they had noticed that there were among us men full and gorged with all sorts of good things, and that their other halves were beggars at their doors, emaciated with hunger and poverty; and they thought it strange that these needy halves could endure such injustice.

QUESTIONS

1. What practices in the two cultures is Montaigne commenting on in this excerpt?

2. In what ways does he find Native American culture admirable by comparison to his own? What aspects of his own culture is he criticizing?

3. How are contemporary events and conditions in France reflected in Montaigne's remarks?

Source: Donald M. Frame, trans., *The Complete Essays of Montaigne* (Stanford, Calif.: Stanford University Press, 1948), pp. 153, 155–159. Reprinted by permission of the publisher.

themes—evident in *Hamlet* and *Macbeth*—is the legitimacy of rulers. He also explored the contradictions in values between the growing commercial world he saw around him and the older, seemingly more stable world of feudal society. Subtle political commentary distinguishes Shakespeare's later writings near and shortly after the death of Elizabeth in 1603, when political and economic problems were becoming increasingly troublesome. In *Coriolanus*, he portrays commoners as poor but not ignorant; they are in fact fully rational and capable of analyzing their situation—perhaps more capable, Shakespeare hints, than their ruler. The play is safely set in ancient Rome, but the social and political tensions it depicts clearly applied to the Elizabethan present.

Shakespeare's extraordinary career was possible because his life coincided with the rise of professional theater. In the capitals of England and Spain, professional theaters first opened in the 1570s. Some drama was produced at court or in aristocratic households, but most public theaters drew large and very mixed audiences, including the poorest city dwellers. Playwrights, including Shakespeare, often wrote in teams, under great pressure to keep acting companies supplied with material. The best-known dramatist in Spain, Lope de Vega (LOW-pah day VAY-guh) (1562–1635), wrote more than fifteen hundred works on a wide range of topics. Although religious themes remained popular in Spanish theater, as an echo of medieval drama, most plays in England and Spain treated secular subjects and, as in *Coriolanus*, disguised political commentary.

Over time, theater became increasingly restricted to aristocratic circles. In England, Puritan criticism of the "immorality" of public performance drove actors and playwrights to seek royal patronage. The first professional theater to open in Paris, in 1629, quickly became dependent on Cardinal Richelieu's patronage. Inevitably, as court patronage grew in importance, the wide range of subjects treated in plays began to narrow to those of aristocratic concern, such as family honor and martial glory. These themes are depicted in the works of the Spaniard Pedro Calderón (kall-day-ROHN) (1600–1681), who wrote for his enthusiastic patron, Philip IV, and of the Frenchman Pierre Corneille (kore-NAY) (1606–1684), whose great tragedy of aristocratic life, *Le Cid*, was one of the early successes of the seventeenth-century French theater.

Drama's significance as an art form is reflected in its impact on the development of music: The opera, which weds drama to music, was invented in Italy in the early seventeenth century. The first great work in this genre is generally acknowledged to be *Orfeo* (*Orpheus*, 1607) by Claudio Monteverdi (mon-tay-VAIR-dee) (1567–1643). Opera, like drama, reflected the influence of humanism in its secular themes and in its emulation of Greek drama, which had used both words and music. The practice of music itself changed under the dramatic impulse. Monteverdi was the first master of a new musical style known as "monody," which emphasizes the progression of chords. Monodic music is inherently dramatic, creating a sense of forward movement, expectation, and resolution.

Drama, Art, and Political Thought

Whether produced on a public stage or at court or in a less formal setting, drama was a favored method of communication in this era because people responded to and made extensive use of the spoken word. Dramatic gesture and storytelling to get a message across were commonplace and were important components of politics.

What we might call "street drama" was a common event. When aristocratic governors entered major towns, such as when Margaret of Parma entered Brussels, an ostentatious formal "entry" was often staged. The dignitary would ride through the main gate, usually beneath a canopy made of luxurious cloth. Costumed townspeople staged brief symbolic dramas, such as of the story of David and Goliath, on the streets; the event might end with an elaborate banquet. A remnant of these proceedings survives today in the ceremony of giving distinguished visitors "the keys to the city," which, in the sixteenth century, really were functional.

Royalty made artful use of ceremony. Royal entries into towns took on an added weight, as did royal funerals and other such occasions. These dramas reinforced political and constitutional assumptions in the minds of witnesses and participants and, over time, there were revealing changes in the representations of royal power. In France, for example, the ritual entry of the king into Paris had originally stressed the participation of the leading guilds, judges, and administrators, symbolizing their active role in governing the city and the kingdom. But in the last half of the sixteenth century, the procession began to glorify the king alone.

Speculation about and celebration of power, as well as dramatic emotion, also occurred in the visual arts—most notably in painting and architecture, in the style now known as **baroque**. Baroque (ba-ROKE) style was a new kind of visual language that could project power and grandeur and simultaneously engage viewers' senses. (See the feature "The Visual Record: Baroque Art.")

The very fact that rulers experimented with self-representation suggests that questions about the nature and extent of royal power were far from settled. Queen Elizabeth I had the particular burden of assuming the throne in a period of great instability. Hence, she paid a great deal of attention to the image of herself that she conveyed in words and authorized to be fashioned in painting. Elizabeth styled herself variously as mother to her people and as a warrior-queen (drawing on ancient myths of Amazon women). More formal speculation about constitutional matters also resulted from the tumult

baroque Style of European art and architecture popular from the late sixteenth to early eighteenth centuries. Baroque art modified Renaissance techniques, adding dynamism and emotional energy, which resulted in works that were both impressively grand and emotionally engaging.

An Image of Royalty This dramatic painting of Charles I on horseback was one of several likenesses of the king painted by the baroque artist Anthony Van Dyck. This painting was originally hung at the end of a long gallery in one of the royal palaces, next to similarly triumphal images of Roman emperors. (The Royal Collection © 2003, Her Majesty Queen Elizabeth II)

THE VISUAL RECORD

Baroque Art

If today, you were to walk through the cathedral in the Belgian city of Antwerp and notice this painting, titled *The Raising of the Cross*, it might not strike you as remarkable. The crucifixion of Jesus is a frequent subject of religious painting, after all. But let us look at the image more carefully. First of all, this is a portrayal not of Jesus on the cross, but rather of the raising of the cross. In other words, it captures a moment of action, not its aftermath. The frame of the painting is filled with action as well. The figures on the left and at the center support the cross and push it up. At the bottom right, we see figures straining at ropes as they pull the cross upright. Our eye is drawn to the movement in the painting, partly by the use of light, which floods the figure of Jesus. We also note the unexpected diagonal position of the crucified figure, and we survey the image in order to make sense of it.

This is a dynamic painting, and simultaneously, an emotionally engaging one. We encounter Jesus not as a static, perhaps already dying, figure on the cross, but at the very moment of his crucifixion. There is also a striking similarity between the figure of Jesus and those of the men who are working hard to accomplish his crucifixion: They are all men, whose muscled bodies are more alike than not. The human pathos of the moment is brought to life.

The image you see before you is one of three panels in a triptych, or three-paneled altarpiece. The left-hand panel depicts Saint John, the Virgin Mary, and others witnessing Jesus' crucifixion. The panel on the right shows a Roman officer watching over his soldiers as they crucify two thieves. Whereas most triptychs of the period contained three unrelated images, here the panels combine to form a single story of the crucifixion.

This altarpiece was executed in 1610 by the influential painter Peter Paul Rubens (1577–1640), a native of Antwerp, in the southern Netherlands. Rubens was one of the great masters of what came to be called the baroque style. Baroque techniques were pioneered in the late sixteenth century in Italy, first in church design, and spread slowly, with many regional variations, especially throughout Catholic Europe, during the seventeenth century. The origin of the term *baroque* has been debated; it may have come from the Portuguese *barroco*, used to describe irregularly shaped pearls. The term, as applied to the arts, was initially derogatory, denoting distortion, illogic, and irregularity. Baroque painting was distinguished by the dramatic use of color and shading and by the dynamic energy of figures.

Baroque artists based their work on Renaissance achievements in representing the human form in a convincing three-dimensional space. But with the strong use of light, movement, and more robust and realistic human figures, these artists enhanced the drama and emotional impact of what they depicted.

Like baroque artists, baroque architects modified the precision, symmetry, and orderliness of Renaissance architecture to produce a sense of greater dynamism in space. Baroque churches, for example, were impressively grand and monumental, yet emotionally engaging at the same time. Façades and interiors were both massive and, through the clever use of architectural and decorative components, suggestive of movement. A good example of this is the work of Gianlorenzo Bernini (bare-NEE-nee) (1598–1680), who designed the portico outside Saint Peter's Basilica in Rome, as well as the highly ornate bronze canopy over the altar inside the basilica. Dramatic illusion in the interior of buildings—such as painting a chapel ceiling with figures receding as if ascending to heaven—was a common device in baroque architecture. One of the primary purposes of baroque architecture and art was to create simultaneously a display of power and an invitation to sensory experience. Baroque art encouraged piety that was not only emotionally involved, and thus satisfying, but also awe-inspired. In this way, it reflected the aims of the Counter-Reformation church, whose leaders were among its most important patrons.

Peter Paul Rubens's early training in Italy shaped him as an artist and established his secondary career as a diplomat. Throughout his life, he undertook diplomatic missions for the Habsburg viceroys in the Spanish Netherlands, gaining artistic commissions wherever he went. Rubens's subject matter varied widely, including church design and decoration, portraiture, and landscape painting, reflecting the fact that baroque art also had important secular applications. Indeed, magnificent baroque palaces symbolized the wealth and power of the elites (see the photos on pages 450 and 458).

Rulers began to employ artists as portrait painters, such as Rubens's pupil Anthony Van Dyck (1599–1641), whose painting of Charles I of England appears on page 435. Because portraits have become so common, we cannot fully appreciate how arresting this image would have been in its day. Like Rubens's *Raising of the Cross*, Van Dyck's image of Charles was an innovative rendering of familiar elements.

of the sixteenth and seventeenth centuries. As we have seen, the Protestant faction in France advanced arguments for the limitation of royal power. Alternative theories enhancing royal authority were offered, principally in support of the Catholic position, though also simply to buttress the beleaguered monarchy itself. The most famous of these appeared in *The Six Books of the Republic* (1576), by the legal scholar Jean Bodin (bo-DAHN) (1530–1596). Bodin was a Catholic, but offered a fundamentally secular perspective on the purposes and source of power within a

Rubens: The Raising of the Cross
(*Onze Lieve Vrouwkwerk, Antwerp Cathedral, Belgium/ Peter Willi/Bridgeman Art Library*)

The image of a ruler on horseback was well known, but it had never been exploited as fully by English monarchs as it had been by rulers on the Continent. This large portrait of the king was designed to be hung at the end of a long palace corridor so that, from a distance, a courtier would have the illusion of actually seeing the king riding proudly through a triumphal arch.* Compare this portrait with the much more stilted one of Elizabeth I on page 422. It is striking how effective the technical and stylistic innovations of baroque art and architecture were in expressing secular, as well as spiritual, power.

QUESTIONS

1. How does baroque art involve the viewer by appealing to senses and emotions?

2. Why was baroque painting effective for conveying political messages, as in Van Dyck's portrait of Charles I?

---

* This discussion draws on the work of Roy Strong, *Van Dyck: Charles I on Horseback* (New York: Viking, 1972), pp. 20–25.

state. His special contribution was a vision of a truly sovereign monarch. Bodin offered a theoretical understanding that is essential to states today and is the ground on which people can claim rights and protection from the state—namely, that there is a final sovereign authority. For Bodin, that authority was the king. Contract theory, devised by French Protestants to legitimize resistance to the monarchy, was abandoned when Henry IV granted toleration to the Huguenots in 1598. In England, theoretical justification of resistance to Charles I was initially limited to

SECTION SUMMARY

- Literacy and access to printed books enabled new levels of self-consciousness and self-reflection, as in the work of Montaigne.

- The rise of professional theater began in the 1570s; drama was a favored means of communication by writers as well as political leaders.

- Shakespeare and other writers and artists reflected on many of the current concerns about legitimate authority, religion, and human life in this period.

- Baroque art appealed to viewers' emotions, but also expressed power and grandeur.

- Political theorist Bodin developed the notion of sovereign authority within the state.

invoking tradition and precedent. Contract theory, as well as other sweeping claims regarding subjects' rights, would be more fully developed later in the century.

Bodin's theory of sovereignty, however, was immediately echoed in other theoretical works, most notably, that of Hugo Grotius (GROW-shus) (1583–1645). A Dutch jurist and diplomat, Grotius developed the first principles of modern international law. He accepted the existence of sovereign states that owed no loyalty to higher authority (such as the papacy) and thus needed new principles to govern their interactions. His major work, *De Jure Belli ac Pacis* (*On the Law of War and Peace*, 1625), was written in response to the turmoil of the Thirty Years' War. Grotius argued that relations between states could be based on respect for treaties voluntarily reached between them. In perhaps his boldest move, he argued that war must be justified, and he developed criteria to distinguish just wars from unjust ones.

CHAPTER SUMMARY

The late sixteenth and early seventeenth centuries were an era of intense struggle over political and religious authority. Rulers everywhere, through a variety of means, tried to buttress and expand their power. They were resisted by traditional centers of power, such as independent-minded nobles and wealthy townspeople. But they were also resisted by the novel challenge of religious dissent, which empowered even common people both to claim a greater right to question authority and to risk more in their attempts to oppose it.

The most powerful monarch of the day, the king of Spain, could not defeat a religious and political rebellion in the prosperous Netherlands, even with the resources of treasure from the New World. France was torn apart by decades of civil war before the Crown was able to impose a workable peace and reassert royal authority. In England, political and religiously inspired challenges to royal authority were contained by Elizabeth I, but not as effectively addressed by her successors. Meanwhile, the various states of the Holy Roman Empire were engulfed in a thirty-year war that also had political and religious roots and which became one of the most bitter and complex conflicts of the period.

War itself became more destructive, owing to new technologies and increasing resources devoted to it. Ordinary people also coped with the price revolution, which caused their wages to lose value and many to lose their land. The difficult economic circumstances of these decades meant that working people, desperate for secure livelihood, rioted or took up arms out of economic, as well as religious, concerns.

FOCUS QUESTIONS

- What circumstances permitted Spain's ambitious policies and to what degree were they successful?

- What conditions led to civil war in France? How did religious and political conflict develop differently in England?

- Why did war erupt again within the Holy Roman Empire and what was the significance of the conflict?

- What caused the economic stresses of these decades and how did ordinary people cope with them?

- In what ways do the literature and art of this period reflect the political, social, and religious conflicts of the age?

Yet, however grim the circumstances people faced, the technology of print and the spread of literacy helped spur speculative and creative works by providing the means for reflection and the audiences to receive and appreciate it. Ironically, the increased importance and grandeur of court life, though a cause of political strain, resulted in a new wave of patronage for art, literature, and drama. Other works, such as Shakespeare's plays, both reflect and reflect on the conflicts in the society of the day. Baroque art expressed both the religious passions of the era and the claims to authority by rulers.

KEY TERMS

Philip II (p. 410)

United Provinces (p. 414)

Armada (p. 414)

Huguenots (p. 417)

Edict of Nantes (p. 419)

Elizabeth I (p. 421)

Puritans (p. 421)

Thirty Years' War (p. 425)

Peace of Westphalia (p. 429)

price revolution (p. 430)

gentry (p. 431)

baroque (p. 437)

 This icon will direct you to additional materials on the website: www .cengage.com/history/ noble/westciv6e.

e See our interactive eBook for map and primary source activities.

NOTES

1. Geoffrey Parker, *The Dutch Revolt* (London: Penguin, 1985), p. 288, n. 5.

2. Quoted in A. W. Lovett, *Early Habsburg Spain, 1517–1598* (Oxford: Oxford University Press, 1986), p. 212.

3. Quoted in R. J. Knecht, *The French Wars of Religion, 1559–1598* (London: Longman, 1989), p. 109.

4. Quoted in Jean Berenger, *A History of the Habsburg Empire, 1273–1700*, trans. C. A. Simpson (London and New York: Longman, 1990), p. 239.

16

Louis XIV in Roman Armor
(Scala/Art Resource, NY)

Europe in the Age of Louis XIV, ca. 1640–1715

The portrait of King Louis XIV of France as a triumphant warrior, to the left, was one of hundreds of such images of the king that decorated his palace at Versailles and other sites around his kingdom—where they made his subjects aware of his presence, regardless of whether he was in residence. In this painting, the contemporary artist Charles Le Brun depicts Louis as a Roman warrior, and his power is represented by a mixture of other symbols—Christian and pagan, ancient and contemporary. An angel crowns him with a victor's laurel wreath and carries a banner bearing the image of the sun. In his hand, Louis holds a marshal's baton—a symbol of military command—covered with the royal emblem of the fleur-de-lys (flur-duh-LEE). In the background, behind the "Roman" troops following Louis, is an idealized city.

These trappings symbolized the significant expansion of royal power during Louis's reign. He faced down the challenges of warrior-nobles, suppressed religious dissent, and tapped the nation's wealth to wage a series of wars of conquest. A period of cultural brilliance early in his reign and the spectacle of an elaborate court life crowned his achievements. In his prime, his regime was supported by a consensus of elites; such harmony was made possible by the lack of institutional brakes on royal authority. However, as his attention to symbolism suggests, Louis's power was not unchallenged. By the end of the Sun King's reign, the glow was fading: France was struggling under economic distress brought on by the many wars fought for his glory and had missed opportunities for commercial success abroad. Elites throughout France who had once accepted, even welcomed, his rule became critics, and common people outright rebels.

In England, by contrast, the Crown faced successful rebellion by subjects claiming religious authority and political legitimacy for their causes. Resistance to the expansion of royal authority, led by Parliament, resulted in the execution of the king and the establishment of a short-lived republic, the Commonwealth. Although the monarchy was restored, it became permanently weaker after the civil war. After the Thirty Years' War, vigorous rulers in central and eastern Europe undertook a program of territorial expansion and state building that led to the dominance in the region of Austria, Brandenburg-Prussia, and Russia. The power of these states derived, in part, from the economic relationship of their lands to the wider European economy. In all the major states of continental Europe, princely governments were able to monopolize military power for the first time, in return for economic and political concessions to noble landholders.

The seventeenth century also witnessed a dynamic phase of European expansion overseas, following on the successes of the Portuguese and the Spanish in the

FOCUS QUESTIONS

- How did Louis XIV successfully expand royal power in France and what were some of the achievements of his reign?

- What were the long-term consequences of the English civil war?

- Which states began to dominate central and eastern Europe and why were they successful?

- How and why did Europe's overseas trade and colonization expand in the seventeenth century and what effects did this expansion have on Europe itself?

This icon will direct you to additional materials on the website: www.cengage.com/history/noble/westciv6e.

See our interactive eBook for map and primary source activities.

fifteenth and sixteenth centuries. The Dutch created the most successful trading empire. Eager migrants settled in the Americas in ever-increasing numbers, while forced migrants—enslaved Africans—were transported by the thousands to work on the profitable plantations of European colonizers. Aristocrats, merchants, and peasants back in Europe jockeyed to take advantage of—or to mitigate the effects of—the local political and economic impact of Europe's expansion.

FRANCE IN THE AGE OF ABSOLUTISM

How did Louis XIV successfully expand royal power in France and what were some of the achievements of his reign?

Absolutism Extraordinary concentration of power and symbolic authority in royal hands, achieved particularly by the king of France (Louis XIV) in the seventeenth century.

Louis XIV Longest-reigning ruler in European history, he imposed "absolute" rule in France and his reign witnessed a great flowering of French culture.

Absolutism is a term often used to describe the extraordinary concentration of power in royal hands achieved by the kings of France, most notably **Louis XIV** (r. 1643–1715), in the seventeenth century. Louis continued the expansion of state power begun by his father's minister, Cardinal Richelieu (see page 421). The extension of royal power, under Louis as well as his predecessor, was accelerated by his desire to sustain an expensive and aggressive foreign policy. The policy itself was partly traditional—fighting the perpetual enemy, the Habsburgs, and seeking military glory—and partly new—expanding the borders of France. Louis XIV's successes in these undertakings made him both envied and emulated by other rulers: The French court became a model of culture and refinement. But increased royal authority was not accepted without protest: Common French people as well as elites dug in their heels over the cost of Louis's policies to them.

The Last Challenge to Absolutism: The Fronde, 1648–1653

Louis inherited the throne at the age of five in 1643. His mother, Anne of Austria (1601–1666), acted as regent, together with her chief minister and personal friend, Cardinal Jules Mazarin (mah-zah-RAHN) (1602–1661). They immediately faced revolts against the concentration of power in royal hands and the exorbitant taxation that had prevailed under Louis's father. The most serious revolt began in 1648, led by the Parlement (par-luh-MAWNH) of Paris and the other sovereign law courts in the capital.

The source of the Parlement's leverage over the monarchy was its traditional right to register laws and edicts, which amounted to judicial review. Now, the Parlement attempted to extend this power by debating and even initiating government policy. The sovereign courts sitting together drew up a reform program abolishing most of the machinery of government established under Richelieu and calling for consent to future taxation. The citizens of Paris rose to defend the courts when royal troops were sent against them in October.

Civil war waxed and waned around France from 1648 to 1653. Fighting was led by great aristocrats in the name of the parlements and other law courts. At the same time, further reform proposals were offered. For example, middling nobles in the region around Paris worked on their own reform program and made preparations for a meeting of the Estates General—a representative assembly—to enact it.

These revolts begun in 1648 were derided with the name "Fronde," which was a popular children's game. However, the Fronde (FRAWND) was not child's play; it constituted a serious challenge to the legacy of royal government as it had developed under Richelieu. It ended without a noteworthy impact on the growth of royal power for several reasons. First, Mazarin made strategic concessions to individual aristocrats, who were always eager to trade their loyalty for the fruits of royal service. Meanwhile, the Parlement of Paris accepted a return to royal authority when the civil war caused starvation as well as threatened its control of reform.

Moreover, the Parlement of Paris was a law court, not a representative assembly. Its legitimacy derived from its role as upholder of royal law, and it could not, over time, challenge the king on the pretext of upholding royal tradition in his name. Parlementaires saw the Estates General as a rival institution and helped quash the proposed meeting of representatives. They especially wanted to avoid reform that included abolition of the paulette, a fee guaranteeing the hereditary right to royal office (see page 420).

Unlike England, France had no single institutional focus for resistance to royal power. A strong-willed and able ruler, as Louis XIV proved to be, could counter challenges to royal power, particularly when he satisfied the ambitions of aristocrats and those bureaucrats who profited from the expansion of royal power.

France Under Louis XIV, 1661–1715

Louis XIV fully assumed control of government in 1661, at a propitious moment. The Peace of the Pyrenees in 1659 had ended, in France's favor, the wars with Spain that had dragged on since the end of the Thirty Years' War. As part of the peace agreement, Louis married a Spanish princess, Maria Theresa. In the first ten years of his active reign, Louis achieved a degree of control over the mechanisms of government unparalleled in the history of monarchy in France or anywhere else in Europe. Louis was an extremely vigorous and diligent king. He put in hours a day at a desk, while sustaining the ceremonial life of the court, with its elaborate hunts, balls, and other public events.

GOVERNMENT REFORMS

Louis did not invent any new bureaucratic devices, but rather used existing ranks of officials in new ways that increased government efficiency and further centralized control. He radically reduced the number of men in his High Council, the advisory body closest to the king, to include only three or four great ministers of state affairs. This intimate group, with Louis's active participation, handled all policymaking. The ministers of state, war, and finance were chosen exclusively from nonnoble men of bourgeois origin, whose training and experience fitted them for such positions. Jean-Baptiste Colbert (coal-BEAR) (1619–1683), perhaps the greatest of them, served as minister of finance and supervised most domestic policy from 1665 until his death. He was from a merchant family and had served for years under Mazarin.

Several dozen other officials, picked from the ranks of up-and-coming lawyers and administrators, drew up laws and regulations and passed them to the intendants for execution at the provincial level. Sometimes these officials at the center were sent to the provinces on short-term supervisory missions. The effect of this system was to bypass many entrenched provincial bureaucrats, particularly those known as tax farmers. Tax farmers were freelance businessmen who bid for the right to collect taxes in a region in return for a negotiated fee they paid to the Crown. The Crown, in short, did not control its own tax revenues. The money Louis's regime saved by the more efficient collection of taxes (revenues almost doubled in some areas) enabled the government to streamline the bureaucracy: Dozens of the offices created over the years to bring cash in were bought back by the Crown from their owners.

The system still relied on the bonds of patronage and personal service—political bonds borrowed from aristocratic life. Officials rose through the ranks by means of service to the great, and family connection and personal loyalty still were essential. Of the seventeen different men who were part of Louis XIV's High Council during his reign, five were members of the Colbert family, for example.

CHRONOLOGY

1602	Dutch East India Company formed
1607	Jamestown colony founded in Virginia
1608	Champlain founds Quebec City
1613	Michael becomes first Romanov tsar in Russia
1620	Pilgrims settle at Plymouth (Massachusetts)
1642–1648	Civil war in England
1643	Louis XIV becomes king of France
1648–1653	Fronde revolts in France
1649	Execution of Charles I
1649–1660	English Commonwealth
1659	Peace of the Pyrenees
1660	Monarchy restored in England
1661	Louis XIV assumes full control of government
1672–1678	Dutch War
1682	Peter the Great becomes tsar of Russia
1685	Edict of Nantes revoked
1688	Glorious Revolution
1699	Treaty of Carlowitz
1700–1721	Great Northern War
1701–1714	War of the Spanish Succession
1713	Peace of Utrecht
1715	Death of Louis XIV

**ECONOMIC
DEVELOPMENT**

Colbert and the other ministers began to develop the kind of planned government policymaking that we now take for granted. Partly by means of their itinerant supervisory officials, they tried to formulate policy based on carefully collected information. How many men of military age were available? How abundant was this year's harvest? Answers to such questions enabled not only the formulation of economic policy, but also the deliberate management of production and services to achieve certain goals—above all, the recruitment and supply of the king's vast armies.

Colbert actively encouraged France's economic development in other ways. He reduced the internal tolls and customs barriers, which were relics of medieval landholders' rights. He encouraged industry with state subsidies and protective tariffs. He set up state-sponsored trading companies—the two most important being the East India Company and the West India Company, established in 1664.

mercantilism Economic policy pursued by western European states in the seventeenth and eighteenth centuries that stressed self-sufficiency in manufactured goods, tight government control of trade, and the absolute value of bullion.

Mercantilism is the term historians use to describe the theory behind Colbert's efforts. This economic theory stressed self-sufficiency in manufactured goods, tight control of trade to foster the domestic economy, and the absolute value of bullion. Both capital for development—in the form of hard currency, known as bullion—and the amount of world trade were presumed to be limited in quantity. Therefore, state intervention in the form of protectionist policies was believed necessary to guarantee a favorable balance of payments.

This static model of national wealth did not wholly fit the facts of growing international trade in the seventeenth century. Nevertheless, mercantilist philosophy was helpful to France. France became self-sufficient in the all-important production of woolen cloth, and French industry expanded notably in other sectors. Colbert's greatest success was the systematic expansion of the navy and merchant marine. By the end of Louis XIV's reign, the French navy was virtually the equal of the English navy.

RELIGIOUS LIFE

Beginning in 1673, Louis tried to bring the religious life of the realm more fully under royal control. He claimed some of the church revenues and powers of ecclesiastical appointment within France that the pope still exercised. Partly to bolster his position with the pope, he also began to attack the Huguenot community in France. First, he offered financial rewards for conversion to Catholicism. Then, he took more drastic steps, such as destroying Protestant churches and quartering troops in Huguenots' homes to force them to convert. In 1685, he revoked the Edict of Nantes. A hundred thousand Protestant subjects—including some six hundred army and navy officers—refused even nominal conversion to Catholicism and chose to emigrate.

Meanwhile, Louis faced resistance to his claims against the pope from within the ranks of French Catholics. These laypeople and clerics represented a movement within French Catholicism known as Jansenism, after Cornelius Jansen, a professor of theology whose writings inspired it. Jansenists practiced an austere style of Catholic religiosity that was akin to some Protestant doctrine in its notions about human will and sinfulness. Louis was wary of any challenge to either the institutional or symbolic unity of his regime and was particularly suspicious of Jansenism because its adherents included many of his political enemies, particularly among families of parlement officials. Late in Louis's reign, another pope obligingly declared many Jansenist doctrines to be heretical as part of a compromise agreement with Louis on matters of church governance and finance.

Despite these successes, the power of the Crown was still greatly limited by modern standards. The "divine right" of kingship, a notion formulated by Louis's chief apologist, Bishop Jacques Bossuet (BOS-soo-way) (1627-1704), did not mean unlimited power to rule; rather, it meant that hereditary monarchy was the divinely ordained form of government, best suited to human needs. *Absolutism* was not iron-fisted control of the realm, but rather the successful focusing of energy, loyalties, and symbolic authority in the Crown. The government functioned well in the opening decades of Louis's reign because his role as the focal point of power and loyalty was both logical, after the preceding years of unrest, and skillfully exploited. Much of the glue holding together the absolutist state lay in informal mechanisms, such as patronage and court life, as well as in the traditional hunt for military glory—all of which Louis amply supplied.

The Life of the Court

An observer comparing the lives of prominent noble families in the mid-sixteenth and mid-seventeenth centuries would have noticed striking differences. By the second half of the seventeenth century, most sovereigns or territorial princes had the power to crush revolts. The nobility relinquished its former independence but retained economic and social supremacy and, as a consequence, considerable political clout. Nobles also developed new ways to symbolize their privilege by means of cultural refinement. This process was particularly dramatic in France.

One sign of Louis's success in marshaling the loyalty of the aristocracy was the brilliant court life that his regime sustained. No longer able to wield independent political power, aristocrats lived at court whenever they could. There, they competed for patronage and prestige—for commands in the royal army and for honorific positions at court itself. A favored courtier might, for example, participate in the elaborate daily *lever* (LEV-ay) (arising) of the king; he might be allowed to hand the king his shirt—a demeaning task, yet a coveted one for the access to the king that it guaranteed. Courtiers now defended their honor with private duels, not warfare, and relied on precise etiquette and clever conversation to mark their political and social distinctiveness. (See the feature, "The Visual Record: Table Manners.")

Noblewomen and noblemen alike began to reflect on their new roles in letters, memoirs, and the first novels. A prominent theme of these works is the increasing need for a truly private life of affection and trust, with which to counterbalance the public façade necessary to an aspiring courtier. The most influential early French novel was *The Princess of Cleves* by Marie-Madeleine Pioche de la Vergne (1634–1693), best known by her title, Madame de Lafayette. Mme. de Lafayette's novel treats the particular difficulties faced by aristocratic women who, without military careers to bring glory and provide distraction, were more vulnerable than men to gossip and slander at court and more trapped by their arranged marriages.

Louis XIV's court is usually associated with the palace he built at Versailles (vare-SIGH), southwest of Paris. Some of the greatest talent of the day worked on the design and construction of Versailles from 1670 through the 1680s. It became a masterpiece of luxurious, but restrained, baroque style—a model for royal and aristocratic palaces throughout Europe for the next one hundred years.

Before Louis's court, in his later years, withdrew to Versailles, it traveled among the king's other châteaux around the kingdom, and in this itinerant period, court life was actually at its most creative. These early years of Louis's personal reign were the heyday of French drama. The comedian Jean-Baptiste Poquelin, known as Molière (mole-YARE) (1622–1673), impressed the young Louis with his productions in the late 1650s and was rewarded with the use of a theater in the main royal palace in Paris. Like Shakespeare earlier in the century, Molière explored the social and political tensions of his day. He satirized the pretensions of the aristocracy and the social climbing of the bourgeoisie. Some of his plays were banned, but most were not only tolerated, but extremely popular with the elite audiences they mocked. Their popularity is testimony to the confidence of Louis's regime in its early days.

Also popular at court were the tragedies of Jean Racine (rah-SEEN) (1639–1699), who was to the French theater what Shakespeare was to the English: the master of poetic language. His plays focus on the emotional and psychological lives of the characters and stress the unpredictable, usually unhappy, role of fate, even among royalty. The pessimism in Racine foreshadowed the less successful second half of Louis's reign.

The Burdens of War and the Limits of Power

Louis XIV started wars that dominated the attention of most European states in the second half of the seventeenth century. His wars sprang from traditional causes: the importance of the glory and dynastic aggrandizement of the king and the preoccupation of the aristocracy with military life. But if Louis's wars had familiar motives, they were far more demanding on state resources than any previous wars.

The new offensive tactics developed during the Thirty Years' War (see page 429) changed the character of armies in ways that demanded more resources for training. A higher proportion of soldiers became gunners, and their effectiveness lay in how well they operated as a unit. Armies began to train seriously off the field of battle because drill and discipline were vital to success. France's victories in the second half of the seventeenth century are partly traceable to the regime's attention to these tasks, as well as to recruitment and supply, which together constituted another phase of the "military revolution." The numbers of men on the battlefield increased somewhat as training increased the effectiveness of large numbers of infantry, but the total numbers of men in arms supported by the state at any time increased dramatically once the organization to support them was in place. Late in the century, France kept more than 300,000 men in arms when at war (which was most of the time).

Table Manners

If you were to sit down in a fancy restaurant, order a juicy steak, and then eat it with your bare hands, other diners would undoubtedly stare, shocked by your bad manners. It has not always been the case that table manners meant very much—were able to signal social status, for example. In fact, table manners did not always exist at all in the sense that we know them. How did they evolve? How did they come to have the importance that they do? And why should historians pay any attention to them?

Imagine that you have been invited to dinner at a noble estate in the year 1500. As you sit down, you notice that there are no knives, forks, and spoons at your place, and no napkins either. A servant (a young girl from a neighboring village) sets a roast of meat in front of you and your fellow diners.

Table Manners of the Upper Class in the Seventeenth Century
(Courtesy of the Trustees of the British Museum)

In 1667, Louis invoked rather dubious dynastic claims to demand from Spain lands in the Spanish Netherlands and the large independent county on France's eastern border called the Franche-Comté (FRAWNSH–con-TAY) (see **MAP 16.1**). After a brief conflict, the French obtained only some towns in the Spanish Netherlands.

Louis's focus then shifted to a new enemy, the Dutch. The Dutch had been allied with France since the beginning of their existence as provinces in rebellion against Spain. But the French now turned against them because of Dutch dominance of seaborne trade in the growing international economy. At first, the French tried to offset the Dutch advantage with tariff barriers against Dutch goods. But confidence in the French army led Louis's generals to urge action against the vulnerable Dutch lands. "It is impossible that his Majesty should tolerate any longer the insolence and arrogance of that nation," rationalized the usually pragmatic Colbert in 1670.[1]

The lords and ladies on either side of you hack off pieces of meat with the knives that they always carry with them, and then, they eat the meat with their fingers. Hunks of bread on the table in front of them catch the dripping juices.

One hundred fifty years later, in 1650, dinner is a much more "civilized" meal. Notice the well-to-do women dining in this engraving by the French artist Abraham Bosse (1602–1676). The table setting, with tablecloths, napkins, plates, and silverware, is recognizable to us. The lady at the extreme right holds up her fork and napkin in a somewhat forced and obvious gesture. These diners have the utensils that we take for granted, but the artist does not take them for granted: They are intended to be noticed by Bosse's elite audience.

In the seventeenth century, aristocrats and gentry signaled their political and social privilege with behavior that distinguished them from the lower classes in ways their more powerful ancestors had found unnecessary. Historians have called this the invention of civility. As we have seen, proper courtesy to one's superiors at court was considered essential. Rituals of honor and deference were increasingly taking the place of armed conflict as the routine behavior of the upper classes. Also essential, however, were certain standards of physical privacy and delicacy. Something as seemingly trivial as the use of a fork became charged with symbolic significance. As the actual power of the aristocrats was circumscribed by the state, they found new expressions of status. Since the sixteenth century, new kinds of manners had been touted in handbooks, reflecting changes that already had occurred at Italian courts. During the seventeenth century, these practices became more widespread and opened up a gulf between upper- and lower-class behavior.

Some of the new behaviors concerned bodily privacy and discretion. A nobleman now used a handkerchief instead of his fingers or coat sleeve, and he did not urinate in public. The new "rules" about eating are particularly interesting. Why did eating with a fork seem refined and desirable to aristocrats trying to buttress their own self-images? As any 3-year-old knows, eating with a fork is remarkably inefficient.

Using a fork kept you at a distance—literal and symbolic—from the animal you were eating. Napkins wiped away all trace of bloody juices from your lips. Interestingly, as diners began to use utensils, other eating arrangements changed in parallel ways. Sideboards had been in use for a long time, but pieces of meat were now discreetly carved on the sideboard and presented to diners in individual portions. The carcass was brought to the sideboard cut into roasts instead of unmistakably whole, and it was often decorated—as it is today—to further disguise it.

The new aristocrat was increasingly separated from the world of brute physical force, both in daily life and on the battlefield. In warfare, brute force was no longer adequate. Training, discipline, and tactical knowledge were more important and heightened the significance of rank, which separated officers from the vast numbers of common soldiers. Aristocrats now lived in a privileged world where violence—except for an occasional duel—was no longer a fact of life. Their new behavior codes signaled their new invulnerability to others. Above all, they worked to transform a loss—of the independence that had gone hand in hand with a more violent life—into a gain: a privileged immunity to violence.

Specific manners became important, then, because they were symbols of power. The symbolic distance between the powerful and the humble was reinforced by other changes in habits and behavior. A sixteenth-century warrior customarily traveled on horseback and often went from place to place within a city on foot, attended by his retinue. A seventeenth-century aristocrat was more likely to travel in a horse-drawn carriage. The presence of special commodities from abroad—such as sugar—in the seventeenth century created further possibilities for signaling status.

It is interesting to note that other personal habits still diverged dramatically from what we would consider acceptable today. Notice the large, stately bed in the same room as the dining table in Bosse's engraving. Interior space was still undifferentiated by our standards, and it was common for eating, talking, sleeping, and estate management all to go on in a single room. The grand bed is in the picture because, like the fork, it is a mark of status. Like virtually everything else, what is "proper" varies with historical circumstance.

QUESTIONS

1. Why did elites become interested in table manners in the seventeenth century?

2. How did manners function as effective symbols of power?

The Dutch War began in 1672, with Louis personally leading one of the largest armies ever fielded in Europe—perhaps 120,000 men. The English had also fought the Dutch over trade in the 1650s and now Louis secretly paid the English king, Charles II, to join an alliance against the Dutch.

At first, the French were spectacularly successful, but the Dutch opened dikes and flooded the countryside, and the land war became a soggy stalemate. At the same time, the Dutch beat combined English and French forces at sea and gathered allies who felt threatened by Louis's aggression. The French soon faced German and Austrian forces along their frontier, and by 1674, the English had joined the alliance against France as well. A negotiated peace in 1678 gave France further territory areas in the Spanish Netherlands, as well as control of the Franche-Comté, but it was an illusion of victory only.

Ensconced at Versailles since 1682, Louis seemed to be at the height of his powers. Yet, the Dutch War had in fact cost him more than he had gained. Reforms in government and finance ended under the pressure of paying for war, and old habits of borrowing money and selling offices were revived.

Versailles Palace, The Hall of Mirrors This ornate gallery, more than 75 yards long, connects the two wings of the palace. Seventeen huge windows and opposing walled mirrors flood the gallery with light. In addition to these dramatic effects, the designers included many thematic details, such as miniature fleur-de-lys entwined with suns to symbolize the union of France and Louis, in the gilded work near the ceiling. (Réunion des musées nationaux/Art Resource, NY)

Other government obligations, such as encouraging overseas trade, were neglected. Colbert's death in 1683 dramatically symbolized the end of an era of innovation in the French regime.

THE NINE YEARS' WAR A new war, now known as the Nine Years' War, or King William's War, was touched off late in 1688 by a French invasion of Germany to claim an inheritance there. In his ongoing dispute with the pope, Louis also seized the papal territory of Avignon (ah-veen-YOHN) in southern France. Boldest of all, he helped the exiled Catholic claimant to the English crown, James II, mount an invasion to reclaim his throne (see page 455). Louis's unforgiving Dutch opponent, William of Orange, king of England from 1689 to 1702, led an alliance of all the major powers—Spain, the Netherlands, England, Austria, and the major German states—against the French. As with the Dutch War, the Nine Years' War was costly and, on most fronts, inconclusive. This time, though, there was no illusion of victory for Louis. In the Treaty of Ryswick (1697), Louis gave up most of the territories he had claimed or seized, as well as his contentious claim to papal revenues. The terrible burden of war taxes, combined with crop failures in 1693 and 1694, caused widespread starvation in the countryside. French courtiers began to criticize Louis openly.

THE WAR OF THE SPANISH SUCCESSION The final and most devastating war of Louis's reign, called the War of the Spanish Succession, broke out in 1701. It was a straightforward dynastic clash between France and its perennial enemy, the Habsburgs. Both Louis and Habsburg Holy Roman emperor Leopold I (r. 1657–1705) hoped to claim, for their heirs, the throne of Spain, left open at the death in 1700 of the last Spanish Habsburg, Charles II. Charles II bequeathed the throne to Louis's grandson, Philip of Anjou, by reason of Louis's marriage to the Spanish princess Maria Theresa and Philip had quickly entered Spain to claim his new kingdom. War was made inevitable when, in an act of sheer belligerence, Louis

🌐 **Map 16.1—Territorial Gains of Louis XIV, 1667–1715**
Louis's wars, though enormously expensive for France, produced only modest gains of territory along France's eastern and northern frontiers.

renounced one of the conditions of Charles's will: Philip's accession to the throne of Spain, Louis insisted, did not prevent his becoming king of France as well. The Dutch and English responded to the prospect of so great a disruption of the balance of power in Europe by allying with the emperor against France. The Dutch and English also wanted to defend their colonial interests, since the French had already begun to profit from new trading opportunities with the Spanish colonies.

Again, the French fought a major war on several fronts on land and at sea. Again, the people of France felt the cost in crushing taxes that multiplied the effects of harvest failures. Major revolts inside France forced Louis to divert troops from the war. For a time, it seemed that the French would be soundly defeated, but they were saved by the superior organization of their forces and by dynastic accident: Unexpected deaths in the Habsburg family meant that the Austrian claimant to the Spanish throne suddenly was poised to inherit rule of Austria and the empire as well. The English, more afraid of a revival of unified Habsburg control of Spain and Austria than of French domination of Spain, quickly called for peace negotiations.

The Peace of Utrecht in 1713 helped to set the agenda of European politics for the eighteenth century. Philip of Anjou was recognized as Philip V, the first Bourbon king of Spain, but on the condition that the Spanish and French crowns would never be worn by the same monarch. To maintain the balance of power against French interests, the Spanish Netherlands and Spanish territories in Italy were ceded by a second treaty in 1714 to Austria, which for many decades would be France's major continental rival. The Peace of Utrecht also marked the beginning of England's dominance of overseas trade and colonization. The French gave to England certain lands in Canada and the Caribbean and renounced any privileged relationship with Spanish colonies. England was allowed to control the highly profitable slave trade with Spanish colonies.

SECTION SUMMARY

- The Fronde were revolts against royal power early in Louis XIV's reign.

- Louis successfully rebuilt royal power using control of taxation, a reformed bureaucracy, and traditional political bonds, such as aristocratic patronage.

- The power Louis wielded has been labeled "absolutism" because there were no formal institutional limits on his authority.

- Court life in Louis's reign sponsored artistic creativity and encouraged a new emphasis on cultural refinement in the aristocracy.

- Louis started a series of costly wars from which the French state gained little.

Louis XIV had added small pieces of territory along France's eastern border (see **MAP 16.1**), and a Bourbon ruled in Spain. But the costs in human life and resources were great for the slim results achieved. The army and navy had swallowed up capital that might have fueled investment and trade; strategic opportunities overseas were lost, never to be regained. Louis's government had been innovative in its early years, but remained constrained by traditional ways of imagining the interest of the state.

THE ENGLISH CIVIL WAR AND ITS AFTERMATH

What were the long-term consequences of the English civil war?

Parliament   English legislative institution, which used control over monies to bargain with the Crown over foreign and domestic policies, leading to civil war and the deposition of Charles I.

In England, unlike in France, a representative institution—**Parliament**—became an effective, permanent brake on royal authority. The process by which Parliament gained a secure role in governing the kingdom was neither easy nor peaceful, however. As we saw in Chapter 15, conflicts between the English crown and its subjects, culminating in the Crown-Parliament conflict, concerned control over taxation and the direction of religious reform. Beginning in 1642, England was beset by civil war between royal and parliamentary forces. The king was eventually defeated and executed, and for a time, the monarchy was abolished altogether. It was restored in 1660, but Parliament retained a crucial role in governing the kingdom—a role that was confirmed when, in 1688, it again deposed a monarch and established limits on future monarchs' power.

Civil War, 1642–1649

Fighting broke out between the armies of Charles I and parliamentary armies in the late summer of 1642. The Long Parliament (see page 424) continued to represent a broad coalition of critics and opponents of the monarchy, ranging from aristocrats, concerned primarily with abuses of royal prerogative, to radical Puritans, eager for thorough religious reform and determined to defeat the king. Fighting was halfhearted initially, and the tide of war at first favored Charles.

In 1643, however, the scope of the war broadened. Charles made peace with Irish rebels and brought Irish troops to England to bolster his armies. Parliament, in turn, received military aid from the Scots in exchange for promises that Presbyterianism would become the religion of England. Meanwhile, **Oliver Cromwell** (1599–1658), a Puritan member of the Long Parliament and a cavalry officer, helped reorganize parliamentary forces. The eleven-hundred-man cavalry, trained by Cromwell and known as the "Ironsides" and supported by parliamentary and Scottish infantry, defeated the king's troops at Marston Moor in July 1644. The victory made Cromwell famous.

Oliver Cromwell   English Puritan general, during the English civil war, who governed as Lord Protector during the interregnum from 1653 to 1658.

Shortly afterward, Parliament further improved its forces by creating the New Model Army, rigorously trained like Cromwell's Ironsides. Sitting members of Parliament were barred from commanding troops; hence, upper-class control of the army was reduced. This army played a decisive role not only in the war, but also in the political settlement that followed the fighting.

The New Model Army won a convincing victory over royal forces at Naseby in 1645. In the spring of 1646, Charles surrendered to a Scottish army in the north. In January 1647, Parliament paid the Scots for their services in the war and took the king into custody. In the negotiations that followed, Charles tried to play his opponents off against one another, and, as he had hoped, divisions among them widened.

Most members of Parliament were Presbyterians, Puritan gentry who favored a strongly unified and state-controlled church along Calvinist lines. They wanted peace with the king in return for acceptance of the new church structure and parliamentary control of standing militias for a specified period. They did not favor wider political changes, such as extending the right to vote to ordinary people. These men were increasingly alarmed by the appearance of multiple religious sects and by the actual religious freedom that many ordinary people were claiming for themselves. With the weakening of royal authority and the disruption of civil war, censorship was relaxed, and public preaching by ordinary men, and even women, who felt divinely inspired was becoming commonplace.

Above all, Presbyterian gentry in Parliament feared more radical groups in the army and in London who had supported them up to this point, but who favored more sweeping political and religious change. Most officers of the New Model Army, such as Cromwell, were Independents, Puritans who, unlike the Presbyterians, favored a decentralized church, a degree of religious toleration, and a wider sharing of political power among men of property, not just among the very wealthy gentry. In London, a well-organized artisans' movement known as the "Levellers" went even further; Levellers favored universal manhood suffrage, equality under the law, better access to education, and decentralized churches—in short, the separation of political power from wealth and virtual freedom of religion. Many of the rank and file of the army were deeply influenced by Leveller ideas.

In May 1647, the majority in Parliament voted to offer terms to the king and to disband the New Model Army—without first paying most of the soldiers' back wages. This move provoked the first direct intervention by the army in politics. Representatives of the soldiers were chosen to present grievances to Parliament; when this failed, the army seized the king and, in August, occupied Westminster, Parliament's meeting place. Independent and Leveller elements in the army debated the direction of possible reform to be imposed on Parliament. One Leveller argued for universal manhood suffrage: "Every man that is to live under a government ought first by his own consent to put himself under that government; and I do think that the poorest man in England is not at all bound ... to that government that he hath not had a voice to put himself under."[2]

In November, however, their common enemy Charles escaped from his captors and raised a new army with his former enemies, the Scots, who were also alarmed by the growing radicalism in England. Civil war began again early in 1648. Although it ended quickly with a victory by Cromwell and the New Model Army in August, the renewed war further hardened political divisions and enhanced the power of the army. The king was widely blamed for the renewed bloodshed, and the army did not trust him to keep any agreement he might now sign. When Parliament, still dominated by Presbyterians, once again voted to negotiate with the king, army troops, led by Colonel Thomas Pride, prevented members who favored Presbyterianism or negotiating with the king from attending sessions. The "Rump" Parliament that remained after "Pride's Purge" voted to try the king. A hasty trial followed and, on January 30, 1649, Charles I was executed for "treason, tyranny and bloodshed" against his people.

The Interregnum, 1649–1660

A Commonwealth—a republic—was declared. Executive power resided in a council of state. The House of Lords was abolished and legislative power resided in the one-chamber Rump Parliament. Declaring a republic proved far easier than running one, however. The execution of the king shocked most English and Scots and alienated many elites from the new regime. The legitimacy of the Commonwealth government would always be in question.

The tasks of making and implementing policy were hindered by the narrow political base on which the government now rested. Excluded were the majority of the reformist Presbyterian or Anglican gentry who had been purged from Parliament. Also excluded were the more radical Levellers; Leveller leaders in London were arrested when they published tracts critical of the new government. Within a few years, many disillusioned Levellers would join a new religious movement called the Society of Friends, or Quakers, which espoused complete religious autonomy. Quakers declined all oaths or service to the state, and they refused to acknowledge social rank.

Above all, the new government was vulnerable to the power of the army, which had created it. In 1649 and 1650, Cromwell led punitive expeditions to Ireland and Scotland, partly for sheer revenge and partly to put down resistance to Commonwealth authority. In Ireland, where Cromwell's forces were particularly ruthless, the English dispossessed more Irish landholders, which

Popular Preaching in England Many women took advantage of the collapse of royal authority to preach in public—a radical activity for women at the time. This print satirizes the Quakers, a religious movement that attracted many women. (Mary Evans Picture Library)

served to pay off the army's wages. Meanwhile, Parliament could not agree on systematic reforms, particularly the one reform Independents in the army insisted on: more broadly based elections for a new Parliament. Fresh from his victories, Cromwell led his armies to London and dissolved Parliament in the spring of 1652.

In 1653, a cadre of army officers drew up the "Instrument of Government," England's first—and still, today, only—written constitution. It provided for an executive, the Lord Protector, and a Parliament to be based on somewhat wider male suffrage. Cromwell was the natural choice for Lord Protector. Cromwell was an extremely able leader who was not averse to compromise, either in politics or religion. He believed in a state church, but, unlike his Presbyterian opponents, one that allowed for local control, including choice of minister, by individual congregations. He also believed in toleration for Catholics and Jews, as long as no one disturbed the peace.

As Lord Protector, Cromwell oversaw impressive reforms in law that reflected his belief in the limits of governing authority. For example, contrary to the practice of his day, he opposed capital punishment for petty crimes. The government of the Protectorate, however, accomplished little, given Parliament's internal divisions. The population at large still harbored royalist sympathizers; after a royalist uprising in 1655, Cromwell divided England into military districts and vested governing authority in army generals.

After Cromwell died of a sudden illness in September 1658, the Protectorate could not survive the strains over policy and the challenges to its legitimacy. In February 1660, the decisive action of one army general enabled all the surviving members of the Long Parliament to rejoin the Rump. The Parliament summarily dissolved itself and called for new elections. The newly elected Parliament recalled Charles II, son of Charles I, from exile abroad and restored the monarchy. The chaos and radicalism of the late civil war and "interregnum"—the period between reigns, as the years from 1649 to 1660 came to be called—now spawned a conservative reaction.

The Restoration, 1660–1685

Charles II (r. 1660–1685) claimed his throne at the age of 30. He had learned from his years of uncertain exile and from the fate of his father. He did not seek retribution, but rather offered a general pardon to all but a few rebels (mostly those who had signed his father's death warrant), and he suggested to Parliament a relatively tolerant religious settlement that would include Anglicans as well as Presbyterians.

That the reestablished royal government was not more tolerant than it turned out to be was not Charles's doing, initially, but Parliament's. During the 1660s, the "Cavalier" Parliament, named for royalists in the civil war, passed harsh laws aimed at religious dissenters. Anglican orthodoxy was reimposed, including the reestablishment of bishops and the Anglican Book of Common Prayer. All officeholders and clergy were required to swear oaths of obedience to the king and to the established church. As a result, hundreds of non-Anglican Protestants were forced out of office. Holding nonconformist religious services became illegal, and Parliament passed a "five-mile" act to prevent dissenting ministers even from traveling near their former churches. Property laws were tightened and the criminal codes made more severe.

The king's behavior, however, began to mimic prerevolutionary royalist positions. Charles II began to flirt with Catholicism, and his brother and heir, James, openly converted. Charles promulgated a declaration of tolerance that would have included Catholics, as well as nonconformist Protestants, but Parliament would not accept it. In 1678, Charles's secret treaties with the French became known (see page 449), and rumors of a Catholic plot to murder Charles and reimpose Catholicism became widespread. No firm evidence of the "Popish Plot" was ever unearthed, although thirty-five people were executed for alleged participation. Parliament passed the Test Act, which barred all but Anglicans from public office. As a result, the Catholic James was forced to resign as Lord High Admiral.

When Parliament then moved to exclude James from succession to the throne, Charles dissolved it. A subsequent Parliament, worried by the possibility of a new civil war, backed down. But the legacy of the previous civil war and interregnum was a potent one. After two decades of religious pluralism and broadly based political activity, it was impossible to reimpose religious conformity or to silence all dissent, even with harsh new laws on the books. It was also impossible to silence Parliament. Though reluctant to press too far, Parliament tried to assert its policies against the desires of the king.

However, by the end of his reign, Charles was financially independent of Parliament, thanks to increased revenue from overseas trade and secret subsidies from France, his recent ally against the Dutch. If he had been followed by an able successor, Parliament might have lost a good measure of its confidence and independence. But his brother James's reign and its aftermath further enhanced Parliament's power.

The Glorious Revolution, 1688

When James II (r. 1685–1689) succeeded Charles, Parliament was wary but initially cooperative. For example, it granted James customs duties for life, as well as funds to suppress a rebellion by one of Charles's illegitimate sons. James did not try to impose Catholicism on England as some had feared, but he did try to achieve toleration for Catholics in two declarations of indulgence in 1687 and 1688. However admirable his goal—toleration—he had essentially changed the law of the realm without Parliament's consent. He further undermined his position with heavy-handed tactics. When several leading Anglican bishops refused to read the declarations from their pulpits, he had them imprisoned and tried for seditious libel. However, a sympathetic jury acquitted them.

James also failed because of the coincidence of other events. In 1685, at the outset of James's reign, Louis XIV of France had revoked the Edict of Nantes. The possibility that subjects and monarchs in France and, by extension, elsewhere could be of different faiths seemed increasingly unlikely. Popular fears of James's Catholicism were thus heightened early in his reign, and his later declarations of tolerance, though they benefited Protestant dissenters too, were viewed with suspicion. Then, in 1688, the king's second wife, who was Catholic, gave birth to a son. The birth raised the specter of a Catholic succession.

In June 1688, to put pressure on James, leading members of Parliament invited William of Orange, husband of James's Protestant daughter, Mary, to come to England. William mounted an invasion that became a rout and James sought protection in France. William called Parliament, which declared James to have abdicated and offered the throne jointly to William and Mary. With French support, James invaded the British Isles in 1690, but was defeated by William at the Battle of Boyne, in Ireland, that year.

The substitution of William (r. 1689–1702) and Mary (r. 1689–1694) for James, known as the **Glorious Revolution**, was engineered by Parliament and confirmed its power. Parliament presented the new sovereigns with a Declaration of Rights upon their accession and, later that year, with a Bill of Rights that defended freedom of speech, called for frequent Parliaments, and required all future monarchs to be Protestant (see the feature, "The Written Record: The English Bill of Rights"). Parliament's role in the political process was ensured by its power of the purse, since William sought funds for his ambitious military efforts, particularly the Netherlands' ongoing wars with France.

The issues that had faced the English since the beginning of the century were common to all European states: religious division and elite power, fiscal strains and resistance to taxation.

Glorious Revolution
Bloodless English revolution in 1688 in which Parliament replaced the Catholic King James II with William (of Orange) and his wife, Mary (James's Protestant daughter), and imposed, on the new rulers, a Bill of Rights that confirmed Parliament's power.

SECTION SUMMARY

- In England, unlike in France, a representative institution controlled taxation and could effectively challenge royal policies.

- A civil war between Charles I and parliamentary forces ended with the defeat and execution of the king in 1649.

- Several groups, including wealthy gentry and ordinary townspeople, had allied to support Parliament, but they did not agree on a program of political and religious reform.

- The government of the interregnum did not last after the death of the Lord Protector, Oliver Cromwell, because too few of the original supporters of Parliament believed it legitimate or approved of its policies.

- The Crown was restored under Charles II but began to conflict again with Parliament over political and religious policy under his successor James II.

- The role of Parliament in English government was confirmed when William and Mary accepted the Crown under conditions stated in the Bill of Rights.

The English Bill of Rights

After King William and Queen Mary accepted the throne, they signed this Bill of Rights presented to them by Parliament in 1689. They therefore accepted not only the limits of royal power enshrined in the document but also the fact that Parliament could legislate how the monarchy was to function.

Whereas the Lords Spiritual and Temporal and Commons assembled at Westminster, lawfully, fully and freely representing all the estates of the people of this realm, did upon the thirteenth of February ... present unto their Majesties, then called and known by the names and style of William and Mary, prince and princess of Orange, being present in their proper persons, a certain declaration in writing made by the said Lords and Commons in the words following, viz.:

Whereas the late King James the Second, by the assistance of diverse evil counselors, judges and ministers employed by him, did endeavor to subvert and extirpate the Protestant religion and the laws and liberties of this kingdom;

By assuming and exercising a power of dispensing with and suspending of laws and the execution of laws without consent of Parliament; ...

By levying money for and to the use of the Crown by pretense of prerogative for other time and in other manner than the same was granted by Parliament;

By raising and keeping a standing army within this kingdom in time of peace without consent of Parliament, and quartering soldiers contrary to law;

By causing several good subjects being Protestants to be disarmed at the same time when papists were both armed and employed contrary to law;

By violating the freedom of election of members to serve in Parliament;

By prosecutions in the Court of King's Bench for matters and causes cognizable only in Parliament, and by diverse other arbitrary and illegal courses; ...

And excessive bail hath been required of persons committed in criminal cases to elude the benefit of the laws made for the liberty of the subjects;

And excessive fines have been imposed;

And illegal and cruel punishments inflicted; ...

All which are utterly and directly contrary to the known laws and statutes and freedom of this realm;

And whereas the said late King James the Second having abdicated the government and the throne being thereby vacant, his Highness the prince of Orange (whom it hath pleased Almighty God to make the glorious instrument of delivering this kingdom from popery and arbitrary power) did ... cause letters to be written to the Lords Spiritual and Temporal being Protestants, and other letters to the several counties, cities, universities, boroughs and cinque ports,

Yet, the cataclysmic events in England—the interregnum, the Commonwealth, the Restoration, the Glorious Revolution—had set it apart from other states. A representative institution had become a partner of the monarchy.

NEW POWERS IN CENTRAL AND EASTERN EUROPE

Which states began to dominate central and eastern Europe and why were they successful?

By the end of the seventeenth century, three states dominated central and eastern Europe: Austria, Brandenburg-Prussia, and Russia. After the Thirty Years' War, the Habsburgs' dominance in the splintering empire waned, and they focused on expanding and consolidating their power in their hereditary possessions, centered in what became modern Austria. Brandenburg-Prussia, in northeastern Germany, emerged from obscurity to rival the Habsburg state. The rulers of Brandenburg-Prussia had gained lands in the Peace of Westphalia, and astute management transformed their relatively small and scattered holdings into one of the most powerful states in Europe. Russia's new stature in eastern Europe resulted in part from the weakness of its greatest rival, Poland, and the determination of one leader, Peter the Great, to assume a major role in European affairs. Sweden controlled valuable Baltic territory through much of the century, but eventually was also eclipsed by Russia as a force in the region.

The internal political development of states was dramatically shaped by their relationship to the wider European economy: They were sources of grain and raw materials for the more densely urbanized West. The development of and the competition among states in central and eastern Europe were closely linked to developments in western Europe.

for the choosing of such persons to represent them as were of right to be sent to Parliament. . . .

And thereupon the said Lords Spiritual and Temporal and Commons, pursuant to their respective letters and elections, being now assembled in a full and free representative of this nation, taking into their most serious consideration the best means for attaining the ends aforesaid, do in the first place (as their ancestors in like case have usually done) for the vindicating and asserting their ancient rights and liberties declare;

That the pretended power of suspending of laws or the execution of laws by regal authority without consent of Parliament is illegal;

That the pretended power of dispensing with laws or the execution of laws by regal authority, as it hath been assumed and exercised of late, is illegal; . . .

That levying money for or to the use of the Crown by pretense of prerogative, without grant of Parliament, for longer time, or in other manner than the same is or shall be granted, is illegal;

That it is the right of the Subjects to petition the king, and all commitments and prosecutions for such petitioning are illegal;

That the raising or keeping a standing army within the kingdom in time of peace, unless it be with consent of Parliament, is against law;

That the subjects which are Protestants may have arms for their defense suitable to their conditions and as allowed by law;

That election of members of Parliament ought to be free;

That the freedom of speech and debates or proceedings in Parliament ought not to be impeached or questioned in any court or place out of Parliament;

That excessive bail ought not to be required, nor excessive fines imposed nor cruel and unusual punishments inflicted; . . .

And that for redress of all grievances, and for the amending, strengthening and preserving of the laws, Parliaments ought to be held frequently.

QUESTIONS

1. How, specifically, does this document limit royal power?

2. What rights were the creators of this document most concerned to protect, in your view?

3. Would any of the rights protected here have been useful to common English people?

Source: *The Statutes: Revised Edition*, vol. 1 (London: Eyre and Spottiswoode, 1871), pp. 10–12.

The Consolidation of Austria

The Thirty Years' War (see pages 427–430) weakened the Habsburgs as emperors but strengthened them in their own lands. The main Habsburg lands in 1648 were a collection of principalities comprising modern Austria, the kingdom of Hungary (largely in Turkish hands), and the kingdom of Bohemia (see **MAP 16.2**). In 1714, Austria acquired the Spanish Netherlands (modern Belgium), which were renamed the Austrian Netherlands. Although language and ethnic differences prevented an absolutist state along French lines, Leopold I (r. 1657–1705) made political and institutional changes that enabled the Habsburg state to become one of the most powerful in Europe through the eighteenth century.

Much of the coherence that already existed in Leopold's lands had been achieved by his predecessors after the Thirty Years' War. The lands of rebels in Bohemia had been confiscated and redistributed among loyal, mostly Austrian, families. In return for political and military support for the emperor, these families were given the right to exploit their newly acquired land and the peasants who worked it. The desire to recover population and productivity after the destruction of the Thirty Years' War gave landlords further incentive to curtail peasants' autonomy, particularly in devastated Bohemia. Austrian landlords throughout the Habsburg domains provided grain and timber for the export market and foodstuffs for the Austrian armies, while elite families provided the army with officers. This political-economic arrangement provoked numerous serious peasant revolts, but the peasants were not able to force changes in a system that suited both the elites and the central authority.

Although Leopold had lost much influence within the empire itself, an imperial government including a war ministry, financial bureaucracy, and the like still functioned in his capital, Vienna. Leopold worked to extricate the government of his own lands from the apparatus of imperial institutions, which were staffed largely by Germans more loyal to imperial, than to Habsburg, interests.

Baroque Splendor in Austria   The Belvedere Palace (whose name means "beautiful view") was built near Vienna as the summer residence of the great aristocratic general Prince Eugene of Savoy, who had successfully led Habsburg armies against the Turks and had reaped many rewards from Leopold and his successors. The palace shares many features in common with Louis XIV's palace of Versailles.   (Erich Lessing/Art Resource, NY)

In addition, Leopold used the Catholic Church as an institutional and ideological support for his state. Leopold's personal ambition was to reestablish devout Catholicism throughout his territories. Acceptance of Catholicism became the litmus test of loyalty to the Habsburg regime, and Protestantism vanished among elites. Leopold encouraged the work of Jesuit teachers and members of other Catholic religious orders. These men and women helped staff his government and administered religious life down to the most local levels.

Leopold's most dramatic success, as a Habsburg and a religious leader, was his reconquest of the kingdom of Hungary from the Ottoman Empire. Since the mid-sixteenth century, the Habsburgs had controlled only a narrow strip of the kingdom. Preoccupied with fighting France, Leopold did not himself choose to begin a reconquest. His centralizing policies, however, alienated nobles and townspeople in the portion of Hungary he did control, as did his repression of Protestantism, which had flourished in Hungary. Hungarian nobles began a revolt, aided by the Turks, aiming for a reunited Hungary under Ottoman protection.

The Habsburgs won, instead, in part because they received help from the Venetians, the Russians, and especially the Poles, whose lands in Ukraine were threatened by the Turks. The Turks overreached their supply lines to besiege Vienna in 1683. When the siege failed, Habsburg armies slowly pressed east and south, recovering Buda, the capital of Hungary, in 1686 and Belgrade (modern Serbia) in 1688. The **Treaty of Carlowitz** ended the fighting in 1699, after the first conference where European allies jointly dictated terms to a weakening Ottoman Empire. Austria's allies had also gained at the Ottomans' expense: The Poles recovered the threatened Ukraine, and the Russians gained a vital foothold on the Black Sea.

Leopold gave control of reclaimed lands to loyal Austrian officers but could not fully break the traditions of Hungarian separatism. Hungary's great aristocrats—whether they had defended the Habsburgs against Turkish encroachment or guarded the frontier for Turkish overlords—retained their independence. The peasantry, as elsewhere, suffered a decline in status as a result of the Crown's efforts to ensure the loyalty of elites. In the long run, Hungarian independence weakened the Habsburg state, but in the short run, Leopold's victory over the Turks and the recovery of Hungary were momentous events, confirming the Habsburgs as the preeminent power in central Europe.

The Rise of Brandenburg-Prussia

Several German states, in addition to Austria, gained territory and stature after the Thirty Years' War. By the end of the seventeenth century, the strongest was **Brandenburg-Prussia**, a conglomeration of small territories held, by dynastic accident, by the Hohenzollern family. The two principal territories were electoral Brandenburg, in northeastern Germany, with its capital, Berlin, and the duchy of Prussia, a fief of the Polish crown along the Baltic coast east of Poland proper (see **Map 16.2**). In addition, the Hohenzollerns ruled a handful of small principalities near the Netherlands. These unpromising lands became a powerful state, primarily because of the work of Frederick William, known as "the Great Elector" (r. 1640–1688).

Frederick William used the occasion of a war to effect a permanent change in the structure of government. He took advantage of a war between Poland and its rivals, Sweden and Russia (described in the next section), to win independence for the duchy of Prussia from Polish overlordship. When his involvement in the war ended in 1657, he kept intact the general war commissariat, a combined civilian and military body that had efficiently directed the war effort, bypassing traditional councils and representative bodies. He also used the standing army to force the payment of high taxes. Most significantly, he established a positive relationship with the Junkers (YUNG-kurz), hereditary landholders, which ensured him both revenue and loyalty. The Junkers surrendered their accustomed political independence in return for greater economic and social power over the peasants who worked their lands. The freedom to control their estates led many nobles to invest in profitable agriculture for the export market. The peasants were serfs who received no benefits from the increased productivity of the land.

Frederick William further enhanced his state's power by sponsoring industry. These industries did not have to fear competition from urban producers because the towns had been frozen out of the political process and saddled with heavy taxes. Though an oppressive place for many Germans, Brandenburg-Prussia attracted many skilled refugees, such as Huguenot artisans fleeing Louis XIV's France.

Other German states, such as Bavaria and Saxony, had vibrant towns, largely free peasantries, and weaker aristocracies but were relative nonentities in international affairs. Power on the European stage depended on military force. Whether in a large state like France or in a small one like Brandenburg-Prussia, that power usually came at the expense of the people.

Competition Around the Baltic

The rivers and port cities of the Baltic coast were conduits for the growing trade between the Baltic hinterland and the rest of Europe. Trade in grain, timber, furs, iron, and copper was vital to the entire European economy and caused intense competition, especially between Poland-Lithuania and Sweden, to control the coast and inland regions. In 1600, a large portion of the Baltic hinterland lay under the control of Poland-Lithuania, a vast state at the height of its power, but one that would prove an exception to the pattern of expanding royal power in the seventeenth century.

Poland and Lithuania had been jointly governed since a marriage united their ruling families in the late Middle Ages. Even so, the two states retained distinct traditions. Like some of the Habsburgs' territories, Poland-Lithuania was a multiethnic state, particularly the huge duchy of Lithuania, which included Ruthenia (modern Belarus and Ukraine). Poles spoke Polish, a Slavic language, and were primarily Catholic, although there were also large minorities of Protestants,

Treaty of Carlowitz
Treaty imposed by the European allies on the Ottoman Empire, by which the Austrians, Venetians, Russians, and Poles gained territory at the Turks' expense.

Brandenburg-Prussia
Group of German territories ruled by the Hohenzollern family that became one of Europe's most powerful states in the seventeenth century.

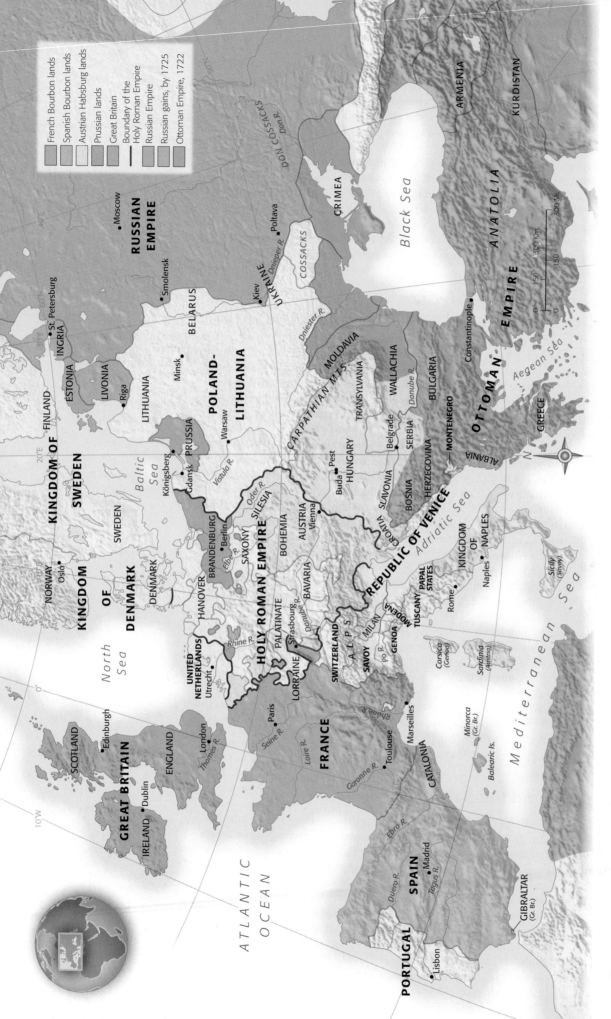

MAP 16.2 — New Powers in Central and Eastern Europe, to 1725

The balance of power in central and eastern Europe shifted with the strengthening of Austria, the rise of Brandenburg-Prussia, and the expansion of Russia at the expense of Poland and Sweden.

Legend:
- French Bourbon lands
- Spanish Bourbon lands
- Austrian Habsburg lands
- Prussian lands
- Great Britain
- Boundary of the Holy Roman Empire
- Russian Empire
- Russian gains, by 1725
- Ottoman Empire, 1722

ATLANTIC OCEAN

North Sea

Baltic Sea

Black Sea

Mediterranean Sea

Adriatic Sea

Aegean Sea

GREAT BRITAIN
SCOTLAND · Edinburgh
ENGLAND · London
Thames R.
IRELAND · Dublin

PORTUGAL · Lisbon
Tagus R.
Duero R.

SPAIN · Madrid
CATALONIA
Ebro R.
GIBRALTAR (Gr. Br.)

FRANCE · Paris
Seine R.
Loire R.
Garonne R.
Toulouse ·
Marseilles ·
Rhône R.

Minorca (Gr. Br.)
Balearic Is.

NORWAY · Oslo
KINGDOM OF DENMARK
DENMARK
KINGDOM OF SWEDEN
SWEDEN
FINLAND
St. Petersburg ·
INGRIA
ESTONIA
LIVONIA · Riga

Moscow ·
RUSSIAN EMPIRE
Smolensk ·
BELARUS
Minsk ·
LITHUANIA
POLAND-LITHUANIA
Warsaw ·
Kiev ·
UKRAINE
Dnieper R.
Poltava ·
DON COSSACKS
Don R.
COSSACKS
Dniester R.
CRIMEA

UNITED NETHERLANDS
Utrecht ·
HANOVER
BRANDENBURG
Berlin ·
Elbe R.
SAXONY
Königsberg
Gdansk
PRUSSIA
Vistula R.
Oder R.
SILESIA
BOHEMIA
HOLY ROMAN EMPIRE
Rhine R.
PALATINATE
Strasbourg ·
LORRAINE
SWITZERLAND
ALPS
Danube R.
BAVARIA
AUSTRIA · Vienna
Buda · Pest
HUNGARY
CARPATHIAN MTS.
TRANSYLVANIA
MOLDAVIA
WALLACHIA
Danube R.
BULGARIA

SAVOY
MILAN
GENOA
Po R.
MODENA
TUSCANY
PAPAL STATES
Rome ·
KINGDOM OF NAPLES
Naples ·
Corsica (Genoa)
Sardinia (Austria)
Sicily (Savoy)
REPUBLIC OF VENICE
CROATIA
SLAVONIA
BOSNIA
SERBIA · Belgrade
HERZEGOVINA
MONTENEGRO
ALBANIA
GREECE
OTTOMAN EMPIRE
Constantinople ·
ANATOLIA
ARMENIA
KURDISTAN

0   150   300 Km
0   150   300 Mi

Orthodox Christians, and Jews in Poland. Lithuanians, whose language was only distantly related to the Slavic languages, were mostly Catholic as well, although Orthodox Christianity predominated among the Ruthenians, who spoke a Slavic language related to both Russian and Polish.

The state commanded considerable resources, including the ports of Gdansk and Riga on the Baltic and grain-producing lands in the interior. However, Poland-Lithuania had internal weaknesses. It was a republic of the nobility, with a weak elected king at its head. The great nobles, whose fortunes increased with the grain trade, ran the affairs of state through the national parliament, the Sejm (SAME). They drastically limited the ability of the Crown to tax and to grant new titles of nobility, as was the practice throughout Europe. These limitations meant that the king could not reward the loyalty of wealthy gentry or the small numbers of urban elites, so that they might be a counterweight to noble power. Limited funds also meant that the Polish crown would be hard put to defend its vast territories when challenged by its rivals.

Strains began to mount within Poland-Lithuania in the late sixteenth century. The spread of the Counter-Reformation, encouraged by the Crown, created tensions with both Protestant and Orthodox subjects in the diverse kingdom. As the power of landholding nobles grew with Poland's expanding grain exports, impoverished peasants were bound to the land, and lesser gentry, particularly in Lithuania, were shut out of political power. In Ukraine, communities of **Cossacks**, nomadic farmer-warriors, grew as Polish and Lithuanian peasants fled harsh conditions to join them. The Cossacks had long been tolerated because they served as a military buffer against the Ottoman Turks to the south, but now Polish landlords wanted to reincorporate the Cossacks into the profitable political-economic system they controlled.

In 1648, the Polish crown faced revolt and invasion that it could not fully counter. The Cossacks led a major uprising, which included Ukrainian gentry as well as peasants. In 1654, the Cossacks tried to assure their autonomy by transferring their allegiance to Moscow. They became part of a Russian invasion of Poland-Lithuania that, by the next year, had engulfed much of the eastern half of the dual state. At the same time, Poland's perennial rival, Sweden, seized central Poland in a military campaign marked by extreme brutality. Many Polish and Lithuanian aristocrats continued to act like independent warlords and cooperated with the invaders to preserve their own local power.

Operating with slim resources, Polish royal armies eventually managed to recover much territory—most important, the western half of Ukraine (see **Map 16.2**). But the invasions and subsequent fighting were disastrous. The population of Poland declined by as much as 40 percent, and vital urban economies were in ruins. The Catholic identity of the Polish heartland had been a rallying point for resistance to the Protestant Swedes and the Orthodox Russians, but the religious tolerance that had distinguished the diverse Polish kingdom and had been mandated in its constitution was now abandoned. In addition, much of its recovery of Lithuanian territory was only nominal.

The elective Polish crown passed in 1674 to the military hero Jan Sobieski (so-BYESS-key) (r. 1674–1696), known as "Vanquisher of the Turks" for his role in raising the siege of Vienna in 1683. Given Poland's internal weakness, however, Sobieski's victories, in the long run, helped the Ottomans' other foes—Austria and Russia—more than they helped the Poles. After his death, Poland would be vulnerable to the political ambitions of its more powerful neighbors. The next elected king, Augustus II of Saxony (r. 1697–1704, 1709–1733), dragged Poland back into war, from which Russia would emerge the clear winner in the power struggle in eastern Europe.

The Swedes, meanwhile, successfully vied with the Poles for control of the lucrative Baltic coast. Swedish efforts to control Baltic territory had begun in the sixteenth century, first to counter the power of its perennial rival, Denmark, in the western Baltic. Sweden then competed with Poland to control Livonia (modern Latvia) and its major port city, Riga. By 1617, under Gustav Adolf, the Swedes gained the lands to the north of Livonia surrounding the Gulf of Finland (the most direct outlet for Russian goods), and in 1621, they displaced the Poles in Livonia itself. Swedish intervention in the Thirty Years' War (see page 428) had been part of this campaign to secure Baltic territory. And the Treaty of Westphalia (1648, see page 429) confirmed Sweden's gains on the Baltic.

The port cities held by Sweden were profitable but simply served to pay for the costly wars necessary to seize and defend them. Indeed, Sweden did not have the resources to hold Baltic territory over the long term, and it gained little from its aggression against Poland in the 1650s. Owing to its earlier gains, Sweden managed to reign supreme on the Baltic coast until the end of the century, when it was supplanted by the powerful Russian state.

Cossacks Russian term meaning "free men" originally applied to people of central Asian origin in the hinterland of the Black Sea. After 1500, many peasants escaping serfdom in Poland-Lithuania and Russia fled and became "Cossacks."

Russia Under Peter the Great

The Russian state grew dramatically in the sixteenth century, under Ivan IV (r. 1533–1584), the first Russian ruler to routinely use the title "Tsar" (Russian for "Caesar"). Ivan's use of the title reflected his imperial intentions. He expanded the territory under Moscow's control south to the Caspian Sea and east into Siberia. Within his expanding empire, Ivan ruled as an autocrat. The need to gather tribute money for Mongol overlords in medieval times had concentrated many resources in the hands of Muscovite princes. Ivan was able to bypass noble participation and create ranks of officials loyal only to him.

Ivan came to be called "the Terrible," from a Russian word meaning "awe-inspiring." Although a period of disputed succession to the throne, known as the "Time of Troubles," followed Ivan's death in 1584, the foundations of the large and cohesive state he had built survived until a new dynasty of rulers was established in the seventeenth century.

The Romanovs, an aristocratic family related to Ivan's, became the new ruling dynasty in 1613. Michael (r. 1613–1645) was named tsar by an assembly of aristocrats, gentry, and commoners who were more alarmed by the civil wars and recent Polish invasions than by a return to strong tsarist rule. Michael was succeeded by his son, Alexis (r. 1645–1676), who presided over the extension of Russian control to eastern Ukraine in 1654, following the wars in Poland, and developed an interest in cultivating relationships with the West.

Peter the Great   Energetic and tyrannical Russian tsar who forcibly westernized Russian state and society and made Russia into a great power.

A complete shift of the balance of power in eastern Europe and the Baltic, in Russia's favor, was achieved by Alexis's son, Peter I (r. 1682–1725), "the Great." **Peter the Great** accomplished this by military successes against his enemies and by forcibly reorienting Russian government and society toward involvement with the rest of Europe.

Peter was almost literally larger than life. Nearly 7 feet tall, he towered over most of his contemporaries and had physical and mental energy to match his size. He set himself to learning trades and studied soldiering by rising through the ranks of the military like a common soldier. He traveled abroad to learn as much as he could about western European economies and governments. He wanted the revenue, manufacturing output, technology and trade, and, above all, up-to-date army and navy that other rulers enjoyed.

Immediately on his accession to power, Peter initiated a bold series of changes in Russian society. His travels had taught him that European monarchs coexisted with a privileged, but educated, aristocracy and that a brilliant court life symbolized and reinforced their authority. So, he set out to refashion Russian society in what amounted to an enforced cultural revolution. He provoked a direct confrontation with Russia's traditional aristocracy over everything from education to matters of dress. He elevated numerous new families to the ranks of gentry and created an official ranking system for the nobility to encourage and reward service to his government.

Peter's effort to reorient his nation culturally, economically, and politically toward Europe was most obvious in the construction of the city of St. Petersburg on the Gulf of Finland, which provided access to the Baltic Sea (see **MAP 16.2**). In stark contrast to Moscow, dominated by the medieval fortress of the Kremlin, St. Petersburg was a modern European city with wide avenues and palaces designed for a sophisticated court life.

Although Peter was highly intelligent, practical, and determined to create a more productive and better governed society, he was also cruel and authoritarian. Peasants already bore the brunt of taxation, but their tax burden worsened when they were assessed arbitrarily by head and not by output of the land. The building of St. Petersburg cost staggering sums in both money and workers' lives. Peter's entire reform system was carried out tyrannically; resistance was brutally suppressed. Victims included his own son, who died after torture while awaiting execution for questioning his father's policies. Peter faced rebellions by elites, as well as common people, against the exactions and the cultural changes of his regime.

A major reason for the high cost of Peter's government to the Russian people was his ambition for territorial gain—hence, his emphasis on an improved, and costly, army and navy. He

Peter the Great   This portrait by a Dutch artist captures the tsar's "westernizing" mission by showing Peter in military dress according to European fashions of the day.
(Bildarchiv Preussischer Kulturbesitz/Art Resource, NY)

recruited experienced foreign technicians and created the Russian navy from scratch. At first, ships were built in the south to contest Turkish control of the Black Sea. Later, they were built in the north to secure and defend the Baltic. Peter also modernized the Russian army by employing tactics, training, and discipline he had observed in the West. He introduced military conscription and built munitions plants. By 1709, Russia was able to manufacture most of the up-to-date firearms its army needed.

Russia waged war virtually throughout Peter's reign. He struck at the Ottomans and their client state in the Crimea. Peter was most successful against his northern competitor, Sweden, for control of the weakened Polish state and the Baltic Sea. The conflicts between Sweden and Russia, known as the Great Northern War, raged from 1700 to 1709 and, in a less intense phase, lasted until 1721. By the Treaty of Nystadt in 1721, Russia gained its present-day territory in the Gulf of Finland near St. Petersburg, plus Livonia and Estonia. These acquisitions gave Russia a secure window on the Baltic and, in combination with its gains of Lithuanian territory earlier in the century, made Russia the preeminent Baltic power, at Sweden's and Poland's expense.

SECTION SUMMARY

- After the Thirty Years' War, Austria, Brandenburg-Prussia, and Russia became the dominant states in central and eastern Europe.

- Central and eastern Europe provided raw materials for the wider European economy, which enhanced elites' power over peasants, increased revenues to states, and caused wars between states over these resources.

- The Austrian Habsburgs consolidated their power in their territories within the Holy Roman Empire and reconquered Hungary from the Ottoman Turks.

- Although composed of a collection of small principalities, Brandenburg-Prussia became a powerful state.

- Poland-Lithuania declined in the seventeenth century because the elective monarchy could not defend itself against independent aristocrats, rebellious Cossacks, or powerful neighboring states.

- Russia was forcibly modernized by Peter the Great and became the most powerful state in eastern Europe under his reign, eclipsing Sweden in control of Baltic territories.

THE EXPANSION OF OVERSEAS TRADE AND SETTLEMENT

How and why did Europe's overseas trade and colonization expand in the seventeenth century and what effects did this expansion have on Europe itself?

By the beginning of the seventeenth century, competition from the Dutch, French, and English was disrupting the Spanish and Portuguese trading empires in the New World and in Asia. During the seventeenth century, the Dutch not only became masters of the spice trade, but broadened the market to include many other commodities. In the Americas, a new trading system linking Europe, Africa, and the New World came into being with the expansion of tobacco and, later, sugar production. French and English colonists began settling in North America in increasing numbers. Overseas trade also had a crucial impact on life within Europe: on patterns of production and consumption, on social stratification, and on the distribution of wealth.

The Growth of Trading Empires: The Success of the Dutch

By the end of the sixteenth century, the Dutch and the English were making incursions into the Portuguese-controlled spice trade with areas of India, Ceylon, and the East Indies. Spain had annexed Portugal in 1580, but the drain on Spain's resources, from its wars with the Dutch and French, prevented Spain from adequately defending its enlarged trading empire in Asia. The Dutch and, to a lesser degree, the English rapidly supplanted Portuguese control of this lucrative trade (see **MAP 16.3**).

The Dutch were particularly well placed to dominate overseas trade. They already dominated seaborne trade within Europe, including the most important long-distance trade, which linked Spain and Portugal—with their wine and salt, as well as spices, hides, and gold from abroad—with the Baltic seacoast, where these products were sold for grain and timber produced in Germany, Poland-Lithuania, and Scandinavia. The geographic position of the Netherlands and the fact that the Dutch consumed more Baltic grain than any other area, because of their large urban population, help to explain their dominance of this trade. In addition, the Dutch had improved the design of their merchant ships to maximize their profits. By 1600, they had

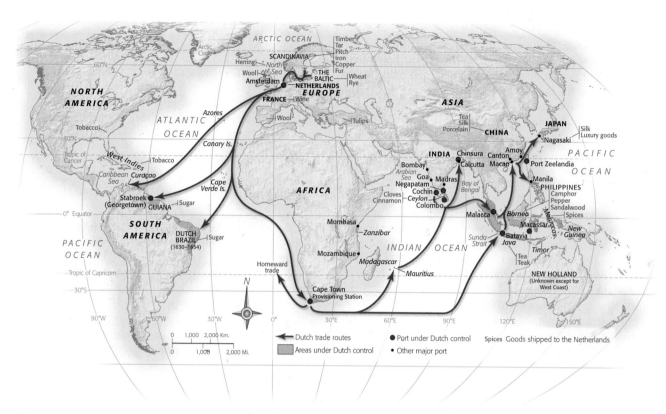

🌐 **MAP 16.3—Dutch Commerce in the Seventeenth Century**
The Dutch supplanted Portuguese control of trade with Asia and dominated seaborne trade within Europe.

Dutch East India Company   Commercially innovative Dutch company, formed in 1602, that combined government management of trade with both public and private investment.

developed the *fluitschip* (flyship), a cheaply built vessel with a long, flat hull and simple rigging, that carried goods economically.

The Dutch succeeded in Asia because of institutional, as well as technological, innovations. In 1602, the **Dutch East India Company** was formed. The company combined government management of trade, typical of the period, with both public and private investment. In the past, groups of investors had funded single voyages or small numbers of ships on a one-time basis. The formation of the Dutch East India Company created a permanent pool of capital to sustain trade. After 1612, investments in the company were negotiable as stock. These greater assets allowed proprietors to spread the risks and delays of longer voyages among larger numbers of investors. In addition, more money was available for warehouses, docks, and ships. The English East India Company, founded in 1607, also supported trade, but more modestly. It had one-tenth the capital of the Dutch company and did not use the same system of permanent capital held as stock by investors until 1657. The Bank of Amsterdam, founded in 1609, became the depository for the bullion that flowed into the Netherlands with the flood of trade. The bank established currency exchange rates and issued paper money and instruments of credit to facilitate commerce.

A dramatic expansion of trade with Asia resulted from the Dutch innovations, so much so that by 1650, the European market for spices was glutted, and traders' profits had begun to fall. To control the supply of spices, the Dutch seized some of the areas where they were produced. The Dutch and English also responded to the oversupply of spices by diversifying their trade. The proportion of spices in cargoes from the East fell from about 70 percent at mid-century to just over 20 percent by the century's end. New consumer goods, such as tea, coffee, and silk and cotton fabrics, took their place. Eventually, the Dutch and the English, alert for fresh opportunities, entered the local carrying trade among Asian states. This enabled them to make profits even without purchasing goods, and it slowed the drain of hard currency from Europe—currency in increasingly short supply, as silver mines in the Americas were depleted.

The "Golden Age" of the Netherlands

The prosperity occasioned by the Dutch trading empire created social and political conditions within the Netherlands unique among European states. The concentration of trade and shipping sustained a healthy merchant oligarchy and also a prosperous artisanal sector. Disparities of wealth were smaller here than anywhere else in Europe. The shipbuilding and fishing trades, among others, supported large numbers of workers with a high standard of living for the age.

The Netherlands appeared to contemporaries to be an astonishing exception to the normal structures of politics. Political decentralization in the Netherlands persisted. The Estates General (representative assembly) for the Netherlands as a whole had no independent powers of taxation. Each of the seven provinces retained considerable autonomy. Wealthy merchants in the Estates of the province of Holland, in fact, constituted the government for the entire nation for long periods because of Holland's economic dominance. The head of government was the executive secretary, known as the pensionary, of Holland's Estates.

Holland's only competition in the running of affairs came from the House of Orange, aristocratic leaders of the revolt against Spain (see pages 410–413). They exercised what control they had by means of the office of *stadtholder* (STAHT-hole-der)—a kind of military governorship—to which they were elected in individual provinces. Their principal interest, traditional military glory and dynastic power, accounted for some of their influence, since they led the Netherlands' defense against Spanish attacks until the Peace of Westphalia in 1648 and against French aggression after 1672. Their power also came from their status as the only counterweight within the Netherlands to the dominance of Amsterdam's (in Holland) mercantile interests. Small towns, dependent on land-based trade or rural areas dominated by farmers and gentry, looked to the stadtholders of the Orange family to defend their interests.

As elsewhere, religion was a source of political conflict. The stadtholders and the leading families of Holland, known as regents, vied for control of the state church. Regents of Holland generally favored a less rigid and austere form of Calvinism than did the stadtholders. Their view reflected the needs of the diverse urban communities of Holland, where thousands of Jews, as well as Catholics and various Protestants, lived. Dutch commercial dominance involved the Netherlands in costly wars throughout the second half of the century. Between 1657 and 1660, the Dutch fought the Swedes to safeguard the sea-lanes and port cities of the Baltic. The most costly conflicts came from the rivalry of England and France. Under Cromwell, the English attempted to close their ports to the Dutch carrying trade. In 1672, the English, under Charles II, allied with the French, hoping that together they could destroy Dutch commercial power and even divide the Netherlands' territory between them. The Dutch navy, rebuilt since Cromwell's challenge, soon forced England out of the alliance.

But there were long-term consequences of these wars for the Dutch state. As a result of the land war with France, the Estates in Holland lost control of policy to William of Nassau (d. 1702), prince of Orange, after 1672. William drew the Netherlands into his family's long-standing close relationship with England. Like previous members of his family, William had married into the English royal family: His wife was Mary, daughter of James II. After William and Mary assumed the English throne, Dutch commerce actually suffered more when allied with England than in its previous rivalry. William used Dutch resources for the land war against Louis XIV and reserved, for the English navy, the fight at sea. By the end of the century, Dutch maritime strength was being eclipsed by English sea power.

The Growth of Atlantic Commerce

In the seventeenth century, the Dutch, the English, and the French joined the Spanish as colonial and commercial powers in the Americas. The Spanish colonial empire, in theory a trading system closed to outsiders, was in fact vulnerable to other European traders. Spanish treasure fleets were themselves a glittering attraction. In 1628, for example, a Dutch captain seized the entire fleet. But by then, Spain's goals and those of its competitors had begun to shift. The limits of an economy based on the extraction, rather than the production, of wealth became clear with the declining output of the Spanish silver mines during the 1620s. In response, the Spanish and their Dutch, French, and English competitors expanded the production of cash crops: tobacco, dyestuffs, and, above all, sugar.

Vermeer: The Letter
This is a later work by one of the great artists of the Dutch "Golden Age." Dutch art was distinguished by common, rather than heroic, subjects–here, a merchant-class woman writes a letter. The masterful use of lighting and perspective in paintings such as this one would not be equaled until the age of photography. (Bridgeman-Giraudon/Art Resource, NY)

plantation system
Agricultural system, first developed by the Portuguese, in which forced labor produced cash crops on large estates owned by absentee landlords.

The European demand for tobacco and sugar, both addictive substances, grew steadily in the seventeenth century. The **plantation system**—the use of forced labor to produce cash crops on vast tracts of land—had been developed on Mediterranean islands in the Middle Ages by European entrepreneurs, using slaves procured in Black Sea ports by Venetian and Genoese traders. Sugar production by this system had been established on Atlantic islands, such as the Cape Verde Islands, using African labor, and then in the Americas, by the Spanish and Portuguese. Sugar production in the New World grew from about 20,000 tons a year in 1600 to about 200,000 tons by 1770.

In the 1620s, while the Dutch were exploiting Portuguese weakness in the Eastern spice trade, they were also seizing sugar regions in Brazil and replacing Portuguese slave traders in African ports. The Portuguese were able to retake most of their Brazilian territory in the 1650s. But the Dutch, because they monopolized the carrying trade, were able to become the official supplier of slaves to Spanish plantations in the New World and the chief supplier of slaves, as well as other goods, to most other regions. (See the feature, "The Global Record: Journal of a Dutch Slave Ship.") The Dutch made handsome profits dealing in human cargo until the end of the seventeenth century, when they were supplanted by the British.

The Dutch introduced sugar cultivation to the French and English after learning it themselves in Brazil. Sugar plantations began to supplant tobacco cultivation, as well as subsistence farming, on the Caribbean islands the English and French controlled. Beginning in the late sixteenth century, English and French seamen had seized islands in the Caribbean to use as provisioning stations and staging points for raids against or commerce with Spanish colonies. Some island outposts had expanded into colonies and attracted European settlers—some, as in North America, coming as indentured servants—to work the land. Sugar cultivation drastically transformed the character of these island settlements because it demanded huge outlays of capital

Sugar Manufacture in Caribbean Colonies Production of sugar required large capital outlays, in part because the raw cane had to be processed quickly, on-site, to avoid spoilage. This scene depicts enslaved workers operating a small sugar mill on the island of Barbados in the seventeenth century. In the background, a press crushes the cane; in the foreground, the juice from the cane is boiled down until sugar begins to crystallize. (Mary Evans Picture Library)

and continual supplies of unskilled labor. Large plantations, owned by wealthy, often absentee landlords and dependent on slave labor, replaced smaller-scale independent farms. The most profitable sugar colonies were, for the French, the islands of Martinique and Guadeloupe and, for the English, Barbados and Jamaica.

Early Colonies in North America

Aware of the overwhelming Spanish advantage in the New World, and still hoping for treasures, such as the Spanish had found, the English, French, and Dutch were also eager to explore and settle North America. From the early sixteenth century on, French, Dutch, English, and Portuguese seamen had fished and traded off Newfoundland. By 1630, small French and Scottish settlements in Acadia (near modern Nova Scotia) and on the St. Lawrence River and English settlements in Newfoundland were established to systematically exploit the timber, fish, and fur of the North Atlantic coasts.

In England, rising unemployment and religious discontent created a large pool of potential colonists, some of whom were initially attracted to early farming and trading settlements in the Caribbean. The first of the English settlements to endure, in what was to become the United States, was established at Jamestown, named for James I, in Virginia in 1607. ("Virginia," named for Elizabeth I, the "Virgin Queen," was an extremely vague designation for the Atlantic coast of North America and its hinterland.)

ENGLISH SETTLEMENTS

The Crown encouraged colonization, but a private company, similar to those that financed long-distance trade, was established to organize the enterprise. The directors of the Virginia Company were London businessmen. Investors and would-be colonists purchased shares. Shareholders among the colonists could participate in a colonial assembly, although the governor appointed by the company was the final authority.

The colonists arrived in Virginia with ambitious and optimistic instructions: to open mines, establish profitable agriculture, and search for sea routes to Asia. But at first, the colonists struggled even to survive in the unfamiliar environment. "Though there be fish in the seas ... and beasts in the woods ... they are so wild and we so weak and ignorant, we cannot trouble them much," wrote Captain John Smith from Virginia to the directors in London.[3] The native peoples in Virginia, unlike those in Spanish-held territories, were not organized in urbanized, rigidly

Journal of a Dutch Slave Ship

These excerpts from a journal kept by the captain of the Dutch ship St. Jan record a 1659 slave-trading voyage that began in Africa and ended on Curaçao, a Dutch island colony in the Caribbean.

The 8th [of March]. We arrived with our ship on Saturday before Arda [in modern Benin] to take onboard the surgeon's mate, and tamarinds as refreshment for the slaves. We set sail the next day to continue our voyage to Rio Reael.

The 22nd [of May]. We weighed anchor again and sailed out of the Rio Reael. . . . We acquired there in trade two hundred and nineteen slaves, men and women, boys as well as girls; and we set our course for [islands in the Gulf of Biafra] in order to seek food for the slaves, because nothing was to be had in Rio Reael.

The 26th ditto. On Monday we arrived [on the islands]. We spent seven days there looking but barely obtained enough for the slaves' daily consumption; therefore we decided to sail [up a nearby river] to see whether any food could be found there.

The 29th [of June]. On Sunday we decided to continue our voyage because there was also little food [up the river mouth] for the slaves because of the heavy rain which we had daily and because many slaves were suffering from dysentery caused by the bad food supplied to us at [St. George del Mina, a Dutch fort established to serve the slave trade]. . . .

The 11th [of August]. We lay sixteen days at Cape Lopez [modern Gabon] in order to take on water and firewood. Among the water barrels some forty were taken apart to be repaired because our cooper died . . . [and] we had no one who could repair them.

The 24th [of September]. On Friday we arrived at the island of Tobago [in the Caribbean] where we took on water and also bought some bread for our crew because for three weeks they have had no rations.

The 1st of November. We lost our ship on the reef [east of Curaçao] and our crew fled in the boat immediately. There was no chance to save the slaves because we had to abandon the ship on account of heavy surf.

The 4th ditto. We arrived with the boat at . . . Curaçao. The [governor] dispatched two sloops to retrieve the slaves from the shipwreck. One of the sloops was taken by a pirate together with eighty-four slaves.

QUESTIONS

1. Note the dates in the captain's journal. How much time was devoted to trade and provisioning in Africa? How much time to the transatlantic journey?

2. Note the details the captain includes. What do these details reveal about how the voyage was planned? For whom is he recording these details, and why?

3. A companion document reveals that 110 of the 219 captive men, women, and children died during the voyage across the Atlantic. Does knowing this information change how you interpret this document? What happened to the captives who survived the journey?

Source: Charles T. Gehring and J. A. Schiltkamp, eds., *New Netherlands Documents*, vol. 17 (Interlaken, N.Y.: Heart of the Lakes Publishing, 1987), pp. 128–131. Used by permission from the *New Netherlands Project*, The New York State Library.

hierarchical societies that, after conquest, could provide the invaders with a labor force. In fact, most of the native population was quickly wiped out by European diseases. The introduction of tobacco as a cash crop a few years later saved the colonists economically—although the Virginia Company had already gone bankrupt and the Crown had assumed control of the colony. With the cultivation of tobacco, the Virginia colony, like the Caribbean islands, became dependent on forced, eventually slave, labor.

Among the Virginia colonists were impoverished men and women who came as servants, indentured to those who had paid their passage—that is, they were bound by contract to pay off their debts by several years of labor. Colonies established to the north, in what was called "New England," also drew people from the margins of English society. Early settlers there were religious dissidents. The first to arrive were the Pilgrims, who arrived at Plymouth (modern Massachusetts) in 1620. They were a community of religious Separatists who had originally immigrated to the Netherlands from England for freedom of conscience.

Following the Pilgrims, came Puritans, escaping escalating persecution under Charles I. The first, in 1629, settled under the auspices of another royally chartered company, the Massachusetts Bay Company. Among their number were many prosperous Puritan merchants and landholders. Independence from investors in London allowed them an unprecedented degree of self-government once the Massachusetts Bay colony was established.

Nevertheless, the colonies in North America were disappointments to England because they generated much less wealth than expected. Shipping timber back to Europe proved too expensive, although New England forests did supply some of the Caribbean colonists' needs. The fur trade became less lucrative, as English settlement pushed the Native Americans, who did most of the trapping, west and as French trappers to the north encroached on the trade. Certain colonists profited enormously from the tobacco economy, but the mother country did so only moderately because the demand in Europe for tobacco never matched the demand for sugar. The English settlements did continue to attract more migrants than other colonizers' outposts. By 1640, Massachusetts had some fourteen thousand European inhabitants. Through most of the next century, the growth of colonial populations in North America would result in an English advantage over the French in control of New World territory.

FRENCH SETTLEMENTS

The French began their settlement of North America at the same time as the English, in the same push to compensate for their mutual weakness in comparison to the Spanish (see **MAP 16.4**). The French efforts, however, had very different results, owing partly to the sites of their settlements, but mostly to the relationship between the mother country and the colonies. The French hold on territory was always tenuous because of the scant number of colonists who could be lured from home. There seems to have been less economic impetus for colonization from France than from England. After the French crown took over the colonies, the religious impetus also evaporated, since only Catholics were allowed to settle in New France. Moreover, the Crown forced a hierarchical political organization on the French colonies. A royal governor directed the colony, and large tracts of land were set aside for privileged investors. Thus, North America offered little to tempt French people of modest means who were seeking a better life.

The first successful French colony was established in Acadia in 1605. This settlement was an exception among the French efforts because it was founded by Huguenots, not by Catholics. A few years later, the explorer Samuel de Champlain (1567?–1635) navigated the St. Lawrence River and founded Quebec City (1608). He convinced the royal government, emerging from its preoccupations with religious wars at home, to promote the development of the colony. French explorers went on to establish Montreal, farther up the St. Lawrence (1642), and to explore the Great Lakes and the Mississippi River basin (see **MAP 16.4**).

Such investment as the French crown was able to attract went into profitable trade, mainly in furs, and not into the difficult business of colonization. French trappers and traders who ventured into wilderness areas were renowned for their hardiness and adaptability, but they did not bring their families and establish settled, European-style towns. Quebec remained more of a trading station, dependent on shipments of food from France, than a growing urban community. Much of the energy of French colonization was expended by men and women of religious orders—the "Black Robes"—bringing their zeal to new frontiers. By the middle of the seventeenth century, all of New France had only about three thousand European inhabitants.

The seeming weakness of the French colonial effort in North America was not much noticed at the time. French and English fishermen, trappers, and traders competed intensely, and the French often reaped the greater share of profits, owing to their closer ties with Native American trading systems. Outright battles occasionally erupted between English and French settlements. But for both England and France, indeed for all colonial powers, the major profits and strategic interests in the New World lay to the south, in the sugar-producing Caribbean. For example, in 1674, the Dutch gave up their trading center, New Amsterdam (modern-day New York City) to the English in return for recognition of the Dutch claims to sugar-producing Guiana (modern Suriname) in South America.

The growth of the plantation system meant that, by far, the largest group of migrants to European-held territories in the Americas was forced migrants: African men and women sold

🌐 **MAP 16.4—The English and French in North America, ca. 1700**

By 1700, a veritable ring of French-claimed territory encircled the coastal colonies of England. English-claimed areas, however, were more densely settled and more economically viable.

into slavery and shipped, like other cargo, across the Atlantic to work on Caribbean islands, in South America and southern North America. A conservative estimate is that approximately 1.35 million Africans were forcibly transported as slave labor to the New World during the seventeenth century.

The Impact of Trade and Warfare Within Europe

Within Europe, the economic impact of overseas trade was profound. Merchants and investors in a few of Europe's largest cities reaped great profits. Mediterranean ports, such as Venice, once the heart of European trade, did not share in the bonanza from the new trade with Asia or the Americas. Atlantic ports, such as Seville, through which most Spanish commerce with the New World flowed, and, above all, Amsterdam began to flourish. The population of Amsterdam increased from about 30,000 to 200,000 in the course of the seventeenth century.

All capital cities, however, not just seaports, grew substantially during the 1600s. Increasing numbers of government officials, courtiers and their hangers-on, and people involved in trade lived and worked in capital cities. These cities also grew indirectly from the demand such people generated for workers, such as carters and domestic servants, and products, ranging from fashionable clothing to exotic foodstuffs. For the first time, large numbers of country people found work in cities. Perhaps as much as one-fifth of the population of England passed through London at one time or another, creating the mobile, volatile community so active in the English civil war and its aftermath.

But social stratification intensified despite the expanding economy. Poverty increased in cities, even in vibrant Amsterdam, because cities attracted people fleeing rural unemployment with few skills and fewer resources. As growing central governments heaped tax burdens on peasants, many rural people were caught in a cycle of debt; the only escape was to abandon farming and flock to cities. Patterns of consumption reflected the economic gulf between city dwellers; most people could not afford to buy the spices or sugar that generated such profits.

Peasant rebellions occurred throughout the century as a result of depressed economic conditions and the heavy taxation that accompanied expanded royal power and extensive warfare. Some small-scale revolts involved direct action, such as seizing the tax collector's grain or stopping the movement of grain to the great cities. Urban demand often caused severe food shortages in rural areas in western Europe, despite the booming trade in grain with eastern Europe via the Baltic.

The scale of popular revolts, especially against taxation, meant that thousands of troops sometimes had to be diverted from a state's foreign wars. As a matter of routine, soldiers accompanied tax officials and enforced collection all over Europe. As the ambitions of rulers grew, so too did the resistance of ordinary people to the exactions of the state.

SECTION SUMMARY

- The Dutch innovations in ship design and forms of investment helped them dominate overseas trade.

- The wealth from trade supported a higher standard of living, wider political participation, and more religious tolerance in the Netherlands than elsewhere in Europe.

- The Dutch, the English, and the French expanded their trade and colonization in the Americas, following Spain and Portugal's earlier successes.

- Most European profits from trade and settlement in the Americas came from plantation agriculture, using slave labor, established on Caribbean islands.

- Overseas trade, together with more centralized governments, resulted in the spectacular growth of coastal and capital cities, wider divisions between rich and poor, and increased peasant rebellions.

CHAPTER SUMMARY

Following the most powerful monarchy in Europe, France, most states had moved from internal division—with independent provinces and aristocrats going their own way—to greater coherence. In France, Louis XIV's brand of government, which has been labeled "absolutism," arose from successful use of traditional political mechanisms, such as patronage, plus the defeat of any institutional brakes on his authority. Court life in Louis's reign sponsored artistic creativity and encouraged a new emphasis on cultural refinement in the aristocracy. In the military realm, however, Louis started a series of costly wars from which the French state gained little.

In England, a civil war over the very issue of parliamentary participation in government led to the temporary abolition of the monarchy itself. The Crown was restored under Charles

II, but conflicts arose again over political and religious policy under his successor James II. The year 1688 marked the "Glorious Revolution," in which Parliament helped bring William and Mary to the throne. Parliament's power was ensured by the Declaration of Rights and Bill of Rights, which have lasting significance today.

States, troubled by religious and political turmoil or on the political margins early in the century, evolved into secure and dynamic centers of power: the Netherlands, the Habsburg domains, Brandenburg-Prussia, and Russia. This stability was both cause and consequence of rulers' desires to make war on an ever larger scale. The Austrian Habsburgs reconquered Hungary from the Ottoman Turks, while the power of Poland-Lithuania declined in the seventeenth century because it was unable to defend itself against independent aristocrats, rebellious Cossacks, or powerful neighboring states. Russia was forcibly modernized by Peter the Great and became the most powerful state in eastern Europe, eclipsing Sweden in control of Baltic territories. By the end of the century, only those states able to field massive armies were competitive on the European stage. The Netherlands, a stark exception to the pattern of centralized royal control, began more closely to resemble other states under the pressure of warfare by century's end.

At the beginning of the century, overseas trade and colonization had been the near monopoly of Spain and Portugal. At the end of the century, the English, French, and Dutch had supplanted them in controlling trade with Asia and were reaping many profits in the Americas, especially from the extension of plantation agriculture. The Dutch were a successful trading empire because of their innovations in ship design and forms of investment. With their wealth from trade, they supported a higher standard of living, wider political participation, and more religious tolerance. Beneath all these developments lay significant economic, social, and cultural shifts. One effect of the increased wealth generated by overseas trade and the increased power of governments to tax their subjects was a widening gulf between rich and poor. New styles of behavior and patterns of consumption highlighted differences between social classes.

FOCUS QUESTIONS

- How did Louis XIV successfully expand royal power in France and what were some of the achievements of his reign?

- What were the long-term consequences of the English civil war?

- Which states began to dominate central and eastern Europe and why were they successful?

- How and why did Europe's overseas trade and colonization expand in the seventeenth century and what effects did this expansion have on Europe itself?

KEY TERMS

absolutism (p. 444)

Louis XIV (p. 444)

mercantilism (p. 446)

Parliament (p. 452)

Oliver Cromwell (p. 452)

Glorious Revolution (p. 455)

Treaty of Carlowitz (p. 459)

Brandenburg-Prussia (p. 459)

Cossacks (p. 461)

Peter the Great (p. 462)

Dutch East India Company (p. 464)

plantation system (p. 466)

 This icon will direct you to additional materials on the website: www .cengage.com/history/ noble/westciv6e.

See our interactive eBook for map and primary source activities.

NOTES

1. Quoted in D. H. Pennington, *Europe in the Seventeenth Century*, 2d ed. (London: Longman, 1989), p. 508.

2. G. E. Aylmer, ed., *The Levellers in the English Revolution* (Ithaca, N.Y.: Cornell University Press, 1975), pp. 100–101.

3. Philip A. Barbour, ed., *The Complete Works of Captain John Smith (1580–1631)*, vol. 2 (Chapel Hill: University of North Carolina Press, 1986), p. 189.

CHAPTER OUTLINE

Descartes and Queen Christina
René Descartes (*second from the right*) instructs Queen Christina of Sweden and her courtiers. (Réunion des musées nationaux/Art Resource, NY)

A Revolution in Worldview

The year is 1649. Queen Christina of Sweden welcomes us with her gaze and her gesture to witness a science lesson at her court. Her instructor, the French philosopher René Descartes, clutches a compass and points to an astronomical drawing. The young queen, 23 years old at the time, was already well known as a patron of artists and scholars. Christina had invited Descartes to her court because of his achievements in physics and philosophy. This painting depicts the fact that during Christina's lifetime, new theories in the field of astronomy revolutionized the sciences and required new definitions of matter to explain them. Descartes earned fame both for his new theories about matter and for his systematic approach to using human reason to understand the universe. This painting celebrates both Descartes's work and Christina's sponsorship of it.

The revolution within the sciences had been initiated in the sixteenth century by the astronomical calculations and hypotheses of Nicholas Copernicus, who theorized that the earth moves around the sun. The work of the Italian mathematician and astronomer Galileo Galilei, as well as others, added evidence to support this hypothesis. Their work overturned principles of physics and philosophy that had held sway since ancient times. Later generations of scientists and philosophers, beginning with Descartes, labored to construct new principles to explain the way nature behaves. The readiness of scientists, their patrons, and educated laypeople to push Copernicus's hypothesis to these conclusions came from several sources: their exposure to the intellectual innovations of Renaissance thought, the intellectual challenges and material opportunities represented by the discovery of the New World, and the challenge to authority embodied in the Reformation. They advanced and discussed scientific theories in print for the first time. Also, the new science offered prestige and technological advances to the rulers, such as Christina, who sponsored it.

By the end of the seventeenth century, a vision of an infinite but orderly cosmos appealing to human reason had, among educated Europeans, largely replaced the medieval vision of a closed universe centered on the earth and suffused with Christian purpose. Religion became an increasingly subordinate ally of science as confidence in an open-ended, experimental approach to knowledge came to be as strongly held as religious conviction. It is because of this larger shift in worldview, not simply because of particular scientific discoveries, that the seventeenth century can be called the era of the Scientific Revolution.

Because religious significance had been attached to previous scientific explanations and religious authority had defended them, the new astronomy automatically led to an enduring debate about the compatibility of science and religion. But the revolution in worldview was not confined to astronomy or even to science generally. As philosophers gained confidence in human reason and the intelligibility of the world, they turned to new speculation about human affairs. They began to challenge traditional justifications for the hierarchical nature of society and the sanctity of authority, just as energetically as Copernicus and his followers had overthrown old views about the cosmos.

FOCUS QUESTIONS

- How did the Copernican theory challenge traditional views of the universe?

- How and why did new theories about astronomy lead to a broader Scientific Revolution?

- How did the new scientific worldview lead people to challenge traditional notions of society, the state, and religion?

 This icon will direct you to additional materials on the website: www .cengage.com/history/ noble/westciv6e.

 See our interactive eBook for map and primary source activities.

THE REVOLUTION IN ASTRONOMY, 1543–1632

How did the Copernican theory challenge traditional views of the universe?

The origins of the seventeenth-century revolution in worldview lie, for the most part, in developments in astronomy. Because of astronomy's role in the explanations of the world and human life that had been devised by ancient and medieval scientists and philosophers, any advances in astronomy were bound to have widespread intellectual repercussions. By the early part of the seventeenth century, fundamental astronomical beliefs had been successfully challenged. The consequence was the undermining of both the material (physics) and the philosophical (metaphysics) explanations of the world that had been standing for centuries.

The Inherited Worldview

Most ancient and medieval astronomers accepted the perspective on the universe that unaided human senses support—namely, that the earth is fixed at the center of the universe and the celestial bodies, such as the sun and the planets, rotate around it. The regular movements of heavenly bodies and the obvious importance of the sun for life on earth made astronomy a vital undertaking for both scientific and religious purposes in many ancient societies. Astronomers in ancient Greece carefully observed the heavens and learned to calculate and to predict the seemingly circular motion of the stars and the sun about the earth. The orbits of the planets were more difficult to explain, for the planets seemed to travel both east and west across the sky at various times and with no regularity that could be mathematically understood. Indeed, the word *planet* comes from a Greek word meaning "wanderer."

We now know that all the planets simultaneously orbit the sun at different speeds in paths that are at different distances from the sun. The relative positions of the planets constantly change; sometimes other planets are "ahead" of the earth and sometimes "behind." In the second century A.D., the Greek astronomer Ptolemy (TAHL-eh-mee) attempted to explain the planets' occasional "backward" motion by attributing it to "epicycles"—small circular orbits within the larger orbit. Ptolemy's mathematical explanations of the imagined epicycles were extremely complex, but neither Ptolemy nor medieval mathematicians and astronomers were ever able fully to account for planetary motion.

Ancient physics, most notably the work of the Greek philosopher Aristotle (384–322 B.C.), explained the fact that some objects (such as cannonballs) fall to earth but others (stars and planets) seem weightless relative to earth because of their composition: Different kinds of matter have different inherent tendencies and properties. In this view, all earthbound matter (like cannonballs) falls because it is naturally attracted to earth—heaviness being a property of earthbound things.

In the Christian era, the Aristotelian explanation of the universe was infused with Christian meaning and purpose. The heavens were said to be made of different, pure matter because they were the abode of the angels. Both the earth and the humans who inhabited it were changeable and corruptible. Yet, God had given human beings a unique and special place in the universe, which was thought to be a closed world with the stationary earth at the center. Revolving around the earth in circular orbits were the sun, moon, stars, and planets. The motion of all lesser bodies was caused by the rotation of all the stars together in the vast crystal-like sphere in which they were embedded.

A few ancient astronomers theorized that the earth moved about the sun. Some medieval philosophers also adopted this heliocentric thesis (*helios* is the Greek word for "sun"), but it remained a minority view because it seemed to contradict both common sense and observed data. The sun and stars *appeared* to move around the earth with great regularity. Moreover, how could objects fall to earth if the earth was moving beneath them? Also, astronomers detected no difference in angles from which observers on earth viewed the stars at different times. Such differences would exist, they thought, if the earth changed positions by moving around the sun. It was inconceivable that the universe could be so large and the stars so distant that the earth's movement would produce no measurable change in the earth's position with respect to the stars.

Several conditions of intellectual life in the sixteenth century encouraged new work in astronomy and led to the revision of the earth-centered worldview. The most important was the work of Renaissance humanists in recovering and interpreting ancient texts. Now able to work with new Greek versions of Ptolemy, mathematicians and astronomers noted that his explanations for the motion of the planets were imperfect and not simply inadequately transmitted, as they had long believed. Also, the discovery of the New World dramatically undercut the assumption that ancient knowledge was superior. The existence of the Americas specifically undermined Ptolemy's authority once again, for it disproved many of the assertions in his *Geography*, which had just been recovered in Europe the previous century.

The desire to explain heavenly movements better was still loaded with religious significance in the sixteenth century and was heightened by the immediate need for reform of the Julian calendar (named for Julius Caesar). Ancient observations of the movement of the sun, though remarkably accurate, could not measure the precise length of the solar year. By the sixteenth century, the cumulative error of this calendar had resulted in a change of ten days: The spring equinox fell on March 11 instead of March 21. An accurate and uniform system of dating was necessary for all rulers and their tax collectors and record keepers. And because the calculation of the date of Easter was at stake, a reliable calendar was the particular project of the church.

Impetus for new and better astronomical observations and calculations arose from other features of the intellectual and political landscape as well. Increasingly, as the century went on, princely courts became important sources of patronage for and sites of scientific activity. Rulers, eager to buttress their own power by symbolically linking it to dominion over nature, sponsored investigations of the world, as Ferdinand and Isabella had so successfully done, and displayed the marvels of nature at their courts. Sponsorship of science also yielded practical benefits: better mapping of the ruler's domains and better technology for mining, gunnery, and navigation.

Finally, schools of thought fashionable at the time, encouraged by the humanists' critique of tradition, hinted at the possibilities of alternative physical and metaphysical systems. The ancient doctrine of Hermeticism (named for the mythical originator of the ideas, Hermes Trismegistos), revived since the Renaissance, claimed that matter is universally imbued with divine (or magical) spirit. Drawing on Hermeticism was Paracelsianism, named for the Swiss physician Philippus von Hohenheim (1493–1541), who called himself Paracelsus (literally "beyond Celsus," an acclaimed Roman physician whose works had just been recovered). Paracelsus (pair-uh-SEL-sus) scoffed at the notion that ancient authorities were the final word on the workings of nature. Paracelsus offered an alternative to accepted medical theory, put forth by the ancient physician Galen (ca. 131–201), who was as revered as Aristotle. Galen (GAY-len) believed that an imbalance of bodily "humors" caused illness. Paracelsus substituted a theory of chemical imbalance that anticipated our modern understanding of pathology. He was wildly popular wherever he taught because he successfully treated many illnesses and lectured openly to laymen.

Neo-Platonism, another school of thought, had a more systematic and far-reaching impact. Neo-Platonism was a revival, primarily in Italian humanist circles, of certain aspects of Plato's thought. It contributed directly to innovation in science because it emphasized the abstract nature of true knowledge and thus encouraged mathematical investigation. This provided a spur to astronomical studies, which, since ancient times, had been concerned more with mathematical analysis of heavenly movements than with physical explanations for them. Also, like Hermeticism and Paracelsianism, Neo-Platonism had a mystical dimension that encouraged creative speculation about the nature of matter and the organization of the universe. Neo-Platonists were particularly fascinated by the sun as a symbol of the one divine mind or soul at the heart of all creation.

CHRONOLOGY

1543	Copernicus, *De Revolutionibus Orbium Caelestium* Vesalius, *On the Fabric of the Human Body*
1576	Construction of Brahe's observatory begins
1603	Accadèmia dei Lincei founded in Rome
1609	Kepler's third law of motion
1610	Galileo, *The Starry Messenger*
1620	Bacon, *Novum Organum*
1628	Harvey, *On the Motion of the Heart*
1632	Galileo, *Dialogue on the Two Chief Systems of the World*
1633	Galileo condemned and sentenced to house arrest
1637	Descartes, *Discourse on Method*
1651	Hobbes, *Leviathan*
1660	Boyle, *New Experiments Physico-Mechanical* Royal Society of London founded
1666	Académie Royale des Sciences founded in France
1686	Fontenelle, *Conversations on the Plurality of Worlds*
1687	Newton, *Principia (Mathematical Principles of Natural Philosophy)*
1690	Locke, *Two Treatises of Government and Essay on Human Understanding*
1702	Bayle, *Historical and Critical Dictionary*

The Traditional Universe
In this print from around 1600, heavenly bodies are depicted orbiting the earth in perfectly circular paths. Notice the horse-drawn chariot near the top of the image, which represents the Greek god of the sun circling the earth. (Bettmann/Corbis)

The Challenge by Copernicus

Nicholas Copernicus
Polish astronomer who initiated the Scientific Revolution by proposing that the earth and other planets orbit the sun.

Nicholas Copernicus (1473–1543), son of a German merchant family in Poland, pursued wide-ranging university studies in philosophy, law, astronomy, mathematics, and medicine—first in Cracow in Poland and then in Bologna and Padua in Italy. In Italy, he was exposed to Neo-Platonic ideas. Copernicus (kuh-PURR-nih-kus) took a degree in canon (church) law in 1503 and became a cathedral canon (a member of the cathedral staff) in the city of Frauenburg (modern Poland), where he pursued his own interests in astronomy, while carrying out administrative duties. When the pope asked Copernicus to assist with the reform of the Julian calendar, he replied that reform of the calendar required reform in astronomy. His major work, *De Revolutionibus Orbium Caelestium (On the Revolution of Heavenly Bodies*, 1543), was dedicated to the pope in the hopes that it would help with the task of calendar reform—as indeed it did. The Gregorian calendar, issued in 1582 during the pontificate of Gregory XIII (r. 1572–1585), was based on Copernicus's calculations.

Copernicus postulated that the earth and all the other planets orbit the sun. He did not assert that the earth does in fact move around the sun, but offered the heliocentric system as a mathematical construct, useful for predicting the movements of planets, stars, and the sun. However, he walked a thin line between making claims for a mathematical construct, on the one hand, and physical reality, on the other. Scholars now believe that Copernicus was himself persuaded that the **heliocentric theory** was correct. He had searched in ancient sources for thinkers who believed the earth moved. Other astronomers, familiar with his work and reputation, urged him to publish the results of his calculations. But not until 1542, twelve years after finishing the work, did he send *De Revolutionibus* to be published. He received a copy just before his death the next year.

heliocentric theory
Means "sun-centered." Theory of Nicholas Copernicus that the earth and other planets orbit the sun.

By affirming the earth's movement around the sun, while also salvaging features of the old system, Copernicus faced burdens of explanation not faced by Ptolemy. For example, Copernicus still assumed that the planets traveled in circular orbits, so he was forced to retain some epicycles in his schema to account for the circular motion. In general, however, the Copernican account of planetary motion was simpler than the Ptolemaic account. But his work only slowly led to conceptual revolution, as scientists worked with his calculations and assembled other evidence to support the heliocentric theory.

The most important reason that fundamental conceptual change followed Copernican theory so gradually was that Copernicus did not resolve the physical problems his ideas raised. If Copernicus were right, the earth would have to be made of the same material as other planets. How, then, would Copernicus explain the motion of objects on earth—the fact that they fall to earth—if it was not in their nature to fall toward the heavy, stationary earth? In Copernicus's system, the movement of the earth caused the *apparent* motion of the stars. But if the stars did not rotate in their crystalline sphere, what made all other heavenly bodies move?

Copernicus was not as troubled by these questions as we might expect him to have been. Since ancient times, mathematical astronomy—the science of measuring and predicting the movements of heavenly bodies—had been far more important than, and had proceeded independently of, physical explanations of observed motion. Nevertheless, as Copernicus's own efforts to support his hypothesis reveal, his theories directly contradicted many of the supposed laws of motion. The usefulness of his theories to other astronomers meant that the contradictions between mathematical and physical models for the universe would have to be resolved. Copernicus himself might be best understood as the last Ptolemaic astronomer, working within inherited questions and with known tools. His work itself did not constitute a revolution, but it did start one.

The First Copernican Astronomers

In the first generation of astronomers after the publication of *De Revolutionibus* in 1543, we can see the effects of Copernicus's work. His impressive computations rapidly won converts among fellow astronomers who continued to develop Copernican theories. By the second quarter of the seventeenth century, they and many others accepted the heliocentric theory as a reality and not just as a useful mathematical fiction. The three most important astronomers to build on Copernican assumptions, and on the work of one another, were the Dane Tycho Brahe (1546–1601), the German Johannes Kepler (1571–1630), and the Italian Galileo Galilei (1564–1642).

Like generations of observers before him, **Tycho Brahe** (BRAH) had been stirred by the majesty of the regular movements of heavenly bodies. After witnessing a partial eclipse of the sun, he abandoned a career in government, befitting his noble status, and became an astronomer. Brahe was the first truly post-Ptolemaic astronomer because he was the first to improve on the data that the ancients and all subsequent astronomers had used. Ironically, no theory of planetary motion could have reconciled the data that Copernicus had used: They were simply too inaccurate, based, as they were, on naked-eye observations, even when errors of translation and copying, accumulated over centuries, had been corrected.

In 1576, the king of Denmark showered Brahe with properties and pensions enabling him to build an observatory, Uraniborg, on an island near the capital, Copenhagen. At Uraniborg, Brahe improved on ancient observations with large and very finely calibrated instruments that permitted precise measurements of celestial movements by the naked eye. His attention to precision and frequency of observation produced results that were twice as accurate as any previous data had been.

As a result of his observations, Brahe agreed with Copernicus that the various planets did rotate around the sun, not around the earth. He still could not be persuaded that the earth itself moved, for none of his data supported such a notion. Brahe's lasting and crucial contribution was his astronomical data. They would become obsolete as soon as observations from telescopes were accumulated about a century later. But in the meantime, they were used by **Johannes Kepler** to further develop Copernicus's model and arrive at a more accurate heliocentric theory.

Kepler was young enough to be exposed to Copernican ideas from the outset of his training, and he quickly recognized in Brahe's data the means of resolving the problems in Copernican analysis. Though trained in his native Germany, Kepler went to Prague, where Brahe spent the last years of his life at the court of the Holy Roman emperor after a quarrel with the Danish king. There, Kepler became something of an apprentice to Brahe. After Brahe's death in 1601, Kepler kept his mentor's records of astronomical observations and continued to work at the imperial court as Rudolf II's court mathematician.

TYCHO BRAHE

Tycho Brahe Danish astronomer and first European to collect new astronomical data by using instruments to observe the celestial bodies.

Johannes Kepler German astronomer who developed three laws of planetary motion, known as Kepler's laws, which mathematically confirmed the Copernican heliocentric theory.

JOHANNES KEPLER

Tycho Brahe's Observatory   Brahe gathered the best talent, including German instrument makers and Italian architects, to build his state-of-the-art observatory near Copenhagen. Brahe named the complex Uraniborg, for Urania, the muse of astronomy.   (General View of the Observatory of Uraniborg, constructed c. 1584 by Tycho Brahe (1546–1601) on the island of Hven, Denmark from 'Le Theatre du Monde' or 'Nouvel Atlas', published in Amsterdam, 1645 (coloured engraving) by Willem Blaeu (1571–1638) and Joan (1596–1673)/Private Collection/Archives Charmet/The Bridgeman Art Library)

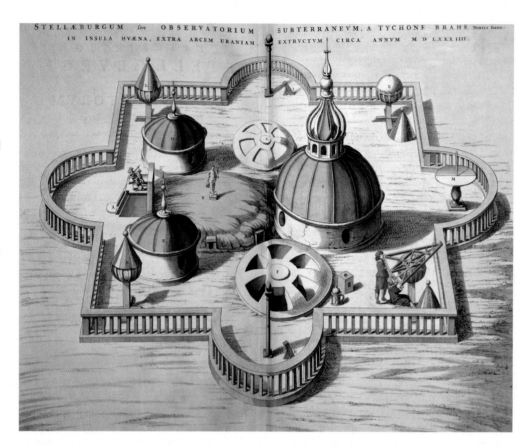

Kepler's contribution to the new astronomy, like that of Copernicus, was fundamentally mathematical. In it, we can see the stamp of the Neo-Platonic conviction about the purity of mathematical explanation. Kepler spent ten years working to apply Brahe's data to the most intricate of all the celestial movements—the motion of the planet Mars—as a key to explaining all planetary motion. Mars is close to the earth, but its orbital path is farther from the sun. This combination produces dramatic and puzzling variations in the apparent movement of Mars to an earthly observer.

The result of Kepler's work was laws of planetary motion that, in the main, are still in use. First, Kepler eliminated the need for epicycles by correctly asserting that planets follow elliptical, and not circular, orbits. Elliptical orbits could account, both mathematically and visually, for the motion of the planets when combined with Kepler's second law, which describes the *rate* of a planet's motion around its orbital path. Kepler noted that the speed of a planet in its orbit slows proportionally as the planet's distance from the sun increases. A third law demonstrates that the distance of each planet from the sun and the time it takes each planet to orbit the sun are in a constant ratio.

Kepler's work was a breakthrough because it mathematically confirmed the Copernican heliocentric hypothesis. In so doing, the work directly challenged the ancient worldview, in which heavenly bodies constantly moved in circular orbits around a stationary earth. Kepler's laws invited speculation about the properties of heavenly and terrestrial bodies alike. In fact, a new physics would be required to explain the novel motion that Kepler had posited. Kepler himself, in Neo-Platonic fashion, attributed planetary motion to the sun: "[The sun] is a fountain of light, rich in fruitful heat, most fair, limpid and pure ... called king of the planets for his motion, heart of the world for his power ... Who would hesitate to confer the votes of the celestial motions on him who has been administering all other movements and changes by the benefit of the light which is entirely his possession?"[1]

Galileo Galilei   Italian physicist and astronomer who provided evidence supporting the heliocentric theory and helped develop the science of mechanics.

Galileo and the Triumph of Copernicanism

Galileo Galilei holds a preeminent position in the development of astronomy because, first, he provided compelling new evidence to support Copernican theory and, second, he contributed to the development of a new physics—or, more precisely, mechanics—that could account for the movements of bodies in new terms. In short, he began to close the gap between the new astronomy and new explanations for the behavior of matter. Just as important, his efforts to publicize his findings and his condemnation by the church spurred popular debate about Copernican ideas in literate society and helped to determine the course science would take.

Galileo's career also illustrates, in dramatic fashion, the dependence of scientists on and their vulnerability to patronage relationships. Born to a minor Florentine noble family, Galileo began studying medicine at the nearby University of Pisa at the age of 17, but became intrigued by problems of mechanics and mathematics. He began studying those disciplines at Pisa under the tutelage of a Florentine court mathematician and became a lecturer in mathematics there in 1589, at age 25, after publishing promising work in mechanics. Three years later, well-connected fellow mathematicians helped him secure a more prestigious professorship at the University of Padua, where Copernicus had once studied. Galileo skillfully cultivated the learned Venetian aristocrats (Venice ruled Padua at this time) who controlled academic appointments and secured renewals and salary raises over the next eighteen years.

During his years at Pisa and Padua, Galileo pursued his revolutionary work in mechanics, although he did not publish the results of his experiments until much later. Galileo's principal contribution to mechanics lay in his working out of an early theory of inertia. As a result of a number of experiments with falling bodies (balls rolling on carefully constructed inclines—not free-falling objects that, according to myth, he dropped from the Leaning Tower of Pisa), Galileo ventured a new view of what is "natural" to objects. Galileo's view was that uniform motion is as natural as a state of rest. In the ancient and medieval universe, all motion needed a cause, and all motion could be explained in terms of purpose. "I hold," Galileo countered, "that there exists nothing in external bodies … but size, shape, quantity and motion."[2] Galileo retained the old assumption that motion was somehow naturally circular. Nevertheless, his theory was a crucial step in explaining motion according to new principles and in fashioning a worldview that accepted a mechanical universe devoid of metaphysical purpose.

The results of this work were, for the most part, not published until the end of his life. In the meantime, Galileo became famous for his astronomical observations, which he began in 1609 and which he parlayed into a position back at the Florentine court. Early that year, Galileo learned of the invention of a primitive telescope (which could magnify distant objects only three times) and quickly improved on it to make the first astronomically useful instrument. In *Sidereus Nuncius (The Starry Messenger*, 1610), he described his scrutiny of the heavens with his telescope in lay language. He documented sighting previously undetectable stars, as well as moons orbiting the planet Jupiter. In another blow to ancient descriptions of the universe, he noted craters and other "imperfections" on the surface of the moon. Three years later, he published his solar observations in *Letters on Sunspots*. Sunspots are regions of relatively cool gaseous material that appear as dark spots on the sun's surface. For Galileo, sunspots and craters on the moon proved that the heavens are not perfect and changeless, but rather are like the supposedly "corrupt" and changeable earth. His telescopic observations also provided further support for Copernican heliocentrism. Indeed, Galileo's own acceptance of Copernicanism can be dated to this point because magnification revealed that each heavenly body rotates on its axis: Sunspots, for example, can be tracked across the visible surface of the sun as the sun rotates.

Galileo had already been approached by various Italian princes and in turn sought to woo their support with gifts of some of his earlier inventions, such as a military compass. He aimed his *Starry Messenger* at the Medici dukes of Florence, naming Jupiter's moons the "Medicean Stars" and publishing the work to coincide with the accession of the young Cosimo II, whom he had tutored as a youth. In 1610, he returned in triumph to his native Tuscany as court philosopher to the grand duke. Soon, however, his own fame and the increasing acceptance of Copernicanism aroused opposition. In 1615, Galileo was denounced to the Inquisition by a Florentine friar. Galileo defended himself to his patrons and to the wider scientific community by arguing, in print, that the new science did not challenge religion. (See the feature, "The Written Record: Galileo Asserts Science and Religion Are Compatible.") After an investigation, the geokinetic theory (that the earth moves) was declared heretical, but Galileo himself was allowed to continue to use Copernican theory, but only as a theory. Indeed, a number of the most fervent practitioners of the new science continued to be clergymen who followed Galileo's work with interest. A new pope, elected in 1623, was a Tuscan aristocrat and an old friend of Galileo. Galileo dedicated his work on comets, *The Assayer* (1624), to Urban VIII in honor of his election.

Galileo Asserts Science and Religion are Compatible

After Galileo Galilei's work on sunspots was released, many learned followers grew anxious about the implications of the new science. In the letter excerpted here, published in 1615 and widely circulated, Galileo reassures the mother of Cosimo II, the dowager grand duchess of Tuscany, that the new science does not contradict Christianity. The Catholic Church would eventually condemn Galileo for his beliefs, arguing that it was wrong to contradict established knowledge about the heavens. Although the church's actions constrained the development of science in some (predominantly Catholic) regions, throughout Europe investigators continued to find ways to make the new science fully compatible with their faiths.

Some years ago, as Your Serene Highness well knows, I discovered in the heavens many things that had not been seen there before our own age. The novelty of these things, as well as some consequences which followed from them ... stirred up against me no small number of professors—as if I had placed these things in the sky with my own hands in order to upset nature and overturn the sciences ... [These professors] go about invoking the Bible, which they would have minister to their deceitful purposes. Contrary to the sense of the Bible and the intention of the holy Fathers, if I am not mistaken, they would extend such authorities until even in purely physical matters—where faith is not involved—they would have us altogether abandon reason and the evidence of our own senses in favor of some biblical passage, though under the surface meaning of its words this passage may contain a different sense. ...

I think that in discussions of physical problems we ought to begin not from the authority of scriptural passages, but from sense experience and necessary demonstrations. ... I should judge that the authority of the Bible was designed to persuade men of those articles and propositions which, surpassing all human reasoning, could not be made credible by science, or by any means other than through the very mouth of the Holy Spirit. ...

But I do not feel obliged to believe that the same God who has endowed us with senses, reason and intellect has intended to forgo their use and by some other means to give us knowledge which we can attain by them. He would not require us to deny sense and reason in physical matters which are set before our eyes and minds by direct experience or necessary demonstrations. This must be especially true in those sciences of which but the faintest trace ... is to be found in the Bible. Of astronomy, for instance, so little is found that none of the planets except Venus are so much as mentioned. ...

Now, if the Holy Spirit has purposely neglected to teach us propositions of this sort as irrelevant to the highest goal (that is, to our salvation), how can anyone affirm that it is obligatory to take sides on them, and that one belief is required by faith, while another side is erroneous? ... I would assert here something that was heard from [a respected cleric]: ... "the intention of the Holy Ghost is to teach us how to go to heaven, not how heaven goes." ... [And] in St. Augustine we read: "If anyone shall set the authority of Holy Writ against clear and manifest reason, ... he opposes to the truth not the meaning of the Bible, which is beyond his comprehension, but rather his own interpretation. ... "

Moreover, we are unable to affirm that all interpreters of the Bible speak with divine inspiration, for if that were so there would exist no differences between them about the sense of a given passage. Hence [it would be wise] not to permit anyone to usurp scriptural texts and force them in some way to maintain any physical conclusion to be true, when at some future time the senses ... may show the contrary. Who indeed will set bounds to human ingenuity? Who will assert that everything in the universe capable of being perceived is already discovered and known?

QUESTIONS

1. How does Galileo justify pursuing scientific investigation against certain claims of faith?

2. Do you think that Galileo's arguments would have been reassuring to the grand duchess? Why or why not?

3. Why might the arguments have further angered those church officials already hostile toward Galileo's work?

Source: *Discoveries and Opinions of Galileo*, by Galileo Galilei, translated by Stillman Drake, copyright © 1957 by Stillman Drake. Used by permission of Doubleday, a division of Random House, Inc.

Now in his 60s, Galileo began to work on a book that summarized his life's work—*Dialogue on the Two Chief Systems of the World* (1632), structured as a conversation among three characters debating the merits of Copernican theory. Given the work's sensitive subject matter, Galileo obtained explicit permission from the pope to write it and cleared some portions with censors before publication. The work was the most important single source in its day for the popularization of Copernican theory, but it led to renewed concerns in Rome. Galileo had clearly overstepped the bounds of discussing Copernicanism in theory only and appeared to advocate it. Simplicio, the character representing the old worldview, was, as his name suggests, an example of ignorance, not wisdom.

Moreover, the larger political context affecting Galileo's patrons and friends had changed. The pope was being threatened by the Spanish and Austrian Habsburg rulers for his tepid support in the Thirty Years' War, in which Catholic forces were now losing to Protestant armies (see page 428). He could no longer be indulgent towards his friend, Galileo. Galileo was forced to stand trial for heresy in Rome in 1633. When, in a kind of plea-bargain arrangement, he pled guilty to a lesser charge of inadvertently advocating Copernicanism, Pope Urban intervened to insist on a weightier penalty. Galileo's book was banned, he was forced to formally renounce his "error," and he was sentenced to house arrest. Galileo lived confined and guarded, continuing his investigations of mechanics, until his death eight years later.

- The Scientific Revolution began in 1543 with the publication of Copernicus's mathematical calculations supporting the heliocentric theory.

- Tycho Brahe and Johannes Kepler confirmed Copernicus's hypothesis with new data and more thorough mathematical explanations of the motions of planets.

- Galileo's observations with his telescope provided new evidence to support Copernican theory; his experiments in mechanics contributed to new explanations for the behavior of matter.

- Galileo's advocacy of Copernicanism led to his condemnation by the church.

THE SCIENTIFIC REVOLUTION EXPANDS, CA. 1600–1700

How and why did new theories about astronomy lead to a broader Scientific Revolution?

Galileo's work found such a willing audience in part because Galileo, like Kepler and Brahe, was not working alone. Dozens of other scientists were examining old problems from the fresh perspective offered by the breakthroughs in astronomy. Some analyzed the nature of matter, now that it appeared that all matter in the universe was somehow the same, despite its varying appearances. Many of these thinkers addressed the metaphysical issues that their investigations inevitably raised. They began the complex intellectual and psychological journey toward a new worldview, one that accepted the existence of an infinitely large universe of undifferentiated matter with no obvious place in it for humans.

The Uses of the New Science

No less a man than **Francis Bacon** (1561–1626), lord chancellor of England during the reign of James I, wrote a utopian essay extolling the benefits of science for a peaceful society and for human happiness. In *New Atlantis*, published one year after his death, Bacon argued that science would produce "things of use and practice for man's life."[3] In *New Atlantis* and *Novum Organum* (1620), Bacon reveals his faith in science by advocating patient, systematic observation and experimentation to accumulate knowledge about the world. He argues that the proper method of investigation "derives axioms from . . . particulars, rising by gradual and unbroken ascent, so that it arrives at the most general axioms of all. This is the true way but untried."[4]

Bacon did not undertake experiments himself, although his widely read works were influential in encouraging both the **empirical method** (relying on observation and experimentation) and inductive reasoning (deriving general principles from particular facts). Given the early date of his writings, it might seem difficult to account for his confidence in the benefits of science. Bacon was a visionary, but his writings reflect the widespread interest in science within his elite milieu, an interest actively encouraged by the state. In another of his writings, he argues that a successful state should concentrate on effective "rule in religion *and* nature, as well as civil administration."[5]

Bacon's pronouncements reflect the fact that an interest in exploring nature's secrets and exercising "dominion over nature" had become an indispensable part of princely rule. Princely courts were the main sources of financial support for science and the primary sites of scientific work during Bacon's lifetime. Part of the impetus for this development had come from the civic humanism of the Italian Renaissance, which had celebrated the state and service to it and had provided models both for educated rulers and for cultivated courtiers. Attention to science and to its benefits for the state also reflects the scope, and pragmatism, of princely resources and ambitions: the desire of rulers for technical expertise in armaments, fortification, construction, navigation, and mapmaking. (See the feature, "The Visual Record: Modern Maps.")

Francis Bacon England's lord chancellor during the reign of James I and author of influential works encouraging the empirical scientific method and inductive reasoning.

empirical method Philosophical view developed by Bacon and Locke, which holds that all knowledge is based on observation and experimentation and that general principles should be derived from particular facts.

The lure of the New World and the drive for overseas trade and exploration especially encouraged princely support of scientific investigation. A renowned patron of geographic investigation, from mapmaking to navigation, was Henry, prince of Wales (d. 1612), eldest son of James I. Prince Henry patronized technical experts such as gunners and seamen, as well as those with broader and more theoretical expertise. One geographer at his court worked on the vital problem of calculating longitude, sketched the moon after reading and emulating Galileo's work with the telescope, and, in the spirit of empiricism associated with Bacon, compiled information about the new territory Virginia, including the first dictionary of any Native American language.

Science was an ideological, as well as a practical, tool for power. Most courts housed collections of marvels, specimens of exotic plants and animals, and mechanical contrivances. These collections demonstrated the ruler's interest in investigation of the world—in other words, his or her status as an educated individual. Collections and the work of court experts also enhanced the ruler's reputation as a patron and person of power. Galileo was playing off such expectations when he named his newly discovered moons of Jupiter "Medicean Stars." Like all patronage relationships, the status was shared by both partners; indeed, the attention of a patron was a guarantee of the researcher's scientific credibility.

By the beginning of the seventeenth century, private salons and academies where investigators might meet on their own were another significant milieu of scientific investigation. These, too, had their roots in the humanist culture of Italy, where circles of scholars without university affiliations had formed. Though also dependent on private resources, these associations were an important alternative to princely patronage, since a ruler's funds might wax and wane according to his or her other commitments. Private organizations could avoid the stark distinctions of rank that were inevitable at courts, yet mimicked courts in the blend of scholars and educated courtiers they included. This more collegial, but still privileged, environment also fostered a sense of legitimacy for the science pursued there: Legitimacy came from the recognition of fellow members and, in many cases, from publication of work by the society itself.

The earliest academy dedicated to scientific study was the *Accadèmia Segreta* (Secret Academy), founded in Naples in the 1540s. The members pursued experiments together in order, in the words of one member, "to make a true anatomy of the things and operations of nature itself."[6] During the remainder of the sixteenth century and on into the seventeenth, such academies sprang up in many cities. The most celebrated was the *Accadèmia dei Lincei* (ack-uh-DAY-mee-uh day-ee lin-CHAY-ee), founded in Rome by an aristocrat in 1603. Its most famous member, Galileo, joined in 1611. The name "Lincei," from *lynx*, was chosen because of the legendary keen sight of that animal, an appropriate mascot for "searchers of secrets." Galileo's fame and the importance of his discoveries forced all such learned societies to take a stand for or against Copernicanism. Throughout the seventeenth century, the investigation of nature would continue in increasingly sophisticated institutional settings.

Scientific Thought in France

René Descartes French philosopher and mathematician who emphasized skepticism and deductive reasoning in his most influential treatise, *Discourse on Method*. He offered the first alternative physical explanation of matter after the Copernican revolution.

Philosophers, mathematicians, and educated elites thus engaged in lively debate and practical investigation throughout Europe in the first half of the seventeenth century. In France, the great questions about cosmic order were being posed, ironically, at a time of political disorder. The years following the religious wars saw the murder of Henry IV, another regency, and further civil war in the 1620s (see pages 419–420). In this environment, questions about order in the universe and the possibilities of human knowledge took on particular urgency. It is not surprising that a Frenchman, **René Descartes** (1596–1650), created the first fully articulated alternative worldview.

DESCARTES AND A NEW WORLDVIEW

Descartes (day-KART) developed and refined his thinking in dialogue with a circle of other French thinkers. His work became more influential among philosophers and laypeople than the work of some of his equally talented contemporaries because of its thoroughness and rigor, grounded in Descartes's mathematical expertise, and because of his graceful, readable French. His system was fully presented in his *Discours de la méthode* (*Discourse on Method*, 1637). Descartes described some of his intellectual crises in his later work, *Meditations* (1641).

Descartes accepted Galileo's conclusion that the heavens and the earth are made of the same elements. He drew on ancient atomic models (that had not, then, been generally accepted) to create a new theory about the nature of matter. His theory that all matter is made up of identical bits, which he named "corpuscles," is a forerunner of modern atomic and quantum theories. Descartes believed that all the different appearances and behaviors of matter (for example, why stone is always hard and water is always wet) could be explained solely by the size, shape,

A Collection of Naturalia   Collections of exotic specimens, such as this display in Naples, symbolized the ruler's authority by suggesting his or her power over nature.   (From *Hevelius*, *Machinae coelestis*. By permission of the Houghton Library, Harvard University)

and motion of these "corpuscles." Descartes's was an extremely mechanistic explanation of the universe. It nevertheless permitted new, more specific observations and hypotheses and greater understanding of inertia. For example, because he reimagined the universe as being filled with "corpuscles" free to move in any direction, "natural" motion no longer seemed either circular (Galileo's idea) or toward the center of the earth (Aristotle's idea). The new understanding of motion would be crucial to Isaac Newton's work later in the century.

In his works, Descartes tries to resolve the crisis of confidence that the new discoveries about the universe had produced. The collapse of the old explanations about the world made Descartes and other investigators doubt not only what they knew, but also their capacity to know anything at all. Their physical senses—which denied that the earth moved, for example—had been proved untrustworthy. Descartes's solution was to reenvision the human rational capacity, the mind, as completely distinct from the world—that is, as distinct from the human body and its unreliable sense perceptions. In a leap of faith, Descartes presumed that God would not have given humans a mind if that mind consistently misled them. For Descartes, God became the guarantor of human reasoning capacity, and humans were distinguished by that capacity. This is the significance of his famous claim "I think, therefore I am."

Descartes thus achieved a resolution of the terrifying doubt about the world—a resolution that exalted the role of the human knower. The Cartesian universe was one of mechanical motion, not purpose or mystical meaning, and the Cartesian human being was preeminently a mind that could apprehend that universe. In what came to be known as "Cartesian dualism," Descartes proposed that the human mind is detached from the world and yet, at the same time, can objectively analyze the world.

Modern Maps

Modern mapping was developed during the Scientific Revolution. Like most of the changes associated with the Scientific Revolution, changes in mapping were the result of several influences: innovations in Renaissance art, knowledge gleaned from voyages of exploration, the impact of new astronomical discoveries, the interest and support of princely patrons, and the spread of new ideas by means of print. All of these factors enabled Europeans of this era to have a literally new view of their world. Yet, as in the work of Copernicus, developments in mapping also depended on the continued use of data accumulated in previous centuries. In the examples shown here, we can see the dramatic progress in mapmaking over the course of the sixteenth and seventeenth centuries.

Consider the brightly colored map of western Europe and North Africa reproduced here. It is a reproduction from a 1584 atlas of printed sea charts made by a Dutchman, Lucas Waghenauer. To our eye, the map may look decorative, even quaint. Sailing ships and sea monsters, not drawn to scale, populate the oceans. Most of the major states, such as England and France, are adorned with a crest identifying their ruling dynasties.

Because some of its features appear decorative to us, we may not realize the considerable innovation that the map represented in its day. First, it is an example of the revolutionary method of depicting space achieved in the Renaissance. The discovery of linear perspective by Renaissance artists enabled them to create the illusion of three-dimensional space in their paintings and to likewise depict territory, on a map, as imagined from the perspective of a distanced observer. In addition, the landforms appear in relatively accurate relationship to one another because mapmakers, following the newly recovered *Geography* by Ptolemy, used increasingly accurate projections of the globe to represent landforms on a two-dimensional map.*

The projection used for this map was particularly useful because compass bearings could be represented as straight lines. The many straight lines that crisscross this map are called "rhumb" lines; they represent compass headings that could be used to navigate between two points. Compass bearings between points on coastlines appeared on hand-drawn medieval sea charts (after the invention of the compass in about 1250). So, this sixteenth-century map combines medieval knowledge with new knowledge of geography and of how to depict landforms accurately. In addition, the information in this map was all the more useful because it was published, along with many other sea charts, in book form.

Europe and North Africa, 1584 (The Art Archive/John Webb/Picture Desk)

Now, let us look at the apparently simpler map of the coastline of France, made about one hundred years later, in 1693. We immediately note that virtually all the decorative elements are gone. There are no sea monsters and no ships to sail the abundant seas. The map is a line drawing; it is not even colored. The simplified style of the map by itself testifies to further progress in mapmaking, and to the ability of users to absorb information from maps. To make sense of this map, the viewer would need to be familiar with the representation of France from other maps since, for example, the land borders are not sketched in.

Indeed, the map conveys abundant information, all of which reflects scientific advancement over the intervening 100 years. The figure of a compass marks the Paris meridian, advertising that the site of the city has been precisely determined by means of its longitude. A horizontal line

Descartes's ambitious view of human reason emphasizes deductive reasoning (a process of reasoning in which the conclusion follows necessarily from the stated premises), a natural consequence of his philosophical rejection of sense data. The limits of deductive reasoning for scientific investigation would be realized and much of Cartesian physics rejected by the end of the century. Nevertheless, Descartes's assumption about the objectivity of the observer would become an enduring part of scientific practice. In Descartes's day, the most radical aspect of his thought was the reduction of God to the role of guarantor of knowledge. Many fellow scientists

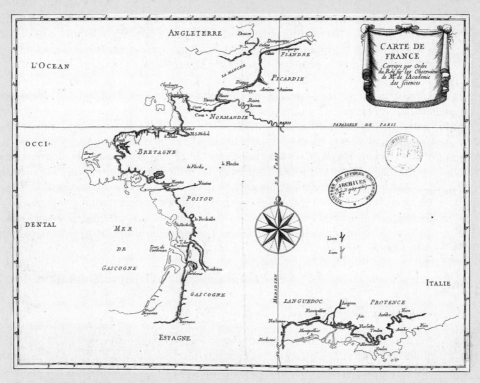

The French Coastline, 1693 (Bibliothèque nationale de France)

marks its latitude. More accurate calculation of longitude had been made possible by the work of Johannes Kepler and Galileo Galilei, whose mapping of heavenly bodies provided known points in the night sky from which to calculate the longitude of the observer's position on earth. Calculation of latitude had always been easier, since it involved only determining the angle of the sun above the horizon, but it also became more precise by use of better instrumentation in the seventeenth century. (Note: Above and to the right of the compass symbol are modern circular and oval stamps identifying the archive where the map is housed; these marks would not have appeared when the map was originally published.)

After 1650, French cartographers, among others, systematically collected astronomical observations from around the world so they could map all known lands more precisely. In addition to claiming the correct coordinates for Paris, this map also dramatically corrects earlier maps of the coastline of France. The map superimposes a corrected view (the darker line) of the coastline over an older rendering (the fainter line, mostly outside of the darker line). Thus, this map not only provides information, but also boldly demonstrates the progress of mapmaking itself.

The legend of the map calls attention to this progress. It reads, "Map of France, corrected by order of the King by the observations of Messieurs of the Academy of Sciences." The map thus also documented royal patronage of scientific work. It is interesting, however, that the king is mentioned discreetly, in what is coming to be a standardized label on the map. The information in the map stands alone, without royal crests or decorations, because the public that viewed the map by now accepted and expected updated knowledge about the world.

QUESTIONS

1. What different types of information does the first map supply? Identify as many as you can.

2. What would have appeared most impressive about the second map, to a contemporary?

---

*This discussion of the evolution of mapmaking and of these examples draws on the work of Norman J. W. Thrower, *Maps and Civilization* (Chicago: University of Chicago Press, 1996). chaps. 5 and 6.

and interested laypeople were fearful of Descartes's system because it seemed to encourage "atheism." In fact, Descartes's faith had been necessary for the construction of his new world system—but the system did work without God.

Descartes would have been surprised and offended by charges of atheism, but he knew that his work would antagonize the church. He moved to the Netherlands to study in 1628, and his *Discourse* was first published there. His long residence in the Netherlands led him to advocate religious toleration late in his life. In 1649, at the urging of an influential friend with contacts at the Swedish court, Descartes accepted the invitation of Queen Christina to visit there. Christina was an eager but demanding patron, who required Descartes to lecture on scientific topics at 5:00 a.m. each day. The long hours of work and harsh winter weather took their toll on his health, and Descartes died of pneumonia after only a few months in Sweden.

PASCAL AND THE LIMITS OF SCIENTIFIC KNOWLEDGE

A contemporary of Descartes, fellow Frenchman Blaise Pascal (1623–1662), drew attention in his writings and in his life to the limits of scientific knowledge. The son of a royal official, Pascal (pahss-KAHL) was perhaps the most brilliant mind of his generation. A mathematician like Descartes, he stressed the importance of mathematical representations of phenomena, built one of the first calculating machines, and invented probability theory. He also carried out experiments to investigate air pressure, the behavior of liquids, and the existence of vacuums.

Pascal's career alternated between periods of intense scientific work and religious retreat. Today, he is well known for his writings justifying the austere Catholicism known as Jansenism (see page 446) and for his explorations of the human soul and psyche. His *Pensées* (*Thoughts*, 1657) consists of the published fragments of his defense of Christian faith, which remained unfinished at the time of his death. Pascal's appeal for generations after him may lie in his attention to matters of faith and of feeling. His most famous statement, "The heart has its reasons which reason knows not," can be read as a declaration of the limits of the Cartesian worldview.

Science and Revolution in England

The new science had adherents and practitioners throughout Europe by 1650. Dutch scientists in the commercial milieu of the Netherlands, for example, had the freedom to pursue practical and experimental interests. The Dutch investigator Christiaan Huygens (HI-ghenz) (1629–1695) worked on a variety of problems, including air pressure and optics. In 1657, he invented and patented the pendulum clock, the first device to measure accurately small units of time, essential for a variety of measurements.

England proved a unique environment for the development of science in the middle of the century. In a society torn by civil war, differing positions on science became part and parcel of disputes over Puritanism, church hierarchy, and royal power. Scientific, along with political and religious, debate was generally encouraged by the collapse of censorship, beginning in the 1640s.

During the 1640s, natural philosophers with Puritan leanings were encouraged in their investigations by dreams that science, of the practical Baconian sort, could be the means by which the perfection of life on earth could be brought about and the end of history—the reign of the saints preceding the return of Christ—could be accelerated. Their concerns ranged from improved production of gunpowder (for the armies fighting against Charles I) to surveying and mapmaking. Perhaps the best-known member of this group was Robert Boyle (1627–1691). In his career, we can trace the evolution of English science through the second half of the seventeenth century.

Boyle and his colleagues were theoretically eclectic, drawing on Cartesian mechanics and even Paracelsian chemical theories. They attacked the English university system, still under the sway of Aristotelianism, and proposed widespread reform of education. They were forced to moderate many of their positions, however, as the English civil wars proceeded. Radical groups, such as the Levellers, used Hermeticism and the related Paracelsianism as part of their political and religious tenets. The Levellers and other radical groups drew on the Hermetic notion that matter is imbued with divine spirit; they believed that each person was capable of divine knowledge and a godly life without the coercive hierarchy of church and royal officials.

Boyle and his colleagues responded to these challenges. They gained institutional power when they accepted positions at Oxford and Cambridge. They formed the core of the Royal Society of London, which they persuaded Charles II to recognize and charter on his accession to the throne in 1660. They worked out a theoretical position that combined the orderliness of mechanism, a continued divine presence in the world, and a Baconian belief in scientific progress. This unwieldy set of notions was attractive to the educated elite of the day, who wanted the certainties of science, but did not want to give up certain authoritarian aspects of the old Christian worldview.

Their most creative contribution, both to their own cause and to the advancement of science, was their refinement of experimental philosophy and practice. In 1660, Boyle published *New Experiments Physico-Mechanical*. The work describes the results of his experiments with an air pump he had designed, and it lays out general rules for experimental procedure. Descartes had accounted for motion by postulating that "corpuscles" of matter interact, thereby eliminating the possibility of a vacuum in nature. Recent experiments on air pressure suggested otherwise, however, and Boyle tried to confirm their findings with his air pump.

Boyle's efforts to demonstrate that a vacuum could exist—by evacuating a sealed chamber with his pump—were not successes by modern standards because his experiments could not readily be duplicated. Boyle tied the validity of experimental results to the agreement of witnesses to the experiment—a problematic solution, since only investigators sympathetic to his hypothesis and convinced of his credibility usually witnessed the results. In response to a Cambridge scholar who criticized his interpretation of one experiment, Boyle replied that he could not understand his critic's objections, "the experiment having been tried both before our whole society [the Royal Society of London], and very critically, by its royal founder, his majesty himself."[7] In other words, rather than debate differing interpretations, Boyle appealed to the authority and prestige of the participants. In English science of the mid-seventeenth century, therefore, we have a further example of the fact that new truths, new procedures for determining truth, and new criteria for practitioners were all being established simultaneously.

The Achievement of Isaac Newton

The Copernican revolution reached its high point with the work of the Englishman **Isaac Newton** (1643–1727), born one year almost to the day after Galileo died. Newton completed the new explanation for motion in the heavens and on earth that Copernicus's work had required and that Kepler, Galileo, and others had sought.

After a difficult childhood and an indifferent education, Newton entered Cambridge University as a student in 1661. Copernicanism and Cartesianism were being hotly debated, though not yet officially studied. Newton made use of Descartes's work in mathematics to develop his skill on his own, and by 1669, he had invented calculus. (He did not publish his work at the time, and another mathematician, Gottfried von Leibniz [LIBE-nits], later independently developed calculus and vied with Newton for credit.)

Isaac Newton   English physicist, mathematician, and natural philosopher. His mathematical computation of the laws of gravity and planetary motion, which he combined with a fully developed theory of inertia, completed the explanation for motion initiated by Nicholas Copernicus.

Newton won a fellowship at Cambridge in 1667 and became a professor of mathematics in 1669, at the recommendation of a retiring professor with whom he had shared his work on calculus. With less demanding teaching assignments, he was able to devote much of the next decade to work on optics—an important area of study for testing Descartes's corpuscular theory of matter.

Isaac Newton   Pictured here about fifteen years after the publication of *Principia*, Newton was also one of the developers of calculus. The cumbersome mathematics he still relied on, however, has led one scholar to ponder: "What manner of man he was who could use as a weapon what we can scarcely lift as a burden."[8]   (By courtesy of the National Portrait Gallery, London)

In the 1680s, Newton experienced a period of self-imposed isolation from other scientists after a particularly heated exchange with one colleague, provoked by Newton's difficult temperament. During this decade, he returned to the study of alternative theories about matter. As a student at Cambridge, he had been strongly influenced by the work of a group of Neo-Platonists who were critical of Cartesian theory that posited God as a cause of all matter and motion but removed God, or any other unknown or unknowable force, as an explanation for the behavior of matter. The Neo-Platonists' concerns were both religious and scientific. As Newton says in some of his early writing, while a student, "However we cast about we find almost no other reason for atheism than this [Cartesian] notion of bodies having … a complete, absolute and independent reality."[9]

Newton now read treatises in alchemy and Hermetic tracts and began to imagine explanations for the behavior of matter (such as for bits of cloth fluttered from a distance by static electricity) that Cartesian corpuscular theory could not readily explain. Precisely what the forces were that caused such behavior, he was not sure, but his eclectic mind and his religious convictions enabled him to accept their existence.

It was this leap that allowed him to propose the existence of gravity—a mysterious force that accounts for the movements of heavenly bodies in the vacuum of space. Others had speculated about the existence of gravity; indeed, the concept of inertia worked out by Galileo, Descartes, and others suggested the need for the concept of gravity. Otherwise, if a planet were "pushed" (say, in Kepler's view, by the "motive force" of the sun), it would continue along that course forever unless "pulled back" by something else.

Newton's extraordinary contribution to a new mechanistic understanding of the universe was the mathematical computation of the laws of gravity and planetary motion, which he combined with a fully developed concept of inertia. In 1687, Newton published *Philosophia Naturalis Principia Mathematica* (*Mathematical Principles of Natural Philosophy;* usually called *Principia*). In this mathematical treatise—so intricate that it was baffling to laypeople, even those able to read Latin—Newton laid out his **laws of motion** and expressed them as mathematical theorems that can be used to test future observations of moving bodies. Then he demonstrated that these laws also apply to the solar system, confirming the data already gathered about the planets and even predicting the existence of an, as yet, unseen planet. His supreme achievement was his law of gravitation, with which he could predict the discovery of the invisible planet. This law states that every body, indeed every bit of matter, in the universe exerts over every other body an attractive force proportional to the product of their masses and inversely proportional to the square of the distance between them. Newton not only accounted for motion, but definitively united heaven and earth in a single scheme and created a convincing picture of an orderly nature.

Neither Newton nor anyone else claimed that his theorems resolved all questions about motion and matter. Exactly what gravity is and how it operates were not clear, as they still are not. Newton's laws of motion are taught today because they still adequately account for most problems of motion. The fact that so fundamental a principle as gravity remains unexplained in no way diminishes Newton's achievement but is clear evidence of the nature of scientific understanding: Science provides explanatory schemas that account for many—but not all—observed phenomena. No schema explains everything, and each schema contains open doorways that lead both to further discoveries and to blind alleys. Newton, for example, assumed that the forces that accounted for gravity would mysteriously work on metals so that, as alchemists predicted, they might "quickly pass into gold."[10]

After the publication of *Principia*, Newton was more of a celebrated public figure than a practicing scientist. He helped lead resistance to James II's Catholicizing policies in the university, and he became the familiar of many other leading minds of his day, such as John Locke (see page 495). Newton became the president of the Royal Academy of Sciences in 1703 and was knighted in 1705, the first scientist to be so distinguished. By the end of his life, universities in England were dominated by men who acclaimed and built on his work. The transformation of the institutional structure of science in England was complete.

laws of motion The laws of gravity, planetary motion, and inertia first laid out in the seventeenth century by Isaac Newton.

Developments In Chemistry, Biology, and Medicine

The innovations in astronomy that led to the new mechanistic view of the behavior of matter did not automatically spill over to other branches of science. In astronomy, innovation came after the ancient and medieval inheritance had been fully assimilated and its errors disclosed. Other branches of science followed their own paths, though all were strongly influenced by the **mechanistic worldview**.

In chemistry, the mechanistic assumption that all matter was composed of small, equivalent parts was crucial to understanding the properties and behaviors of compounds (combinations of elements). But knowledge of these small units of matter was not yet precise enough to be of much use in advancing chemistry conceptually. Nevertheless, the flawed conceptual schema did not hold back all chemical discovery and development. Lack of understanding of gases, and of the specific elements in their makeup, for example, did not prevent the improvement of gunpowder. Indeed, unlike the innovations in astronomy, conceptual breakthroughs in chemistry and biology owed a great deal to the results of plodding experiment and the slow accumulation of data.

A conceptual leap forward was made in biology in the sixteenth and seventeenth centuries as a result of practical knowledge, because biological knowledge was mostly a by-product of the practice of medicine. The recent discovery of *On Anatomical Procedures*, a treatise by the ancient physician Galen, encouraged dissection and other research. Andreas Vesalius (1514–1564), in particular, made important advances by following Galen's example. Born in Brussels, Vesalius (vuh-SAY-lee-us) studied at the nearby University of Louvain and then at Padua, where he was appointed professor of surgery. He ended his career as physician to Emperor Charles V and his son, Philip II of Spain. In his teaching at Padua, Vesalius acted on the newly recovered Galenic teachings by doing dissections himself rather than giving the work to technicians. In 1543, he

mechanistic worldview Seventeenth-century philosophical view that saw the world as a machine that functions in strict obedience to physical laws, without purpose or will.

Vesalius on Human Anatomy The meticulous illustrations in Vesalius's work helped ensure its success. The medium of print was essential for accurate reproduction of scientific drawings. Note also the way the human body, in this drawing of musculature, is depicted as dominating the landscape. (Terri Torretto/Dover Publications)

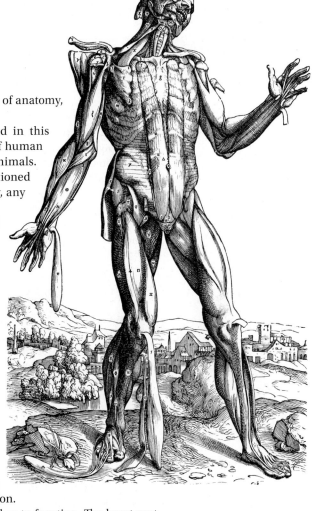

published versions of his lectures as an illustrated compendium of anatomy, *De Humani Corporis Fabrica* (*On the Fabric of the Human Body*).

The results of his dissections of human corpses, revealed in this work, demonstrated a number of errors in Galen's knowledge of human anatomy, much of which had been derived from dissection of animals. Neither Vesalius nor his immediate successors, however, questioned overall Galenic theory about the functioning of the human body, any more than Copernicus had utterly rejected Aristotelian physics.

The slow movement from new observation to changed explanation is clearly illustrated in the career of the Englishman William Harvey (1578–1657). Much like Vesalius, Harvey was educated first in his own land and then at Padua, where he benefited from the tradition of anatomical research. Also like Vesalius, he had a career as a physician, first in London and later at the courts of James I and Charles I.

Harvey postulated the circulation of the blood—postulated rather than discovered, because owing to the technology of the day, he could not observe the tiny capillaries where the movement of arterial blood into the veins occurs. After conducting vivisectional experiments on animals that revealed the actual functioning of the heart and lungs, he reasoned that circulation of the blood must occur. He carefully described his experiments and his conclusions in *Exercitatio Anatomica de Motu Cordis et Sanguinis in Animalibus* (1628), usually shortened to *De Motu Cordis* (*On the Motion of the Heart*).

Harvey's work challenged Galenic anatomy and, like Copernicus's discoveries, created new burdens of explanation. According to Galenic theory, the heart and lungs helped each other to function. The heart sent nourishment to the lungs through the pulmonary artery, and the lungs provided raw material for the "vital spirit," which the heart gave to the blood to sustain life. The lungs also helped the heart sustain its "heat." This heat was understood to be an innate property of organs, just as "heaviness," in traditional physics, had been considered an innate property of earthbound objects.

From his observations, Harvey came to think of the heart in mechanistic terms: as a pump to circulate the blood. But he adjusted, rather than abandoned, Galenic theories concerning "heat" and "vital spirit." The lungs had been thought to "ventilate" the heart by providing air to maintain "heat," just as a bellows blows air on a fire. In light of his discovery of the pulmonary transit (that all of the blood is pumped through the lungs and back through the heart), Harvey suggested instead that the lungs carried out some of these functions for the blood, helping it to concoct the "vital spirit." Only in this sense did he think of the heart as a machine, circulating this life-giving material throughout the body.

Harvey's explanation of bodily functions, in light of his new knowledge, did not constitute a rupture with Galenic tradition. But by the end of his life, Harvey's own adjustments of Galenic theory were suggesting new conceptual possibilities. His work inspired additional research in physiology, chemistry, and physics. Robert Boyle's efforts to understand vacuums can be traced in part to questions Harvey raised about the function of the lungs and the properties of air.

SECTION SUMMARY

- Interest in the new science spread in the seventeenth century as many scholars accepted Copernican theory and as rulers realized the possible advantages of scientific advances.

- René Descartes built on the work of Galileo to formulate a new theory about the nature of matter.

- Descartes believed that humans could understand nature by using reason, not by trusting sensory data.

- English scientists, such as Robert Boyle, began to use experimental methods.

- Isaac Newton developed new laws of motion, still in use today, that explain the behavior of matter on earth and in space with a single set of mathematical principles.

- Advances in the life sciences included new anatomical discoveries by Andreas Vesalius and work by William Harvey on the circulation of the blood.

THE NEW SCIENCE IN CONTEXT: SOCIETY, POLITICS, AND RELIGION

How did the new scientific worldview lead people to challenge traditional notions of society, the state, and religion?

Scientists wrestled with questions about God and human capacity every bit as intently as they attempted to find new explanations for the behavior of matter and the motion of the heavens. Eventually, the profound implications of the new scientific worldview would affect thought and behavior throughout society. Once people no longer thought of the universe in hierarchical terms, they could question the hierarchical organization of society. Once people questioned the authority of traditional knowledge about the universe, the way was clear for them to begin to question traditional views of the state, the social order, and even the divine order. Such profound changes of perspective took hold very gradually, however. The advances in science did lead to revolutionary cultural change, but until the end of the seventeenth century, traditional institutions and ideologies limited its extent.

The Beginnings of Scientific Professionalism

Institutions both old and new supported the new science developing in the sixteenth and seventeenth centuries. Some universities were the setting for scientific breakthroughs, but court patronage, a well-established institution, also sponsored scientific activity. The development of the Accadèmia dei Lincei, to which Galileo belonged, and of other academies was a step toward modern professional societies of scholars, although these new organizations depended on patronage.

In England and France, royally sponsored scientific societies were founded in the third quarter of the century, reflecting rulers' keen interest in science. The Royal Society of London, though charted by the king in 1660, received no money. It remained an informal institution sponsoring amateur scientific interests, as well as specialized independent research. The Académie Royale des Sciences in France, established in 1666 by Jean-Baptiste Colbert, Louis XIV's minister of finance (see page 445), sponsored research but also supported chosen scientists with pensions. These associations were extensions to science of traditional kinds of royal recognition and patronage. Thus, the French Académie was well funded but tightly controlled by the government of Louis XIV, while the Royal Society of London received little of Charles II's scarce resources or precious political capital. Like the earlier academies, these royally sponsored societies published their fellows' work; in England, the *Philosophical Transactions of the Royal Society* began in 1665.

The practice of seventeenth-century science took place in so many diverse institutions—academies, universities, royal courts—that neither *science* nor *scientist* was rigorously defined. Science, as a discipline, was not yet detached from broad metaphysical questions. Boyle, Newton, Pascal, and Descartes all concerned themselves with questions of religion, and all thought of themselves not as scientists but, like their medieval forebears, as natural philosophers. These natural philosophers were still members of an elite who met in aristocratic salons to discuss literature, politics, or science with equal ease and interest. Nevertheless, the beginnings of a narrowing of the practice of science to a tightly defined, truly professional community are evident in these institutions.

Women Scientists and Institutional Constraints

The importance of court life and patronage to the new science had, at first, enabled women to be actively involved in the development of science. Women ran important salons in France; aristocratic women everywhere were indispensable sources of patronage for scientists; and women themselves were scientists, combining, as did men, science with other pursuits. Noblewomen and daughters of gentry families had access to education in their homes, and a number of such women were active scientists—astronomers, mathematicians, and botanists. The astronomer Maria Cunitz (KOO-nits) (1610–1664), from Silesia (a Habsburg-controlled province, now in modern Poland), learned six languages with the encouragement of her father, a physician. Later, she published a useful simplification of some of Kepler's mathematical calculations. Women from some artisanal families also received useful training at home. Such was the case of the German entomologist Maria Sibylla Merian (1647–1717). Merian learned the techniques of illustration in the workshop of her father, an artist in Frankfurt. She later used her artistic training and her refined powers of observation to study and record the features and behaviors of insects and plants in the New World.

Margaret Cavendish, duchess of Newcastle (1623–1673), wrote several major philosophical works, including *Grounds of Natural Philosophy* (1668). She was a Cartesian but was influenced by Neo-Platonism. She believed matter to have "intelligence" and thus disagreed with Descartes's views on matter, but she criticized fellow English philosophers on the grounds that, like Descartes, she distrusted sensory knowledge as a guide to philosophy.

Margaret Cavendish was aware of the degree to which her participation in scientific life depended on informal networks and on the resources available to her because of her aristocratic status. Women scientists from more modest backgrounds, without Cavendish's resources, had to fight for the right to employment, as public institutions gained importance as settings for the pursuit of science. The German astronomer Maria Winkelman (VINK-el-mahn) (1670–1720), for example, tried to succeed her late husband in an official position in the Berlin Academy of Sciences in 1710, after working as his unofficial partner during his tenure as astronomer to the academy. The academy withheld an official position from Winkelman after her husband's death, however, despite her experience and accomplishments (she had discovered a new comet, for example, in 1702). The secretary of the academy stated: "That she be kept on in an offcial capacity to work on the calendar or to continue with observations simply will not do. Already during her husband's lifetime the society was burdened with ridicule because its calendar was prepared by a woman. If she were now to be kept on in such a capacity, mouths would gape even wider."[11] Winkelman worked in

Astronomers Elisabetha and Johannes Hevelius   The Heveliuses were one of many collaborating couples among the scientists of the seventeenth century. Women were usually denied pensions and support for their research when they worked alone, however.   (Houghton Library)

private observatories but was able to return to the Berlin Academy only as the unofficial assistant to her own son, whose training she herself had supervised. As the new science gained in prestige, women scientists often found themselves marginalized. While women were routinely accepted as members of Italian academies, they were excluded from formal membership in the academies in London and Paris, although they could use the academies' facilities and received prizes from the societies for their work.

The New Science, the State, and the Church

The new natural philosophy had implications for traditional notions about the state. The new worldview that all matter, whether in the heavens or on earth, was identical and answerable to discernible natural laws gradually undermined political systems resting on a belief in the inherent inequality of persons and on royal prerogative. By the middle of the eighteenth century, a fully formed alternative political philosophy would argue for more "rational" government in keeping with the rational, natural order of things. But the change came slowly, and while it was coming, traditional rulers found much to admire and utilize in the new science.

Technological possibilities of the new science were very attractive to governments. Experiments with vacuum pumps had important applications in the mining industry, for example. Governments also sponsored pure, and not only applied, scientific research. A French naval expedition to Cayenne, in French Guiana, led to refinements of the pendulum clock but had, as its main purpose, progressive observations of the sun to permit the calculation of the earth's distance from the sun. Members of the elite saw the opportunity not only for practical advances, but also for prestige and, most important, confirmation of the orderliness of nature. It is hard to overestimate the psychological impact and intellectual power of this fundamental tenet of the new science—namely, that nature is an inanimate machine that reflects God's design not through its purposes, but simply by its orderliness. Thus, in the short run, the new science supported a vision of order that was very pleasing even to an absolute monarch, such as Louis XIV.

As we have seen, scientists themselves flourished in close relationships with princes and actively sought their patronage. Christiaan Huygens left the Netherlands to accept the patronage of Louis XIV and produced, in France, some of his most important work in optics and mechanics. Huygens had learned from his father, secretary to the princes of Orange in the Netherlands, that a princely court not only offered steady support, but also opened doors to other royal academies and salons. Huygens published some of his early research through the Royal Society in London, thanks to contacts his father had established. When Galileo left his position at Padua for the Medici court in Florence, he wrote to a friend, "It is not possible to receive a salary from a Republic [Venice] ... without serving the public, because to get something from the public one must satisfy it and not just one particular person; ... no one can exempt me from the burden while leaving me the income; and in sum I cannot hope for such a benefit from anyone but an absolute prince."[12]

Scientists and scientific thought also remained closely tied to religion in both practical and institutional ways during the seventeenth century. Both religion and the Catholic Church, as an institution, were involved with scientific advancement from the time of Copernicus. Copernicus himself was a cleric, as were many philosophers and scientists after him. This is not surprising, for most research in the sciences to this point had occurred within universities sponsored and staffed by members of religious orders, who had the education, time, and resources necessary for scientific investigation. Some of Descartes's closest collaborators were clerics, as were certain of Galileo's aristocratic patrons and his own protégés. Moreover, religious and metaphysical concerns were central to the work of virtually every scientist. The entire Cartesian process of reasoning about the world, for example, was grounded in Descartes's certainty about God. Copernicus, Kepler, Newton, and others believed they perceived God's purpose in the mathematical regularity of nature.

The notion that religion was the opponent of science in this era is a result of Galileo's trial and represents a distortion even of that event. It is true that the new astronomy and mechanics challenged traditional interpretations of Scripture, as well as the fundamentals of physics and metaphysics that were taught in universities. Thus, in its sponsorship of universities, the church was literally invested in the old view, even though individual churchmen investigated and taught Copernican ideas. The rigid response of the church hierarchy to Galileo is partially explained by the aftermath of the Protestant Reformation, which, in the minds of many churchmen—including Galileo's accusers and some of his judges—had demonstrated the need for a firm response to any challenge to the church's authority. Galileo seemed particularly threatening because he was well known, wrote for a wide audience, and, like the Protestants, presumed to interpret the Scriptures. Galileo may well have escaped punishment entirely had it not been for the political predicament faced by the pope at the time of his trial, however.

The condemnation of Galileo shocked many clerics, including the three who had voted for leniency at his trial. Clerics who were also scientists continued to study and teach the new science where and when they could. Copernicanism was taught by Catholic missionaries abroad. (See the feature, "The Global Record: Jesuits and Astronomy in China.") To be sure, Galileo's trial did have a chilling effect on scientific investigation in many Catholic regions of Europe. Investigators could and did continue their research, but many could publish results only by smuggling manuscripts to Protestant lands. After the middle of the seventeenth century, many of the most important empirical and theoretical innovations in science occurred in Protestant regions. However, Protestant leaders had also not been receptive to Copernican ideas at first because the ideas seemed to defy scriptural authority as well as common sense. In 1549, one of Martin Luther's associates wrote: "The eyes are witnesses that the heavens revolve in the space of twenty four hours. But certain men, either from love of novelty or to make a display of ingenuity, have concluded that the earth moves. ... Now it is want of honesty and decency to assert such notions. ... It is part of a good mind to accept the truth as revealed by God and to acquiesce in it."[13]

Protestant thinkers were also as troubled as Catholics by the metaphysical dilemmas that the new theories seemed to raise. In 1611, one year after Galileo's *Starry Messenger* appeared,

Science and Royal Power   This painting memorializes the founding of the French Académie des Sciences and the building of the royal observatory in Paris. Louis himself is at the center of the painting, reflecting the symbolic importance of royal power in the sponsorship of science.   (Erich lessing/Art Resource, NY)

the English poet John Donne (1573–1631) reflected on the confusion that now reigned in human affairs, with the heavenly hierarchy dismantled:

> *[The] new Philosophy calls all in doubt,*
> *The Element of fire is quite put out,*
> *The Sun is lost, and th'earth, and no man's wit*
> *Can well direct him where to look for it*
> *… … … …*
> *Tis all in pieces, all coherence gone;*
> *All just supply, and all Relation:*
> *Prince, Subject, Father, Son, are things forgot,*
> *For every man alone thinks he hath got*
> *To be a Phoenix, and that then can be*
> *None of that kinde, of which he is, but he.*[14]

The challenge of accounting, in religious terms, for the ideas of Copernicus and Descartes became more urgent for Protestants as the ideas acquired an anti-Catholic status after the trial of Galileo in 1633 and as they became common scientific currency by about 1640. As we have seen, Newton was able to develop his theories on motion and gravity in part because of a religious certainty about divine force that could account for the motion of bodies in a vacuum. In short, religion did not merely remain in the scientists' toolbox of explanations; it remained a

Jesuits and Astronomy in China

The Italian Matteo Ricci (1552–1610) was one of the first Jesuit missionaries to establish himself at the imperial court in China. Ricci's willingness to learn the Chinese language and his own scientific knowledge was crucial to his acceptance at the Chinese court. Jesuit missionaries who followed Ricci in the seventeenth century found their scientific expertise equally valued, and several openly taught Copernican theory in the East. Chinese interest in European knowledge was itself new. In previous centuries, Europeans had eagerly borrowed from China, including knowledge of papermaking and printing.

The Chinese have not only made considerable progress in moral philosophy but in astronomy and in many branches of mathematics as well. At one time they were quite proficient in arithmetic and geometry, but in the study and teaching of these branches of learning they labored with more or less confusion. They divide the heavens into constellations in a manner somewhat different from that which we employ. Their count of the stars outnumbers the calculations of our astronomers by fully four hundred, because they include in it many of the fainter stars which are not always visible. And yet with all this, the Chinese astronomers take no pains whatever to reduce the phenomena of celestial bodies to the discipline of mathematics. Much of their time is spent in determining the moment of eclipses and the mass of the planets and the stars, but here, too, their deductions are spoiled by innumerable errors. Finally they center their whole attention on that phase of astronomy which our scientists term astrology, which may be accounted for by the fact that they believe that everything happening on this terrestrial globe of ours depends upon the stars.

Some knowledge of the science of mathematics was given to the Chinese by the Saracens [Mongols], who penetrated into their country from the West, but very little of this knowledge was based upon definite mathematical proofs. What the Saracens left them, for the most part, consisted of certain tables of rules by which the Chinese regulated their calendar and to which they reduced their calculations of planets and the movements of the heavenly bodies in general. The founder of the family which at present regulates the study of astrology prohibited anyone from indulging in the study of this science unless he were chosen for it by hereditary right. The prohibition was founded upon fear, lest he who should acquire a knowledge of the stars might become capable of disrupting the order of the empire and seek an opportunity to do so.

QUESTIONS

1. In what ways is Ricci both appreciative and critical of Chinese science?

2. What do Ricci's comments about Chinese science reveal about his own assumptions concerning astronomy and mathematics and how to study them appropriately?

Source: Louis J. Gallagher, trans., *China in the Sixteenth Century: The Journals of Matthew Ricci: 1583–1610* (New York: Random House, 1953), pp. 30–31. Copyright 1942, 1953 and renewed 1970 by Louis J. Gallagher, S.J. Used by permission of Random House, Inc.

fundamental building block of scientific thought and central to most scientists' lives, whether they were Catholic or Protestant.

Thomas Hobbes English philosopher who argued in *Leviathan* that people are made up of mechanistic appetites and so need a strong ruler to govern them. However, he also envisioned citizens as potentially equal and constrained neither by morality nor by natural obedience to authority.

The New Science and Political Thought at the End of the Seventeenth Century

Traditional institutions and ideologies checked the potential effects of the new science for a time, but by the middle of the seventeenth century, political theory was beginning to reflect the impact of the mechanistic worldview. Political philosophers began to doubt that either the world or human society was an organic whole in which each part was distinguished in nature and function from the rest. Thomas Hobbes, John Locke, and others reimagined the bonds that link citizens to one another and to their rulers.

THOMAS HOBBES

Because of the political turmoil in England, **Thomas Hobbes** (1588–1679) spent much of his productive life on the Continent. After the beginnings of the parliamentary rebellion, he joined a group of royalist émigrés in France. He met Galileo and lived for extended periods in Paris, in contact with the circle of French thinkers that included Descartes. Like Descartes, he theorized about the nature and behavior of matter and published a treatise on his views in 1655.

Hobbes is best known today for *Leviathan* (1651), his treatise on political philosophy. In *Leviathan*, Hobbes applies to the world of human beings his largely Cartesian view of nature as composed of "self-motivated," atom-like bits of matter. Hobbes viewed people as mechanistically as he viewed the rest of nature. In his view, people are made up of appetites of various sorts—the same kind of innate forces that drive all matter. The ideal political system, he concluded, is one in which a strong ruler controls the disorder that inevitably arises from the clash of people's desires. Unlike medieval philosophers, Hobbes did not draw analogies between the state and the human body (the king as head, judges and magistrates as arms, and so forth). Instead, he compared the state to a machine that "ran" by means of laws and was kept in good working order by a skilled technician—the ruler.

Hobbes's pessimism about human behavior and his insistence on the need for restraint imposed from above reflect, as does the work of Descartes, a concern for order in the wake of upheaval—in Hobbes's case, civil war in his native England. This concern was one reason he was welcomed into the community of French philosophers, who were naturally comfortable with royalty as a powerful guarantor of order. But Hobbes's work, like theirs, was a radical departure because it envisioned citizens as potentially equal and constrained neither by morality nor by natural obedience to authority.

Another Englishman, **John Locke** (1632–1704), offered an entirely different vision of natural equality among people and, consequently, of social order. Locke's major works, *Essay on Human Understanding* (1690) and *Two Treatises of Government* (1690), reflect the experimentalism of Robert Boyle, the systematizing rationality of Descartes, and other strands of the new scientific thought. In his *Essay*, Locke provides a view of human knowledge more pragmatic and utilitarian than the rigorous mathematical model of certainty used by many other philosophers. He argues that human knowledge is largely the product of experience. He agrees with Descartes that reason orders and explains human experience, but unlike Descartes, he doubts that human reason has unlimited potential to comprehend the universe. Locke, however, offered a more optimistic vision of the possible uses of reason. Whereas Descartes was interested in mentally ordering and understanding the world, Locke was interested in actually functioning *in* the world.

Locke's treatises on government reflect his notion of knowledge based on experience, as well as his particular experiences as a member of elite circles following the Restoration in England. Trained in medicine, he served as personal physician and general political assistant to one of the members of Parliament most opposed to Charles II's pretensions to absolutist government. When James II acceded to the throne in 1685, Locke remained in the Netherlands, where he had fled to avoid prosecution for treason. He became an adviser to William of Orange and returned to England with William and Mary in 1688. Locke's view of the principles of good government came to reflect the pro-parliamentary stance of his political milieu.

Unlike Hobbes, Locke argued that people are capable of self-restraint and mutual respect in their pursuit of self-interest. The state arises, he believed, from a contract that individuals freely enter into to protect themselves, their property, and their happiness from possible aggression by others. They can invest the executive and legislative authority to carry out this protection in monarchy or any other governing institution, though Locke believed that the English Parliament was the best available model. Because sovereignty resides with the people who enter into the contract, rebellion against the abuse of power is justified. At the core of Locke's schema is thus a revolutionary vision of political society based on human rights.

Locke's experience as an English gentleman is apparent in his emphasis on private property, which he considered a fundamental human right. Nature, he believed, cannot benefit humankind unless it is worked by human hands, as on a farm, for example. Private ownership of property guarantees its productivity and entitles the owner to participate in Locke's imagined contract. Indeed, Locke's political vision is unequivocal, and unbending, on the nature of property. Locke even found a justification for slavery. He also did not consider women to be independent beings in the same way as men. The family, he felt, is a separate domain from the state, not bound by the same contractual obligations. Locke and many other seventeenth-century thinkers were unable to imagine a new physical or political reality without invoking a notion of gender as a "natural" principle of order and hierarchy. Margaret Cavendish, among others, disputed the validity of such arbitrary distinctions in capacities and rights between men and women; nevertheless, men frequently used them. Locke's use of gender as an arbitrary organizing principle gave his bold new vision of rights for certain men a claim to being "natural." The use of gender-specific vocabulary to describe nature itself had the effect of making the new objective attitude toward the world seem "natural." Works by seventeenth-century scientists are filled with references to nature as a woman who must be "conquered," "subdued," or "penetrated."

JOHN LOCKE

John Locke English philosopher who asserted that the state arises from a contract that individuals freely endorse. Therefore, because sovereignty resides with the people, rebellion against abuse of power is justified—a revolutionary vision of a political society based on human rights.

SKEPTICISM AND
THE SPREAD
OF SCIENTIFIC
RATIONALITY

Although traditional gender distinctions limited and reinforced most facets of political thought, in other areas, the fact of uncertainty and the need for tolerance were embraced. In another of Locke's influential works, the impassioned *Letter on Toleration* (1689), he argues that religious belief is fundamentally private and that only the most basic Christian principles need be accepted by everyone. Others went further than Locke by entirely removing traditional religion as necessary to morality and public order. Fostering this climate of religious skepticism were religious pluralism in England and the self-defeating religious intolerance of Louis XIV's persecution of Protestants.

Pierre Bayle (1647–1706), a Frenchman of Protestant origins, argued that morality can be wholly detached from traditional religion. Indeed, Bayle concluded, one need not be a Christian at all to be a moral being. Bayle cited as an example of morality the philosopher Baruch Spinoza (1632–1677), a Dutch Jew who had been cast out of his local synagogue for supposed atheism. Even so, Spinoza believed the state to have a moral purpose and human happiness to have spiritual roots.

Bayle's skepticism toward traditional knowledge was more wide-ranging than his views on religion. His best-known work, *Dictionnaire historique et critique* (*Historical and Critical Dictionary*, 1702), was a compendium of observations about and criticisms of virtually every thinker whose works were known at the time, including such recent and lionized figures as Descartes and Newton. Bayle was the first systematic skeptic, and he relentlessly exposed errors and shortcomings in all received knowledge. His works were very popular with elite lay readers. Bayle's countryman Bernard de Fontenelle (fon-tuh-NEL) (1657–1757), secretary to the Académie des Sciences from 1699 to 1741, was the greatest popularizer of the new science of his time. His *Entretiens sur la Pluralités des Mondes* (*Conversations on the Plurality of Worlds*, 1686) went through numerous editions and translations. It was, as the title implies, an informally presented description of the infinite universe of matter. He also helped spread the new science by publishing descriptions of the work of the Académie's scientists. Fontenelle is a fitting figure with whom to end a discussion of the Scientific Revolution because he represents, and worked to accomplish, the transfer of the new science into political and social philosophy—a movement we know as the "Enlightenment." A fully developed secular worldview, with revolutionary implications for human affairs, would be the product of the Enlightenment in the next century.

SECTION SUMMARY

- New institutions, such as academies, supported scientific work and were forerunners of modern scientific associations.

- European rulers were eager to sponsor scientific work both for its practical benefits and for its symbolic importance for their power.

- Scientific work remained closely tied to religion in both intellectual and institutional ways. Political thought in the seventeenth century, as represented by Locke and Bayle, began to reflect the new science's confidence in human reason.

- Women scientists were disadvantaged by the institutional settings for the new science and by the way notions about gender were used in the new science and political philosophy.

CHAPTER SUMMARY

The Scientific Revolution began with developments in astronomy. Because of astronomy's role in explanations of the world and human life that prevailed in the Middle Ages, changes in astronomical theory were bound to have widespread effects on other knowledge and beliefs. Copernicus's heliocentric theory led to wider scientific and philosophical innovation also because of the context in which it was received. Recent recoveries of new ancient texts in the Renaissance and the discovery of previously unknown lands in the New World made it possible to imagine challenging ancient scientific authority. The interest of princes in both the prestige and the practical use of science helped support the work of scientists. Other scientists, following Copernicus, built on his theories, culminating in the work of Galileo, who supported Copernican theory with additional data and widely published his findings.

The Frenchman Descartes was the first to fashion a systematic explanation for the operations of nature to replace the

FOCUS QUESTIONS

- How did the Copernican theory challenge traditional views of the universe?

- How and why did new theories about astronomy lead to a broader Scientific Revolution?

- How did the new scientific worldview lead people to challenge traditional notions of society, the state, and religion?

medieval view. The political and intellectual climate in England, meanwhile, encouraged the development of experimental science and inductive reasoning. Isaac Newton provided new theories to explain the behavior of matter and expressed them in mathematical terms that could apply to either the earth or the cosmos. With his work, traditional astronomy and physics were overturned, replaced by a vision of a universe of matter that behaves not according to a higher purpose, but rather as a machine.

New institutions in the form of private, as well as officially sponsored, scientific societies rose up to support scientists' work. These societies were particularly important before the new science became accepted in universities, although they excluded some practitioners of the new science, particularly women. Rulers made use of the new science for the practical results it offered, despite the ideological challenges it presented to their power. The relationship of religion to the new science was equally complex and contrary. Some religious leaders scorned the new science; most scientists, whether Catholic or Protestant, worked to accommodate both the new science and their religious beliefs. Indeed, religious faith—in the case of Newton, for example—was a spur to innovation. By the end of the seventeenth century, the hierarchical Christian worldview, grounded in the old science, was being challenged on many fronts, most notably in the work of the political philosophers Hobbes and Locke, who both challenged traditional justifications for royal authority. Locke's work was particularly important for the future because he argued that governments can exist only with the consent of the governed.

KEY TERMS

Nicholas Copernicus
(p. 476)

heliocentric theory (p. 476)

Tycho Brahe (p. 477)

Johannes Kepler (p. 477)

Galileo Galilei (p. 478)

Francis Bacon (p. 481)

empirical method (p. 481)

René Descartes (p. 482)

Isaac Newton (p. 487)

laws of motion (p. 488)

mechanistic worldview
(p. 488)

Thomas Hobbes (p. 494)

John Locke (p. 495)

 This icon will direct you to additional materials on the website: www .cengage.com/history/ noble/westciv6e.

NOTES

1. Quoted in Thomas S. Kuhn, *The Copernican Revolution* (Cambridge, Mass.: Harvard University Press, 1985), p. 131.

2. Quoted in Margaret C. Jacob, *The Cultural Meaning of the Scientific Revolution* (Philadelphia: Temple University Press, 1988), p. 18.

3. Quoted ibid., p. 33.

4. Quoted in Alan G. R. Smith, *Science and Society in the Sixteenth and Seventeenth Centuries* (New York: Science History Publications, 1972), p. 72.

5. Quoted in Jacob, p. 32 (emphasis added).

6. Quoted in Bruce T. Moran, ed., *Patronage and Institutions: Science, Technology and Medicine at the European Court* (Rochester, N.Y.: Boyden Press, 1991), p. 43.

7. Quoted in Steven Shapin, *A Social History of Truth* (Chicago: University of Chicago Press, 1994), p. 298.

8. Quoted in Smith, p. 130.

9. Quoted in Jacob, p. 89.

10. Quoted ibid., p. 25.

11. Quoted in Londa Schiebinger, *The Mind Has No Sex?* (Cambridge, Mass.: Harvard University Press, 1989), p. 92.

12. Quoted in Richard S. Westfall, "Science and Patronage," *ISIS* 76 (1985): 16.

13. Quoted in Kuhn, p. 191.

14. *Complete Poetry and Selected Prose of John Donne*, ed. John Hayward (Bloomsbury, England: Nonesuch Press, 1929), p. 365, quoted in Kuhn, p. 194.

See our interactive eBook for map and primary source activities.

18

CHAPTER OUTLINE

The Enlightenment

European States in the Age of Enlightenment

The Widening World of Trade and Production

The Widening World of Warfare

Café Society in the Eighteenth Century
(G. Dagli Orti/The Art Archive)

Europe on the Threshold of Modernity, ca. 1715–1789

D rinks are set before these gentlemen on their table, but this is more than just a social gathering. The men are absorbed in intense conversation. One man raises his hand, perhaps to emphasize his point, while another listens with a skeptical smirk. Several others eagerly follow their conversation. Other animated discussions go on at nearby tables. The setting depicted here was altogether new in the eighteenth century, when this picture was made, and a caption that originally accompanied the illustration reveals its importance: "Establishment of the new philosophy: our cradle was the café."

Cafés—coffeehouses—were as revolutionary in their day as the Internet is in our own. They were one of the principal places where educated people could debate the "new philosophy"—what we now call Enlightenment philosophy—and could explore its implications for social and political life. Men gathered in clubs and cafés; women directed private gatherings known as salons. Both men and women read more widely than ever before.

What the new science did to physics, the Enlightenment did to politics. The Enlightenment transferred into political and social thought the intellectual revolution that had already occurred in the physical sciences. Hence, it constituted a revolution in political philosophy, but it was also much more. The era witnessed the emergence of an informed body of public opinion, critical of the prevailing political system. The relationship between governments and the governed had begun to change: Subjects of monarchs were becoming citizens of nations.

The notion that human beings, using their rational faculties, could not only understand nature but might also transform their societies was appealing to rulers as well, in part for the traditional reason—strengthening state power. Frederick the Great of Prussia, Catherine the Great of Russia, and other monarchs self-consciously tried to use Enlightenment precepts to guide their efforts at governing. They had mixed success because powerful interests opposed their efforts at reform and because, ultimately, their own hereditary and autocratic power was incompatible with Enlightenment ideals.

Profound changes in economic and social life accompanied this revolution in intellectual and political spheres. The increasing economic and strategic importance of overseas colonies made them important focal points of international conflict. Economic growth spurred population growth, which in turn stimulated industry and trade. As the century closed, Europe was on the threshold of truly revolutionary changes in politics and production that had their roots in the intellectual, economic, and social ferment of eighteenth-century life.

FOCUS QUESTIONS

- What were the most important ideas in Enlightenment thought, and what were some of the intellectual, social, and political conditions that favored its development?

- To what extent did the activities of rulers, particularly "enlightened despots," reflect Enlightenment ideals, and to what extent did they reflect traditional concerns of state power?

- How and why did trade and production increase in the eighteenth century?

- How did warfare and its consequences change in the eighteenth century?

 This icon will direct you to additional materials on the website: www .cengage.com/history/ noble/westciv6e.

See our interactive eBook for map and primary source activities.

THE ENLIGHTENMENT

What were the most important ideas in Enlightenment thought, and what were some of the intellectual, social, and political conditions that favored its development?

The Enlightenment was an intellectual movement that brought to political and social questions the confidence in the intelligibility of natural law that Newton and other scientists had recently achieved. Following Descartes and Locke, Enlightenment thinkers believed that human beings could discern and work in concert with the laws of nature for the betterment of human life. Above all, Enlightenment thought gave people the confidence to question tradition. A belief grew that society must be grounded on rational foundations to be determined by humans, not arbitrary foundations determined by tradition and justified by religious authority.

Enlightenment thought was debated in increasingly widespread publications, such as newspapers. There were new opportunities for exchanging views in literary societies, salons, and cafés. These new means of sharing information ensured that informed public opinion would become a new force in political and cultural life. Given this broad base, Enlightenment thinking was certain to challenge the very foundations of social and political order.

Voltaire: The Quintessential Philosophe

philosophes French term referring to thinkers and critics of the Enlightenment era, including Voltaire and Rousseau.

Voltaire French writer, critic, and reformer who embodied the spirit of eighteenth-century rationalism: its confidence, its increasingly practical bent, its wit and sophistication.

In France, Enlightenment thinkers were known as **philosophes** (fee-low-ZOHFS), a term meaning not a formal philosopher but rather a thinker and critic. The most famous of the philosophes was **Voltaire** (1694-1778). A prolific writer, critic, and reformer, Voltaire embodied the spirit of eighteenth-century rationalism: its confidence, its increasingly practical bent, its wit and sophistication. He was widely admired throughout Europe, including by several rulers. Born François-Marie Arouet to a middle-class family, he took the pen name Voltaire in 1718, after one of his early plays was a critical success. Like many philosophes, Voltaire moved in courtly circles but was often on its margins. His mockery of the regent for the young French king earned him a year's imprisonment in 1717, and an exchange of insults with a leading courtier some years later led to enforced exile in Great Britain for two years.

After returning from Britain, Voltaire published his first major philosophical work. *Lettres philosophiques (Philosophical Letters*, 1734) revealed the influence of his British sojourn and helped to popularize Isaac Newton's achievements in mathematics and science. To confidence in the laws governing nature, Voltaire added cautious confidence in humans' attempts to discern truth. From the Englishman Locke's work, he was persuaded to value education. These elements gave Voltaire's philosophy both its passionate conviction and its sensible practicality.

Voltaire portrayed Great Britain as a more rational society than France. The British government had a more workable set of institutions; the economy was less crippled by the remnants of feudal privilege, and education was not in the hands of the church. He was particularly impressed with the relative religious and intellectual toleration evident across the Channel. Voltaire was one of many French thinkers who singled out the Catholic Church as the archenemy of progressive thought. Philosophes constantly collided with the church's negative views of human nature and resented its control over most education and its influence in political life. Typical of Voltaire's criticism of the church is his stinging satire of the clerics who had condemned Galileo: "I desire that there be engraved on the door of your holy office: Here seven cardinals assisted by minor brethren had the master of thought of Italy thrown into prison at the age of seventy, made him fast on bread and water, because he instructed the human race."

After the publication of his audacious *Letters*, Voltaire was again forced into exile from Paris, and he lived for some years in the country home of a woman with whom he shared a remarkable intellectual and emotional relationship: Emilie, marquise du Châtelet (shot-uh-LAY) (1706-1749). Châtelet was a mathematician and a scientist. She prepared a French translation of Newton's *Principia*, while Voltaire worked on his own writing projects, which included a commentary on Newton's work. Because of Châtelet's influence, Voltaire became more knowledgeable about the sciences and more serious in his efforts to apply scientific rationality to human affairs. He was devastated by her sudden death in 1749.

Shortly afterward he accepted the invitation of the king of Prussia, Frederick II, to visit Berlin. His stay was stormy and brief because of disagreements with other court philosophers. He then lived for a time in Geneva, Switzerland, until his criticisms of the city's moral codes forced yet another exile on him. He spent most of the last twenty years of his life at his estates on the Franco-Swiss border, where he could be relatively free from interference by any government. These were productive years. He produced his best-known satirical novelette, *Candide*, in 1758. It criticized aristocratic privilege and the power of the church as well as the naiveté of philosophers who took "natural law" to mean that the world was already operating as it should.

In contrast, Voltaire believed that only by struggle could the accumulated habits of centuries be overturned. This belief led to his political activities. He became involved in several celebrated legal cases in which individuals were pitted against the authority of the church, which was still backed by the authority of the state. Voltaire's pursuit of justice in these cases was relentless. In addition to writing plays, novelettes, and essays, he published a stream of political tracts to champion specific causes and to argue for reform. He also worked close to home, initiating agricultural reform on his estates and working to improve the status of peasants in the vicinity.

Voltaire died in Paris in May 1778, after a triumphal welcome for the staging of one of his plays. By then, he was no longer leader of the Enlightenment in strictly intellectual terms. Thinkers and writers more radical than he had become prominent during his long life. They dismissed some of his beliefs, such as the notion that a monarch could introduce reform. But Voltaire had provided a crucial stimulus to French thought with his *Philosophical Letters* and through the example of his own prolific writing and political involvement. Until the end of his life, Voltaire remained a bridge between the increasingly diverse body of Enlightenment thought and the literate elite audience.

CHRONOLOGY

1715–1774	Reign of Louis XV in France
1722–1742	Walpole first British "prime minister"
1734	Voltaire, *Philosophical Letters*
1740–1748	War of the Austrian Succession
1740–1780	Reign of Maria Theresa of Austria
1740–1786	Reign of Frederick the Great of Prussia
1746	Battle of Culloden
1748	Montesquieu, *The Spirit of the Laws* Hume, *An Enquiry Concerning Human Understanding*
1751–1765	Diderot, *Encyclopedia*
1756-1763	Seven Years' War
1758	Voltaire, *Candide*
1762	Rousseau, *The Social Contract*
1762–1796	Reign of Catherine the Great of Russia
1772	First partition of Poland
1776	Smith, *The Wealth of Nations*
1780–1790	Reign of Joseph II of Austria
1792	Wollstonecraft, *A Vindication of the Rights of Woman*

The Variety of Enlightenment Thought

A variety of thinkers contributed to the development of Enlightenment ideas. There were differences among philosophes about major issues. For example, though there was virtual unanimity in criticism of the Catholic Church, there was no unanimity about the existence or nature of God. Voltaire was a theist who believed in a creator of the universe, but not a specifically Christian God. Some philosophes were outright atheists, arguing that a universe operating according to discoverable laws needs no divine presence to explain or justify its existence. In spite of—and partly because of—their disagreements, a number of the philosophes remain among the most important political thinkers in modern times.

MONTESQUIEU

Charles de Secondat (1689–1755), baron of Montesquieu (mawn-tess-KYUH), a French judge and legal philosopher, combined the belief that human institutions must be rational with Locke's assumption of human educability. Montesquieu's treatise, *De L'Esprit des lois (The Spirit of the Laws*, 1748), published in twenty-two printings within two years, argued that laws were not meant to be arbitrary rules but derived naturally from human society: The more evolved a society was, the more liberal were its laws. This notion that progress is possible within society and government deflated Europeans' pretensions with regard to other societies, for a variety of laws could be equally "rational" given different conditions. Montesquieu is perhaps best known to Americans as the advocate of the separation of legislative, executive, and judicial powers that became enshrined in the U.S. Constitution later in the century. To Montesquieu, this scheme seemed to parallel in human government the balance of forces observable in nature; moreover, the arrangement seemed best to guarantee liberty.

Voltaire Visits Frederick the Great of Prussia Voltaire leans forward, at left, to discuss a point of philosophy with Frederick. Skill at witty conversation enabled philosophes such as Voltaire to advance fundamental criticisms of society even to elite audiences. (Bildarchiv Preussischer Kulturbesitz/Art Resource, NY)

ECONOMIC THOUGHT AND THE SCOTTISH ENLIGHTENMENT

Adam Smith Scottish economist who developed the doctrine of "laissez-faire" in his treatise, *The Wealth of Nations* (1776).

Enlightenment philosophers also investigated the "laws" of economic life. For example, French thinkers, known as *physiocrats*, proposed ending "artificial" control over land in order to free productive capacity and permit the flow of crops to market. Their target was traditional forms of land tenure, including collective control of village lands by peasants and traditional rights over land and labor by landlords. The freeing of restrictions on manufacture and trade, as well as agriculture, was proposed by the Scotsman **Adam Smith** in his treatise, *An Inquiry into the Nature and Causes of the Wealth of Nations* (1776).

Smith (1723–1790) was a professor at the University of Glasgow. Scottish universities did not require specialization in subject matter and were open to ideas from abroad, enabling Smith's and others' unique contributions to Enlightenment thought.

Smith is best known in modern times as the originator of "laissez-faire" economics. *Laissez-faire* (LESS-ay-fair), or "let it run on its own," assumes that an economy will regulate itself, without interference by government and, of more concern to Smith, without the monopolies and other economic privileges common in his day. But this schema was not merely a rigid application of natural law to economics. His ideas grew out of an optimistic view of human nature and rationality that was heavily indebted to Locke. Humans, Smith believed, have drives and passions that they can direct and govern by means of reason and inherent mutual sympathy. Thus, Smith suggested, in seeking their own achievement and well-being, people are often "led by an invisible hand" simultaneously to benefit society as a whole. Smith's countryman and friend David Hume (1711–1776) investigated economics, politics, and religion but is best known today for his radical critique of the human capacity for knowing. He was the archskeptic, taking Locke's view of the limitations on human reason to the point of doubting the efficacy of any sensory data. His major exposition of these views, *An Enquiry Concerning Human Understanding* (1748), led to important innovations later in the century in the work of the German philosopher Immanuel Kant. At the time, though, Hume's arguments were almost contrary to the prevailing spirit that embraced empirical knowledge. Hume himself separated this work from his other writings on moral, political, and economic philosophy, which were more in tune with contemporary views.

THE ENCYCLOPEDIA

Mainstream confidence in empirical knowledge and in the intelligibility of the world is evident in the multiauthored *Encyclopédie (Encyclopedia)*. This seventeen-volume compendium of knowledge, criticism, and philosophy was assembled by leading philosophes in France and published there between 1751 and 1765. The volumes were designed to contain state-of-the-art knowledge about arts, sciences, technology, and philosophy. The guiding philosophy of the project, set forth by its chief editor, Denis Diderot (DEED-uh-row) (1713–1784), was a belief in the advancement of human happiness through the advancement of knowledge. The *Encyclopedia* was revolutionary in that it not only intrigued and inspired intellectuals, but also assisted thousands of government officials and professionals.

The encyclopedia project illustrates the political context of Enlightenment thought as well as its philosophical premises. The Catholic Church placed the work on the *Index of Prohibited Books*, and the French government might have barred its publication but for the fact that the official who would have made the decision was himself drawn to Enlightenment thinking. Many other officials, however, worked to suppress it. Thus, like Voltaire, the contributors to the *Encyclopedia* were admired by certain segments of the elite and persecuted by others in their official functions.

GENDER INEQUALITIES

The *Encyclopedia* reflects the complexities and limitations of Enlightenment thought on another issue: the position of women. One might expect that challenging accepted knowledge and traditional power arrangements would lead to arguments for the equality of women with men, and thus, for extending women's rights. Indeed, some contributors to the *Encyclopedia* blamed women's inequality with men not on inherent gender differences, but rather on laws and customs that had excluded women from education. However, other contributors blamed women, and not society, for their plight, or they argued that women had talents that fit them only for the domestic sphere.

Both positions were represented in Enlightenment thought as a whole. The assumption of the natural equality of all people provided a powerful ground for arguing the equality of women with men. Some thinkers, such as Mary Astell (1666–1731), challenged Locke's separation of family life from the public world of free, contractual relationships. "If absolute authority be not necessary in a state," she reasoned, "how comes it to be so in a family?" Most such thinkers advocated increased education for women, if only to make them fit to raise enlightened children. By 1800, the most radical thinkers were advocating full citizenship rights for women and equal rights to property, along with enhanced education.

The best-known proponent of those views was an Englishwoman, Mary Wollstonecraft (1759–1797), who wrote *A Vindication of the Rights of Woman* (1792). She assumed that most elite women would devote themselves to domestic duties, but she argued that without the responsibilities of citizenship, the leavening of education, and economic independence, women could be neither fully formed individuals nor worthy of their duties. "[F]or how can a being be generous who has nothing of its own? Or virtuous, who is not free?" she asked.[1] Working women, she concluded, needed political and economic rights simply to survive.

ROUSSEAU

A notion of women's limited capacities was one element in the deeply influential writings of **Jean-Jacques Rousseau** (1712–1778). Like Locke, Rousseau (roo-SO) could conceive of the free individual only as male, and he grounded both his criticism of the old order and his novel political ideas in an arbitrary division of gender roles. Rousseau's view of women was linked to a critique of the artificiality of elite, cosmopolitan society in which Enlightenment thought was then flourishing, and in which aristocratic women were fully involved. Rousseau believed in the educability of men but was as concerned with issues of character and emotional life as with cognitive knowledge. Society—particularly artificial courtly society—was corrupting, he believed. The

Jean-Jacques Rousseau
French philosophe who imagined an egalitarian society governed by the "general will" in *The Social Contract* and was a sharp critic of aristocratic society.

Rousseau Discusses the Benefits of Submitting to the General Will

In this excerpt from his Social Contract, Rousseau describes the relationship of individuals to the general will. Notice the wider-ranging benefits Rousseau believes men will enjoy in society as he envisions it. Rousseau is clearly interested in intellectual, moral, and emotional well-being.

I assume that men reach a point where the obstacles to their preservation in a state of nature prove greater than the strength that each man has to preserve himself in that state. Beyond this point, the primitive condition cannot endure, for then the human race will perish if it does not change its mode of existence ...

"How to find a form of association which will defend the person and goods of each member with the collective force of all, and under which each individual, while uniting himself with the others, obeys no one but himself, and remains as free as before." This is the fundamental problem to which the social contract holds the solution. ...

The passing from the state of nature to the civil society produces a remarkable change in man; it puts justice as a rule of conduct in the place of instinct, and gives his actions the moral quality they previously lacked. ... And although in civil society man surrenders some of the advantages that belong to the state of nature, he gains in return far greater ones; his faculties are so exercised and developed, his mind is so enlarged, his sentiments so ennobled, and his whole spirit so elevated that ... he should constantly bless the happy hour that lifted him for ever from the state of nature and from a stupid, limited animal made a creature of intelligence and a man. ...

For every individual as a man may have a private will contrary to, or different from, the general will that he has as a citizen. His private interest may speak with a very different voice from that of the public interest; his absolute and naturally independent existence may make him regard what he owes to the common cause as a gratuitous contribution, the loss of which would be less painful for others than the payment is onerous for him; and fancying that the artificial person which constitutes the state is a mere fictitious entity (since it is not a man), he might seek to enjoy the rights of a citizen without doing the duties of a subject. The growth of this kind of injustice would bring about the ruin of the body politic.

Hence, in order that the social pact shall not be an empty formula, it is tacitly implied in that commitment—which alone can give force to all others—that whoever refuses to obey the general will shall be constrained to do so by the whole body, which means nothing other than that he shall be forced to be free; for this is the necessary condition which, by giving each citizen to the nation, secures him against all personal dependence, it is the condition which shapes both the design and the working of the political machine, and which alone bestows justice on civil contracts—without it, such contracts would be absurd, tyrannical and liable to the grossest abuse.

QUESTIONS

1. What benefits will citizens find in society as Rousseau envisions it?

2. In what ways is Rousseau concerned with freedom?

Source: Jean-Jacques Rousseau, *The Social Contract*, translated by Maurice Cranston. Reprinted by permission of PFD on behalf of The Estate of Maurice Cranston. Copyright © 1968 by Maurice Cranston.

worthy citizen had to cultivate virtue and sensibility, not manners or refinement as courtiers do. Rousseau believed women should be the guarantors of the "natural" virtues of children and nurturers of the emotional life and character of men.

Rousseau's emphasis on the education and virtue of citizens was the underpinning of his larger political vision, set forth in *Du Contrat social* (*The Social Contract*, 1762). He imagined an egalitarian republic—possible particularly in small states, such as his native Geneva—in which men would consent to be governed because the government would determine and act in accordance with the "general will" of the citizens. The "general will" was not majority opinion, but rather what each citizen *would* want if he were fully informed and were acting in accordance with his highest nature. The "general will" became apparent whenever the citizens met as a body and made collective decisions, and it could be imposed on all inhabitants. (See the feature, "The Written Record: Rousseau Discusses the Benefits of Submitting to the General Will.") This was a breathtaking vision of direct democracy—but one with ominous possibilities, for Rousseau rejected the institutional checks on state authority proposed by Locke and Montesquieu.

Rousseau's work reflects, to an extreme degree, a central tension in Enlightenment thought: It was part of elite culture as well as its principal critic. The son of a humble family, Rousseau always sensed himself an outcast in the sophisticated world of Parisian salons. However, he depended on the patronage of several aristocratic women, even as he criticized the influence of such women. His own personal life did not match his prescriptions for others. He completely neglected to give his four children the education that he argued was vital; indeed, he abandoned them all to an orphanage. He was nevertheless profoundly important as a critic of an elite society still dominated by status and privilege.

The Growth of Public Opinion

It is impossible to appreciate the significance of the Enlightenment without understanding the degree to which it was a part of public life. Most of the philosophes came from modest backgrounds. They influenced the privileged elite of their day because of the social and political environment in which their ideas were elaborated. Indeed, one of the most important features of the Enlightenment was the creation of an informed body of public opinion that stood apart from court society.

THE READING PUBLIC

Increased literacy and access to books and other printed materials are an important part of the story. Perhaps more important, the kinds of reading that people favored began to change. We know from inventories made of people's belongings at the time of their deaths (required for inheritance laws) that books in the homes of ordinary people were no longer just traditional works such as devotional literature. Ordinary people now read secular and contemporary philosophical works. As the availability of such works increased, reading itself evolved from a reverential encounter with old ideas to a critical encounter with new ideas. Solitary reading for reflection and pleasure became more widespread.

New kinds of reading material were available. Regularly published periodicals in Great Britain, France, and Italy served as important means for the spread of enlightened opinion in the form of reviews, essays, and published correspondence. Some of these journals had been in existence since the second half of the seventeenth century, when they had begun as a means to circulate the new scientific work. Now subscribers included Americans anxious to keep up with intellectual life in Europe. In addition to newsletters and journals, newspapers, which were regularly published even in small cities throughout western and central Europe, circulated ideas. Newspapers were uniquely responsive to their readers. They began to carry advertisements, which both produced revenue for papers and widened readers' exposure to their own communities. Even more important was the inauguration of letters to the editor. Newspapers thus became venues for the often rapid exchange of news and opinions.

Habits of reading and responding to written material changed not only because of this increased and changing reading matter, but also because of changes in the social environment. In the eighteenth century, forerunners of the modern lending libraries made their debut. In Paris, for a fee, one could join a *salle de lecture* (sahl duh lek-TOOR) (literally, a "reading room") where the latest works were available to any member. Booksellers, whose numbers increased dramatically, found ways to meet readers' demands for inexpensive access to reading matter. One might pay for the right to read a book in the bookshop itself. Newspapers were available in such shops and in cafés. In short, new sites encouraged people to see themselves not just as readers, but as members of a reading public.

THE SALONS

Among the most famous and most important of these venues were the Parisian **salons**, regular gatherings in private homes, where Voltaire and others read their works-in-progress aloud and discussed them. Several Parisian women—mostly wealthy, but of modest social status—invited courtiers, bureaucrats, and intellectuals to meet in their homes at regular times each week. The *salonnières* (sal-on-YAIR) (salon leaders) themselves read widely in order to facilitate the exchange of ideas among their guests. This mediating function was crucial to the success of the salons. Manners and polite conversation had been a defining feature of aristocratic life since the seventeenth century, but they had largely been means of displaying status and safeguarding honor. The leadership of the salonnières and the protected environment they provided away from court life enabled a further evolution of "polite society" to occur: Anyone with appropriate manners could participate in conversation as an equal. The assumption of equality in turn enabled conversation to turn away from maintaining the status quo to questioning it.

salons Regular gatherings in eighteenth-century Parisian private homes, where Voltaire and other philosophes read and discussed their works; the exchange of ideas was facilitated by female *salonnières* (salon leaders).

The influence of salons was extended by the wide correspondence networks the salonnières maintained. Perhaps the most famous salonnière in her day, Marie-Thérèse Geoffrin (zhoh-FRAN) (1699–1777) corresponded with Catherine the Great, the reform-minded empress of Russia, as well as with philosophes outside Paris and with interested would-be members of her circle. The

The Growth of the Book Trade   Book ownership dramatically increased in the eighteenth century, and a wide range of secular works—from racy novelettes to philosophical tracts—was available in print. In this rendering of a bookshop, shipments of books have arrived from around Europe. Notice the artist's optimism in the great variety of persons, from the peasant with a scythe to a white-robed cleric, who are drawn to the shop by "Minerva" (the Roman goddess of wisdom).   (Musée des Beaux-Arts de Dijon)

ambassador of Naples regularly attended her salon while in Paris and exchanged weekly letters with her when home in Italy. He reflected on the importance of salon leaders such as Geoffrin when he wrote from Naples lamenting, "[Our gatherings here] are getting farther away from the character and tone of those of France, despite all [our] efforts. … There is no way to make Naples resemble Paris unless we find a woman to guide us, organize us, *Geoffrinise* us."[2]

Various clubs, local academies, and learned and secret societies, such as Masonic lodges, copied some features of the salons of Paris. Hardly any town was without a private society that functioned both as a forum for political and philosophical discussion and as an elite social club. Here mingled doctors, lawyers, and local officials—some of whom enjoyed the fruits of the political system in offices and patronage. In Scotland, universities were flourishing centers of Enlightenment thought, but political clubs in Glasgow and Edinburgh also were centers of debate.

Ideas circulated beyond the membership of salons and clubs, in turn, by means of print. Newsletters reporting the goings-on at salons in Paris were produced by some participants. The exchange and spread of Enlightenment ideas, regardless of the method used, encouraged a type of far-reaching political debate that had never before existed, except possibly in seventeenth-century England. The greatest impact of the Enlightenment, particularly in France, was not the creation of any specific program for political or social change. Rather, its supreme legacy was an informed body of public opinion that could generate change.

The Arts in the Age of Reason

The Enlightenment reverberated throughout all aspects of cultural life. Just as the market for books and the reading public expanded, so did the audience for works of art in the growing leisured urban circles of Paris and other great cities. The modern cultured public—a public of concertgoers and art gallery enthusiasts—began to make its first appearance and constituted another arena in which public opinion was shaped. Courts around Europe continued to sponsor composers, musicians, and painters by providing both patronage and audiences. Yet some performances began to take place in theaters and halls outside the courts in venues more accessible to the public. And, beginning in 1737, one section of the Louvre (LOO-vruh) palace in Paris was devoted annually to public exhibitions of painting and sculpture (though by royally sponsored and approved artists). In both France and Britain, public discussion of art began to occur in published reviews and criticisms: The role of art critic was born. Works of art were also sold by public means, such as auctions. As works became more available, demand grew and production increased.

The Moralizing Message of Neoclassical Art   The French painter Jacques-Louis David portrays the mourning of the Trojan hero Hector by his wife, Andromache. This kind of art tried to depict and encourage virtuous feelings. David was well known for depicting his subjects with simple gestures—such as the extended arm of Andromache here—that were intended to portray sincere emotion.   (Private Collection/The Stapleton Collection/ Bridgeman Art Library International)

In subject matter and style, these various art forms exhibited great variety. A favorite theme of painters was an exploration of private life and emotion sometimes called the "cult of sensibility." Frequently, these works depicted private scenes of upper-class life, especially moments of intimate conversation or flirtation.

The cult of sensibility was also nurtured by increased literacy, greater access to books, and the need to retreat from the elaborate artifice of court life. The novel became an increasingly important genre for exploring social problems and human relationships. Daniel Defoe, in *Robinson Crusoe* (1717), used realism for purposes of social commentary, while the novels of Samuel Richardson (1689–1761)—*Pamela* (1740) and *Clarissa* (1747–1748)—explored personal psychology and passion. The cult of sensibility was not mere entertainment; it also carried the political and philosophical message, echoing Rousseau's work, that honest emotion was a "natural" virtue and that courtly manners, by contrast, were both irrational and degrading. The enormous popularity of Rousseau's own novels, *La Nouvelle Héloïse* (1761) and *Emile* (1762), for example, came from the fact that their intense emotional appeal was simultaneously felt to be uplifting.

A revival of classical subjects and styles after the middle of the century evoked what were thought to be the pure and timeless values of classical heroes. This revival revealed the influence of Enlightenment thought because the artists assumed the educability of their audience by means of example. Classical revival architecture illustrated a belief in order, symmetry, and proportion. Americans are familiar with its evocations because it became the architecture of their public buildings, but even churches were built in this style in eighteenth-century Europe. The classical movement in music reflected both the cult of sensibility and the classicizing styles in the visual arts. Embodied in the works of Austrians Franz Josef Haydn (1732–1809) and Wolfgang Amadeus Mozart (1756–1791), this movement saw the clarification of musical structures, such as the modern sonata and symphony, and enabled melody to take center stage.

Another trend in art and literature was a fascination with nature and with the seemingly "natural" in human culture—less "developed" or more historically distant societies. One of the most popular printed works in the middle of the century was the alleged translation of the poems of Ossian (AHSH-un), a third-century Scots Highland poet. Early English, German, Norse, and other folktales were also "discovered" (in some cases invented) and published, some in several editions during the century. Folk life, other cultures, and untamed nature itself thus began to be celebrated at the very time they were being more definitively conquered. (See the feature, "The Visual Record: Gardens.") Ossian, for example, was celebrated just as the Scottish Highlands were being pillaged and pacified by the English after the clans' support for a rival claimant to the English throne. Once purged of any threat, the exotic image of another culture (even the folk culture of one's own society) could be a spur to the imagination. The remote became romantic and offered a sense of distance from which to measure one's own sophistication and superiority.

SECTION SUMMARY

- The "Enlightenment" was an intellectual movement that brought confidence in human reason and the workings of natural law from the sciences into political and social thought.

- A wide range of thinkers, known as philosophes, contributed to Enlightenment thought; opinions about religion, the limits of human reason, the equality of the sexes, and other issues were energetically debated.

- Enlightenment ideas were spread by publications, such as newspapers, and were discussed in cafés and salons; an informed body of public opinion independent of government and the court was created for the first time.

- Art became more accessible to the public; works of art became more thematically varied than before, though many explored "natural" emotion.

EUROPEAN STATES IN THE AGE OF ENLIGHTENMENT

To what extent did the activities of rulers, particularly "enlightened despots," reflect Enlightenment ideals, and to what extent did they reflect traditional concerns of state power?

Mindful of the lessons to be learned from the civil war in England, and eager to repeat the achievements of Louis XIV, European rulers in the eighteenth century continued their efforts to govern with greater effectiveness. Some, like the rulers of Prussia and Russia, were encouraged in their efforts by Enlightenment ideas that stressed the need for reforms in law, economy, and government. Like Voltaire, they believed that monarchs could be agents for change. The changes were uneven, however, and at times, owed as much to traditional efforts at better government as to "enlightened" opinion. However limited their "enlightened" policies, monarchs were changing their views of themselves and their public images from self-aggrandizing absolutist to diligent servant of the state. The state was increasingly seen as separate from the ruler, with dramatic consequences for the future.

France During the Enlightenment

It is one of the seeming paradoxes of the era of the Enlightenment that critical thought about society and politics flourished in France, an autocratic state. Yet France was blessed with a well-educated elite, a tradition of scientific inquiry, and a legacy of cultured court life that, since the early days of Louis XIV, had become the model for all Europe (see pages 446–447). French was the international intellectual language, and France was the most fertile center of cultural life. Both Adam Smith and David Hume, for example, spent portions of their careers in Paris and were welcomed into Parisian salons. In fact, the French capital was an environment that encouraged debate precisely because of the juxtaposition of the vibrant new intellectual climate with the institutional rigidities of its political system. In France, patronage and privilege were the sole avenues to power, a system that excluded many talented and eager members of the elite.

The French state continued to embody fundamental contradictions. As under Louis XIV, the Crown sponsored scientific research, subsidized commerce and exploration, and tried to rationalize the royal administration. Royal administrators tried to chip away at the traditional privileges that hampered effective government—such as the exemption most nobles enjoyed from taxation. However, the Crown also continued to claim the right to govern autocratically, and the king was supported both ideologically and institutionally by the Catholic Church. A merchant in the bustling port of Bordeaux might be glad of the royal navy's protection of the colonies, and of the Crown's efforts to build better roads for trade within France. However, with his fellow Masons, he would fume when church officials publicly burned the works of Rousseau and resent his exclusion from any formal voice in politics.

The problems facing the French government were made worse by two circumstances: first, the strength of the elites' defense of their privileges, and second, mounting government debt from foreign wars. Fiscal reform was increasingly urgent, yet entrenched elites stood in the way of change. Louis XIV was followed on the throne by his 5-year-old great-grandson, Louis XV (r. 1715–1774). During the regency early in his reign, the supreme law courts, the parlements, reclaimed the right to object to royal edicts and thus to exercise some control over the enactment of law. Throughout Louis XV's reign, his administration often locked horns with the parlements, particularly as royal ministers tried various schemes to cope with financial crises.

The power of the parlements came not only from their routine role in government, but also from the fact that parlementaires were all legally noble and owned their offices, just as a great nobleman owned his country estate. In addition, the parlements were the only institutions that could legitimately check royal power. As such, they were often supported in their opposition to royal policies by the weight of public opinion. On the one hand, enlightened opinion believed in the rationality of doing away with privileges, such as the ownership of offices. On the other hand, the role of consultative bodies and the separation of powers touted by Montesquieu, himself a parlementaire, were much prized. And even our Bordeaux merchant, who had little in common with privileged officeholders, might nevertheless see the parlementaires' resistance as his best protection from royal tyranny. The parlementaires, however, usually used their power for protecting the status quo.

A further check on reform was the character of the king himself. Louis XV displayed none of the kingly qualities of his great-grandfather. He was neither pleasant nor affable, and he was lazy. He did not give the "rationality" of royal government a good name. By the end of his reign, he was roundly despised. By the late 1760s, the weight of government debt from foreign wars finally forced the king into action. He threw his support behind the reforming schemes of his chancellor, Nicolas de Maupeou (mo-POO), who dissolved the parlements early in 1771 and created new law courts whose judges would not enjoy independent power.

The Crown lost control of reform when Louis died soon after, in 1774. His 20-year-old grandson, Louis XVI, well-meaning but insecure, allowed the complete restoration of the parlements. Further reform efforts, sponsored by the king and several talented ministers, came to nothing because of parlementary opposition. Not surprisingly, from about the middle of the century,

Gardens

What is a garden? Like most of the art forms that we see habitually, the garden is difficult to analyze or even to think of as an art form. Like the buildings they surround, however, gardens have much to tell us about human habits and values. Let us examine these eighteenth-century gardens for evidence of contemporaries' attitudes toward nature and their relationship with it.

Look at the two English-style gardens illustrated here. The first is next to the Governor's Mansion in Williamsburg, the capital of the English colony of Virginia. Construction of this garden began at the end of the seventeenth century; the photograph shows the restored gardens that tourists may visit today. The second garden, from the private estate of West Wycombe in England, looks very different—much more like a natural landscape. The engraving reproduced here dates from the 1770s. The two gardens represent distinct epochs in the development of the garden, hence the differences between them. However, each of these gardens in its own way celebrates human domination of nature.

This symbolic domination of nature is more obvious to us in the Williamsburg garden. The lawns and hedges are trimmed in precise geometrical shapes and are laid out, with the walkways, in straight lines. This "palace garden"

was a small English variant of the classical garden developed in France—most spectacularly at the Versailles Palace—and then imitated throughout Europe during the seventeenth century. The garden at Versailles is so vast that at many points, all of nature visible to the eye is nature disciplined by humans.

We can think of such gardens as pieces of architecture, because that is how they were originally conceived. The design originated in the enclosed courtyard gardens of the homes of classical antiquity. The straight lines and square shapes of these gardens mimic the buildings they are attached to. In fact, these seventeenth- and eighteenth-century gardens were usually laid out as an extension of the buildings themselves. Notice the wide staircase that descends from the central axis of the Governor's Mansion into the central walkway of the garden. Other architectural details, such as the benches positioned at the ends of various walkways, add to the sense of the garden as an exterior room. The garden symbolizes the taming of nature into a pleasing vision of order and regularity.

However, the later eighteenth-century garden represents even greater confidence in the human relationship with nature, although it does not appear to do so at first glance. The extensive garden at first seems to be nature itself

Governor's Mansion and Formal Gardens at Williamsburg, Virginia (© Robert Llewellyn)

Landscape Garden at West Wycombe, England (Courtesy of the Trustees of the British Museum)

plus a few added details, such as the statuary, and a few improvements, such as the grass kept trim by the workers in the foreground. Our familiarity with such landscapes—in our own suburban yards—keeps us from immediately perceiving how contrived such a landscape is. Nature, however, does not intersperse dense stands of trees or clumps of shrubbery with green expanses of lawns. Nor does nature conveniently leave portions of a hillside bare of trees to provide a view of the water from a palatial house on the hill (to the left). Note also that the waterfall cascading over rocks and statuary flows from an artificial lake, neatly bordered by a path.

This kind of garden reflects Enlightenment optimism about humans' ability to understand and work with nature. Such gardens were asymmetrical: Paths were usually curved, and lakes and ponds were irregularly shaped, as they would be in nature. Trees and shrubs were allowed to maintain their natural form. Nevertheless, this landscaping conveys a powerful message of confidence and order. Humans cannot bend or distort nature to their own ends, but they can live in harmony with it as they manage it and enjoy its beneficence. People were freed from regarding nature as hostile and needing to be fought. In this garden, one lives with nature but improves on it. The workers cutting the

grass do not detract from the engraving but rather make the scene more compelling.

This brand of landscape gardening appeared in the English colonies across the Atlantic by the end of the eighteenth century. One of the best examples is at Monticello, Thomas Jefferson's Virginia estate, first designed in the 1770s and constructed and improved over the remainder of Jefferson's life (1743–1826). If you tour Monticello, you will notice a curving garden path bordered by flowers in season, with mature trees scattered here and there. Jefferson planned every inch of this largely random-looking outdoor space, just as he planned the regimented fruit and vegetable garden that borders it. The older, classical style of the Williamsburg garden is partly explained by its earlier date and also because this more aggressively controlling style lasted longer in the American colonies than in Europe, perhaps because "nature" seemed more wild and more formidable in the New World.

QUESTIONS

1. How do the two gardens depicted here reflect two different visions of human power over nature?

2. What explains the evolution of styles, over the eighteenth century, in this art form?

there had been calls to revive the Estates General, the representative assembly last convened in 1614. By the time an Estates General was finally called in the wake of further financial problems in 1788, the enlightened elites' habit of carrying on political debate and criticism outside the actual corridors of power, as well as their accumulated mistrust of the Crown, had created a volatile situation.

Monarchy and Parliament in Great Britain

After the deaths of William (d. 1702) and Mary (d. 1694), the British crown passed to Mary's sister, Anne (r. 1702–1714), and then to a collateral line descended from Elizabeth Stuart (d. 1662), sister of the beheaded Charles I. Elizabeth had married Frederick, elector of the Palatinate (and had reigned with him briefly in Bohemia at the start of the Thirty Years' War; see page 427), and her descendants were Germans, now electors of Hanover. The new British sovereign in 1714, George I (r. 1714–1727), was both a foreigner and a man of mediocre abilities. Moreover, his claim to the throne was immediately contested by Catholic descendants of James II (see page 455), who attempted to depose him in 1715 and later his son, George II (r. 1727–1760), in 1745.

The 1745 uprising was the more serious threat. The son of the rival Stuart claimant to the throne, Charles (known in legend as Bonnie Prince Charlie), landed on the west coast of Scotland, with French assistance. He led his forces south into England. Most of the British army and George II himself were on the Continent, fighting in the War of the Austrian Succession (see page 522). Scotland had been formally united with England in 1707 (hence, the term *Great Britain* after that time), and Charles had found some support among Scots dissatisfied with the economic and political results of that union.

But the vast majority of Britons, Scottish or English, did not want the civil war that Charles's challenge inevitably meant, especially on behalf of a Catholic claimant who relied on support from Britain's great rival, France. Charles's army, made up mostly of poor Highland clansmen, was destroyed at the Battle of Culloden (cull-UH-dun) in April 1746 by British army units, hastily returned from abroad. Charles fled back to France, and the British government used the failed uprising as justification for the brutal and forceful integration of the still-remote Scottish Highlands into the British state.

Despite this serious challenge to the new dynasty and the harsh response it occasioned, the British state, overall, enjoyed a period of relative stability as well as innovation in the eighteenth century. The civil war of the seventeenth century had reaffirmed both the need for a strong monarchy and the role of Parliament in defending elite interests. The power of Parliament had recently been reinforced by the Act of Settlement, by which the German Protestant heir to Queen Anne had been chosen in 1701. By excluding the Catholic Stuarts from the throne and establishing the line of succession, this document reasserted that Parliament determined the legitimacy of the monarchy. In fact, the act claimed greater parliamentary authority over foreign and domestic policy in the aftermath of William's constant involvement in war (see page 450).

In the eighteenth century, cooperation between monarchy and Parliament evolved further as Parliament became a more sophisticated and secure institution. Political parties—that is, distinct groups within the elite favoring certain foreign and domestic policies—came into existence. Two groups, the Whigs and the Tories, had begun to form during the reign of Charles II (d. 1685). The Whigs (named derisively by their opponents with a Scottish term for horse thieves) had resisted Charles's pro-French policies and his efforts to tolerate Catholicism. They had wholly opposed his brother and successor, James II. Initially, the Whigs favored an aggressive foreign policy against continental opponents, particularly France. The Tories (whose name was also a taunt, referring to Irish cattle rustlers) leaned toward a conservative view of their own role, favoring isolationism in foreign affairs and deference toward monarchical authority. Whigs generally represented the interests of the great aristocrats or wealthy merchants or gentry. Tories more often represented the interests of provincial gentry and the traditional concerns of landholding and local administration.

The Whigs were the dominant influence in government through most of the century to 1770. William and Mary, as well as Queen Anne, favored Whig religious and foreign policies. The loyalty of many Tories was called into question by their support for a Stuart, not Hanoverian, succession at Anne's death in 1714. The long Whig dominance of government was also ensured by the talents of Robert Walpole, a member of Parliament who functioned virtually as a prime minister from 1722 to 1742.

Walpole (1676–1745) was from a minor gentry family and was brought into government in 1714 with other Whig ministers in George I's new regime. An extremely talented politician, he took advantage of the mistakes of other ministers over the years and, in 1722, became both the first lord of the treasury and chancellor of the exchequer. No post or title of "prime minister" yet existed, but the great contribution of Walpole's tenure was to create that office in fact, if not officially. He chose to maintain peace abroad when and where he could and thus presided over a period of recovery and relative prosperity.

Initially, Walpole was helped in his role as go-between for king and Parliament by George I's own limitations. The king rarely attended meetings of his own council of ministers and was hampered by his limited command of English. Gradually, the Privy Council of the king became something resembling a modern cabinet dominated by a prime minister. By the end of the century, the notions of "loyal opposition" to the Crown within Parliament and parliamentary responsibility for policy had taken root.

In some respects, the maturation of political life in Parliament resembled the lively political debates in the salons of Paris. In both cases, political life was being legitimized on a new basis. In England, however, that legitimation was enshrined in a legislative institution, which made it especially effective and resilient. Parliament was not yet in any sense representative of the British population, however. Because of strict property qualifications, only about 200,000 adult men could vote. In addition, representation was very uneven and heavily favored traditional landed wealth. Some constituencies with only a few dozen voters sent members to Parliament. Many of these "pocket boroughs" were under the control of (in the pockets of) powerful local families who could intimidate the local electorate, particularly in the absence of secret ballots.

Political Satire in England This gruesome image, showing England being disemboweled by members of the government, criticizes the government's acceptance of a treaty with France. Satirical images such as this one were increasingly part of the lively and more open political life in eighteenth-century England. (Courtesy of the Trustees of the British Museum)

Movements for reform of representation in Parliament began in the late 1760s as professionals, such as doctors and lawyers, with movable (as opposed to landed) property and merchants in booming but underrepresented cities began to demand the vote. As the burden of taxation grew—the result of the recently concluded Seven Years' War (discussed later in this chapter)—these groups felt increasingly deprived of representation. Indeed, many felt kinship with the American colonists who opposed increased taxation by the British government on these same grounds and revolted in 1775.

However, the reform movement faltered over the issue of religion. In 1780, a tentative effort by Parliament to extend some civil rights to British Catholics provoked rioting in London (known as the Gordon Riots, after one of the leaders). The riots lasted for eight days and claimed three hundred lives. Pressure for parliamentary reform had been building, but this specter of a popular movement out of control temporarily ended the drive for reform by disenfranchised elites.

"Enlightened" Monarchy

Arbitrary monarchical power might seem antithetical to Enlightenment thought. After all, the Enlightenment stressed the reasonableness of human beings and their capacity to discern and act in accord with natural law. Yet, monarchy seemed an ideal instrument of reform to Voltaire and to many of his contemporaries. The work of curtailing the influence of the church, reforming legal codes, and eliminating barriers to economic activity might be done more efficiently by a powerful monarch than by other available means. Historians have labeled a number of rulers of this era "enlightened despots" because of the arbitrary nature of their power, yet the enlightened or reformist uses to which they put it.

SCANDINAVIA

In Denmark, in 1784, a reform-minded group of nobles, led by the young crown prince Frederick (governing on behalf of his mentally ill father), began to apply Enlightenment remedies to the kingdom's economic problems. This move was a bold departure from the past because, in Denmark, the Crown had governed without significant challenge from the landholding nobility since the mid-seventeenth century and the nobility enjoyed ironclad domination of the peasantry. The reformers encouraged freer trade and sought, above all, to improve agriculture by elevating the status of the peasantry. With improved legal status and with land reform, which enabled some peasants to own the land they worked for the first time, agricultural productivity in Denmark rose dramatically. These reforms constitute some of the clearest achievements of any of the "enlightened" rulers.

In contrast to Denmark, Sweden had a relatively unbroken tradition of noble involvement in government, stemming in part from its marginal economy and the consequent stake of the nobility in the Crown's aggressive foreign policy. Since Sweden's eclipse as a major power after the Great Northern War (see page 462), factions of the Swedish parliament, the Diet, had fought over the reins of government, somewhat like the emerging political parties in Britain. Ironically, it was in Sweden, and not Denmark, that an "enlightened despot" emerged. King Gustav III (r. 1771–1796) staged a coup to regain control of policy from the Diet and began an ambitious program of reform of the government. Restrictions on trade in grain and other economic controls were liberalized, the legal system was rationalized, the death penalty was strictly limited, and legal torture was abolished.

Despite his achievements, Gustav III suffered the consequences of advancing reform by autocratic means in a kingdom with a strong tradition of representative government. Gustav eventually tried to deflect the criticisms of the nobility by reviving grandiose—but completely unrealistic—schemes for the reconquest of Baltic territory. In 1796, he was mortally wounded by an assassin hired by disgruntled nobles.

PRUSSIA

Enlightened despotism
Term for the reform-oriented rule of eighteenth-century monarchs. Enlightened despots applied Enlightenment remedies to economic problems and encouraged education and legal reform, but did not dismantle elites' privileges or share their own power.

Frederick the Great
Autocratic king of Prussia who transformed the country into a major military power and also sponsored "enlightened" reforms.

"Enlightened despotism" aptly describes the rule of Frederick II of Prussia (r. 1740–1786), known as **Frederick the Great**. Much of the time, Frederick resided in his imperial electorate of Brandenburg, near its capital, Berlin. His scattered states, which he extended by seizing new lands, are referred to as Prussia rather than Brandenburg-Prussia because members of his family were now kings of Prussia thanks to their ambitions and the weakness of the Polish state, of which Prussia had once been a dependent duchy. In many ways, the Prussian state *was* its military victories, for Frederick's bold moves and the policies of his father, grandfather, and great-grandfather committed the state's resources to a military presence of dramatic proportions. Prussia was on the European stage at all only because of that driving commitment.

The institutions that constituted the state and linked the various provinces under one administration were dominated by the needs of the military. Frederick II's father, Frederick William (r. 1713–1740), had added an efficient provincial recruiting system to the state's central institutions, which he also further consolidated. But in many other respects, the Prussian state was in its infancy. There was no tradition of political participation—even by elites—and little chance of cultivating any. Nor was there any political or social room for maneuver at the lower part of the social scale. The rulers of Prussia had long ago given in to the aristocracy's demand for tighter control over peasant labor on their own lands in return for their support of the monarchy. The rulers relied on the nobles for local administration and army commands. Thus, the kinds of social, judicial, or political reforms that Frederick could hope to carry out without undermining his own power were starkly limited.

Frederick tried to modernize agricultural methods and simultaneously to improve the condition of the peasants, but he met stiff resistance from the noble landholders. He did succeed in abolishing serfdom in some regions. He tried to stimulate the economy by sponsoring state industries and trading monopolies, but too few resources and too little initiative from the tightly controlled merchant communities stymied his plans. Simplifying and codifying the inherited jumble of local laws was a goal of every ruler. A law code published in 1794, after Frederick's death, was partly the product of his efforts.

Frederick's views of the role of Enlightenment thought reflect the limitations of his situation. One doesn't have to lead a frontal assault on prejudices consecrated by time, he believed; instead, one must be tolerant of superstition because it will always have a hold on the masses. Perhaps his most distinctive "enlightened" characteristic was the seriousness with which he took his task as ruler. He was energetic and disciplined to a fault. In his book, *Anti-Machiavel* (1741), he argued that a ruler has a moral obligation to work for the betterment of the state. He styled himself as the "first servant" or steward of the state. However superficial this claim may appear, Frederick compares favorably with Louis XV of France, who, having a far more wealthy and flexible society to work with, did much less.

AUSTRIA

The Habsburg ruler **Maria Theresa** of Austria (r. 1740–1780) was guided more by traditional concerns for effective rule and compassion for her subjects than by Enlightenment ideas. After surviving the near dismemberment of Austrian territories in the War of the Austrian Succession (see page 522), she embarked on an energetic program of reform to improve the administration of her territories. "Austria," it must be remembered, is a term of convenience; the state was a very medieval-looking hodgepodge that included present-day Austria, the kingdoms of Bohemia and Hungary, the Austrian Netherlands, and lands in northern Italy. Among her more successful reforms were improved assessment and collection of taxes to tap the wealth of her subjects more effectively and thus better defend all her domains. She improved her subjects' access to justice and limited the exploitation of serfs by landlords. She made primary schooling universal and compulsory, in order to better train peasants for the army. Although the policy was far from fully implemented at the time of her death, hers was the first European state with so ambitious an education policy. Maria Theresa accomplished all of this without being particularly "enlightened" personally. She was a devout Catholic who cherished orthodoxy in religious matters. She did not welcome Enlightenment philosophy to her court and feared freedom of the press.

Maria Theresa Habsburg archduchess of Austria and queen of Hungary and Bohemia who reformed and centralized the administration of her Austrian and Bohemian lands.

Many of the ministers and bureaucrats who implemented Maria Theresa's reforms were themselves well versed in "enlightened" ideas. The diverse character of the Habsburg lands meant that some members of the governing elite came from the Netherlands and from Italy, where sympathy for the Enlightenment was well rooted by comparison with the relatively poorer and more rural society of the Austrian hinterland. Moreover, the language of the Habsburg court was French (Maria Theresa spoke it fluently); thus, no amount of local censorship—which, in any case, Maria Theresa relaxed—could prevent the governing class from reading and absorbing Enlightenment philosophy in its original language.

Maria Theresa was followed on the throne by her two sons, Joseph II (r. 1780–1790) and Leopold II (r. 1790–1792), each of whom counted himself a follower of the Enlightenment. After his mother's death, Joseph II carried out bold initiatives that she had not attempted, including freedom of the press, significant freedom of religion, and the abolition of serfdom in Habsburg lands.

Like Frederick the Great, Joseph regarded himself as a servant of the state. Also like Frederick, he was limited in his reform program by the economic and social rigidities of the society he ruled; he could not directly assault the privileges of great landholders, on whose wealth the state depended. His despotic methods—he imposed reforms autocratically—antagonized many of these powerful subjects. His more able brother, Leopold, spent much of his two-year reign dexterously saving reforms enacted by his mother and, especially, his brother in the face of mounting opposition.

RUSSIA

Perhaps the most powerful ruler with a claim to the title "enlightened despot" was Catherine, empress of Russia (r. 1762–1796). **Catherine the Great**, as she came to be called, was the true heir of Peter the Great in her abilities, policies, and ambitions. Her determination and political acumen were evident soon after she was brought to the Russian court from her native Germany in 1745. After enduring brutal treatment by her husband, Tsar Peter III, Catherine engineered a coup in which he was killed, and then ruled alone for more than thirty years.

Catherine the Great Empress of Russia who, through an astute policy of wars and alliances, expanded her country's borders. An "enlightened despot," she advanced the westernizing reforms begun by Peter the Great.

Like any successful ruler of her age, Catherine counted territorial aggrandizement among her chief achievements: she expanded Russian territory at the expense of the Ottoman Empire and Poland-Lithuania.

Nevertheless, Catherine counted herself a sincere follower of the Enlightenment. Like Frederick, she attempted to take an active role in the European intellectual community; she corresponded with Voltaire over the course of many years and acted as patron to the encyclopedist Diderot. One of Catherine's boldest political moves was the secularization of church lands. Although Peter the Great had extended government control of the Russian Orthodox Church, he had not touched church lands. Catherine also licensed private publishing houses; the number of books published in Russia tripled during her reign. This enriched cultural life was one of the principal causes of the flowering of Russian literature that began in the early nineteenth century.

The stamp of the Enlightenment on Catherine's policies is also clearly visible in her attempts at legal reform. In 1767, she convened a legislative commission and provided it with a guiding

Catherine the Great as a young woman   This portrait of Catherine was painted when she first came to the Russian court from her native Germany in 1745. Catherine wears formal court dress and the portrait introduces her as a "Grand Duchess," a Russian title reserved for the royal family. (Portrait of Grand Duchess Yekatrina Alexeyevna, later Catherine II, c.1745, Grooth, Georg Christoph (1716-49)/Hermitage, St. Petersburg, Russia/The Bridgeman Art Library)

document, the *Instruction*, which she had written herself. The commission was remarkable because it included representatives of all classes, including peasants. Catherine hoped for a general codification of law as well as reforms, such as the abolition of torture and capital punishment—reforms that made the *Instruction* radical enough to be banned from publication in other countries. She did not propose changing the legal status of serfs, however, and class conflict made the commission unworkable in the end. Most legal reforms were eventually accomplished piecemeal and favored the interests of landed gentry.

Like the Austrian rulers, Catherine undertook far-reaching administrative reform to create more effective local units of government but, again, political imperatives were fundamental, and reforms in local government strengthened the hand of the gentry. The legal subjection of peasants in serfdom was also extended as a matter of state policy to help win the allegiance of landholders in newly acquired areas. In Russia, as in Prussia and Austria, oppression of the peasantry continued because the monarch wanted to ensure the allegiance of the elites who lived from the peasants' labor. Catherine particularly valued the cooperation of elites because the expanding Russian state was incorporating new peoples, such as the Tatars in the Crimea, and attempting to manage its relationships with border peoples such as the Cossacks. Catherine's reign witnessed one of the most massive and best-organized peasant rebellions of the century. Occurring in 1773, the rebellion expressed the grievances of the thousands of peasants who joined its ranks and called for the abolition of serfdom. The revolt took its name, however, from its Cossack leader, Emelian Pugachev (poo-guh-CHOFF) (d. 1775), and reflected also the Cossacks' resistance to centralized control. The dramatic dilemmas faced by Catherine illustrate both the promise and the costs of state formation throughout Europe. State consolidation permitted the imposition of internal peace, coordinated economic policy, and reform of justice, but it came at the price of greater—in some cases much greater—control and coercion of the population.

SECTION SUMMARY

- In France, the royal government tried unsuccessfully to eliminate the privileges of nobility, which limited state revenue and kept most people shut out of the political process.

- The Parliament in England was securely established as a part of government; political parties, representing differing interests among the elite, began to develop.

- "Enlightened despots," such as Frederick the Great in Prussia, ruled autocratically but used their power for some reforms in law, education, and public welfare.

THE WIDENING WORLD OF TRADE AND PRODUCTION

How and why did trade and production increase in the eighteenth century?

The importance of international trade and colonial possessions to the states of western Europe grew enormously in the eighteenth century (see **MAP 18.2**). Between 1715 and 1785, Britain's trade with North America rose from 19 to 34 percent of its total trade, and its trade with Asia and Africa rose from 7 to 19 percent of the total. By the end of the century, more than half of all British trade was carried on outside Europe; for France, the figure was more than a third. Plantation agriculture based on slave labor in European colonies created profits and products that drove much of this trade. Equally profound changes were occurring in the European countryside. Population, production, and consumption were beginning to grow beyond the bounds that all preceding generations had lived within and taken for granted.

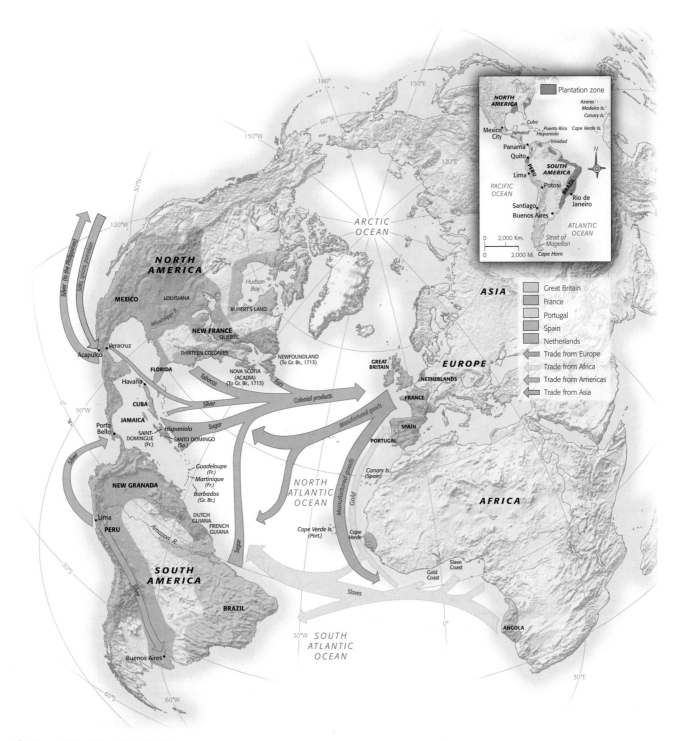

🌐 **Map 18.1—The Atlantic Economy, ca. 1750**

The triangle trade linked Europe, Africa, and European colonies in the Americas. The most important component of this trade for Europe was the plantation agriculture of the Caribbean islands, which depended on enslaved Africans for labor.

The Atlantic World: Expanding Commerce and the Slave Trade

European commercial and colonial energies were concentrated in the Atlantic world in the eighteenth century because the profits were greatest there. The colonial population of British North America grew from about 250,000 in 1700 to about 1.7 million by 1760. The densely settled New England colonies provided a market for manufactured goods from the mother country, although

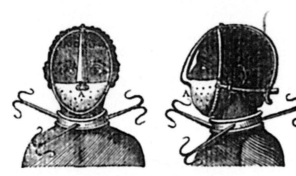

The Treatment of Slaves on Caribbean Plantations
These images of the brutal treatment of slaves on West Indian plantations come from a report published in England designed to convince the British public of the horrors of slavery. At top, a husband and wife are violently separated after being sold to different slave owners. At bottom, a mouthpiece and neck guard are used to prevent escape. The treatment of slaves described here is also documented in other surviving accounts from the eighteenth century. (New York Public Library/Art Resource, NY)

they produced little by way of raw materials or bulk goods on which traders could make a profit. The colonies of Maryland and Virginia produced tobacco, the Carolinas rice and indigo (a dyestuff). England re-exported all three throughout Europe at considerable profit.

The French in New France, only 56,000 in 1740, were vastly outnumbered by British colonists. Nevertheless, the French had successfully expanded their control of territory in Canada. Settlements sprang up between the outposts of Montreal and Quebec on the St. Lawrence River. Despite resistance, the French extended their fur trapping—the source of most of the profits New France generated—west and north along the Great Lakes, consolidating their hold by building forts at strategic points. They penetrated as far as the modern Canadian province of Manitoba, where they cut into the British trade run out of Hudson Bay. The French also contested the mouth of the St. Lawrence River and the Gulf of St. Lawrence with the British. The British held Nova Scotia and Newfoundland, the French controlled parts of Cape Breton Island, and both states fished the surrounding waters.

The commercial importance of these North American holdings, as well as those in Asia, was dwarfed by the European states' Caribbean possessions, however. The British held Jamaica, Barbados, and the Leeward Islands; the French, Guadeloupe and Martinique; the Spanish, Cuba and Santo Domingo; and the Dutch, a few small islands. Sugar, produced on plantations by slave labor, was the major source of profits, along with other cash crops such as coffee, indigo, and cochineal (another dyestuff). The concentration of shipping to this region indicates the region's importance in the European trading system. For example, by the 1760s, the British China trade occupied seven or eight ships a year. In the 1730s, British trade with Jamaica alone drew three hundred ships.

The economic dependence of the colonies on slave labor meant that the colonies were tied to their home countries not with a two-way commercial exchange, but with a three-way, or "triangle," trade (see **Map 18.1**). Certain European manufactures were shipped to ports in western Africa, where they were traded for slaves. Captive Africans were transported to South America, the Caribbean, or North America, where planters bought and paid for them with profits from their sugar and tobacco plantations. (See the feature, "The Global Record: An African Recalls the Horrors of the Slave Ship.") Sugar and tobacco were then shipped back to the mother country to be re-exported at great profit throughout Europe.

This plantation economy in the Caribbean was vulnerable to slave revolts, as well as to competition among the Europeans. Often, wars over control of the islands significantly disrupted production and lessened profits for the European planters on the islands and for their trading partners back in Europe. The growing demands by Europeans for sugar and other products kept the plantation system expanding, despite these challenges, throughout the eighteenth century. The **slave trade** grew dramatically as a result. Approximately five times as many Africans— perhaps as many as seven million people—were forcibly transported to the Americas as slaves in the eighteenth century as in the seventeenth.

slave trade Europeans' trade with Africa in which involuntary laborers were shipped to the Americas to be sold to owners of, especially, sugar plantations. The trade reached its peak in the eighteenth century, when approximately seven million Africans were shipped across the Atlantic.

The slave trade became an increasingly specialized form of oceangoing commerce (for example, slave traders throughout Europe adopted a standardized ship design) and, at the same time, one increasingly linked to the rest of European commerce by complex trade and financial ties. In England, London merchants who imported Asian goods, exported European manufactures, or distributed Caribbean sugar could provide credit for slave traders based in the northern city of Liverpool to fund their journeys to Africa and then the Americas.

An African Recalls the Horrors of the Slave Ship

Olaudah Equiano (ca. 1750–1797) was an Ibo from the Niger region of West Africa. He first experienced slavery as a boy when kidnapped from his village by other Africans, but nothing prepared him for the brutality of the Europeans who bought and shipped him to Barbados, in the British West Indies. His narration of the horrors of the "Middle Passage" between Africa and the Americas may represent a composite story of others' experiences as well as his own. Nevertheless, his account remains one of the few written records by an African survivor of a slave ship.

The first object which saluted my eyes when I arrived on the [African] coast was the sea and a slave ship, which was then riding at anchor, and waiting for its cargo. ... When I was carried on board I was immediately handled, and tossed up, to see if I were sound, by some of the crew. ... When I looked around the ship ... and saw ... a multitude of black people of every description chained together, every one of their countenances expressing dejection and sorrow, I no longer doubted of my fate. ...

I was not long suffered to indulge my grief; I was soon put down under the decks, and there I received such a salutation in the nostrils as I had never experienced in my life; so that with the loathsomeness of the stench ... I became so sick and low that I was not able to eat. ... I now wished for the last friend, death, to relieve me; but soon, to my grief, two of the white men offered me eatables; and, on my refusing to eat, one of them held me fast by the hands and laid me across, I think, the windlass, and tied my feet while the other flogged me severely.

One day, when we had a smooth sea and a moderate wind, two of my wearied countrymen, who were chained together ... , preferring death to such a life of misery, somehow made through the nettings and jumped into the sea; immediately another dejected fellow who [was ill and so not in irons] followed their example; and I believe many more would very soon have done the same, if they had not been prevented by the ship's crew who were instantly alarmed. Those of us that were the most active were in a minute put down under the deck; and there was such a noise and confusion amongst the people of the ship as I have never heard before, to stop her, and get the boat to go after the slaves. However, two of the wretches were drowned, but they got the other and afterwards flogged him unmercifully for thus attempting to prefer death to slavery. In this manner we continued to undergo more hardships than I can now relate; hardships which are inseparable from this accursed trade.

QUESTIONS

1. What particular horrors of the Middle Passage seem to stand out in Equiano's mind? What is the significance of these vignettes?

2. What clues in this excerpt reveal the audience Equiano had in mind for his narrative?

Source: *The Interesting Narrative of the Life of Olaudah Equiano, or Gustavus Vassa, the African* (London, 1793); reprinted in David Northrup, ed., *The Atlantic Slave Trade* (Boston: Houghton Mifflin, 2002), pp. 68–70.

MORE FOOD AND MORE PEOPLE

Throughout European history, there had been a delicate balance between available food and numbers of people to feed. Population growth had accompanied increases in the amount of land under cultivation. From time to time, however, population growth surpassed the ability of the land to produce food, and people became malnourished and prey to disease. In 1348, the epidemic known as the Black Death struck just such a vulnerable population in decline. After this catastrophic decline in the fourteenth century, the European population experienced a prolonged recovery, and in the eighteenth century, the limits that had previously been reached began to be exceeded for the first time.

The cause was not a decline in infant mortality, which remained as high as ever. Even Queen Anne of England outlived every one of the seventeen children she bore (and all but one of them died in infancy). Instead, population growth occurred because of a decline in the death rate for adults and a simultaneous increase in the birthrate in some areas, owing to earlier marriages. Adults began to live longer partly because of a decline in the incidence of plague. However, the primary reason adults were living longer was that more and different kinds of food began to be produced. Adults were better nourished and thus better able to resist disease. The increase in the food supply also meant that more new families could be started.

Food production increased because new crops were introduced and agricultural methods changed. The cumulative effect of these changes was so dramatic that historians have called them an **agricultural revolution**. In the past, peasants safeguarded the fertility of the land by alternately cultivating some portions while letting others lie fallow or using them as pasture. Manure provided fertilizer, but during the winter, livestock could not be kept alive in large numbers. Limited food for livestock meant limited fertilizer, which in turn meant limited production of food for both humans and animals.

agricultural revolution
Dramatic increase in food production from the sixteenth to eighteenth centuries, brought about by changes in agricultural practices and cultivation of new crops. The agricultural revolution allowed the population of Europe to expand beyond historic limits.

519

Gérard Dou: The Vegetable Seller   The specialization of agriculture meant that a more varied diet was available to increasing numbers of Europeans.   (Musée des Beaux-Arts, Nimes/Giraudon/Art Resource, NY)

The new crops now being planted included fodder, such as clover, legumes, and turnips, that did not deplete the soil and could be fed to livestock over the winter. The greater availability of animal manure in turn boosted grain production. In addition, the nutrient-dense potato was introduced from the Americas in the sixteenth century. It could feed more people per acre than could grain. In certain areas, farming families produced potatoes to feed themselves, while they grew grain to be sold and shipped elsewhere.

More food being produced meant more food available for purchase. The opportunity to buy food freed up land and labor. A family that could purchase food might decide to convert its farm to specialized use, such as raising dairy cattle, which meant, in turn, that several families might be supported by a piece of land that had previously supported only one. Over a generation or two, a number of children might share the inheritance of what had previously been a single farm, yet each could make a living from his or her share, and population could grow as it had not done before.

Farmers had known about and experimented with many of the crops used for fodder for centuries. However, widespread planting of these crops and other changes were long in coming and happened in scattered areas because a farmer had to have control over land in order to make changes. In the traditional open-field system, peasants had split up all the land in the community so that each family might have a piece of each field. Dramatic change was unlikely when an entire community had to act together. Only prosperous farmers had spare capital to invest in new crops and few were inclined to take risks with the production of food and to trust the workings of the market. The bad condition of roads was reason enough not to rely on distant markets.

Yet, where both decent roads and growing urban markets existed, some farmers—even entire villages working together—were willing to produce for urban populations. Booming capital cities, such as London and Amsterdam, and trading centers, such as Glasgow and Bordeaux, demanded not only grain, but also specialized produce, such as dairy products and fruits and vegetables. Urbanization and improved transportation networks also encouraged agriculture because human waste produced by city dwellers—known as "night soil"—could be collected and distributed in the surrounding agricultural regions as fertilizer. By the late eighteenth century, pockets of intensive, diversified agriculture existed in England, northern France, the Rhineland in Germany, the Po Valley in Italy, and Catalonia in Spain.

In some areas, changes in agriculture were accompanied by a shift in power in the countryside. Where the traditional authority of the village to regulate agriculture was weak, peasants were vulnerable to wealthy landlords who wanted to reap the profits of producing for the new markets. In England, a combination of weak village structure and high demand from urban centers created a climate that encouraged landlords to treat land speculatively. They raised the rents that farmers paid for land and changed cultivation patterns on the land that they controlled directly. They appropriated the village common lands, a process known as "enclosure," and used them for cash crops such as sheep (raised for their wool) or beef cattle.

As a result, although the agricultural revolution increased the food supply to sustain more people in Europe, it did not create general prosperity. Many rural people were driven off the land or made destitute by the loss of the resources of common lands. Charitable institutions run by cities, churches, and central governments expanded to care for them—often in poorhouses where people received food and shelter but were forced to work and to live isolated against their will. Peasants in eastern Europe produced grain for export to the growing urban centers in western Europe, but usually by traditional methods. In both eastern and western Europe, the power and profits of landlords were a major force in structuring the rural economy.

The Growth of Industry

Agricultural changes led to further changes in economic and social life. As more food was grown with less labor, that labor was freed to take on other productive work. If enough people could be kept employed making useful commodities, the nonagricultural population could continue to grow. If population grew, more and more consumers would be born, and the demand for more goods would help continue the cycle of population growth, changes in production, and economic expansion. This is precisely what happened in the eighteenth century: A combination of forces increased the numbers of people who worked at producing a few key materials and products (see **MAP 18.2**).

Especially significant was the expansion of the putting-out system. Also known as cottage industry, putting out involved the production of thread and cloth by spinners and weavers working in their own homes, usually in a farming village. An entrepreneur bought the raw materials and "put them out" to be finished by these workers. The putting-out system expanded in the eighteenth century, as the agricultural economy was transformed. All agricultural work was seasonal, demanding intensive effort and many hands at certain times but not others. The labor demands of the new crops meant that an even larger number of people periodically needed work away from the fields to make ends meet.

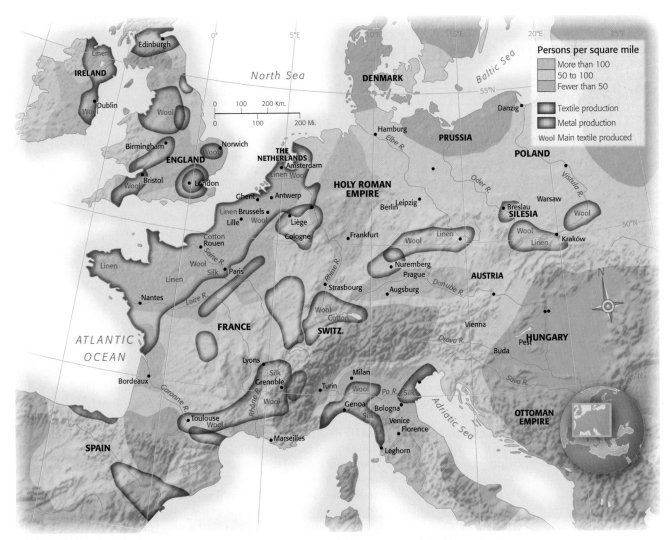

MAP 18.2—Population and Production in Eighteenth-Century Europe

The growth of cottage industry helped to support a growing population. With changes in agriculture, more land-poor workers were available in the countryside to accept work as spinners, knitters, and weavers.

SECTION SUMMARY

- The involvement of European states in international trade and overseas colonization grew markedly in the eighteenth century.

- Approximately seven million Africans were forcibly transported to work on plantations producing cash crops in the Americas.

- The introduction of new crops and changes in cultivation led to increases in food production and what has been called the "agricultural revolution."

- Changes in agriculture enabled the European population to grow beyond previous limits.

- Industrial production, especially of cloth, increased because more people were available for the work, markets for the products expanded, and new technologies arose to meet the demand.

Overseas trade also stimulated production by increasing both the demand in Europe's colonies for cloth and other finished products and the demand at home for manufactured items, such as nails to build the ships that carried the trade. The production of cloth expanded, particularly, because heightened demand led to changes in the way cloth was made. Wool was increasingly combined with other fibers to make less expensive fabrics. By the end of the century, wholly cotton fabrics were being made cheaply in Europe from cotton grown in America by slave labor.

The invention of machines to spin thread, also in the late eighteenth century, markedly increased the rate of production. Cloth production became a spur to a transformed industrial economy because cheaper kinds of cloth could be made for mass consumption. The regions of England, France, and the Low Countries where the new technologies were introduced stood, by the end of the century, on the verge of a massive industrial transformation that would have unprecedented social consequences.

THE WIDENING WORLD OF WARFARE

How did warfare and its consequences change in the eighteenth century?

In the eighteenth century, a new constellation of states emerged to dominate politics in Europe. Alongside the traditional powers of England, France, and Austria were Prussia in central Europe and Russia to the east (see **MAP 18.3**); these five states would dominate European politics until the twentieth century. Common to all these states was their ability to field effective armies and, especially in the case of Britain, navies. Eighteenth-century rulers launched most wars to satisfy traditional territorial ambitions. Now, however, the increasing significance of overseas trade and colonization also made international expansion an important source of conflict, particularly between England and France. As warfare widened in scope, governments increasingly focused on recruiting and maintaining large navies and armies, with increasingly serious effects on ordinary people.

The Pattern of War Within Europe

Wars between European states in the eighteenth century still reflected a dynastic, rather than wholly strategic, view of territory. Although rational and defensible "national" borders were important, collecting isolated bits of territory was also still the norm. The wars between European powers thus became extremely complex strategically. France, for example, might choose to strike a blow against Austria by invading an Italian state in order to use the conquered Italian territory as a bargaining chip in eventual negotiations. Wars were carried out with complex systems of alliances and were followed by the adjustments of many borders and the changing control of small, scattered territories. Rulers of lesser states in Germany and Italy, particularly, remained important as allies and as potential rivals of the Great Powers.

Major wars during the mid-eighteenth century decided the balance of power in German-speaking Europe for the next hundred years. Prussia emerged as the equal of Austria in the region. The first of these wars, now known as the War of the Austrian Succession, began after the death of the Habsburg emperor Charles VI in 1740. Charles died without a male heir, and his daughter, Maria Theresa, succeeded him. Charles had worked to shore up his daughter's position as his heir by means of a treaty of sorts called the Pragmatic Sanction, which he had persuaded allies and potential opponents to accept. Nevertheless, when Charles VI died, rival heiresses and their husbands challenged Maria Theresa for control of her various lands. They were supported by France, the Habsburgs' perennial rival. Worst of all, Prussia, Austria's rival to the north, seized

The Partition of Poland and the Expansion of Russia
Catherine the Great acquired present-day Lithuania, Belarus, and Ukraine, which had once constituted the duchy of Lithuania, part of the multiethnic Polish kingdom.

the wealthy Bohemian province of Silesia (sigh-LEE-zhuh). Austrian lands were threatened with dismemberment.

Though her father had not left his armies or his treasury well equipped to fight a war, Maria Theresa proved a more tenacious opponent than anyone had anticipated. She was helped by Great Britain, which saw the possibility of gains against its colonial rival, France. Fighting eventually spread throughout Habsburg territories, including the Netherlands and in Italy, as well as abroad to British and French colonies. In a preliminary peace signed in 1745, Frederick the Great of Prussia was confirmed in possession of Silesia, but the throne of the Holy Roman Empire was returned to the Habsburgs—given to Maria Theresa's husband, Francis (Franz) I (r. 1745–1765). A final treaty in 1748 ended all the fighting that had continued since 1745, mostly by France and Britain overseas. The Austrian state had survived dismemberment, and Maria Theresa now embarked on the administrative and military reforms necessary to make her state less vulnerable in the future. Prussia, because of the annexation of Silesia and the psychological imprint of victory, emerged as a power of virtually equal rank to the Habsburgs.

The unprecedented threat that Austria now felt from Prussia led to a revolution in alliances across Europe. To isolate Prussia, Maria Theresa agreed to an alliance with France, the Habsburgs' long-standing enemy. Sweden and Russia, with territory to gain at Prussia's expense, joined as well.

Frederick the Great initiated the land phase of what came to be known as the Seven Years' War in 1756, hoping to prevent consolidation of the new alliances. Instead, he found that he had started a war against overwhelming odds. What saved him in part was limited English aid. The English, engaged with France in the overseas conflict that Americans call the French and Indian War, wanted France to be heavily committed on the Continent. Prussia managed to emerge intact—though strained economically and demographically. Prussia and Austria were confirmed as the two states of European rank in German-speaking Europe. Yet, their narrow escapes from being reduced to second-class status reveal how fragile even successful states could be and how dependent on successful armies.

Later in the century, Prussia further expanded its territory by working in concert with Russian expansion. In 1768, Catherine the Great initiated a war against the Ottoman Turks, from which Russia gained much of the Crimean coast. She also continued her predecessors' efforts to dominate the weakened Poland. She was aided in this goal by Frederick the Great, who proposed the deliberate partitioning of Poland to satisfy his own territorial ambitions as well as those of his competitors, Russia and Austria. In 1772, portions of Poland were gobbled up in the first of three successive "grabs" of territory (see **MAP 18.3**). Warsaw eventually landed in Prussian hands, but Catherine gained all of Belarus, Ukraine, and modern Lithuania—which had constituted the duchy of Lithuania.

Great Britain and France: Wars Overseas

The expansion of European trade and settlement abroad in the eighteenth century led to wars between major powers, particularly the British and the French, which were fought primarily overseas. The growth and the proximity of French and British settlements in North America ensured conflict (see **MAP 18.4**). The Caribbean and the coasts of Central and South America were strategic flashpoints as well. At the beginning of the eighteenth century, several substantial islands remained unclaimed by any power. The British were making incursions along the coastline of Central America claimed by Spain and were trying to break into the monopoly of trade between Spain and its vast possessions in the region. Public opinion in both Britain and France became increasingly sensitive to colonial issues.

During the century, England became the dominant naval power in Europe. Its navy protected its far-flung trading networks, its merchant fleet, and the coast of England itself. Within Europe, England's strategic interest lay in promoting a variety of powers there, none of which (or no combination of which) posed too great a threat to England or to its widespread trading system. A second, dynastic consideration in continental affairs was the electorate of Hanover, the large principality in western Germany that was the native territory of the Hanoverian kings of England. Early in the century especially, the interests of this German territory were a significant factor in British foreign policy. Unable to field a large army, given their maritime interests, the British sought protection for Hanover in alliances and subsidies for allies' armies on the Continent and paid for these ventures with the profits on trade. France, on the other hand, was inevitably more committed to affairs on the Continent than were the British. The French were able to hold their own successfully in both arenas during the 1740s, but by 1763, though preeminent on the Continent, they had lost many of their colonial possessions to the English. Conflict between England and France in colonial regions played out in three major phases. The first two coincided with the major land wars in Europe: the War of the Austrian Succession (1740–1748) and the **Seven Years' War** (1756–1763). The third phase coincided with the rebellion of British colonies in North America—the American Revolution—beginning in the 1770s.

In the 1740s, France was heavily involved in the War of the Austrian Succession, while Britain vied with Spain for certain Caribbean territories. Both France and England also tested each other's strength in scattered colonial fighting, which produced a few well-balanced gains and losses. Their conquests were traded back when peace was made in 1748.

Tension was renewed almost immediately at many of the strategic points in North America. The French and British navies harassed each other's merchant shipping in the Gulf of St. Lawrence. The French reinforced their encirclement of British colonies with more forts along the Great Lakes and the Ohio River. When British troops (at one point led by the colonial commander George Washington) attempted to strike at these forts beginning in 1754, open fighting between the French and the English began.

Seven Years' War The first major war between European nations (Britain and France) started and fought largely in their overseas empires.

🌐 Map 18.4—British Gains in North America

The British colonies on the Atlantic coast were effective staging posts for the armies that ousted the French from North America by 1763. However, taxes imposed on the colonies to pay the costs of the Seven Years' War helped spark revolt—the American Revolution—a decade later.

In India, meanwhile, both the French and the British attempted to strengthen their commercial footholds by making military and political alliances with local Indian rulers. The disintegration of the Mogul Empire heightened competition among regional Indian rulers and sparked a new level of ambition on the part of the European powers to gain territorial footholds for the purposes of trade. A British attack on a French convoy provoked a declaration of war by France in May 1756, three months before fighting in the Seven Years' War broke out in Europe. For the first time, a major war between European nations had started in their empires, signifying a profound change in the relation of these nations to the world.

The French had already committed themselves to an alliance with Austria and were increasingly involved on the Continent after Frederick II initiated war there in August 1756. Slowly, the drain of sustaining war both on the Continent and abroad began to tell, and Britain scored major victories against French forces. The cost of involvement on so many fronts meant that French troops were short of money and supplies. They were vulnerable to both supply and personnel shortages—especially in North America—because they were weaker than the British at sea and because New France remained sparsely settled and dependent on the mother country for food.

The French lost a number of fortresses on the Mississippi and Ohio Rivers and on the Great Lakes, and then, they also lost the interior of Canada with the fall of Quebec and of Montreal in 1759 and 1760, respectively (see **Map 18.4**). In the Caribbean, the British seized the French island of Guadeloupe, a vital sugar-producer. Superior resources in India enabled the British to take several French outposts there, including Pondicherry (pon-dih-CHAIR-ee), the most important. By the terms of the Peace of Paris in 1763, France regained Guadeloupe, the most profitable of its American

The Death of General Wolfe at Quebec   General Wolfe commanded British troops that in 1759 defeated the French at Quebec in Canada. Wolfe's death at the battle was memorialized ten years later by American-born artist Benjamin West. This image became widely popular after West sold cheap engraved versions. Notice West's sympathetic treatment of the Native American earnestly focused, like his British allies, on the death of the commander.   (Private Collection/Phillips, Fine Art Auctioneers, New York, USA/The Bridgeman Art Library)

colonies, although Britain gained control of several smaller, previously neutral Caribbean islands to add to its own sugar-producing colonies of Jamaica and Barbados. In India, France retained many of its trading stations but lost its political and military clout. British power in India was dramatically enhanced not only by French losses, but also by victories over Indian rulers who had allied with the French. In the interior, Britain now controlled lands that had never before been under the control of any European power. British political rule in India, as opposed to merely a mercantile presence, began at this time. The British also held Canada. They emerged from the Seven Years' War as the preeminent world power among European states. The dramatic gains led some Britons to speak of the "British Empire" overseas.

The Costs of Warfare

In the eighteenth century, weapons and tactics became increasingly refined and armies more expensive to train and maintain. More reliable muskets were introduced. A bayonet that could slip over a musket barrel without blocking the muzzle was invented. Coordinated use of bayonets required even more careful drill of troops than did volley fire alone to ensure disciplined action in the face of enemy fire and charges. Artillery and cavalry forces also were subjected to greater standardization of training and discipline in action. Increased discipline of forces meant that commanders could exercise meaningful control over a battle for the first time. But such battles were not necessarily decisive, especially when waged against a comparable force. Indeed, training now was so costly that commanders were at times ironically reluctant to hazard their fine troops in battle at all.

In addition, wars could still be won or lost not on the battlefield, but on the supply line. Incentive still existed to bleed civilian populations and exploit the countryside. Moreover, when supply lines were disrupted and soldiers not equipped or fed, the armies of a major power could be vulnerable to smaller, less disciplined armies of minor states. Finally, even supplies, training, and sophisticated tactics could not guarantee success. Not until 1746, at Culloden, could the British army decisively defeat the fierce charge and hand-to-hand fighting of Highland clansmen by holding its position and using disciplined volley fire and bayonet tactics. Warfare became increasingly professional but was still an uncertain business with unpredictable results, despite its staggering cost.

One sure result of the new equipment, discipline, and high costs was that war became an ever greater burden on a state's resources and administration. It became increasingly difficult for small states, such as Sweden, to compete with the forces that others could mount. Small and relatively poor states, such as Prussia, that were able to support large forces did so by means of an extraordinary bending of civil society to the economic and social needs of the army. In Prussia, twice as many people were in the armed forces, proportionally, as in other states, and a staggering 80 percent of its meager state revenue went to sustain the army.

Warfare on this scale also represented an increased burden on common people. Most states introduced some form of conscription in the eighteenth century. Although the very poor often volunteered for army service to improve their lives, conscription of peasants (throughout Europe but particularly in Prussia and Russia) imposed a significant burden on peasant communities and a sacrifice of productive members to the state. Governments everywhere supplemented volunteers and conscripts with mercenaries and even criminals, as necessary, to fill the ranks without tapping the wealthier elements of the community. Men were sometimes taken out of poorhouses and forced to become soldiers. Thus, common soldiers were increasingly seen not as members of society, but as its rejects. Said Frederick II, "useful hardworking people should [not be conscripted but rather] be guarded as the apple of one's eye," and a French war minister agreed that armies had to consist of the "scum of people and of all those for whom society has no use."[3] Brutality became an accepted tool for governments to use to manage such groups of men, and the army increasingly became an instrument of social control used to contain individuals who otherwise might disrupt their own communities.

On the high seas, governments used their navies to suppress piracy. Piracy had been a way of life for hundreds of Europeans and colonial settlers since the sixteenth century. Indentured servants fleeing their obligations, runaway slaves, out-of-work laborers, and adventurers could take up the pirating life, which at least offered autonomy and a chance of some comforts. From the earliest days of exploration, European rulers had authorized men known as privateers to commit acts of war against specific enemies. The Crown took little risk and was spared the cost of arming the ships but shared in the plunder. True piracy—outright robbery on the high seas—was illegal, but in practice, the difference between piracy and privateering was negligible. As governments and merchants grew to prefer regular trade over the irregular profits of plunder, and as national navies developed in the late seventeenth century, a concerted effort to eliminate piracy began.

Because life on the seas was an increasingly vital part of European economic life in the eighteenth century, sea life began to resemble life on land in the amount of compulsion it entailed. Sailors in port were always vulnerable to forcible enlistment in the navy by impressment gangs, particularly during wartime. A drowsy sailor sleeping off a rowdy night could wake up to find himself aboard a navy ship. Press gangs operated throughout England and not just in major ports, for authorities were as interested in controlling "vagrancy" as in staffing the navy.

Like soldiers in the growing eighteenth-century armies, sailors in the merchant marine, as well as the navy, could be subjected to brutal discipline and appalling conditions. Merchant seamen attempted to improve their lot by trying to regulate their relationship with ships' captains. Contracts for pay on merchant ships became more regularized, and seamen often negotiated their terms very carefully, including, for example, details about how rations were to be allotted. Sailors might even take bold collective action aboard ship. The modern term for a work stoppage, *strike*, comes from the sailing expression "to strike sail," meaning to loosen the sails so that they cannot fill with wind. Its use dates from the eighteenth century, from "strikes" of sailors protesting unfair shipboard conditions.

The Idle Apprentice Is Sent to Sea, 1747.
In one of a series of moralizing engravings by William Hogarth, the lazy apprentice is sent away to a life at sea. The experienced seamen in the boat introduce him to some of its terrors: one of them dangles a cat-o'nine tails (used for flogging), while another points out the distant gallows, where pirates and mutineers meet their fate. *(The Idle 'Prentice Turned Away and Sent to Sea*, plate V of 'Industry and Idleness', published 1833 (engraving), Hogarth, William (1697-1764)/Guildhall Library, City of London/The Bridgeman Art Library)

SECTION SUMMARY

- Prussia fought two major wars and emerged as the equal of Austria in German-speaking Europe.

- Russia expanded to the south and partitioned Poland together with Austria and Prussia.

- Britain and France fought over colonial possessions around the world; Britain won many of France's colonies by the end of the Seven Years' War in 1763.

- States recruited soldiers and equipped and trained their armies better than ever before, making war more costly and more demanding on their populations.

- Soldiers, sailors, and peasants found new ways to resist the burdens of forced labor, brutal conditions, and heavy taxation.

Seafaring men were an unusually large and somewhat self-conscious community of wage workers. But economic and political protests by ordinary people also showed interesting parallel changes. Peasant revolts—directly or indirectly a reaction to the costs of armies—had, in the past, ranged from small-scale practical actions against local tax collectors to massive uprisings that only a state's own army could suppress, such as the Pugachev rebellion. Peasant revolts continued to follow these patterns in the eighteenth century but in certain cases, peasants, like sailors, began to confront authority in new ways. They increasingly marshaled legal devices to maintain control over their land and to thwart landlords' efforts to enclose fields and cultivate cash crops. This change, though subtle, was important because it represented an effort to bring permanent structural change to the system and was not simply a temporary redress of grievances. In part, this trend toward "enlightened" revolt reflects increased access to information and the circulation of ideas about reform.

CHAPTER SUMMARY

The Enlightenment was an intellectual movement that applied to political and social thought the confidence in the intelligibility of natural law that Newton and other scientists had recently achieved. Prominent thinkers, called "philosophes," included influential individuals, such as Voltaire and Rousseau. But the Enlightenment was also a more general movement and one of its features was the growth of an informed body of public opinion outside the realm of government. The revolutionary potential of Enlightenment thought came from belief in its rationality and from the fact that it was both critical of its society and fashionable for educated elites to practice.

European rulers in the eighteenth century continued their efforts to govern with greater effectiveness; some self-consciously borrowed Enlightenment ideas to guide their policies, though they remained unwilling to share governing power. In France, although it was the center of the Enlightenment, the Crown failed to eliminate the privileges of nobility and could not adequately tap the wealth of the kingdom. In England, Parliament's role in government was securely established in this century, and new elites wanted to be represented in it.

Though some rulers were inspired by precepts of the Enlightenment, all were guided by traditional concerns of dynastic aggrandizement and strategic advantage. After dramatic expansion of trade, colonization, and the plantation system, conflict over colonial possessions became increasingly important, particularly between England and France. Partly as a result of growing commerce, the European economy was expanding, the population was growing beyond previous limits, and the system of production was being restructured.

FOCUS QUESTIONS

- What were the most important ideas in Enlightenment thought, and what were some of the intellectual, social, and political conditions that favored its development?

- To what extent did the activities of rulers, particularly "enlightened despots," reflect Enlightenment ideals, and to what extent did they reflect traditional concerns of state power?

- How and why did trade and production increase in the eighteenth century?

- How did warfare and its consequences change in the eighteenth century?

KEY TERMS

philosophes (p. 500)

Voltaire (p. 500)

Adam Smith (p. 502)

Jean-Jacques Rousseau (p. 503)

salons (p. 505)

Enlightened despotism (p. 514)

Frederick the Great (p. 514)

Maria Theresa (p. 515)

Catherine the Great (p. 515)

slave trade (p. 518)

agricultural revolution (p. 519)

Seven Years' War (p. 524)

 This icon will direct you to additional materials on the website: www .cengage.com/history/ noble/westciv6e.

NOTES

1. Moira Ferguson, ed., *First Feminists: British Women Writers, 1578-1799* (Bloomington: Indiana University Press, 1985), p. 426.

2. Quoted in Dena Goodman, *The Republic of Letters: A Cultural History of the French Enlightenment* (Ithaca, N.Y.: Cornell University Press, 1994), p. 89.

3. Quoted in M. S. Anderson, *Europe in the Eighteenth Century, 1713-1783*, 3d ed. (London: Longman, 1987), pp. 218-219.

See our interactive eBook for map and primary source activities.

19

A French Citizen Army
The National Guard of Paris leaves to join the army, September 1792
(detail). (Photos12.com-ARJ)

An Age of Revolution, 1789–1815

These militiamen marching off to defend France against the invader in September 1792 appear to be heroes already. Adoring women in the crowd hand them laurel wreaths as they pass; the men march by, resolute and triumphant. Symbols of the ongoing revolution stand out as well: the prominent tricolor flag, the tricolor cockade in each man's hat. In fact, that September, France's citizen armies, for the first time, defeated the army of a foreign monarch poised to breach its borders and snuff out its revolution. The painting celebrates this triumph about to happen and thereby inspires confidence in the Revolution and pride in its citizen-soldiers.

FOCUS QUESTIONS

- What factors led to revolution in France in 1789?
- Why did several phases of revolutionary change occur after 1789 and what were the characteristics of each phase?
- What impact did the Revolution and Napoleonic rule have on France, the rest of Europe, and the wider world?

Today the French Revolution is considered the beginning of modern European, as well as modern French, history. The most powerful monarch in Europe was forced to accept constitutional limits to his power by subjects convinced of their rights. Eventually, the king was overthrown and executed, and the monarchy abolished. Events in France reverberated throughout Europe because the overthrow of one absolute monarchy threatened fellow royals elsewhere. Revolutionary fervor on the part of ordinary soldiers enabled France's armies unexpectedly to best many of their opponents. By the late 1790s, the armies of France would be led in outright conquest of other European states by one of the most talented generals in European history: Napoleon Bonaparte. He brought to the continental European nations that his armies eventually conquered a mixture of imperial aggression and revolutionary change. Europe was transformed both by the shifting balance of power and by the spread of revolutionary ideas.

This icon will direct you to additional materials on the website: www.cengage.com/history/noble/westciv6e.

See our interactive eBook for map and primary source activities.

Understanding the French Revolution means understanding not only its origins, but also its complicated course of events and their significance. Challenging the king's power was not new, but overthrowing the king was revolutionary. A new understanding of the people became irresistible; they were the nation and, as citizens, had the right to representation in government. Louis XVI was transformed from the divinely appointed father of his people to an enemy of the people, worthy only of execution. Central to the Revolution was the complex process by which public opinion was shaped and, in turn, shaped events. Change was driven in part by the power of symbols—flags, rallying cries, inspiring art—to challenge an old political order and legitimize a new one.

THE ORIGINS OF REVOLUTION, 1775–1789

What factors led to revolution in France in 1789?

"I am a citizen of the world," wrote John Paul Jones, captain in the fledgling U.S. Navy, in 1778. He was writing to a Scottish aristocrat, apologizing for raiding the lord's estate while marauding along the British coast during the American Revolution. Jones (1747–1792), born a Scotsman himself, was one of the thousands of cosmopolitan Europeans who were familiar with European cultures on both sides of the Atlantic. As a sailor, Jones literally knew his way around the Atlantic world, but he was a "citizen of the world" in another sense as well. The Scotsman replied to Jones, surprised by the raid, since he was sympathetic to the American colonists; he was a man of "liberal sentiments" like Jones himself.[1] Both Jones and the Scottish lord felt they belonged to an international society of gentlemen who recognized certain Enlightenment principles regarding just and rational government.

The Atlantic world of the late eighteenth century was united both by practical links of commerce and shared ideals about liberty. The strategic interests of the great European powers were also always in play, however. Thus, when the American colonists actively resisted British rule and then in 1776 declared their independence from Britain, the consequences were wide-ranging: British trading interests were challenged, French appetites for gains at British expense were whetted, and illusive notions about liberty seemed more plausible. The victory of the American colonies in 1783, followed by the creation of the U.S. Constitution in 1787, further heightened the appeal of liberal ideas elsewhere. Attempts at liberal reform were mounted in several states, including Ireland, the Netherlands, and Poland. However, the American Revolution had the most direct impact on later events in France because the French had been directly involved in the American effort.

Revolutionary Movements in Europe

While the British government faced the revolt of the American colonies, it also confronted trouble closer to home. Many Britons had divided loyalties, and many who did favor armed force to subdue the American rebellion were convinced that the war was being mismanaged; they demanded reform of the ministerial government. The American rebellion also had ripple effects in other parts of Europe.

A reform movement sprang up in Ireland in 1779. The reformers demanded greater autonomy from Britain. Like the Americans, Irish elites—mostly of English or Scottish origin—felt like disadvantaged junior partners in the British Empire. They objected to policies that favored British imperial interests over those of the Irish ruling class: for example, the exclusion of Irish ports from overseas commerce in favor of English and Scottish ones and the grant of political rights to Irish Catholics so that they might fight in Britain's overseas armies.

The reformers expressed their opposition to British policies not only in parliamentary debates, but also in military defiance. Following the example of the American rebels, they set up a system of local voluntary militia to resist British troops if necessary. The Volunteer Movement was neutralized when greater parliamentary autonomy for Ireland was granted in 1782, following the repeal of many restrictions on Irish commerce. Unlike the Americans, the Irish elites faced an internal challenge to their own authority—the Catholic population whom they had for centuries dominated—which forced them to reach an accommodation with the British government.

Meanwhile, a political crisis with constitutional overtones was also brewing in the Netherlands. The United Provinces (the Netherlands) was governed by a narrow oligarchy of old merchant families, particularly in Amsterdam, and a military governor, the "stadtholder," from the princely House of Orange. The interests of the merchants and of the stadtholder frequently conflicted. Tensions between them deepened during the American Revolution, as merchants favored trade with the colonists and the prince favored maintaining an English alliance.

The conflict changed character when the representatives of the various cities, calling themselves the Dutch "Patriot" Party, defended their positions not merely on the grounds of their traditional political influence within the Netherlands, but also with wider claims to American-style liberty. The Patriots, in turn, were quickly challenged by newly wealthy traders and professionals, long disenfranchised by their closed merchant oligarchy, who demanded liberty too. These challengers briefly took over the Patriot movement. Just as many Irish rebels accepted the concessions of 1782, the Patriot oligarchs in the Netherlands did nothing to resist an invasion in 1787 that restored the power of the stadtholder, the prince of Orange, because it also ended the challenge to their own control of urban government.

Both the Irish volunteers and the Dutch Patriots, though members of very limited movements, echoed the American rebels in practical and ideological ways. Both were influenced by the economic and political consequences of Britain's relationship with its colonies. Both were inspired by the success of the American rebels and their thoroughgoing claims for political self-determination.

Desire for political reform flared in Poland as well during this period. Government reform was accepted as a necessity by Polish leaders after the first partition of Poland in 1772 had left the remnant state without some of its wealthiest territories (see **MAP 18.3** on page 523). Beginning in 1788, however, reforming gentry in the *Sejm* (representative assembly) went further; they established a commission to write a constitution, following the American example. The resulting document, known as the May 3 (1791) Constitution, was the first codified constitution in Europe; it was read and admired by George Washington.

Poles thus established a constitutional monarchy in which representatives of major towns, as well as gentry and nobility, could sit as deputies. The *liberum veto*, or individual veto power, which had allowed great nobles to obstruct royal authority, was abolished. However, Catherine the Great, empress of Russia, would not tolerate a constitutional government operating so close to her own autocratic regime; she ordered an invasion of Poland in 1792. The unsuccessful defense of Poland was led by, among others, a Polish veteran of the American Revolution, Tadeusz Kosciuszko (tah-DAY-oosh kos-USE-ko) (1746–1817). The second, more extensive partition of Poland followed, to be answered in turn in 1794 by a widespread insurrection against Russian rule, spearheaded by Kosciuszko. The uprising was mercilessly suppressed by an alliance of Russian and Prussian troops. Unlike the U.S. Constitution, from which they drew inspiration, the Poles' constitutional experiment was doomed by the power of its neighbors.

The American Revolution and the Kingdom of France

As Britain's greatest commercial and political rival, France naturally was drawn into Britain's struggle with its North American colonies. In the Seven Years' War (1756–1763), the French had lost many of their colonial settlements and trading outposts to the English (see page 526). Stung by this outcome, certain French courtiers and ministers pressed for an aggressive colonial policy that would regain for France some of the riches in trade that Britain now threatened to monopolize. The American Revolution seemed to offer the perfect opportunity. The French extended covert aid to the Americans from the very beginning of the conflict in 1775. After the first major defeat of British troops by the Americans—at the Battle of Saratoga in 1777—France formally recognized the independent United States and committed troops, as well as funds, to the American cause. John Paul Jones's famous ship, the *Bonhomme Richard* (bon-OHM ree-SHARD), was purchased and outfitted by the French government, as were many other American naval vessels. French support was decisive. In 1781, the French fleet kept reinforcements from reaching the British force besieged by George Washington at Yorktown. The American victory at Yorktown effectively ended the war; the colonies' independence was formally recognized by the Treaty of Paris in 1783.

The consequences for France of its American alliance were momentous. Aid for the Americans saddled France with a debt of about 1 billion *livres* (pounds), which represented as much as one-quarter of the total debt that the French government was trying to service. A less tangible impact of the American Revolution came from the direct participation of about nine thousand French soldiers, sailors, and aristocrats. The best known is the Marquis de Lafayette, who became an aide to George Washington and helped command American troops. For many

CHRONOLOGY

1775–1783	American Revolutionary War
1779–1782	Irish Volunteer Movement
1788	U.S. Constitution ratified; Reform movement begins in Poland; "Patriot" movement ends in the Netherlands
1789	French Estates General meets at Versailles (May); Third Estate declares itself the National Assembly (June); Storming of the Bastille (July)
1791	Polish constitution French king Louis XVI captured attempting to flee (June) Slave revolt begins in Saint Domingue
1792	France declares war on Austria; revolutionary wars begin (April); Louis XVI arrested; France declared a republic (August–September)
1793	Louis XVI guillotined
1793–1794	Reign of Terror in France
1799	Napoleon seizes power in France
1801	Concordat with pope
1804	Napoleon crowned emperor Napoleonic Civil Code Independence of Haiti (Saint Domingue) declared
1805	Battle of Trafalgar; Battle of Austerlitz
1806	Dissolution of Holy Roman Empire
1812	French invasion of Russia
1814	Napoleon abdicates and is exiled French monarchy restored
1815	Hundred Days (February–June) Battle of Waterloo

humble men, the war was simply employment. For others, it was a quest of sorts. For them, the promise of the Enlightenment—belief in human rationality, natural rights, and universal laws by which society should be organized—was brought to life in America.

Exposure to the American conflict occurred at the French court, too. Beginning in 1775, a permanent American mission to Versailles lobbied hard for aid. The chief emissary of the Americans was Benjamin Franklin (1706–1790), a philosophe by French standards whose writings and scientific experiments were already known to European elites. His talents—among them, a skillful exploitation of a simple, Quaker-like demeanor—succeeded in promoting the idealization of America at the French court.

The U.S. Constitution, the various state constitutions, and the debates surrounding their ratification were all published in Paris and much discussed in salons and at court, where lively debate about reform of French institutions had been going on for decades. America became the prototype of the rational republic—the embodiment of Enlightenment philosophy. It was hailed as the place where the irrationalities of inherited privilege did not prevail. A British observer, Arthur Young (1741–1820), believed that "the American revolution has laid the foundation of another in France, if [the French] government does not take care of itself."[2]

By the mid-1780s, there was no longer a question of whether the French regime would experience reform but rather a question of what form the reform would take. The royal government was almost bankrupt. A significant minority of the politically active elite was convinced that France's system of government was irrational. Nevertheless, a dissatisfied elite and a financial crisis—even fanned by a successful revolt elsewhere—do not necessarily lead to revolution. Why did the French government—the *Ancien Régime* (ahn-SYEN ray-ZHEEM) or "Old Regime," as it became known after the Revolution—not "take care of itself"?

The Crisis of the Old Regime

The Old Regime was brought to the point of crisis in the late 1780s by three factors: (1) heavy debts that dwarfed an antiquated system for collecting revenue; (2) institutional constraints on the monarchy that defended privileged interests; and (3) public opinion that envisioned thoroughgoing reform and pushed the monarchy in that direction. Another factor was the ineptitude of the king, Louis XVI (r. 1774–1793).

Louis came to the throne in 1774, a year before the American Revolution began. He was a kind, well-meaning man better suited to be a petty bureaucrat than a king. The queen, the Austrian Marie Antoinette (1755–1793), was regarded with suspicion by the many who despised the "unnatural" alliance with Austria the marriage had sealed. She, too, was politically inept, unable to negotiate the complexities of court life, and widely rumored to be selfishly wasteful of royal resources despite the realm's financial crises.

The fiscal crisis of the monarchy had been a long time in the making and was an outgrowth of the system by which the greatest wealth was protected by traditional privileges. At the top of the social and political pyramid were the nobles, a legal grouping that included warriors and royal officials. In France, nobility conferred exemption from much taxation. Thus, the royal government could not directly tax its wealthiest subjects.

This situation existed throughout much of Europe, a legacy of the power of the nobility in medieval times. Unique to France, however, was the strength of the institutions that defended this system. Of particular importance were the royal law courts, the parlements (par-luh-MAWHN), which claimed a right of judicial review over royal edicts. All the parlementaires—well-educated lawyers and judges—were technically noble and loudly defended the traditional privileges of all nobles. Louis XV (d. 1774), near the end of his life, had successfully undermined the power of the parlements by a bold series of moves. Louis XVI, immediately after coming to the throne, buckled under pressure and restored the parlements to full strength.

Deficit financing had been a way of life for the monarchy for centuries. After early efforts at reform, Louis XIV (d. 1715) had reverted to common fund-raising expedients, such as selling offices, which only added to the weight of privileged investment in the old order. England had established a national bank to free its government from the problem, but the comparable French effort early in the century had been undercapitalized and had failed. Late in the 1780s, under Louis XVI, one-fourth of the annual operating expenses of the government was borrowed, and half of all government expenditure went to paying interest on its debt. Short-term economic crises, such as disastrous harvests, added to the cumulative problem of government finance.

The Common People Crushed by Privilege
In this contemporary cartoon, a nobleman in military dress and a clergyman crush a commoner under the rock of burdensome taxes and forced labor *(corvées).* The victim's situation reflects that of the peasantry, but his stylish clothes would allow affluent townspeople to identify with him.   (Musée Carnavalet, Paris/Giraudon/Art Resource, NY)

The king employed able finance ministers who tried to institute fundamental reforms, such as replacing the tangle of taxes with a simpler system in which all would pay and eliminating local tariffs, which were stifling commerce. The parlements and many courtiers and aristocrats, as well as ordinary people, resisted these policies. Peasants and townsfolk did not trust the "free market" (free from traditional trade controls) for grain; most feared that speculators would buy up the grain supply and people would starve. Trying to implement such reforms in times of grain shortage almost guaranteed their failure. Moreover, many supported the parlements simply because they were the only institution capable of standing up to the monarchy. But not all members of the elite joined the parlements in opposing reform. The imprint of "enlightened" public opinion was apparent in the thinking of some courtiers and thousands of educated commoners who believed that the government and the economy had to change. They openly debated the nature and extent of reform at court, in salons, cafes, and other gathering places.

In 1787, the king called an "Assembly of Notables"—an ad hoc group of elites—to support him in facing down the parlements and proceeding with some changes. But he found little support. Some notables, even men sympathetic to reform, either did not support particular proposals or were reluctant to allow the monarchy free rein. Others, reflecting the influence of the American Revolution, maintained that a "constitutional" body such as the Estates General, which had not been called since 1614, needed to make these decisions.

Ironically, nobles and clergy who were opposed to reform supported the call for the Estates General too, confident they could control its deliberations. The three Estates met and voted separately by "order"—clergy (First Estate), nobles (Second Estate), and commoners (**Third Estate**). The combined votes of the clergy and nobles would presumably nullify whatever the Third Estate might propose.

The Estates General

In 1788, mounting pressure from common people, as well as courtiers, led Louis to summon the Estates General. On Louis's orders, deputies were to be elected by local assemblies, which were chosen in turn by wide male suffrage. Louis mistakenly assumed he had widespread support in the provinces and wished to tap it by means of this grassroots voting. Louis also agreed

Third Estate   In France, the common people, as distinct from the clergy (First Estate) and nobles (Second Estate), in the representative body the Estates General.

that the Third Estate should have twice as many deputies as the other two Estates, but he did not authorize voting by head rather than by order, which would have brought about the dominance of the Third Estate. Nevertheless, the king hoped that the specter of drastic proposals put forth by the Third Estate would frighten the aristocrats and clergy into accepting some of his reforms.

Louis's situation was precarious when the Estates General convened in May 1789. Already a groundswell of sentiment confirmed the legitimacy of the Estates General and the authority of the Third Estate to enact change. Political pamphlets circulated arguing that the Third Estate deserved enhanced power because it carried the mandate of the people. The most important of these was *What Is the Third Estate?* (1789) by Joseph Emmanuel Sieyès (1748–1836), a church official from the diocese of Chartres. The sympathies of Abbé Sieyès (say-EZ), as he was known, were with the Third Estate: His career had stalled because he was not noble. Sieyès argued that the Third Estate represented the nation because it did not reflect special privilege.

Among the deputies of the first two Estates—clergy and nobility—were men, such as the Marquis de Lafayette (1757–1834), who were sympathetic to reform. In the Third Estate, a large majority of deputies reflected the most radical political thought possible for men of their standing. Most were lawyers and other professionals who were functionaries in the government but, like Sieyès, of low social rank. They frequented provincial academies, salons, and political societies. They were convinced of the validity of their viewpoints and determined on reform, and they had little stake in the system as it was. When this group convened and met with resistance from the First and Second Estates, and from Louis himself, it seized the reins of government and a revolution began.

1789: A Revolution Begins

As soon as the three Estates convened at the royal palace at Versailles, conflicts surfaced. The ineptness of the Crown was immediately clear. On the first day of the meetings in May, Louis and his ministers failed to introduce a program of reforms for the deputies to consider. This failure raised doubt about the monarchy's commitment to reform. More important, it allowed the political initiative to pass to the Third Estate. The deputies challenged the Crown's insistence that the three Estates meet and vote separately. Deputies to the Third Estate refused to be certified (that is, to have their credentials officially recognized) as members of only the Third Estate rather than as members of the Estates General as a whole.

For six weeks, the Estates General was unable to meet officially, and the king did nothing to break the impasse. During this interlude, the determination of the deputies of the Third Estate strengthened. More and more deputies were won over to the notion that the three Estates must begin in the most systematic way: France must have a written constitution.

THE NATIONAL ASSEMBLY

National Assembly
Legislative body formed in France in June 1789, when members of the Third Estate in the Estates General, joined by some deputies from the clergy, declared themselves the representatives of the nation.

Tennis Court Oath
Pledge signed by all but one deputy of the National Assembly in France on June 20, 1789, to meet until a constitution was drafted.

By the middle of June, more than thirty reformist members of the clergy were sitting jointly with the Third Estate, which had invited all deputies from all three Estates to meet and be certified together. On June 17, the Third Estate simply declared itself the **National Assembly** of France. At first, the king did nothing, but when the deputies arrived to meet on the morning of June 20, they discovered they had been locked out of the hall. Undaunted, they assembled instead in a nearby indoor tennis court and produced the document that has come to be known as the **Tennis Court Oath**. It was a collective pledge to meet until a written constitution had been achieved. Only one deputy refused to support it. Sure of their mandate, the deputies had assumed the reins of government.

The king continued to handle the situation with both ill-timed self-assertion and feeble attempts at compromise. As more and more deputies from the First and Second Estates joined the National Assembly, Louis "ordered" the remaining loyal deputies to join it, too. Simultaneously, however, he ordered troops to come to Paris. He feared disorder in the wake of the recent disturbances throughout France and believed that any challenge to the legitimacy of arbitrary monarchical authority would be disastrous.

The king's call for troops aroused Parisians' suspicions. Some assumed a plot was afoot to starve Paris and destroy the National Assembly. With a population of about 600,000, Paris was one of the largest cities in Europe and it was the political nerve center of the nation—the site of the publishing industry, salons, and the homes of parlementaires and royal ministers. It was also

The Tennis Court Oath   It was raining on June 20, 1789, when the deputies found themselves barred from their meeting hall and sought shelter in the royal tennis court. Their defiance created one of the turning points of the Revolution; the significance was recognized several years later by the creator of this painting.   (Réunion des Musées Nationaux/Art Resource, NY)

a working city, with thousands of laborers of all trades plus thousands more—perhaps one-tenth of the inhabitants—jobless recent immigrants from the countryside. The city was both extremely volatile and extremely important to the stability of royal power.

It took little—news of the dismissal of a reformist finance minister—for Paris to erupt in demonstrations and looting. Crowds besieged City Hall and the royal armory, where they seized thousands of weapons. A popular militia formed as citizens armed themselves. Armed crowds attacked other sites of royal authority, including the huge fortified prison, the Bastille, on the morning of July 14. The Bastille now held only a handful of petty criminals, but it still remained a potent symbol of royal power and, the crowd assumed, held large supplies of arms. The garrison commander at first mounted a hesitant defense, then decided to surrender after citizens managed to secure cannons and drag them to face the prison. Most of the garrison were allowed to go free, although the commander and several officers were murdered by the crowd.

THE STORMING OF THE BASTILLE

The citizens' victory was a great embarrassment to royal authority. The king immediately had to embrace the popular movement. He came to Paris and, in front of crowds at City Hall, donned the red and blue cockade worn by the militia and ordinary folk as a badge of resolve and defiance. This symbolic action signaled the reversal of the Old Regime—politics would now be based on new principles.

Encouraged by events in Paris, inhabitants of cities and towns around France staged similar uprisings. In many areas, the machinery of royal government completely broke down. City councils, officials, and even parlementaires were thrown out of office. Popular militias took control of the streets. A simultaneous wave of uprisings shook the countryside. Most of them

Women's March on Versailles, October 1789 Parisian marketwomen marched the 12 miles to the king's palace at Versailles, some provisioning themselves with tools or weapons as they left the capital. (Réunion des Musées Nationaux/Art Resource, NY)

were the result of food shortages, but their timing added momentum to the more strictly political protests in cities.

TOWARD CONSTITUTIONAL GOVERNMENT

These events forced the members of the National Assembly to work energetically on the constitution and to pass legislation to satisfy popular protests against economic and political privileges. On August 4, the Assembly abolished the remnants of powers that landlords had enjoyed since the Middle Ages, including the right to force peasants to labor on the lord's land and the bondage of serfdom itself. Although largely symbolic, because serfdom and forced labor had been eliminated in much of France, these changes were hailed as the "end of feudalism." A blow was also struck at established religion by eliminating the tithe, the forced payment of one-tenth of a person's income to the church. At the end of August, the Assembly issued the **Declaration of the Rights of Man and the Citizen**. It was a bold assertion of the foundations of a newly conceived government, closely modeled on portions of the U.S. Constitution. Its preamble declared "that [since] the ignorance, neglect or contempt of the rights of man are the sole cause of public calamities and the corruption of governments," the deputies were "determined to set forth in a solemn declaration the natural, inalienable and sacred rights of man."[3]

Declaration of the Rights of Man and the Citizen
Document issued by the National Assembly of France in August 1789. Modeled on the U.S. Constitution, it asserted "the natural, inalienable and sacred rights of man."

In September, the deputies debated the king's role in a new constitutional government. Monarchists favored a government rather like England's, with a two-house legislature, including an upper house representing the hereditary aristocracy and a royal right to veto legislation. More radical deputies favored a single legislative chamber and no veto power for the king. The Assembly compromised: The king was given a three-year suspensive veto—the power to suspend legislation for the sitting of two legislatures. This was still a formidable amount of power but a drastic curtailment of his formerly absolute sovereignty.

THE WOMEN'S MARCH TO VERSAILLES

Again Louis resorted to troops. This time he called them directly to Versailles, where the Assembly sat. News of the troops' arrival provoked outrage, which heightened with the threat of another grain shortage. Early on the morning of October 5, women in the Paris street markets saw the empty grocers' stalls and took immediate collective action. "We want bread!" they shouted at the steps of City Hall. Because they were responsible for procuring their families' food, women often led protests over bread shortages. This protest, however, went far beyond the ordinary. A crowd of thousands gathered and decided to walk all the way to Versailles, accompanied by the popular militia (now called the "National Guard"), to petition the king directly for sustenance.

At Versailles, a joint delegation of the women and deputies from the National Assembly was dispatched to see the king. Some of the women fell at the feet of the king with their tales of hardship, certain that the "father of the people" would alleviate their suffering. He did order stored grain supplies distributed in Paris, and he agreed to accept the constitutional role that the Assembly had voted for him. The king also agreed to return to Paris to reassure the people and was escorted back to the capital by both popular militia and bread protesters. Already, dramatic change had occurred as a result of a complex dynamic among the three Estates, the Crown, and the people of Paris. The king was still assumed to be the fatherly guardian of his people's well-being, but his powers were now limited and his authority badly shaken. The Assembly had begun to govern in the name of the "nation," and so far, it had the support of the people.

SECTION SUMMARY

- Inspired by events in America, elites in Ireland, the Netherlands, and Poland pushed for greater political liberty.

- France's support for the American colonies against Great Britain increased French government debt and exposed French soldiers and courtiers to revolutionary ideas.

- By the late 1780s, French royal government was in crisis owing to bankruptcy, institutions that impeded reform, and agitation for reform within elite society.

- The French Revolution began in 1789 when the Estates General convened, and commoners in the Third Estate claimed a mandate to write a constitution and enact major changes in law.

- French citizens, led by the Parisians, formed popular militias, attacked royal fortresses, and marched to Versailles to confront the king.

THE PHASES OF THE REVOLUTION, 1789–1799

Why did several phases of revolutionary change occur after 1789 and what were the characteristics of each phase?

The French Revolution was a complicated affair. It was a series of changes, in a sense, a series of revolutions, driven not by one group of people but by several groups. Even among elites convinced of the need for reform, the range of opinion was wide. The people of Paris continued to be an important force for change. Country people also became active, primarily in resisting changes forced on them by the central government.

All of the wrangling within France was complicated by foreign reaction to events there. Defending the revolution against foreign enemies soon became a routine burden for the fragile revolutionary governments. In addition, they had to cope with the continuing problems that had precipitated the Revolution in the first place, including the government's chronic indebtedness and frequent grain shortages. Finally, the Revolution itself was an issue in that, once the traditional arrangements of royal government had been altered, momentum for further change was unleashed.

The First Phase Completed, 1789–1791

At the end of 1789, Paris was in ferment, but for a time, forward progress blunted the threat of disastrous divisions between king and Assembly and between either of them and the people of Paris. The capital continued to be the center of lively political debate. Salons continued to meet; academies and private societies proliferated. Deputies to the Assembly joined existing societies or helped to found new ones. Several would be important throughout the Revolution— particularly the Jacobin (JACK-oh-bin) Club, named for the monastic order whose buildings the members used as a meeting hall.

These clubs represented the gamut of revolutionary opinion. Some, in which ordinary Parisians were well represented, focused on economic policies that would directly benefit common people. Women were active in a few of the more radical groups. Monarchists dominated other clubs. At first, similar to the salons and debating societies of the Enlightenment era, the clubs quickly became sources of political pressure on the government. A bevy of popular newspapers also contributed to the vigorous political life in the capital.

The broad front of revolutionary consensus began to break apart as the Assembly made decisions about the constitution and about policies to address France's still-desperate financial situation. The largest portion of the untapped wealth of the nation lay with the Catholic Church, an obvious target of anticlerical reformers. The deputies made sweeping changes: They kept church buildings intact and retained the clergy as salaried officials of the state. They abolished all monasteries, though they pensioned the monks and nuns to permit them to continue as nurses and teachers where possible. Boldest of all, the Assembly seized most of the vast lands of the church and declared them national property *(biens nationaux)* to be sold for revenue for the state.

However, revenue was needed faster than the property could be inventoried and sold, so government bonds *(assignats* [ah-see-NYAH]) were issued against the eventual sale of church lands. Unfortunately, in the cash-strapped economy, the bonds were treated like money, their value became inflated, and the government never realized the hoped-for profits. A greater problem was the political divisiveness generated by the restructuring of the church. Many members of the lower clergy, living as they did near ordinary citizens, were among the most reform-minded of the deputies. These clergy were willing to go along with many changes, but the required oath of loyalty to the state made a mockery of clerical independence.

The Civil Constitution of the Clergy, as these measures were called, was passed by the Assembly in July 1790 because the clerical deputies opposing it were outvoted. More than half of the churchmen did take the oath of loyalty. Those who refused, concentrated among the higher clergy, were in theory thrown out of their offices. A year later (April 1791), the pope declared that clergy who had taken the oath were suspended from their offices. Antirevolutionary sentiment grew among thousands of French people, particularly in outlying regions, to whom the church was still vital as a source of charity and a center of community life.

Meanwhile, the Assembly proceeded with administrative and judicial reform. The deputies abolished the medieval provinces as administrative districts and replaced them with uniform *départements* (departments). They declared that local officials would be elected—a revolutionary dispersal of power that had previously belonged to the king.

As work on the constitution drew to a close in the spring of 1791, the king decided that he had had enough. Royal authority, as he knew it, had been virtually dismantled and Louis himself was now a virtual prisoner in the Tuileries (TWEE-lair-ee) Palace in central Paris. The king and his family attempted to flee France. On June 20, 1791, they set out in disguise. However, the party was stopped—and recognized—in the town of Varennes (vah-REN) near the eastern border of the kingdom.

Louis and his family were returned to Paris under lightly disguised house arrest. It was discovered that he had left behind a document that condemned the constitution and revealed his intention was to invade France with Austrian troops, if necessary. He and the queen had sent money abroad ahead of themselves. Thus, in July 1791, just as the Assembly was completing its proposal for a constitutional monarchy, the monarch himself could no longer be trusted.

Editorials and street protests against the monarchy increased. In one incident, known as the Massacre of the Champ (Field) de Mars (SHOM duh MARSS), government troops led by Lafayette fired on citizens at an antimonarchy demonstration that certain Parisian clubs had organized; about fifty men and women died. This inflammatory incident heightened tensions between moderate reformers satisfied with the constitutional monarchy, such as Lafayette, and outspoken republicans who wanted to eliminate the monarchy altogether.

Nevertheless, on September 14, the king formally swore to uphold the constitution. He had no choice. The event became an occasion for celebration, but suspicion of the monarchy continued. Also, the tension between the interests of common Parisians and the provisions of the new constitution could not be glossed over. Though a liberal document for its day, the constitution reflected the views of the elite deputies who had created it. The right to vote, based on a minimal property qualification, was given to about half of all adult men. However, these men only chose electors, for whom the property qualifications were higher. The electors in turn chose deputies to national bodies as well as local officials. Although, in theory, any eligible voter could be an elected deputy or official, in fact, few ordinary citizens would become deputies or local administrators. A new Declaration of Rights accompanied the constitution; it reflected a fear of the masses that had not existed when the Declaration of the Rights of Man and the Citizen was first promulgated in 1789. Freedom of the press and freedom of assembly, for example, were not fully guaranteed.

Educated women had joined some of the Parisian clubs and had attempted to influence the Assembly to consider women's rights, but the constitution granted neither political rights nor legal equality to women. Nor had the Assembly passed laws beneficial to women, such as the legalization of divorce. A Declaration of the Rights of Woman was drafted by a woman named Olympe de Gouges (oh-LAMP duh GOOZH) to draw attention to the treatment of women in the new constitution.

In any case, very soon after the constitution was implemented, the fragility of the new system became clear. The National Assembly declared that its members could not serve in the first assembly to be elected under the constitution. Thus, the members of the newly elected Legislative Assembly, which began to meet in October 1791, lacked any of the cohesiveness that would have come from collective experience. Also, unlike the previous National Assembly, they did not represent a broad range of opinion but were mostly republicans.

In fact, the Legislative Assembly was dominated by republican members of the Jacobin Club. They were known as Girondins (zhih-ron-DEHN), after the region in southwestern France from which many of the club's leaders came. The policies of these new deputies and continued pressure from the ordinary citizens of Paris would cause the constitutional monarchy to collapse in less than a year.

The Second Phase and Foreign War, 1791–1793

An additional pressure on the new regime soon appeared: a threat of foreign invasion and a war to respond to the threat. Aristocratic émigrés, including the king's brothers, had taken refuge in nearby German states and were planning to invade France. The emperor and other German rulers did little actively to aid the plotters. Austria and Prussia, however, in the Declaration of Pillnitz of August 1791, declared, as a concession to the émigrés, that they would intervene if necessary to support the monarchy in France.

The threat of invasion, when coupled with distrust of the royal family, seemed more real to the revolutionaries in Paris than it may actually have been. But many deputies hoped for war. They assumed that the outcome would be a French defeat, which would lead to a popular uprising that would rid them, at last, of the monarchy. In April 1792, under pressure from the Assembly, Louis XVI declared war against Austria. From this point on, foreign war would be an ongoing factor in the Revolution.

At first, the war was indeed a disaster for France. The army had not been reorganized into an effective fighting force after the loss of many aristocratic officers and the addition of newly self-aware citizens. On one occasion, troops insisted on putting an officer's command to a vote. Early defeats further emboldened critics of the monarchy. Under the direction of the Girondins, the Legislative Assembly began to press for the deportation of priests who had been leading demonstrations against the government. The Assembly abolished the personal guard of the king and summoned provincial National Guardsmen to Paris.

The king's resistance to these measures, as well as fears of acute grain shortages owing to a poor harvest and the needs of the armies, created further unrest. Crowds staged boisterous marches near the royal palace, physically confronted the king, and forced him to don the "liberty cap," a symbol of republicanism. The king's authority and prestige were now thoroughly undermined.

CHRONOLOGY

The French Revolution

May 5, 1789	Estates General meets in Versailles
June 17, 1789	Third Estate declares itself the National Assembly
June 20, 1789	Tennis Court Oath
July 14, 1789	Storming of the Bastille
August 27, 1789	Declaration of the Rights of Man and the Citizen
October 5–6, 1789	Women's march on Versailles Louis XVI returns to Paris
July 1790	Civil Constitution of the Clergy
June 1791	Louis XVI captured attempting to flee
August 1791	Declaration of Pillnitz
September 1791	New constitution implemented
October 1791	Legislative Assembly begins to meet
April 1792	France declares war on Austria
August 10, 1792	Storming of the Tuileries; Louis XVI arrested
September 21, 1792	National Convention declares France a republic
January 21, 1793	Louis XVI guillotined
May 1793	First Law of the Maximum
July 1793	Terror inaugurated
July 1794	Robespierre guillotined; Terror ends
October 1795	Directory established
November 1799	Napoleon seizes power

Louis XVI in 1792   The king, though a kindly man, had neither the character nor the convictions necessary to refashion royal authority symbolically as the Revolution proceeded. When Parisian crowds forced him to wear the "liberty cap," the monarchy was close to collapse. (Metropolitan Museum of Art, The Elisha Whittelsey Collection, The Elisha Whittelsey Fund, 1962 [62.520.333]. Image © The Metropolitan Museum of Art)

By July 1792, tensions had become acute. The grain shortage was severe; Austrian and Prussian troops, committed to saving the royal family, were threatening to invade; and, most important, Parisian citizens were better organized and more determined than ever before. In each of the forty-eight "sections"—administrative wards—of Paris, a miniature popular assembly thrashed out all the events and issues of the day, just as deputies in the nationwide Legislative Assembly did. Derisively called **sans-culottes** (sahn-koo-LOT) ("without knee pants") because they could not afford elite fashions, the ordinary Parisians in the section assemblies included shopkeepers, artisans, and laborers. Their political organization enhanced their influence with the Assembly, the clubs, and Parisian newspapers. By late July, most sections of the city had approved a petition calling for the exile of the king, the election of new city officials, the exemption of the poor from taxation, and other radical measures.

In August, the sans-culottes took matters into their own hands. On the night of August 9, after careful preparations, representatives of the section assemblies constituted themselves as a new city government with the aim of "saving the state." The next day, August 10, they assaulted the Tuileries Palace, where the royal family was living. Hundreds of royal guards and citizens died

sans-culottes Ordinary citizens of revolutionary Paris, whose derisive nickname referred to their inability to afford fashionable knee pants ("culottes").

in the bloody confrontation. The king and his family were imprisoned in one of the fortified towers in the city, under guard of the popularly controlled city government.

With the storming of the Tuileries Palace, the second major phase of the Revolution began: the establishment of republican government in place of the monarchy. By their intimidating numbers, the people of Paris now controlled the Legislative Assembly. Some deputies fled. Those who remained agreed under pressure to dissolve the Assembly and make way for another body to be elected by universal manhood suffrage. On September 20, that assembly, known as the National Convention, began to meet. The next day, the Convention declared the end of the monarchy and set to work crafting a constitution for the new republic.

Coincidentally, that same September day, French forces won their first genuine victory over the allied Austrian and Prussian invasion forces. Though not a decisive battle, it was a profound psychological victory. A citizen army had defeated the professional force of a ruling prince. The victory bolstered the republican government and encouraged it to put more energy into the wars. Indeed, maintaining armies in the field became a weighty factor in the delicate equilibrium of revolutionary government. The new republican regime let it be known that its armies were not merely for self-defense but for the liberation of all peoples in the "name of the French Nation."

Meanwhile, the Convention faced the divisive issue of what to do with the king. Some of the king's correspondence, discovered after the storming of the Tuileries, provided the pretext for charges of treason. The Convention held a trial for him, which lasted from December 11, 1792, to January 15, 1793. He was found guilty of treason by an overwhelming vote (683 to 39); the republican government would not compromise with monarchy. Less lopsided was the sentence: Louis was condemned to death by a narrow majority, 387 to 334.

The consequences for the king were immediate. On January 21, 1793, Louis mounted the scaffold in a public square near the Tuileries and was beheaded. The execution split the ranks of the Convention and soon resulted in the breakdown of the institution itself.

The Faltering Republic and the Terror, 1793–1794

In February 1793, the republic was at war with virtually every state in Europe; the only exceptions were the Scandinavian kingdoms and Russia. Moreover, the regime faced widespread counterrevolutionary uprisings within France. Vigilance against internal and external enemies became a top priority. The Convention established an executive body, the Committee of Public Safety. In theory, this executive council was answerable to the Convention as a whole. But as the months passed, it acted with greater and greater autonomy not only to govern, but also to eliminate enemies. The broadly based republican government represented by the Convention began to disintegrate.

In June 1793, pushed by the Parisian sections, a group of extreme **Jacobins** purged the Girondin deputies from the Convention, arresting many of them. The Girondins were republicans who favored an activist government in the people's behalf, but they were less radical than their fellow Jacobins who now moved against them, less insistent on central control of the Revolution, and less willing to share power with the citizens of Paris. After the purge, the Convention still met, but most authority lay with the Committee of Public Safety.

Now, new uprisings against the regime began as revolts by Girondin sympathizers added to counterrevolutionary revolts by peasants and aristocrats. As resistance to the government mounted and the foreign threat continued, a dramatic event in Paris led the Committee of Public Safety officially to adopt a policy of political repression. A well-known figure of the Revolution, Jean Paul Marat (1743–1793), publisher of a radical newspaper very popular with ordinary Parisians, was murdered on July 13 by Charlotte Corday (1768–1793), an aristocratic woman. Shortly afterward, a longtime member of the Jacobin Club, **Maximilien Robespierre** (ROBES-pee-air) (1758–1794), joined the Committee and called for "Terror"—the systematic repression of internal enemies. He was not alone in his views. Members of the section assemblies of Paris led demonstrations to pressure the government into making Terror the order of the day.

Since the previous autumn, the guillotine had been at work against identified enemies of the regime, but now a more systematic apparatus of Terror was put in place. A Law of Suspects allowed citizens to be arrested simply on vague suspicion of counterrevolutionary sympathies. Revolutionary tribunals and an oversight committee made arbitrary arrests and rendered summary judgments. In October, a steady stream of executions began, beginning with the queen, imprisoned since the storming of the Tuileries the year before. The imprisoned Girondin deputies followed, and then the beheadings continued relentlessly. Paris witnessed about 2,600 executions from 1793 to 1794.

Around France, the verdicts of revolutionary tribunals led to approximately 14,000 executions. Another 10,000 to 12,000 people died in prison. Ten thousand or more were killed, usually by summary execution, after the defeat of counterrevolutionary uprisings. The aim of **the Terror** was not merely to crush active resistance; it was also to silence simple dissent. The victims in Paris included not only aristocrats and former deputies, but also sans-culottes. The radical Jacobins wanted to seize control of the Revolution from the Parisian citizens who had lifted them to power.

ROBESPIERRE AND THE COMMITTEE FOR PUBLIC SAFETY

Jacobins In revolutionary France, a republican political club named for a monastic order.

A Victim of the Terror   Manon Phlipon (1754–1793), known as Madame Roland, led an influential Parisian salon and was married to an important Girondin deputy. She was arrested and guillotined with other Girondins in 1793. Her last words on the scaffold were: "Oh Liberty, what crimes are committed in thy name!"   (Portrait of a Woman, c.1787 (oil on canvas), Labille-Guiard, Adelaide (c.1749-1803)/Musee des Beaux-Arts, Quimper, France/The Bridgeman Art Library)

Robespierre Justifies Terror Against Enemies of the Revolution

In this excerpt from a speech before the National Convention in December 1793, Robespierre justifies the revolutionary government's need to act in a vigorous manner in order to defend itself from challenges within and without.

The defenders of the Republic must adopt Caesar's maxim, for they believe that "nothing has been done so long as anything remains to be done." Enough dangers still face us to engage all our efforts. It has not fully extended the valor of our Republican soldiers to conquer a few Englishmen and a few traitors. A task no less important, and one more difficult, now awaits us: to sustain an energy sufficient to defeat the constant intrigues of all the enemies of our freedom and to bring to a triumphant realization the principles that must be the cornerstone of public welfare. ... Revolution is the war waged by liberty against its enemies; a constitution is that which crowns the edifice of freedom once victory has been won and the nation is at peace. The revolutionary government has to summon extraordinary activity to its aid precisely because it is at war. It is subjected to less binding and less uniform regulations, because the circumstances in which it finds itself are tempestuous and shifting, above all because it is compelled to deploy, swiftly and incessantly, new resources to meet new and pressing dangers. The principal concern of a constitutional government is civil liberty; that of a revolutionary government, public liberty. [A] revolutionary government is obliged to defend the state itself against the factions that assail it from every quarter. To good citizens revolutionary government owes the full protection of the state; to the enemies of the people it owes only death. ...

Is a revolutionary government the less just and the less legitimate because it must be more vigorous in its actions and freer in its movement than ordinary government? No! For it rests on the most sacred of all laws, the safety of the people, and on necessity, which is the most indisputable of all rights. It also has its rules, all based on justice and on public order. It has nothing in common with anarchy or disorder; on the contrary, its purpose is to repress them and to establish and consolidate the rule of law. It has nothing in common with arbitrary rule; it is public interest which governs it and not the whims of private individuals.

QUESTIONS

1. How does Robespierre describe the differences between constitutional and revolutionary government?
2. How does Robespierre defend the legitimacy of revolutionary government?

Source: "Robespierre Justifies the Terror" from *Robespierre*, edited by George Rudé, 1967, 1995, pp. 58–63

Maximilien Robespierre French lawyer and revolutionary leader, influential member of the Committee of Public Safety (1793–1794); advocated Terror to suppress internal dissent.

the Terror Systematic repression of internal enemies undertaken by French revolutionary government from 1793 to 1794. Approximately fourteen thousand people were executed, including aristocrats, Girondins, and sans-culottes.

Robespierre embodied all the contradictions of the policy of Terror. He was an austere, almost prim man who lived very modestly—a model, of sorts, of the virtuous, disinterested citizen. His unbending loyalty to his political principles earned him the nickname "the Incorruptible." The policies followed by the government during the year of his greatest influence, from July 1793 to July 1794, included generous and humane policies to benefit ordinary citizens as well as the atrocities of official Terror. (See the feature, "The Written Record: Robespierre Justifies Terror Against Enemies of the Revolution.") In May 1793, the Convention had instituted the Law of the Maximum, which controlled the price of grain so that city people could afford their staple food—bread. In September, the Committee extended the law to apply to other necessary commodities. Extensive plans were made for a system of free and universal primary education. Slavery in the French colonies was abolished in February 1794. Divorce, first legalized in 1792, was made easier for women to obtain. In addition, the government of the Committee of Public Safety was effective in providing direction for the nation at a critical time. In August 1793, it instituted the first mass conscription of citizens into the army *(levée en masse* [leh-VAY ohn MAHSS]), and a consistently effective popular army came into existence. In the autumn of 1793, this army won impressive victories.

SOCIAL REFORMS IN THE NAME OF REASON

In the name of "reason," traditional rituals and rhythms of life were changed. One reform of long-term significance was the introduction of the metric system of weights and measures. Although people continued to use the old, familiar measures for a very long time, the change was eventually accomplished, leading the way for standardization throughout Europe. Equally "rational," but not as successful, was the elimination of the traditional calendar;

weeks and months were replaced by uniform thirty-day months and *decadi* (ten-day weeks with one day of rest), and all saints' days and Christian holidays were eliminated. The years had already been changed—Year I had been declared with the founding of the republic in the autumn of 1792.

Churches were rededicated as "temples of reason." Robespierre believed that outright atheism left people with no basis for personal or national morality; he promoted a cult of the Supreme Being. New public festivals were solemn civic ceremonies intended to ritualize and legitimize the new political order. But the French people generally resented the elimination of the traditional calendar and the attacks on the church. In the countryside, massive peasant uprisings protested the loss of poor relief, community life, and familiar ritual.

Divorce law and economic regulation were a boon, especially to urban women, but women's participation in section assemblies and in all organized political activity—which had been energetic and widespread—was banned in October 1793. The particular target of the regime was the **Society of Revolutionary Republican Women**, a powerful club representing the interests of female sans-culottes. By banning women from political life, the regime helped to ground its legitimacy, since the seemingly "natural" exclusion of women might make the new system of government appear part of the "natural" order. (See the feature, "The Visual Record: Political Symbols.") Outlawing women's clubs and barring women from section assemblies also eliminated one source of popular power, from which the regime was now trying to distance itself.

Society of Revolutionary Republican Women In revolutionary Paris, a powerful political club that represented the interests of female sans-culottes.

THE END OF THE TERROR

The main policy differences between the Committee and members of the Convention concerned economic matters: how far to go to assist the poor, the unemployed, and the landless. Several of the moderate critics of Robespierre and his allies were guillotined for disagreeing about policy and for doubting the continuing need for the Terror itself. Their deaths helped precipitate the end of the Terror by causing Robespierre's power base to shrink so much that it had no further legitimacy. Also, French armies had soundly defeated Austrian troops on June 26, so there was no longer any need for the emergency status that the Terror had thrived on.

Deputies to the Convention finally dared to move against Robespierre in July 1794. In late July, the Convention voted to arrest Robespierre, the head of the revolutionary tribunal in Paris, and their closest associates and allies in the city government. On July 28 and 29, Robespierre and the others—about a hundred in all—were guillotined, and the Terror ended.

The Thermidorian Reaction and the Directory, 1794–1799

After Robespierre's death, the Convention reclaimed the executive powers that the Committee of Public Safety had seized. It dismantled the apparatus of the Terror, repealed the Law of Suspects, and forced the revolutionary tribunals to adopt ordinary legal procedures. The Convention also passed into law reforms, such as expanded public education, that had been proposed the year before but not enacted. This post-Terror phase of the Revolution is called the "Thermidorian Reaction" because it began in the revolutionary month of Thermidor (July 19–August 17).

Lacking the weapons of the Terror, the Convention was unable to enforce controls on the supply and price of bread. Thus, economic difficulties and a hard winter produced famine by the spring of 1795. The people of Paris tried to retain influence with the new government. In May, crowds marched on the Convention chanting "Bread and the Constitution of '93," referring to the republican constitution drafted by the Convention but never implemented because of the Terror. The demonstrations were met with force and were dispersed.

Members of the Convention remained fearful of a renewed, popularly supported Terror, on the one hand, and royalist uprisings on the other. Counterrevolutionary uprisings had erupted in the fall of 1794, and landings on French territory by émigré forces occurred the following spring. The Convention drafted a new constitution that limited popular participation in government, as had the first constitution of 1791. The new plan allowed fairly widespread (but not universal) male suffrage, but only for electors, who would choose deputies for the two houses of the legislature. The property qualifications for being an elector were very high, so all but elite citizens were effectively disenfranchised. The Convention also decreed that

Political Symbols

During the French Revolution, thousands of illustrations in support of various revolutionary (or counterrevolutionary) ideas were reproduced on posters, on handbills, and in pamphlets. Some satirized their subjects, such as Marie Antoinette, or celebrated revolutionary milestones, such as the fall of the Bastille. The etching here of the woman armed with a pike, dating from 1792, falls into this category. Other pictures, such as the representation from 1795 of Liberty as a young woman wearing the liberty cap, symbolized or reinforced various revolutionary ideals.

Political images like these are an invaluable though problematic source for historians. Let us examine these two images of women and consider how French people during the Revolution might have responded to them. To understand what they meant to contemporaries, we must know something about the other images that these would have been compared to. We must also view the images in the context of the events of the Revolution itself. Immediately, then, we are presented with an interpretive agenda. How ordinary and acceptable was this image of an armed woman? If women were not citizens coequal with men, how could a woman be a symbol of liberty? What, in short, do these political images reveal about the spectrum of political life in their society?

The woman holding the pike stares determinedly at the viewer. Many details confirm what the original caption announced: This is a French woman who has become free. In her hat she wears one of the symbols of revolutionary nationhood: the tricolor cockade. The badge around her waist celebrates a defining moment for the revolutionary nation: the fall of the Bastille. Her pike itself is inscribed with the words "Liberty or death."

The woman appears to be serving not merely as a symbol of free women. She comes close to being the generic image of a free citizen, willing and able to fight for liberty—an astonishing symbolic possibility in a time when women were not yet treated equally under the law or granted the same political rights as the men of their class. Other images prevalent at the time echo this possibility. Many contemporary representations of the women's march on Versailles in 1789 show women carrying arms, active in advancing the Revolution. By the time this image was created (most likely in 1792), many other demonstrations and violent confrontations by ordinary people had

An Armed Citizen, ca. 1792 (Bibliothèque nationale de France)

two-thirds of its members must serve in the new legislature, regardless of the outcome of elections. Although this maneuver enhanced the stability of the new regime, it undermined the credibility of the new vote.

The government under the new constitution, beginning in the fall of 1795, was called the **Directory**, for the executive council of five men chosen by the upper house of the new legislature. To avoid the concentration of authority that had produced the Terror, the members of the Convention had tried to enshrine separation of powers in the new system.

resulted in the creation of dozens of popular prints and engravings that showed women acting in the same ways as men.

Repeatedly during 1792, women proposed to the revolutionary government that they be granted the right to bear arms. Their request was denied, but it was not dismissed out of hand. There was debate, and the issue was in effect tabled. Nevertheless, women's actions in the Revolution had created at least the possibility of envisaging citizenship with a female face.

The image of Liberty from 1795 does not reflect the actions of women but rather represents their exclusion from political participation. It is one of a number of images of Liberty that portray this ideal as a passive, innocent woman, here garbed in ancient dress, surrounded by a glow that in the past had been reserved for saints. Liberty here is envisaged as a pure and lofty goal, symbolized as a pure young woman.

Late in 1793, during the Terror, women were excluded from formal participation in politics with the disbanding of women's organizations. Nor did they gain political rights under the Directory, which reestablished some of the limited gains of the first phase of the Revolution. The justification offered for their exclusion in 1793 was borrowed from Jean-Jacques Rousseau: it is contrary to nature for women to be in public life (see page 503). Women "belong" in the private world of the family, where they will nurture male citizens. Women embody ideal qualities such as patience and self-sacrifice; they are not fully formed beings capable of action in their own right.

Such notions made it easy to use images of women to embody ideals for public purposes. A woman could represent liberty precisely because actual women were not able to be political players.

The two images shown here thus demonstrate that political symbols can have varying relationships to "reality." The pike-bearing citizen is the more "real." Her image reflects the way of thinking about politics that became possible for the first time because of their actions. The other woman reflects not the attributes of actual women, but an ideal type spawned by the use of arbitrary gender distinctions to legitimize political power. In these images, we can see modern political life taking shape: the sophistication of its symbolic language, the importance of abstract ideas, such as liberty and nationhood—as well as the grounding of much political life in rigid distinctions between public and private, male and female.

Liberty as a Young Woman, ca. 1795 (S. P. Avery Collection, Miriam and Ira D. Wallach Division of Arts, Prints, and Photographs, The New York Public Library, Astor, Lenox, and Tilden Foundations/Art Resource, NY)

QUESTIONS

1. What circumstances explain the 1792 image of a woman as an armed citizen?

2. How would an idealized image of a young woman be useful as a symbol of liberty?

---

* This discussion draws on the work of Joan Landes, "Representing the Body Politic: The Paradox of Gender in the Graphic Politics of the French Revolution," and Darlene Gay Levy and Harriet B. Applewhite, "Women and Militant Citizenship in Revolutionary Paris," in Sara E. Melzer and Leslie W. Rabine, eds., *Rebel Daughters: Women and the French Revolution* (New York: Oxford University Press, 1992), pp. 15–37, 79–101.

However, the governments under the Directory were never free from outside plots or from their own extra-constitutional maneuvering. The most spectacular challenge was an attempted coup by the "Conspiracy of Equals," a group of extreme Jacobins who wanted to restore popular government and aggressive economic and social policy on behalf of the common people. The conspiracy ended with arrests and executions in 1797. When elections in 1797 and 1798 returned many royalist, as well as Jacobin deputies, the Directory itself abrogated the constitution: many "undesirable" deputies were arrested, exiled, or denied seats.

SECTION SUMMARY

- The phases of the French Revolution were shaped by elites' desires for change, demands of common people, and the need to defend France against foreign monarchs.

- Between 1789 and 1791, the National Assembly wrote a constitution, seized and sold church property, ended traditional obligations of peasants, and reorganized local government.

- In 1791, the constitution was implemented and a Legislative Assembly elected.

- In 1792, Parisian citizens overthrew the monarchy; the Convention, elected by universal manhood suffrage, governed the republic.

- Control of the government passed to the Committee of Public Safety, which defended France from foreign invasion and gave economic assistance to common people, but also implemented a policy of official Terror in which thousands of French people were killed.

- After the Terror, suffrage was again restricted, but the government of the Directory could not bring stability.

The armies of the republic did enjoy some spectacular successes during these years, for the first time carrying the fighting—and the effects of the Revolution—onto foreign soil. French armies conquered the Dutch in 1795. In 1796–1797, French armies led by the young general **Napoleon Bonaparte** seized control of northern Italy from the Austrians. Both regions were transformed into "sister" republics, governed by local revolutionaries but under French protection. By 1799, however, conditions had once again reached a crisis point. The demands of the war effort, together with rising prices and the continued decline in the value of the assignats, brought the government again to the brink of bankruptcy. The government also seemed to be losing control of the French countryside; there were continued royalist uprisings, local political vendettas between moderates and Jacobins, and outright banditry.

Members of the Directory had often turned to sympathetic army commanders to suppress dissent and to carry out purges of the legislature. They now invited General Bonaparte to help them form a government that they could more strictly control. Two members of the Directory plotted with Napoleon and his brother, Lucien Bonaparte, to seize power on November 9, 1799.

THE NAPOLEONIC ERA AND THE LEGACY OF REVOLUTION, 1799–1815

What impact did the Revolution and Napoleonic rule have on France, the rest of Europe, and the wider world?

Napoleon Bonaparte
French general who took part in a coup in 1799 against the Directory, Napoleon consolidated power as first consul and ruled as emperor from 1804 to 1815.

Talented, charming, and ruthless, Napoleon Bonaparte (1769–1821) was the kind of person who gives rise to myths. His audacity, determination, and personal magnetism enabled him to profit from the political instability in France and to establish himself in power. Once in power, he temporarily stabilized the political scene by fixing in law the more conservative gains of the Revolution. He also used his power and his abilities as a general to continue wars of conquest against France's neighbors, which helped deflect political tensions at home.

Napoleon's troops exported the Revolution as they conquered most of Europe. In most states that came under French control, law codes were reformed, governing elites were opened to talent, and public works were upgraded. Yet French conquest also meant domination, pure and simple, and involvement in France's rivalry with Britain. The Napoleonic era left Europe an ambiguous legacy—war and its enormous costs, yet also revolution and its impetus to positive change.

Napoleon: From Soldier to Emperor, 1799–1804

Napoleon was from Corsica, a Mediterranean island that had passed from Genoese to French control in the eighteenth century. The second son of a large gentry family, he was educated at military academies in France, and he married the politically well-connected widow Joséphine de Beauharnais (Bow-are-NAY) (1763–1814), whose aristocratic husband had been a victim of the Terror.

Napoleon steered a careful course through the political turmoil of the Revolution. By 1799, his military victories had won him much praise and fame. He had demonstrated his ruthlessness in 1795, when he ordered troops guarding the Convention to fire on a Parisian crowd. He had capped his successful Italian campaign of 1796–1797 with an invasion of Egypt in an attempt to strike at British influence and trade connections in the eastern Mediterranean. The Egyptian campaign failed in its goals, but individual victories during the campaign ensured Napoleon's military reputation.

Napoleon's partners in the new government after the November 1799 coup soon learned of his great political skill and ambition. In theory, the new system was a streamlined version of the Directory: Napoleon was to be first among equals in a three-man executive—"First Consul," according to borrowed Roman terminology. But Napoleon quickly asserted his primacy among them and began not only to dominate executive functions, but also to bypass the authority of the regime's various legislative bodies.

His increasingly authoritarian rule was successful in part because he included, among his advisors and ministers, men of many political stripes—Jacobins, reforming liberals, even former Old Regime bureaucrats. He welcomed many exiles back to France, including all but the most ardent royalists. He thus stabilized his regime by healing some of the rifts among ruling elites. Napoleon combined toleration with ruthlessness, however. Between 1800 and 1804, he imprisoned, executed, or exiled dozens of individuals for alleged Jacobin agitation or royalist sympathies, including a prince of the royal family, whom he had kidnapped and coldly murdered.

Under Napoleon's regime, any semblance of free political life ended. Legislative bodies lost all initiative in the governing process, becoming rubber stamps for the consuls' policies. There were no meaningful elections. Voters chose only candidates for a kind of pool of potential legislators, from which occasional replacements were chosen by members of the Senate, an advisory body entirely appointed by Napoleon himself. Political clubs were banned; the vibrant press of the revolutionary years wilted under heavy censorship. Napoleon also further centralized the administrative system, set up by the first wave of revolutionaries in 1789, by establishing the office of prefect to govern the départements. All prefects and their subordinates were appointed by Napoleon, thus extending the range of his power and undermining local government.

Certain administrative changes that enhanced central control, such as for tax collection, had more positive effects. Napoleon oversaw the establishment of the Bank of France, modeled on the Bank of England. The bank provided capital for investment and helped stabilize French currency. Perhaps the most important achievement early in his regime was the Concordat of 1801. This treaty with the pope solved the problem of church-state relations that for years had provoked counterrevolutionary rebellions. The agreement allowed for the resumption of Catholic worship and the continued support of the clergy by the state, but also accepted the more dramatic changes accomplished by the Revolution. Church lands that had been sold were guaranteed to their new owners. Although Catholicism was recognized as the "religion of the majority of Frenchmen," Protestant churches also were allowed, and their clergy were paid. Later, Napoleon granted new rights to Jews as well.

The law code that Napoleon established in 1804 was much like his accommodation with the church in its limited acceptance of revolutionary gains. His **Civil Code** (also known as the *code napoléon*, or Napoleonic Code) honored the revolutionary legacy in its guarantee of equality before the law and its requirement for the taxation of all social classes; it also enshrined modern forms of property ownership and civil contracts. Neither the code nor Napoleon's political regime fostered individual rights, especially for women. Divorce was no longer permitted except in rare instances. Women lost all property rights when they married, and they generally faced legal domination by fathers and husbands.

Civil Code Law code established under Napoleon in 1804 that included limited acceptance of revolutionary gains, such as a guarantee of equality before the law and taxation of all social classes.

Napoleon was careful to avoid heavy-handed displays of power. He cleverly sought ratification of each stage of his assumption of power through national plebiscites (referendums in which all eligible voters could vote for or against proposals)—one plebiscite (pleb-ih-SIGHT) for a new constitution in 1800 and another when he claimed consulship for life in 1802. He approached his final political coup—declaring himself emperor—with similar dexterity. Long before he claimed the imperial title, Napoleon had begun to sponsor an active court life appropriate to imperial pretensions. The empire

Napoleon Crossing the Alps   This stirring portrait by the great neoclassical painter Jacques-Louis David memorializes Napoleon's 1796 crossing of the Alps before his victorious Italian campaign, as a general under the Directory. In part because it was executed in 1801–1802, the painting depicts the moment heroically rather than realistically. (In truth, Napoleon wisely crossed the Alps on a sure-footed mule, not a stallion.) Napoleon, as First Consul, wanted images of himself that would justify his increasingly ambitious claims to power.   (Réunion des Musées Nationaux/Art Resource, NY)

was proclaimed in May 1804 with the approval of the Senate; it was also endorsed by another plebiscite. Napoleon rewarded members of his family and political favorites with noble titles that allowed no legal privilege but carried significant prestige. Old nobles were allowed to use their titles on this basis. Many members of the elite, whatever their origins, tolerated Napoleon's claims to power because he safeguarded fundamental revolutionary gains yet reconfirmed their status.

Conquering Europe, 1805–1810

Napoleon maintained relatively peaceful relations with other nations, while he consolidated power within France, but war soon resumed against political and economic enemies—principally Britain, Austria, and Russia. Tensions with the British quickly reescalated when Britain resumed aggression against French shipping in 1803, and Napoleon countered by seizing Hanover, the ancestral German home of the English king. England was at war at sea with Spain and the Netherlands, client states that Napoleon had forced to support him. Napoleon began to gather a large force on the northern coast of France; his objective was to invade England.

The British fleet, commanded by Horatio Nelson (1758–1805), intercepted a combined French and Spanish fleet that was to have been the invasion force and inflicted a devastating defeat off Cape Trafalgar in southern Spain (see **MAP 19.1**) on October 21, 1805. The victory ensured British mastery of the seas and, in the long run, contributed to Napoleon's demise. In the short run, the defeat at Trafalgar paled for the French beside Napoleon's impressive victories on land. Napoleon abandoned the plans to invade England and, in August, marched his army east through Germany to confront the great continental powers, Austria and Russia.

In December 1805, Napoleon's army routed a combined Austrian and Russian force near Austerlitz (AW-stir-lits), north of Vienna (see **MAP 19.1**). The Battle of Austerlitz was his most spectacular victory. Austria sued for peace. In further battles in 1806, French forces defeated Prussian, as well as Russian, armies once again. Prussia was virtually dismembered, but Napoleon tried to remake Russia into a contented ally. His hold on central Europe would not be secure with a

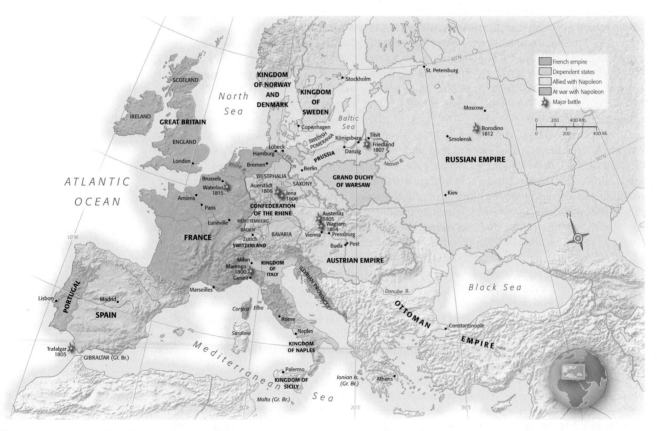

🌐 **MAP 19.1—Napoleonic Europe, ca. 1810**
France dominated continental Europe after Napoleon's victories.

hostile Russia, nor would the anti-British economic system that he envisioned—the Continental System (see page 552)—be workable without Russian participation.

French forces were still trying to prevail in Spain, which had been a client state since its defeat by revolutionary armies in 1795 but was resisting outright rule by a French-imposed king, one of Napoleon's brothers. In 1808, however, Napoleon turned his attention to fully subduing Austria. After another loss to French forces in 1809, Austria, like Russia, accepted French political and economic hegemony in a sort of alliance. Thus, by 1810, Napoleon had transformed most of Europe into allied or dependent states (see **MAP 19.1**). The only exceptions were Britain and the parts of Spain and Portugal that continued, with British help, to resist France.

The states least affected by French hegemony were its reluctant allies: Austria, Russia, and the Scandinavian countries. At the other extreme were territories that had been incorporated into France. These included the Austrian Netherlands, territory along the Rhineland, and sections of Italy that bordered France. These regions were occupied by French troops and were treated as though they were départements of France itself.

In most other areas, some form of French-controlled government was in place, usually headed by a member of Napoleon's family. In both northern Italy and the Netherlands, where "sister" republics had been established after French conquests under the Directory, Napoleon imposed monarchies. Rulers were also installed in the kingdom of Naples and in Spain. Western German states of the Holy Roman Empire that had allied with Napoleon against Austria were organized into the Confederation of the Rhine, with Napoleon as its "Protector." Two further states were created, largely out of the defeated Prussia's territory: the kingdom of Westphalia in western Germany and the Grand Duchy of Warsaw in the east (see **MAP 19.1**).

Napoleon's domination of these various regions had complex, and at times contradictory, consequences. On the one hand, Napoleonic armies essentially exported the French Revolution, in that French domination brought with it the Napoleonic Civil Code, and with it political and economic reform like that of the early phases of the Revolution. Equality before the law was decreed following the French example. This meant the end of noble exemption from taxation in the areas where it existed. The complex snarl of medieval taxes and tolls was replaced with straightforward property taxes that were universally applied. As a consequence, tax revenues rose dramatically—by 50 percent in the kingdom of Italy, for example. Serfdom and forced labor also were abolished, as they had been in France in August 1789.

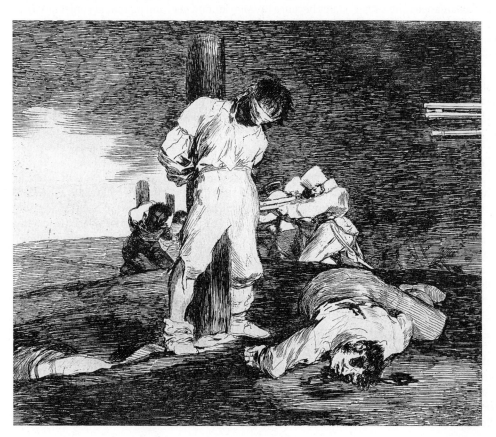

"And It Cannot Be Changed"   This horrifying scene of an execution of rebels against French rule in Spain was one of a series of etchings by Madrid artist Francisco Goya. In the 1810 series, titled "The Disasters of War," Goya was severely critical of French actions, as well as of barbarities committed by the British-backed Spaniards.   (Foto Marburg/Art Resource, NY)

In most Catholic regions, the church was subjected to the terms of the Concordat of 1801. The tithe (forced contributions to support the church) was abolished, church property seized and sold, and monasteries closed. Although Catholicism remained the state-supported religion in these areas, Protestantism was tolerated, and Jews were granted rights of citizenship. Secular education, at least for males, was encouraged.

On the other hand, Napoleon would allow in the empire only those aspects of France's revolutionary legacy that he tolerated in France itself. Just as he had suppressed any meaningful participatory government in France, so too did he suppress it in conquered regions. This came as a blow in states such as the Netherlands, which had experienced its own democratizing "Patriot" movement and which had enjoyed republican self-government after invasion by France during the Revolution itself. Throughout Napoleon's empire, many of the benefits of streamlined administration and taxation were offset by the drain of continual warfare. Deficits rose three- and fourfold, despite increased revenues. And throughout Europe, Napoleon gave away land to reward his greatest generals and ministers, thereby exempting those lands from taxation and control by his own bureaucracy.

If true self-government was not allowed, a broad segment of the elite in all regions was nevertheless won over to cooperation with Napoleon by being welcomed into his bureaucracy or into the large multinational army, called the *Grande Armée* (grawnd are-MAY). Their loyalty was cemented when they bought confiscated church lands.

The impact of Napoleon's Continental System was equally mixed. Under this system, the Continent was in theory closed to all British shipping and goods. The effects were uneven, and smuggling to evade controls on British goods became a major enterprise. Regions heavily involved in trade with Britain or its colonies suffered in the new system, as did overseas trade in general when Britain gained dominance of the seas after Trafalgar. However, the closing of the Continent to British trade, combined with increases in demand to supply Napoleon's armies, spurred the development of continental industries, at least in the short run.

Defeat and Abdication, 1812–1815

Whatever its achievements, Napoleon's empire was ultimately fragile because of the hostility of Austria and Russia, as well as the power of Britain. Russia was a particularly weak link in the chain of alliances and subject states because Russian landowners and merchants objected when their vital trade in timber for the British navy was interrupted and when supplies of luxury goods, brought in British ships, began to dwindle. A century of close alliances with German ruling houses made alliance with a French ruler an extremely difficult political option for Tsar Alexander I.

It was Napoleon, however, who ended the alliance by provoking a breach with Russia. He suddenly backed away from an arrangement to marry one of Alexander's sisters and accepted an Austrian princess instead. (He had divorced Joséphine because their marriage had not produced an heir.) Also, he seized lands in Germany belonging to a member of Alexander's family. When Alexander threatened rupture of the alliance if the lands were not returned, Napoleon mounted an invasion. Advisers warned him about the magnitude of the task he seemed so eager to undertake—particularly about winter fighting in Russia—but their alarms went unheard.

Napoleon's previous military successes had stemmed from a combination of strategic innovations and pure audacity. Napoleon divided his forces into independent corps. Each corps included infantry, cavalry, and artillery. Organized in these workable units, his armies could travel quickly by several separate routes and converge in massive force to face the enemy. Leadership on the battlefield came from a loyal and talented officer corps that had grown up since army commands had been thrown open to nonaristocrats during the Revolution. The final ingredient for success was the high morale of French troops. Since the first victory of the revolutionary armies in September 1792, citizen-soldiers had proved their worth. Complicated troop movements and bravery on the battlefield were possible when troops felt they were fighting for their *nation*, not merely their ruling dynasty. Napoleon's reputation as a winning general added a further measure of self-confidence.

The campaign against Russia began in June 1812. It was a spectacular failure. Napoleon had gathered a force of about 700,000 men—about half from France and half from allied states—a force twice as large as Russia's. But the strategy of quickly moving independent corps and assembling massive forces could not be implemented. Bold victories had often enabled Napoleon's troops to live off the countryside while they waited for supplies to catch up to the front line. But when the enemy attacked supply lines, the distances traveled were very great, the countryside was impoverished, or battles were not decisive, Napoleon's ambitious strategies proved futile. In varying degrees, these conditions prevailed in Russia.

By the time the French faced the Russians in the principal battle of the Russian campaign—at Borodino (bore-uh-DEE-no), west of Moscow (see **MAP 19.1**)—the Grande Armée had been on the march for two and a half months and was already less than half its original strength. After the indecisive but bloody battle, the French occupied and pillaged Moscow but found scarcely enough food and supplies to sustain them. When Napoleon finally retreated from Moscow late in October, the fate of the French forces was all but sealed. As they retreated, the soldiers who had not died in battle died of exposure or starvation or were picked off by Russian peasants as they scavenged for food or fuel. Of the original 700,000 troops of the Grand Armée, fewer than 100,000 made it out of Russia.

Napoleon left his army before it was fully out of Russia to counter a coup attempt in Paris. The collapse of his reign had begun, spurred by a coincidental defeat in Spain. In Spain, a rebel Cortes (national representative assembly) had continued to meet in territory that the French did not control, and British troops supported resistance to the French. In 1812, as Napoleon was advancing against Russia, the collapse of French control accelerated. By the time Napoleon reached Paris at the turn of the new year, an Anglo-Spanish force led by the duke of Wellington was poised to invade France.

Napoleon lost his last chance to stave off a coalition of all major powers against him when he refused an Austrian offer of peace for the return of conquered Austrian territories. With Britain willing to subsidize the allied armies, Tsar Alexander determined to destroy Napoleon, and the Austrians now anxious to share the spoils, Napoleon's empire collapsed. The allies invaded France and forced Napoleon to abdicate on April 6, 1814.

Napoleon was exiled to the island of Elba, off France's Mediterranean coast. He was installed as the island's ruler and was given an income drawn on the French treasury. Meanwhile, however, the restored French king was having his own troubles. Louis XVIII (r. 1814–1824) was the brother of the executed Louis XVI (he took the number eighteen out of respect for Louis XVI's son, who had died in prison in 1795). The new monarch had been out of the country and out of touch with its circumstances since the beginning of the Revolution. In addition to the delicate task of establishing his own legitimacy, he faced enormous practical problems, including pensioning off thousands of soldiers now unemployed and still loyal to Napoleon.

Napoleon, bored and almost penniless in his island kingdom (the promised French pension never materialized), took advantage of the circumstances and returned surreptitiously to France on February 26, 1815. His small band of attendants was joined by the soldiers sent by the king to halt his progress. Louis XVIII abandoned Paris to the returned emperor. Napoleon's triumphant return lasted only one hundred days, however. Though some soldiers welcomed his return, many members of the elite were reluctant to throw in their lot with Napoleon again, and many ordinary French citizens were disenchanted, especially since the defeat in Russia, with the high costs, in conscription and taxation, of his armies. In any case, Napoleon's reappearance galvanized the divided allies, who had been haggling over a peace settlement, into unity. Napoleon tried to strike decisively against the allies, but he lost against English and Prussian troops in his first major battle, at Waterloo (in modern Belgium; see **MAP 19.1**) on June 18, 1815. When Napoleon arrived in Paris after the defeat, he discovered the government in the hands of an ad hoc committee that included the Marquis de Lafayette. Under pressure, he abdicated once again. This time, he was exiled to the tiny, remote island of St. Helena in the South Atlantic, where he died in 1821.

The Legacy of Revolution for France and the World

The process of change in France between 1789 and 1815 was so complex that it is easy to overlook the overall impact of the Revolution. Superficially, the changes seemed to come full circle—with first Louis XVI on the throne, then Napoleon as emperor, and then Louis XVIII on the throne. Even though the monarchy was restored, however, the Revolution had discredited absolute monarchy in theory and practice.

Louis XVIII had to recognize the right of "the people," however narrowly defined, to participate in government and to enjoy due process of law. Another critical legacy of the Revolution and the Napoleonic era was a centralized political system of départements rather than a patchwork of provinces. For the first time, a single code of law applied to all French people. Most officials—from département administrators to city mayors—were appointed by the central government until the late twentieth century. This centralization had a positive side: the government sponsored national

FRANCE

scientific societies, a national library and archives, and a system of teachers' colleges and universities. Particularly under Napoleon, canal- and road-building projects improved transport systems.

Napoleon's legacy, like that of the Revolution itself, was mixed. His self-serving reconciliation of aristocratic pretensions with the opening of careers to men of talent ensured the long-term success of revolutionary principles from which the elite as a whole profited. His reconciliation of the state with the Catholic Church helped to stabilize his regime and cemented some revolutionary gains. The restored monarchy could not renege on these gains. Yet, whatever his achievements, Napoleon's overthrow of constitutional principles worsened the problem of political instability. His brief return to power in 1815 reflects the degree to which his power had always been rooted in military adventurism and in the loyalty of soldiers and officers. Similarly, the swiftness of his collapse suggests that the empire under Napoleon was not an enduring solution to the political instability of the late 1790s; indeed, it was no more secure than any of the other revolutionary governments.

Although Louis XVIII acknowledged the principle of constitutionalism at the end of the Revolution, his regime rested on fragile footing. Indeed, the fragility of new political systems was one of the most profound legacies of the Revolution. There was division over policies, but even greater division over legitimacy—that is, the acceptance by a significant portion of the politically active citizenry of a particular government's right to rule. Before the Revolution started, notions about political legitimacy had undergone a significant shift. The deputies who declared themselves to be the National Assembly in June 1789 already believed that they had a right to do so. In their view, they represented "the nation," and their voice had legitimacy for that reason. These deputies brought to Versailles not only their individual convictions that "reason" should be applied to the political system, but also their experience in social settings where those ideas were well received. In their salons, clubs, and literary societies, they had experienced the familiarity, trust, and sense of community that are essential to effective political action. The deputies' attempt to transplant their sense of community into national politics, however, was not wholly successful, in part because of their naïve refusal to stand for election under the new constitution. The king also actively undermined the system because he disagreed with it in principle. The British parliamentary system, by comparison, though representative only of a tiny elite, had a long history as a workable institution for lords, wealthy commoners, and rulers. This shared experience was an important counterweight to differences over fundamental issues, so that Parliament as an institution both survived political crises and helped resolve them. In France, politics was established on new principles, yet still lacking were the practical means to achieve the promise inherent in those principles.

EUROPE AND ITS COLONIES

France's conquests in Europe were the least enduring of the changes of the revolutionary era. Nevertheless, French domination of Europe had certain lasting effects: Elites were exposed to modern bureaucratic management, and equality under the law transformed social and political relationships. The breakdown of ancient political divisions provided important practical grounding for later cooperation among elites in nationalist movements. In Napoleon's kingdom of Italy, for example, a tax collector from Florence for the first time worked side by side with one from Milan.

The most important legacy of the French Revolution in Europe was the very success of the Revolution. The most powerful absolute monarchy in Europe had succumbed to the demands of its people for dramatic social and political reforms. Throughout Europe in the nineteenth century, ruling dynasties faced revolutionary movements that demanded constitutional government and resorted to force to achieve it.

The most important legacy of the revolutionary wars, however, was the change in warfare itself, made possible by the citizen armies of the French. Citizen-soldiers, who identified closely with their nation, even when conscripts, proved able to maneuver and attack on the battlefield in ways that the brutishly disciplined poor conscripts in royal armies would not. In response, other states tried to build competing armies; the mass national armies that fought the world wars of the twentieth century were the result.

European colonial possessions changed hands during the revolutionary wars. The British took advantage of Napoleon's preoccupation with continental affairs by seizing French colonies and the colonies of the French-dominated Dutch. In 1806, they seized the Dutch colony of Cape Town in southern Africa—crucial for support of trade around Africa—as well as French bases along the African coast. In 1811, they grabbed the island of Java (modern Indonesia).

Indeed, one clear legacy of the Revolution was the expansion of British trade and colonial control, made possible by Britain's sea power. Britain's maritime supremacy and seizure of French possessions expanded British trading networks overseas—though in some cases only temporarily—and closer to home, particularly in the Mediterranean. As long as the British had

Napoleon's Letter to Toussaint-Louverture

In November 1801, Napoleon sent this letter to the governor of the colony of Saint Domingue, Toussaint-Louverture. Toussaint, a former slave, had commanded an army, composed largely of ex-slaves, which had restored order in Saint Domingue following a complicated civil war. As he mentions in the letter, Napoleon had dispatched a force to reestablish French control of the formerly profitable colony. Although Toussaint was captured and later died in a French prison, Napoleon's forces were not successful in reestablishing French control.

To Citizen General Toussaint Louverture, commander in chief of the armies of Saint-Domingue, Peace with England and with other powers in Europe [now] enables France to pay attention to its colony of Saint-Domingue. We are sending General Leclerc, our brother-in-law, to serve as captain general and governor of the colony. He is accompanied by forces suitable to make the sovereignty of France respected. In these circumstances, it pleases us to hope that you will demonstrate to us and to all of France the sincerity of the sentiments that you have continually expressed in your letters to us. We hold you in very high esteem and it pleases us to acknowledge the great service you have rendered to the French people. ... Called by your talents and by the force of circumstance to command, you have ended civil war. ... The constitution you have made contains many good things but also things which are contrary to the dignity and the sovereignty of the French people, of which the people of Saint-Domingue form only a part. The circumstances in which you found yourself, surrounded on all sides by enemies, perhaps made some provisions of the constitution necessary and legitimate. But, happily, now that things have changed you will be able to render homage to the sovereignty of the Nation of which you are one of the most illustrious citizens. ... Any contrary conduct ... would lead you to lose the many rights you have earned to the recognition and the benefits of the Republic [and] would bring you to the edge of a precipice which, in swallowing you up, would contribute to the misery of the brave blacks, whose courage we admire and whose rebellion we would be sorry to have to punish.

Help the new captain general with your counsel, your influence and your talents. What could you want? The freedom of blacks? You know that in every country we have entered we have given liberty to the people who did not have it. Do you want respect, honors and fortune? ... Given the services you have rendered and our esteem for you, you cannot be in doubt that respect, honors and fortune await you.

Make known to the peoples of Saint-Domingue that our concerns for their well-being were often impotent because of the demands of war that we faced. But now, peace and the force of our government will assure them prosperity and liberty. Tell them that if liberty is to them the most important right, that it cannot be enjoyed without the title of "French citizen" and that all acts contrary to the nation, and contrary to the obedience they owe its government and to its representative, the captain general, will be crimes against the national sovereignty. ... And you, General, consider that if you are the first man of color to have arrived at such a pinnacle of power ... you are also, before God and before us, responsible for their good conduct. ...

QUESTIONS

1. What, in your opinion, was Napoleon trying to accomplish with this letter?

2. How would Toussaint-Louverture have interpreted Napoleon's words?

Source: Paul Rossier, ed., *Lettres du Général Leclerc* (Paris: Société de l'Histoire des Colonies Françaises, 1937). Translated by Kristen B. Neuschel.

---

been involved in trade with India, the Mediterranean had been important for economic and strategic reasons because it lay at the end of the land route for trade from the Indian Ocean. Especially after Napoleon's aggression in Egypt in the 1790s, the British redoubled their efforts to control strategic outposts in the Mediterranean.

The British economy would expand dramatically in the nineteenth century as industrial production soared. The roots for growth were laid in this period in the countryside of Britain, where changes in agriculture and in production were occurring. These roots were also laid in Britain's overseas possessions as tighter control of foreign sources of raw materials, notably raw Indian cotton, meant rising fortunes back in Britain. In regions of India, the East India Company was increasing its political domination, and hence, its economic stranglehold on Indian commodities. The export of Indian cotton rose significantly during the revolutionary period as part of an expanding trading system that included China, the source of tea.

On the most productive of the French-controlled Caribbean islands, Saint Domingue (SAHN dome-ANGUE), the French Revolution inspired a successful rebellion by the enslaved plantation workers.

The National Assembly in Paris had delayed abolishing slavery in French colonies, despite the moral appeal of such a move, because of pressure from the white planters and out of fear

François Dominique Toussaint-Louverture
Former slave who governed the island of Saint Domingue (Haiti) as an independent state after the slave revolt of 1791.

REVOLUTION IN THE ATLANTIC WORLD

Haitian Leader Toussaint-Louverture Son of an educated slave, Toussaint-Louverture had himself been freed in 1777 but took on a leadership role when the slave revolt began on Saint Domingue in 1791. His military skill and political acumen were vital to the success of the revolt and to ruling the island's diverse population afterward. (Stock Montage, Inc.)

SECTION SUMMARY

- General Napoleon Bonaparte and two other men seized power from the Directory in a coup in 1799; Napoleon carefully expanded his power and finally declared himself emperor of France in 1804.

- Napoleon's law code and his agreement with the Catholic Church made permanent some of the key changes from the first phase of the Revolution.

- Napoleon recruited former royal officials, old nobility, and recent revolutionaries into his government, thereby resolving some of the political tensions that had resulted from the Revolution.

- The costs associated with Napoleon's foreign conquests resulted in the overthrow of his regime and contributed to the long-term problems of the French government.

- The export of revolution by French armies brought economic costs from war itself and from Napoleon's continental trading system, but also political reform that led, in many cases, to further political liberty.

- In the Americas, the French Revolution inspired movements for independence from colonial rule; in Haiti, slaves and free persons without political rights allied to successfully overthrow French rule.

that the financially strapped French government would lose some of its profitable sugar trade. But the example of revolutionary daring in Paris and confusion about ruling authority as the Assembly and the king wrangled did not go unnoticed in the colonies—in either plantation mansions or slave quarters. White planters on Saint Domingue simply hoped for political and economic "liberty" from the French government and its mercantilist trade policies. White planter rule was challenged, in turn, by wealthy people of mixed European and African descent who wanted equal citizenship, hitherto denied them. A civil war broke out between these upper classes and was followed by a full-fledged slave rebellion, beginning in 1791. Britain sent aid to the rebels when it went to war against the French revolutionary government in 1793. Only when the republic was declared in Paris and the Convention abolished slavery did the rebels abandon alliances with France's enemies and attempt to govern in concert with the mother country.

Although it recovered other colonies from the British, France never regained control of Saint Domingue. Led by a former slave, **François Dominique Toussaint-Louverture** (too-SAHN-loo-ver-TOUR) (1743–1803), the new government of the island tried to run its own affairs, though without formally declaring independence from France. (See the feature, "The Global Record: Napoleon's Letter to Toussaint-Louverture.") Napoleon decided to tighten control of the profitable colonies by reinstituting slavery and ousting the independent government of Saint Domingue. In 1802, French forces fought their way onto the island. They captured Toussaint-Louverture, who died shortly thereafter in prison. But in 1803, another rebellion, provoked by the threat of renewed slavery, expelled French forces for good. A former aide of Toussaint's declared the independence of the colony under the name Haiti—the island's Native American name—on January 1, 1804.

The French Revolution and Napoleonic rule, and the example of the Haitian revolution, had a notable impact on Spanish colonies in the Americas. Like other American colonies, the Spanish colonies wanted to loosen the closed economic relationships with the mother country. In addition, the liberal ideas that had helped spawn the French Revolution spurred moves toward independence in Spanish America. Because of the confusion of authority in Spain, some of these colonies were already governing themselves independently in all but name. Echoes of radical republican ideology and of the Haitian experience were present in two major rebellions in Mexico; participants espoused the end of slavery and championed the interests of the poor against local and Spanish elites. The leaders of these self-declared revolutions were executed (in 1811 and 1815), and their movements were crushed by local elites in alliance with Spanish troops. The efforts of local elites to become self-governing—the attempted liberal revolutions—were little more successful. Only Argentina and Paraguay broke away from Spain at this time.

But as in Europe, a legacy remained of both limited and more radical revolutionary activity. Slave rebellions rocked British Caribbean islands in subsequent decades. On islands dominated by plantation agriculture, such as some British possessions and the Spanish island of Cuba, planters were reluctant to disturb the prevailing order with any liberal political demands on the mother country.

CHAPTER SUMMARY

The French Revolution was a watershed in European history because it successfully challenged the principles of hereditary rule and political privilege by which all European states had previously been governed. The Revolution began when a financial crisis forced the monarchy to confront the desire for political reform by a segment of the French elite. Political philosophy emerging from the Enlightenment and the example of the American Revolution moved the French reformers to action. In its initial phase, the French Revolution established the principle of constitutional government and ended many of the traditional political privileges of the Old Regime.

Then, because of the intransigence of the king, the threat of foreign invasion, and the actions of republican legislators and Parisian citizens, the Revolution moved in more radical directions. Its most extreme phase, the Terror, produced the most effective legislation for ordinary citizens, but also the worst violence of the Revolution. A period of unstable conservative rule that followed the Terror ended when Napoleon seized power.

Although Napoleonic rule solidified some of the gains of the Revolution, it also subjected France and most of Europe to costly wars of conquest. After Napoleon, the French monarchy was restored, but its power would no longer be absolute—and the people would not be refused a voice in government—as a result of the Revolution. The impact of events in France also continued beyond its borders; political and legal reform had been imposed in many parts of Europe and even, in more limited ways, had been embraced in European colonies.

FOCUS QUESTIONS

- What factors led to revolution in France in 1789?

- Why did several phases of revolutionary change occur after 1789 and what were the characteristics of each phase?

- What impact did the Revolution and Napoleonic rule have on France, the rest of Europe, and the wider world?

KEY TERMS

Third Estate (p. 535)

National Assembly (p. 536)

Tennis Court Oath (p. 536)

Declaration of the Rights of Man and the Citizen (p. 538)

sans-culottes (p. 542)

Jacobins (p. 543)

Maximilien Robespierre (p. 544)

the Terror (p. 544)

Society of Revolutionary Republican Women (p. 545)

Directory (p. 546)

Napoleon Bonaparte (p. 548)

Civil Code (p. 549)

François Dominique Toussaint-Louverture (p. 555)

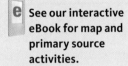 This icon will direct you to additional materials on the website: www .cengage.com/history/ noble/westciv6e.

NOTES

1. Quoted in Samuel Eliot Morrison, *John Paul Jones: A Sailor's Biography* (Boston: Little, Brown, 1959), pp. 149–154.

2. Quoted in Owen Connelly, *The French Revolution and the Napoleonic Era* (New York: Holt, Rinehart, and Winston, 1979), p. 32.

3. James Harvey Robinson, *Readings in European History* (Boston: Ginn, 1906), p. 409.

e See our interactive eBook for map and primary source activities.

INDEX